ADVANCED PLACEMENT
ECONOMICS
MICROECONOMICS

Teacher Resource Manual

4th Edition
Gary L. Stone

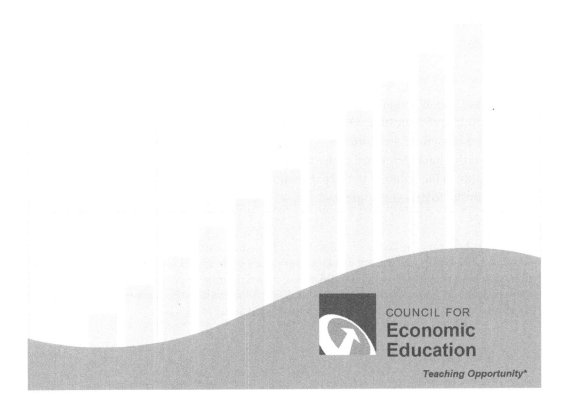

COUNCIL FOR
**Economic
Education**

Teaching Opportunity

Author

Gary L. Stone is a professor of economics and director of the Center for Economic Education at Winthrop University. He has conducted numerous workshops for Advanced Placement Economics teachers and has been a reader and table leader for the AP Economics Examinations for over two decades. Gary received the Bessie B. Moore Service Award from the National Association of Economic Educators for his work in economic education with K–12 teachers in the United States and other countries.

Contributing Author

Margaret A. Ray, author of *Advanced Placement Economics Macroeconomics* and contributor to Unit 1, is a professor of economics and director of the Center for Economic Education at the University of Mary Washington. She taught AP Economics at Collegiate School in Richmond, Virginia, in 2002–2003 and was an economist and director of economic education at the Federal Reserve Bank of Richmond. Margaret has been a reader, table leader, and question leader for the AP Economic Examinations from 1993 to the present and she currently serves on the AP Microeconomics Test Development Committee.

Content Consultant

Dennis Placone is professor emeritus of economics and director of the Center for Economic Education at Clemson University. He has more than 35 years of teaching, research, and administrative experience at Clemson, and has conducted workshops for K–12 teachers including AP teachers since 1989. He served as chair of the AP Economics Test Development Committee from 1997–2003.

Project Director

Kevin Gotchet is the Director for the Excellence in Economic Education program. He has been with the Council for Economic Education for more than eight years and has taken a leading role in several CEE initiatives.

Funding

The Council for Economic Education gratefully acknowledges the funding of this publication by the U.S. Department of Education, Office of Innovation and Improvement, Excellence in Economic Education: Advancing K–12 Economic & Financial Education Nationwide grant award U215B100002. The contents of this book developed under the grant from the Department of Education do not necessarily represent the policy of the Department of Education, and you should not assume endorsement by the federal government.

ISBN: 978-156183-669-7

Contents

Contents

Advanced Placement Economics Microeconomics: Teacher Resource Manual © Council for Economic Education, New York, N.Y.

Contents

Contents

The Council for Economic Education is pleased to introduce this fourth edition of *Advanced Placement Economics*. In the years since its first publication, *Advanced Placement Economics* has become the go-to guide for helping teachers to prepare their students for the AP Microeconomics and Macroeconomics Exams administered by the College Board. We are proud of this accomplishment and believe that this current edition will continue to uphold the high standards set by its predecessors.

AP Economics exams continue to grow in popularity, with more than 90,000 students taking the AP Macroeconomics Exam and more than 56,000 taking the AP Microeconomics Exam in 2011. More test takers means more teachers who must be prepared to teach the relevant content.

This revision of *Advanced Placement Economics* aims to respond to adjustments in the AP Course Outlines and Exams in the nine years since the publication of the third edition. Some changes include paring down content for better emphasis of essential AP economics concepts; revising lessons to utilize contemporary examples; and most importantly, addressing the current state of the test with the addition of new content. In addition, you will see some reorganization of the material in response to teacher feedback. By dividing the macroeconomics and microeconomics teacher's manuals into two separate entities and compartmentalizing various elements, such as student activities solutions and sample multiple-choice question answer keys, the materials provide a more intuitive structure and easier navigation of content. The final product, we believe, will continue to provide teachers with the highest quality economic content and pedagogy for preparing students for success on the exams.

The Council for Economic Education thanks the U.S. Department of Education's Office of Innovation and Improvement for making this revision possible. Additionally, we recognize the authors, Margaret Ray and Gary Stone; our content consultant Dennis Placone; as well as reviewers Gary Petmecky, Margaret Ray, Helen Roberts, and Sandra Wright. Finally, we extend our wholehearted appreciation to John Morton, the intellectual father of these *Advance Placement Economics* resources. John's dogged efforts to advance K–12 economic education have made an immeasurable difference in the field, and we who follow in his footsteps are better off because of his dedicated service.

Acknowledgments

Contributors
Eric Dodge, Hanover College
David Mayer, Churchill High School

Reviewers
Gary Petmecky, Parkview High School, GA
Margaret Ray, University of Mary Washington, VA
Helen Roberts, University of Illinois at Chicago, IL
Sandra Wright, Adlai E. Stevenson High School, IL

Special Acknowledgments
The Council for Economic Education extends special thanks to the authors who helped developed content for the previous editions: John Morton and Rae Jean B. Goodman.

CEE also thanks the contributors to the previous edition:

Blue-Ribbon Committee
Cecelia Conrad
David Hakes
Mike Johanik
Mary Kohelis
Richard MacDonald
N. Gregory Mankiw
Claire Melican
John Morton
Clark Ross
Robert Wedge

Contributors
Clare E. Adkin
Joe Baker
Joanne Beaver
Ike Brannon
Gregory Breuner
Kelly Chaston

Jim Clark
Janice H. Dukes
Rae Jean B. Goodman
Robert Graham
Margaret Hamilton
Robert J. Heffern
W.C. Kerby
Mary Kohelis
Jimmy D. Lee
C. Lee McCarty
Francis McMann
John Morton
Margaret Ray
Phillip Saunders
Pamela Schmitt
David Stark
Mary Jo Thomas
Francis Vottero
Gloria Washington

Advanced Placement Economics is designed to help you teach Advanced Placement (AP) Microeconomics courses and prepare your students for the AP Microeconomics Exam.

The AP program offers two separate examinations in economics: one in microeconomics and one in macroeconomics. Each AP exam is intended for qualified students who wish to complete studies in secondary school that are equivalent to a one-semester college introductory course.

The AP Microeconomics Exam is 2 hours and 10 minutes long and consists of a 70-minute multiple-choice section and a 60-minute free-response section. The free-response section begins with a mandatory 10-minute reading period. The free-response section requires graphical analysis. The multiple-choice section accounts for two-thirds of the student's exam grade and the free-response section for the remaining one-third.

Using *Advanced Placement Microeconomics*

Advanced Placement Microeconomics consists of the Student Resource Manual and the Teacher Resource Manual. Each unit in the Student Resource Manual begins with a key ideas section. The student activities teach basic economic principles and allow students to practice applying economic concepts. Each unit ends with sample multiple-choice questions, which are written in the same format as the questions on the AP exam. It is best for each student to have his or her own Student Resource Manual.

The Teacher Resource Manual provides unit overviews, lesson plans, objectives, Teacher Alerts, Bell Ringer activities to jump-start each class, visuals, and answers to the student activities. The procedures in the lessons include instructional activities that are not in the Student Resource Manual. The Teacher Resource Manual is designed to provide a basic framework around which teachers can design an AP Microeconomics course that best meets the needs of their students.

Advanced Placement Microeconomics is designed to be used with an AP-level economics textbook. The textbook provides the basic content, and the lessons and activities in *Advanced Placement Microeconomics* provide practice, application of the content, and review for the AP Microeconomics Exam.

In addition to *Advanced Placement Microeconomics* and an AP-level textbook, a variety of different resources for teaching AP Microeconomics are available including lesson plans, in-class activities, classroom experiments, videos, and supplemental readings. The Council for Economic Education provides a number of additional resources on the *Advanced Placement Economics* companion website, http://www.councilforeconed.org/ap-economics. You can also find a searchable database of resources for teaching AP Microeconomics on the College Board website, http://apcentral.collegeboard.com.

The New and Improved *Advanced Placement Microeconomics*

The 4th edition of *Advanced Placement Microeconomics* has been significantly updated. The content has been revised to reflect the current AP Course Outline and all activities have been adapted to reflect the mastery of economic principles that students are expected to demonstrate on the AP Microeconomics Exam. We believe it is the most complete and comprehensive supplementary package available for AP Microeconomics.

Both the Student Resource Manual and Teacher Resource Manual reflect the current AP Course Description. They were revised based on input from successful high school AP Economics teachers, college professors of economics, members of the AP Economics Test Development Committee, and AP Economics readers. The activities are designed to prepare students for the AP Microeconomics Exam and

reflect an understanding of the challenges high school students face learning college-level introductory microeconomics. The major changes in the fourth edition are outlined below:

- Content is reorganized using the AP Course Outline.

- Unit 1, "Basic Economic Concepts," is designed to reflect the overlap between AP Microeconomics and AP Macroeconomics for those teachers with students completing both courses in the same year.

- Content not included on the AP Course Outline and AP Microeconomics Exam has been deleted.

- Teacher Alerts and Student Alerts have been added throughout the Student Resource Manual and Teacher Resource Manual to point out areas where students commonly have difficulties.

- Bell Ringers have been added to provide thought-provoking openings for each lesson.

- A list of related practice free response questions (FRQs) from released AP exams (available on the AP Central website with associated rubrics and sample student responses) is provided for the content in each unit.

- New activities have been added that address the following important topics on the AP Microeconomics Course Outline and Exam:

  - ❏ The input and output approaches to comparative advantage

  - ❏ The productivity and cost functions of a firm

  - ❏ Profit-maximizing quantity and price for firms in different market structures

  - ❏ Movement of a firm from short-run equilibrium to long-run equilibrium

  - ❏ Consumer surplus, producer surplus, and deadweight loss

  - ❏ Profit-maximizing price and quantity in factor markets

  - ❏ The effect of government policies intended to correct market failures

Top 10 Keys to Teaching an Effective AP Microeconomics Course

Designing and teaching an AP Microeconomics course is challenging. The course requires teaching college-level material to high school students. Here are a few tips from veteran teachers that will help you be successful.

1. Use the information provided by the College Board.

College Board information and materials are available from AP Central, on the College Board's website: http://apcentral.collegeboard.com. Important information on the site includes:

- The AP Microeconomics Course Description

- The AP Microeconomics Teacher's Guide

- AP Course Audit information

- Exam information

- Released multiple-choice and free-response exam questions, answer keys, sample student responses, and comments

- AP Microeconomic Exam tips

- Information and communications from the AP Microeconomics chief reader

- Curriculum modules, lesson plans, and teaching strategies

- A searchable database of course resources

- Electronic discussion board for AP Economics teachers

- Professional development opportunities

2. Get Teacher Training

The College Board offers several one-day workshops that provide background for AP Microeconomics courses. These workshops focus on the content covered and an analysis of past multiple-choice and free-response questions. The workshop leader, who is often an AP reader, will provide valuable information to improve student performance. It also helps to attend longer summer workshops that focus on the content in AP Microeconomics in more detail. These workshops cover the content more comprehensively and demonstrate activities. State Councils on Economic Education and university Centers for Economic Education offer courses and workshops for AP Economics teachers. Some of these affiliates of the Council for Economic Education can also provide advice to individual teachers. To locate the state council or university center nearest you, log on to the CEE website at http://www. councilforeconed.org/resources/resources-in-your-state/.

3. Use the Best Textbook You Can Get

If you are involved in choosing the textbook for your course, look for a book that matches the AP course content. Especially consider the reading level and readability of the book. If you have the option, also look for a textbook that is compatible with your teaching style. Whichever textbook you use, be sure to ask about ancillary materials such as student activities, teacher's manual, study guide, or test bank. There are reviews of textbooks and other instructional materials on the College Board website.

4. Organize the Course in Advance

The unit plans and lesson plans in this book are based on seventy-five 45-minute class periods each semester. However, every school schedule is different and disruptions always interfere with even the best of plans. So you will need to adapt the plans provided here to meet the needs of your students and the requirements of your school. Make sure you are aware of the exam date and be careful to complete the entire syllabus despite both expected and unexpected disruptions. Also, be sure to allow for plenty of exam review time.

5. Assess Often

Students need lots of practice and frequent assessments to make sure they have mastered the material. Brief but frequent multiple-choice quizzes help students get used to the exam format. Unit tests should have AP-style multiple-choice and free-response questions. Use released AP exam questions, and grade (and have students grade) answers using the rubrics provided by the College Board. Students benefit from learning to answer free-response questions. What is required for students to learn economics and succeed on the AP Microeconomics Exam is very different from what is required in other social science disciplines. Familiarity with past AP questions is a key to student success.

6. Teach an Economic Way of Thinking

Content is very important in AP Economics, but a quality course goes beyond teaching a list of concepts. Economics is a unique way of thinking that helps students develop decision-making skills. The goal of an introductory economics course is to help students develop the economic way of thinking. Even if students don't remember a specific concept covered on the exam, they will be able to use the techniques of thinking they have learned to draw correct conclusions. A good resource of ready-to-use lessons that reinforce the economic way of thinking is *Capstone: Exemplary Lessons for High School Economics* (New York: Council for Economic Education, 2003).

7. Use Active Learning

An AP Microeconomics class will not be effective if the focus is on memorizing definitions, information, and rules. While the lecture-discussion method will be required for initial presentation of course content, economics will be more relevant and stimulating if students are actively involved in the lessons. They will also learn the content at the required, deeper level.

The Council for Economic Education and the companion website for *Advanced Placement Economics* are excellent sources for active-learning activities that can help your students understand concepts critical to their performing well on an AP Economics exam.

8. Practice Makes Perfect

The *Advanced Placement Microeconomics* Student Resource Manual provides students with the practice they will need to be successful on the AP Microeconomics Exam. The goal is not to cover every possible situation but to develop economic reasoning so that students can apply what they have learned to any example they may be given.

9. Graph Early and Often

The students must be able to perform graphical analysis to do well on the AP Microeconomics Exam. Important graphs in microeconomics include production possibilities; demand and supply in both product and factor markets; productivity, cost, revenue, and profit functions of a firm; and externalities.

It is essential for students to understand that they are applying an economic model, not memorizing graphs. Students need to know that graphs must be clearly and correctly labeled to receive credit on AP Economics exams. When you provide feedback on students' graphs, always point out labeling errors and omissions.

10. Emphasize Historically Weak Areas

Each year the AP Microeconomics chief reader identifies areas in which students have done poorly. Because these areas will be covered again in future tests, it pays to review the chief reader's notes. These are available on the College Board's AP Central website for the microeconomics course. Use these notes to design your course and prepare your students for their AP Microeconomics Exam.

Now It's Time to Get Your Act Together and Take Your Show on the Road

Once you have the right tools and the right training, your students should be able to do well on the AP Economics exams. More importantly, you will be giving them a new lens through which to view the world. They will learn a systematic and disciplined way of thinking that will serve them well throughout their lives. This is the real contribution of a well-taught AP Economics course.

On the Web

To download the visuals for each lesson and to find related material, visit:

http://www.councilforeconed.org/ ap-economics

Outline for an Advanced Placement Microeconomics Course

75 class periods of 45 minutes each

	Percentage Goals of Exam
Content Area	*(multiple-choice section)*

I. Basic Economic Concepts (8–14%)

    A. Scarcity, choice, and opportunity cost
    B. Production possibilities curve
    C. Comparative advantage, absolute advantage, specialization, and trade
    D. Economic systems
    E. Property rights and the role of incentives
    F. Marginal analysis

II. The Nature and Functions of Product Markets (55–70%)

    A. Supply and demand (15–20%)
        1. Market equilibrium
        2. Determinants of supply and demand
        3. Price and quantity controls
        4. Elasticity
            a. Price, income, and cross-price elasticities of demand
            b. Price elasticity of supply
        5. Consumer surplus, producer surplus, and allocative efficiency
        6. Tax incidence and deadweight loss
    B. Theory of consumer choice (5–10%)
        1. Total utility and marginal utility
        2. Utility maximization: equalizing marginal utility per dollar
        3. Individual and market demand curves
        4. Income and substitution effects
    C. Production and costs (10–15%)
        1. Production functions: short and long run
        2. Marginal product and diminishing returns
        3. Short-run costs
        4. Long-run costs and economies of scale
        5. Cost minimizing input combination and productive efficiency
    D. Firm behavior and market structure (25–35%)
        1. Profit
            a. Accounting versus economic profits
            b. Normal profit
            c. Profit maximization: MR = MC rule
        2. Perfect competition
            a. Profit maximization
            b. Short-run supply and shutdown decision

    c. Behavior of firms and markets in the short run and in the long run

    d. Efficiency and perfect competition

  3. Monopoly

    a. Sources of market power

    b. Profit maximization

    c. Inefficiency of monopoly

    d. Price discrimination

    e. Natural monopoly

  4. Oligopoly

    a. Interdependence, collusion, and cartels

    b. Game theory and strategic behavior

    c. Dominant strategy

    d. Nash equilibrium

  5. Monopolistic competition

    a. Product differentiation and role of advertising

    b. Profit maximization

    c. Short-run and long-run equilibrium

    d. Excess capacity and inefficiency

III. Factor Markets   (10–18%)

  A. Derived factor demand

  B. Marginal revenue product

  C. Hiring decisions in the markets for labor and capital

  D. Market distribution of income

IV. Market Failure and the Role of Government   (12–18%)

  A. Externalities

    1. Marginal social benefit and marginal social cost

    2. Positive externalities

    3. Negative externalities

    4. Remedies

  B. Public goods

    1. Public versus private goods

    2. Provision of public goods

  C. Public policy to promote competition

    1. Antitrust policy

    2. Regulation

  D. Income distribution

    1. Equity

    2. Sources and measures of income inequality

Lesson Plans

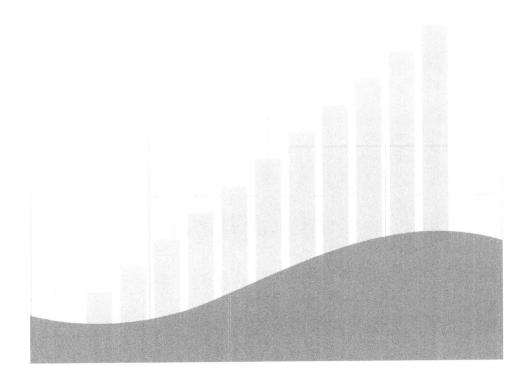

MICROECONOMICS

Basic Economic Concepts

Unit 1

16 class periods or 720 minutes
(21 percent of course time)

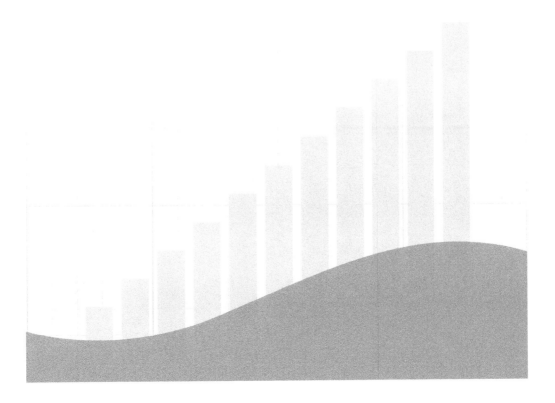

Unit 1 focuses on basic economic concepts, including the framework of demand and supply in a competitive market. These concepts account for 15–24 percent of the Advanced Placement (AP) Microeconomics Exam. More importantly, if students do not understand these concepts, they will have a difficult time throughout the course.

The most important introductory concept is scarcity. In any economy, scarce resources and unlimited wants result in the need to make choices. Students must understand scarcity, opportunity cost, and trade-offs. They should be able to illustrate these concepts on a production possibilities curve (PPC).

Because of scarcity, every economic system must determine which goods and services to produce, how to produce them, and for whom to produce them. Students will learn about how different types of economic systems answer these three questions.

A key part of a microeconomics course focuses on how specialization and exchange increase the total output of goods and services. Students must be able to differentiate between absolute advantage and comparative advantage. Comparative advantage is the key to specialization and trade. Be certain that students understand the difference between input and output examples of comparative advantage.

Unit 1 introduces students to the market forces of demand and supply. It is critical for their success on the AP Microeconomics Exam that students understand how demand and supply determine the market price and quantity, and how changes in demand and supply affect the market equilibrium. Much of the material in the microeconomics course requires students to understand the concepts of demand and supply.

Finally, the foundation of the economic way of thinking is established in Unit 1. This approach to an issue gives students the ability to think critically and make sound decisions. Understanding how marginal analysis leads to wise decisions by individuals, households, firms, and government gives students the flexibility to handle many questions on the AP Microeconomics Exam. Students should not memorize the concepts; instead, they should use the concepts as a framework for organizing the course.

The Lesson Planner

Lesson 1 The Economic Way of Thinking; Activity 1-1 and Visual 1-1

Lesson 2 Scarcity, Opportunity Cost, and Production Possibilities Curves; Activity 1-2 and Visual 1-2

Lesson 3 Absolute Advantage and Comparative Advantage, Specialization, and Trade; Activity 1-3 and Visuals 1-3 and 1-4

Lesson 4 Understanding Demand; Activities 1-4 and 1-5, and Visuals 1-5 and 1-6

Lesson 5 Understanding Supply; Activities 1-6 and 1-7, and Visuals 1-7 and 1-8

Lesson 6 Equilibrium Price and Quantity, Interrelation of Markets; Activities 1-8 and 1-9, and Visuals 1-9 and 1-10

Lesson 7 Economic Systems; Activity 1-10

Lesson 8 Marginal Analysis; Activity 1-11

Practice Free Response Questions (FRQs)

This is a partial list of FRQs that can be used with each unit of the *Advanced Placement Economics: Microeconomics* resource manual. These questions and grading rubrics are available at AP Central on the College Board Web site: http://apcentral.collegeboard.com

2012	Question 2, part (b): change in demand versus change in supply
2012	Question 3: world market demand and supply graph; tariff
2010	Question 3, part (a): demand and supply graph; consumer and producer surplus
2009	Question 2, part (a): demand and supply graph; calculate producer surplus
2006 Form B	Question 2, part (a): draw a demand and supply graph; show consumer and producer surplus

Additional Resources

To download visuals for each lesson and to find related material, visit
http://www.councilforeconed.org/ap-economics

The Economic Way of Thinking

Introduction and Description

AP Economics has many details that can confuse students. Students need a framework to organize these details. This lesson acquaints students with basic economic concepts and methodology. It begins with some key economic ideas that represent a new set of lenses through which students may view the world. The lesson ends with a test of economic myths that should get students' attention. This exercise also gives the teacher a way of reinforcing the economic concepts taught at the beginning of the lesson.

Objectives

1. Define *scarcity*.

2. Define *opportunity cost*.

3. Define the *economic way of thinking*.

4. Apply *scarcity* concepts to a variety of economic and noneconomic situations.

Time Required

Two class periods or 90 minutes

Materials

1. Activity 1-1

2. Visual 1-1

 Bell Ringer

Have you ever been treated to a free lunch? What do economists mean when they say, "There is no such thing as a free lunch"? Explain the TINSTAAFL Principle, and have students give examples of this principle in their own lives.

Teacher Alert: Be sure students understand what "marginal" really means. Reinforce the difference between "marginal" and "total" frequently

throughout your course. Economists work on the *margin* to maximize *total* concepts such as total profit, total utility, and total surplus.

Procedure

1. Display Visual 1-1 and discuss the economic way of thinking. Here are some discussion ideas for each point on the visual.

   ◼ **Everything has a cost.**
   This is the basic idea of the TINSTAAFL Principle. It means that every action costs someone time, effort, or lost opportunities to do something else. Introduce the term *opportunity cost* here. Stress the concept that people incur costs when making decisions, even when people appear to pay nothing. Help students recognize that the true cost of a decision is measured in foregone alternatives rather than in dollars.

   ◼ **People choose for good reasons.**
   Because of scarcity, people always face choices, and they should choose the alternative that gives them the most advantageous combination of costs and benefits. You might stress here that if people have different values, they may make different choices. This might be a good place to discuss *normative* versus *positive economics*. Economists tend to be a tolerant lot because they realize people choose for good reasons. Also stress that *people* choose. Much of the AP Microeconomics course concerns business and government decision making. But business and government decisions are made by people.

   ◼ **Incentives matter.**
   This course is really about incentives. It has been said that economics is about incentives

and everything else is commentary. *Supply and demand analysis* is about incentives. The *theories of the firm* and *factor markets* are about incentives. Government decision making is about incentives. When incentives change, people's behavior changes in predictable ways.

■ **People create economic systems to influence choices and incentives.**
Cooperation among people is governed by written and unwritten rules that are the core of an economic system. As rules change, incentives and behavior change. The success of market systems and the failure of communism are rooted in incentives.

■ **People gain from voluntary trade.**
People trade when they believe the trade makes them better off. If they expect no benefits, they don't trade. Part of the AP Microeconomics course focuses on international trade. However, once again it is people, not countries, that trade. A market system is about voluntary trade. Economics is about voluntary trade between parties that respond to incentives.

■ **Economic thinking is marginal thinking.**
Students must understand the fact that marginal choices involve the effects of additions and subtractions from current conditions. (Should I study another hour for my economics exam? Should I work another hour this weekend?) Much of this course is about comparing marginal costs and marginal benefits to maximize a total concept such as total utility or total profit. Marginal thinking will be stressed in Units 3 and 4, where the theories of the firm and factor markets are discussed. It is important that marginal decision making is discussed in every unit.

■ **The value of a good or service is affected by people's choices.**
Goods and services do not have intrinsic value; their value is determined by the preferences of buyers and sellers. Because of this, trading moves goods and services to higher-valued uses. This is why trading is so important. The price of a good or service is set by supply and demand.

■ **Economic actions create secondary effects.**
Good economics involves analyzing secondary effects. For example, rent controls make apartments more affordable to some consumers, but they also make it less profitable to build and maintain apartments. The secondary effect is a shortage of apartments and houses for rent.

■ **The test of a theory is its ability to predict correctly.**
Students will discuss dozens of theories in an AP Economics course. All these theories have simplifying assumptions. However, the proof of the pudding is in the eating. If the theory correctly predicts the consequences of actions, it is a good theory. Nothing is "good in theory but bad in practice."

2. Tell students that they are going to take a brief quiz. Have students turn to Activity 1-1 in the Student Resource Manual. Give them a few minutes to answer the questions.

3. When everyone is finished, either poll students on their answers, or simply announce that all the answers are false. Some students will think this is a cheap trick.

4. Discuss the answers, and as you do, explain some of the basic laws of economics. Economics is the study of human behavior, and principles have been developed to explain this behavior.

You are laying the foundation for your students' understanding of the economic way of thinking!

The Economic Way of Thinking

■ Everything has a cost.

■ People choose for good reasons.

■ Incentives matter.

■ People create economic systems to influence choices and incentives.

■ People gain from voluntary trade.

■ Economic thinking is marginal thinking.

■ The value of a good or service is affected by people's choices.

■ Economic actions create secondary effects.

■ The test of a theory is its ability to predict correctly.

Scarcity, Opportunity Cost, and Production Possibilities Curves

Introduction and Description

This lesson deals with *opportunity cost*, one of the most important concepts in economics. Start with a lecture on scarcity and *production possibilities curves (PPCs)*. Then reinforce the lecture by using Activity 1-2, which develops the central economic problem of scarcity.

Opportunity costs include not only out-of-pocket expenses (*explicit costs*) but also the value of resources that could be used elsewhere (*implicit costs*). Understanding explicit and implicit costs will be essential as students analyze product markets.

In all societies, people must organize to deal with the basic problems raised by scarcity and opportunity cost. A society must decide which goods and services to produce, how to produce them, and how to distribute them. Societies use three systems—tradition, command, or market—to solve the basic problems. This is the focus of Activity 1-10.

Objectives

1. Define *scarcity*, *opportunity cost*, and *trade-offs*.

2. Identify the conditions that give rise to the economic problem of scarcity.

3. Identify the opportunity costs of various recent decisions made by your school or your community.

4. Construct PPCs from sets of hypothetical data.

5. Apply the concept of opportunity cost to a PPC.

6. Analyze the significance of different locations on, above, and below a PPC.

7. Identify the three questions every economic system must answer.

8. Explain the concept of economic growth. Discuss reasons for such growth and show how it is illustrated using a PPC.

Time Required

Two class periods or 90 minutes

Materials

1. Activity 1-2

2. Visual 1-2

Bell Ringer

Is there any limit to what the United States can produce? Is there any limit to what students can buy?

Teacher Alert: The PPC illustrates three important economic concepts—scarcity, choice, and opportunity cost.

Procedure

1. Give a lecture on scarcity.
   (A) Wants are unlimited.
   (B) A society's resources are limited and fall into four categories: land, labor, capital, and entrepreneurship.
   (C) Society must decide what combination of goods and services to produce this year. The cost of choosing one good is giving up another. This is called opportunity cost.

2. Use Visual 1-2 of a PPC and make points such as these:
   (1) What trade-offs are involved? (*If we want one more unit of one good, we must give up some amount of the other good.*)

(2) Why is the PPC concave, or bowed out, from the origin? *(This is because of the law of increasing opportunity cost.)*

(3) What does a point inside the PPC illustrate? *(It means we are below our potential because of either unemployment or inefficient use of resources.)*

(4) What is a historical example of a point inside the PPC? *(The Great Depression of the 1930s)*

(5) What is the significance of a point outside the PPC? *(It is a point that cannot be achieved with current resources and technology.)*

(6) Under what conditions can a point outside the PPC be reached? *(It will require economic growth with more resources and improved technology.)*

(7) What would a country's PPC look like if it did not have a scarcity of resources? *(Since there would be no limit on what could be produced, there would be no PPC for that country.)*

3. Have students complete Activity 1-2 as homework.

4. Go over Activity 1-2. When discussing the answers, consider these points:

   (A) A linear (straight-line) PPC has constant opportunity costs.

   (B) A concave PPC has increasing opportunity costs. The law of increasing opportunity cost is hard for students to grasp. You can show this concept using Visual 1-2, but be sure to explain the logic behind the increasing cost of producing more of one good. If opportunity cost is constant or increasing for one of the goods, it is constant or increasing, respectively, for both goods.

   (C) The zero opportunity cost (free-good) case is an exercise in graphic interpretation, which can be used to emphasize that there are very few free goods in the world. A free good has zero opportunity cost.

5. Give a lecture on scarcity as the fundamental economic problem and explain that there are several types of economic systems by which countries answer the questions of what to produce, how to produce, and for whom to produce. These economic systems will be discussed in Activity 1-10.

Production Possibilities Curve

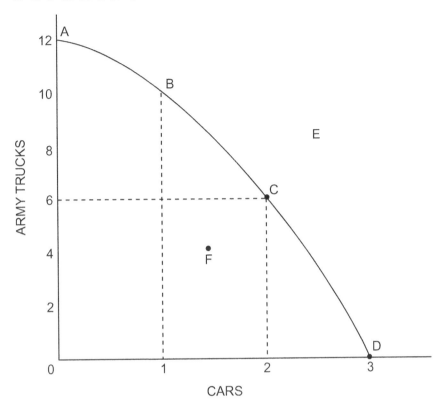

(1) What trade-offs are involved?

(2) Why is the PPC concave, or bowed out, from the origin?

(3) What does a point inside the PPC illustrate?

(4) What is a historical example of a point inside the PPC?

(5) What is the significance of a point outside the PPC?

(6) Under what conditions can a point outside the PPC be reached?

(7) What would a country's PPC look like if it did not have a scarcity of resources?

Absolute Advantage and Comparative Advantage, Specialization, and Trade

Introduction and Description

Activity 1-3 introduces the concepts of *absolute advantage* and *comparative advantage*. Although these concepts are covered in more detail in the international trade unit in Macroeconomics, the concept of comparative advantage is the basis for specialization and voluntary trade as well. Students taking the AP Microeconomics exam need to understand the topic of comparative advantage.

When two parties voluntarily engage in trade, it is because each party feels it will benefit from the trade. It believes the benefit from the exchange will outweigh the cost of the trade. Comparative advantage, which is based on the concept of opportunity cost, demonstrates how voluntary trade produces a net gain for each participant. A person or a nation has a comparative advantage in the production of a product if it can produce that item at a lower opportunity cost than another person or nation. By specializing in the production of goods and services in which it has a comparative advantage, a country can increase its overall level of consumption by trading for items in which it does not have a comparative advantage.

In the examples in this lesson, the cost of producing a good or service is measured in terms of opportunity cost rather than in dollars. By using its resources to produce an extra unit of Good A, a nation gives up the chance to use those same resources to produce some extra amount of Good B. Students need to understand the important role played by opportunity cost in cases of specialization.

Objectives

1. Define *absolute advantage* and *comparative advantage*.

2. Describe and give examples of comparative advantage to which students can relate.

3. Explain why comparative advantage, rather than absolute advantage, is the key to trade.

4. Define *specialization* and *exchange*.

5. Explain how both parties in a trade gain from voluntary exchange.

6. Understand two different approaches to determining comparative advantage: the *input method* and the *output method*.

7. Analyze data to determine which party has the absolute and comparative advantages in different products.

Time Required

Two class periods or 90 minutes

Materials

1. Activity 1-3

2. Visuals 1-3 and 1-4

Bell Ringer

Why does Japan produce so many electronic goods? Why does Brazil produce so much coffee?

Teacher Alert: **Students get confused by the "output method" and the "input method" of determining comparative advantage. Work several examples to demonstrate the two views of a given set of production data.**

Procedure

1. Begin with a discussion of the benefits of trade. Ask students what their lives would be like if they were not able to obtain goods and services from other countries. Ask them how good their standard of living would be if they had to produce everything they eat, wear, watch, and

drive. Emphasize the point that individuals, not nations, trade. However, specialization and trade can be accomplished domestically as well as internationally.

2. Explain the difference between absolute advantage and comparative advantage. Pose this situation to students. Anna is a lawyer who can do word processing faster than any administrative assistant she can hire. Should Anna hire an assistant, or should Anna do word processing in the morning and provide legal services in the afternoon? After all, Anna has an absolute advantage over any administrative assistant in both word processing and legal services. *(Anna should hire the administrative assistant to do the word processing. Anna's comparative advantage is in providing legal services, while the administrative assistant's comparative advantage is in word processing. By specializing according to their comparative advantages, the output of Anna's legal office will be greater than if she did both activities herself.)*

3. Work with students on the examples in Part A of Activity 1-3 to help them understand the output method and input method of determining comparative advantage. They need to see that the person who has the comparative advantage in a particular product will be the same no matter which of the two methods is used.

4. Use Visuals 1-3 and 1-4 to give students more practice with comparative advantage. Have students work with the data in the two charts to answer the questions. Discuss their answers with them.

   Answers to Visual 1-3:

   (1) **Which country has an absolute advantage in producing CDs?**
   (Mexico because it can produce 30 CDs in one hour while Japan can only produce 20 CDs per hour.)

(2) **Which country has an absolute advantage in producing beef?**
(Mexico because it can produce 15 pounds in one hour while Japan can only produce 5 pounds per hour.)

(3) **Which country has a comparative advantage in producing CDs?**
(Japan: 1 CD = $\frac{1}{4}$ B   Mexico: 1 CD = $\frac{1}{2}$ B Japan has the comparative advantage in CDs because it has the lower opportunity cost in producing CDs.)

(4) **Which country has a comparative advantage in producing beef?**
(Japan: 1 B = 4 CDs   Mexico: 1 B = 2 CDs Mexico has the comparative advantage in beef because it has the lower opportunity cost in producing beef.)

(5) **Which country should specialize in CD production?**
(Japan)

(6) **Which country should specialize in beef production?**
(Mexico)

Answers to Visual 1-4:

(1) **Which country has an absolute advantage in producing CDs?**
(Mexico because it can produce one CD in two minutes while it takes Japan three minutes to produce one CD.)

(2) **Which country has an absolute advantage in producing beef?**
(Mexico because it can produce one pound in 4 minutes while it takes Japan 12 minutes to produce one pound.)

(3) **Which country has a comparative advantage in producing CDs?**
(Japan: 1 CD = $\frac{1}{4}$ B   Mexico: 1 CD = $\frac{1}{2}$ B Japan has the comparative advantage in CDs because it has the lower opportunity cost in producing CDs.)

(4) **Which country has a comparative advantage in producing beef?**
(Japan: 1 B = 4 CDs   Mexico: 1 B = 2 CDs
Mexico has the comparative advantage in beef because it has the lower opportunity cost in producing beef.)

(5) **Which country should specialize in CD production?**
(Japan)

(6) **Which country should specialize in beef production?**
(Mexico)

5. Tell students they now are going to work on some additional examples to determine who has the comparative advantage in the production of an item. Refer them to Part B of Activity 1-3. The first example in Part B is worked out for students so they get the idea of what they are to do. There are five more examples in this section. You can have students work on these in class or as homework. Have students present and explain their answers to these problems. Point out that they are determining comparative advantage by using a comparison of opportunity costs rather than a comparison of dollar costs.

6. To be certain that students understand the concept of comparative advantage, ask these questions:

(A) How do you determine who has a comparative advantage in producing a good or service? *(The person who can produce the good at the lower opportunity cost has the comparative advantage for that good.)*

(B) Why is comparative advantage important? *(If people trade on the basis of comparative advantage, they will gain by having more goods at the same cost or the same goods at a lower cost.)*

(C) Why does it matter if two friends save time by specializing in which of two activities they do comparatively better? *(They can do more of these activities in a given period of time, or they can do a given amount of the activities in a shorter amount of time. They both are better off as a result of their specialization.)*

Determining Comparative Advantage (output method)

	Output per hour	
	CDs	Pounds of beef
Japan	20	5
Mexico	30	15

(1) Which country has an absolute advantage in producing CDs?

(2) Which country has an absolute advantage in producing beef?

(3) Which country has a comparative advantage in producing CDs?

(4) Which country has a comparative advantage in producing beef?

(5) Which country should specialize in CD production?

(6) Which country should specialize in beef production?

Advanced Placement Economics Microeconomics: Teacher Resource Manual © Council for Economic Education, New York, N.Y.

Determining Comparative Advantage (input method)

Time required for one unit

	1 CD	1 pound of beef
Japan	3 minutes	12 minutes
Mexico	2 minutes	4 minutes

(1) Which country has an absolute advantage in producing CDs?

(2) Which country has an absolute advantage in producing beef?

(3) Which country has a comparative advantage in producing CDs?

(4) Which country has a comparative advantage in producing beef?

(5) Which country should specialize in CD production?

(6) Which country should specialize in beef production?

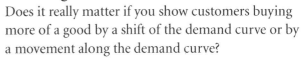

Microeconomics

Understanding Demand

Introduction and Description

In this lesson, students learn about the different aspects of the demand for a good or service. They learn that the typical demand curve is downward sloping. They learn the difference between a *change in the demand* for a good and a *change in the quantity demanded*, a distinction of great importance. They will see what causes a change in demand and what causes a change in quantity demanded. Graphs are essential for analyzing changes in demand and changes in quantity demanded, but manipulating graphs is not enough. Students must understand the actual behavior that is illustrated by a demand curve.

Objectives

1. Describe and analyze what demand is and why consumers buy more of a good or service when the price is lower.

2. Differentiate between a *change in demand* and a *change in quantity demanded*.

3. List and explain the *determinants of demand*.

4. Under specific conditions, determine in which direction a demand curve should shift.

5. Define *consumer surplus*, and know how to show it graphically and calculate its value.

Time Required

Two class periods or 90 minutes

Materials

1. Activities 1-4 and 1-5

2. Visuals 1-5 and 1-6

Bell Ringer

Does it really matter if you show customers buying more of a good by a shift of the demand curve or by a movement along the demand curve?

Teacher Alert: **The distinction between a change in demand and a change in quantity demanded is very important on an AP Economics Exam. Be sure students know what causes each type of change and how to show them graphically.**

Procedure

1. Tell students that the law of demand describes the behavior of consumers. To illustrate this law, give each student a slip of paper with three prices for a popular candy bar or other snack food. Ask each student to write down how many units of the snack food he/she would buy in a one-week period at each of the prices. Collect the slips and add up the quantities at each price. Arrange the prices from the highest to the lowest. In developing the demand curve, point out that the bids are cumulative. That is, a person willing to pay $1.00 for the snack is also willing to pay $0.50. Write the demand schedule and the demand graph on the board. Ask students to describe the behavior of consumers in relation to price and quantity demanded. *(They are inversely related.)*

2. Use Visual 1-5 to illustrate the difference between a change in demand and a change in quantity demanded. A movement from A to B is a change in quantity demanded. This movement along the curve is caused by a change in the price of the product. Only a change in the price of Greebes will cause a change in the quantity of Greebes demanded. A shift in the curve is caused by factors other than a change in the price of Greebes.

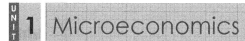

🛈 *Teacher Alert:* Don't let students be lazy and just say "a change in price." They must be specific: Was it the price of this good that changed, or a change in the price of a substitute good or the price of a complementary good? It matters!

3. Still using Visual 1-5, explain the reason a demand curve shifts. *(An increase in demand means people are willing and able to buy more at each price. A decrease in demand means people are willing and able to buy less at each price. A movement from D to D_1 is an increase in demand. A movement from D to D_2 is a decrease in demand.)*

4. Now use Visual 1-6 to discuss the determinants of demand. Give examples in each category.

   ■ Change in consumer tastes

   ■ Change in the number of buyers

   ■ Change in consumer incomes

   ■ Change in the prices of complementary and substitute goods

   ■ Change in consumer expectations

5. Have students complete Parts A and B of Activity 1-4, which ask students to identify changes in demand and changes in quantity demanded. Be sure to point out that the demand price is the maximum price consumers would be willing to pay for a given quantity. Of course, consumers would be willing to pay a lower price than this maximum price.

6. Part C of Activity 1-4 introduces the concept of *consumer surplus*, which is the value received from the purchase of a good in excess of the price paid for it. Use examples that students can relate to as you cover consumer surplus. "You were willing to pay $80 for that pair of shoes but you got them for $60. You have a consumer surplus of $20." Students have frequently missed questions on this concept on past AP exams.

7. Reinforce the determinants of demand and shifts in demand by having students complete Activity 1-5 and discuss it.

Illustrating the Difference between a Change in Demand and a Change in Quantity Demanded

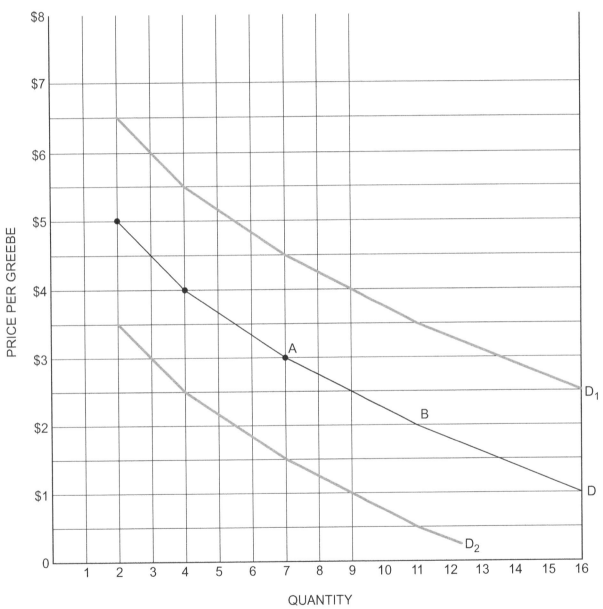

QUANTITY
(hundreds of Greebes per week)

Determinants of Demand

FACTORS THAT SHIFT THE DEMAND CURVE

- ■ Change in consumer tastes

- ■ Change in the number of buyers

- ■ Change in consumer incomes

- ■ Change in the prices of complementary and substitute goods

- ■ Change in consumer expectations

Understanding Supply

Introduction and Description

Prices are determined by demand and supply. This lesson examines the factors that affect supply; these factors are called the *determinants of supply*. Students should also understand the difference between a *change in supply* and a *change in quantity supplied*. Students may have more trouble understanding supply than demand. While the framework of how we study demand and supply is the same, high school students are used to buying things but not so used to supplying things. As buyers, students view a higher price as a bad thing; as sellers, they need to see it as an incentive to produce more.

In this lesson, students learn about the different aspects of the supply of a good or service. They learn that the typical supply curve is upward sloping. They learn the difference between a *change in the supply* of a good and a *change in the quantity supplied*, a distinction of great importance. They will see what causes a change in supply and what causes a change in quantity supplied.

Objectives

1. Describe the behavior of sellers in a competitive market.

2. Differentiate between a *change in supply* and a *change in quantity supplied.*

3. List and explain the determinants of supply.

4. Under specific conditions, determine in which direction a supply curve should shift.

5. Define *producer surplus* and know how to show it graphically and calculate its value.

Time Required

One and a half class periods or 68 minutes

Materials

1. Activities 1-6 and 1-7

2. Visuals 1-7 and 1-8

Bell Ringer

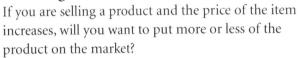

If you are selling a product and the price of the item increases, will you want to put more or less of the product on the market?

Teacher Alert: **The distinction between a change in supply and a change in quantity supplied is very important on an AP Economics Exam. Be sure students know what causes each type of change and how to show them graphically.**

Procedure

1. Tell students that supply describes the behavior of sellers. To illustrate this, give each student a slip of paper with three wages listed. Ask each student to write down how many hours he/she would like to work each week at a local store at these wages. Collect the slips and total the number of hours supplied at each wage. Arrange the wages from the highest to the lowest. In developing the supply curve, point out that the bids are cumulative. That is, a person willing to work for $5.00 an hour is also willing to work for $6.00 an hour. Write the supply schedule and the supply graph on the board. Put "Wage Rate" on the vertical axis and "Hours of Labor" on the horizontal axis. While not all students say they will work more at a higher wage, typically enough do that you will have an upward sloping labor supply curve. While this is an example of a "resource market" rather than a "product market," it is an example that students understand as you are introducing the concept of supply. Ask students to describe the behavior

of suppliers in relation to price (wage) and quantity supplied. *(They are directly related.)*

Now ask students why they would sell more labor at a high wage than at a low wage. Ask them what their opportunity cost is of not working if the wage is $5.00 an hour. Does the opportunity cost of not working increase as the wage increases? *(It does.)* Point out that price (wage) is an incentive to suppliers to provide more of the items consumers want to buy. In this example, the "buyer" was the employer seeking workers.

2. Use Visual 1-7 to illustrate the difference between a change in supply and a change in quantity supplied. A movement from A to B illustrates a change in quantity supplied. This movement along the curve is caused by a change in the price of a good or service. In other words, only a change in the price of Greebes can change the quantity of Greebes supplied.

3. Now illustrate a shift in supply. A shift from S to S_2 is a decrease in supply. Less is supplied at each price. A shift from S to S_1 is an increase in supply. More is supplied at each price.

4. Now use Visual 1-8 to discuss the determinants of supply. Give examples of each determinant. Point out that most determinants of supply relate to the costs of producing the good or service. Explain that the "price" of the product is not the same thing as the "cost" of the product. Any factor that increases costs decreases supply.

Any factor that decreases costs increases supply. The determinants of supply are:

■ Change in resource prices or input prices

■ Change in technology

■ Change in taxes and subsidies

■ Change in the prices of other goods

■ Change in producer expectations

■ Change in the number of suppliers

5. Explain the concept of *producer surplus.* *(Producer surplus is the amount a seller is paid minus the seller's cost. It is the area below the equilibrium price and above the supply curve. The reason that perfectly competitive markets are so good is that the sum of consumer surplus [studied in Activity 1-4] and producer surplus is at a maximum. Things just don't get any better than this. Any interference with the equilibrium quantity under perfectly competitive markets will reduce total surplus [the sum of consumer surplus and producer surplus]. This will be the case with price floors and price ceilings, which students will study later.)*

6. Have students complete Activity 1-6 and go over the answers.

7. Have students complete Activity 1-7 and go over the answers.

Illustrating the Difference between a Change in Supply and a Change in Quantity Supplied

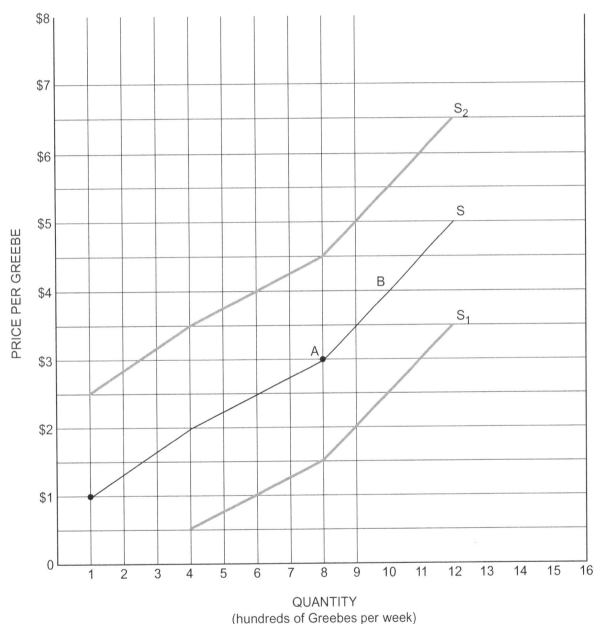

Determinants of Supply

FACTORS THAT SHIFT THE SUPPLY CURVE

- Change in resource prices or input prices

- Change in technology

- Change in taxes and subsidies

- Change in the prices of other goods

- Change in producer expectations

- Change in the number of suppliers

Any factor that *increases* the cost of production *decreases* supply.

Any factor that *decreases* the cost of production *increases* supply.

Equilibrium Price and Quantity, Interrelation of Markets

Introduction and Description

The forces of supply and demand work to establish a price at which the quantity of goods and services people will buy is equal to the quantity suppliers will provide. Activity 1-8 illustrates this interaction between demand and supply. If supply or demand changes, equilibrium price and quantity change. Activity 1-9 drives this point home. Finally, the equilibrium price and quantity of a good or service established by supply and demand in one market can affect the equilibrium price and quantity in other markets. This is demonstrated in Activity 1-9.

Objectives

1. Define *equilibrium price* and *equilibrium quantity*.

2. Determine the equilibrium price and quantity when given the demand for and supply of a good or service.

3. Explain why the price of a good or service and the amount bought and sold in a competitive market will be the equilibrium price and quantity.

4. Predict the effects of changes in supply and demand on equilibrium price and quantity and on the prices of substitute and complementary goods.

5. Given changes in supply and demand, explain which curve has shifted and why.

6. Analyze how buyers and sellers respond to incentives provided by changing market conditions.

Time Required

Two class periods or 90 minutes

Materials

1. Activities 1-8 and 1-9

2. Visuals 1-9 and 1-10

Bell Ringer

Can you explain why the price of gasoline rises sometimes and falls other times?

Teacher Alert: **Students often get confused on when to shift a demand curve or a supply curve. Because this is such an important skill for success on the AP Microeconomics Exam, work with students to be certain they can do it.**

Procedure

1. Before getting to the graphs, it is helpful to define *equilibrium*. Equilibrium is a state of balance between opposing forces. It occurs because everywhere else there is a state of imbalance or *disequilibrium*. In markets, equilibrium is usually a temporary condition. You might illustrate this by putting a ball in a bowl. The ball is at rest at the bottom of the bowl until you hit the bowl, and the ball moves until it comes to rest again. Hitting the bowl is like a shift in demand or supply. The ball movement represents the market forces of demand and supply moving the market back to equilibrium. However, the difference is that equilibrium in the market occurs at different combinations of price and quantity. Each resting place is a different setting, depending on market conditions.

2. Use Visual 1-9 to show how markets reach equilibrium.

   (A) What if the market price were $4? *(There would be a surplus of 800 Greebes.)* How would sellers get rid of the surplus? *(They would lower the price until all the Greebes for* *sale were sold. The lower price is an incentive that brings more buyers into the market. All the Greebes would be sold at $3, the equilibrium price.)*

(B) What if the market price were $2? *(Buyers would demand 800 more Greebes than sellers are willing to sell.)* Which buyers will get the Greebes? *(The ones who will pay more.)* How does the market eliminate the shortage? *(The higher price is an incentive that brings more sellers into the market. Once again, at $3 the number of Greebes offered for sale in a time period is equal to the number of Greebes consumers are willing and able to buy.)*

(C) Only at a price of $3 is the number of Greebes sellers are willing and able to sell equal to the number of Greebes consumers are willing and able to buy. This is why the equilibrium price of Greebes is $3 and the equilibrium quantity of Greebes is 1,000.

⚠ *Teacher Alert:* Students should recognize that equilibrium quantity is both quantity demanded and quantity supplied. They sometimes write "equilibrium quantity demanded" or "equilibrium quantity supplied," when all they need to say is "equilibrium quantity."

3. Have students complete Activity 1-8 and discuss the answers.

4. Now use Visual 1-10 to illustrate shifts in demand and supply. Each shift changes both the equilibrium price and quantity.

    (A) Graph A shows an increase in demand, causing an increase in price, which causes an increase in quantity supplied. Even though the supply curve did not shift, increased

production is shown by a movement along the existing supply curve in response to the higher price. Both equilibrium price and equilibrium quantity increase.

(B) Graph B shows a decrease in demand, causing a decrease in price, which causes a decrease in quantity supplied. Even though the supply curve did not shift, decreased production is shown by a movement along the existing supply curve in response to the lower price. Both equilibrium price and equilibrium quantity decrease.

(C) Graph C shows an increase in supply, causing a decrease in price, which causes an increase in quantity demanded. Even though the demand curve did not shift, increased consumption is shown by a movement along the existing demand curve in response to the lower price. Equilibrium price decreases while equilibrium quantity increases.

(D) Graph D shows a decrease in supply, causing an increase in price, which causes a decrease in quantity demanded. Even though the demand curve did not shift, decreased consumption is shown by a movement along the existing demand curve in response to the higher price. Equilibrium price increases while equilibrium quantity decreases.

(E) In each case, students should distinguish between a shift in demand or supply and a price effect that causes a change in quantity demanded or quantity supplied.

5. Have students complete Activity 1-9 and discuss the answers.

Equilibrium and Disequilibrium

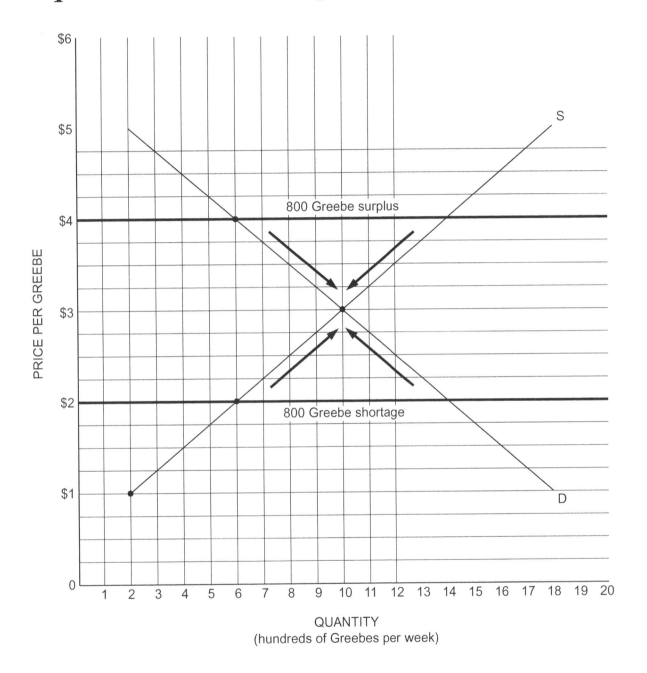

QUANTITY
(hundreds of Greebes per week)

The Effects of Shifts in Demand or Supply

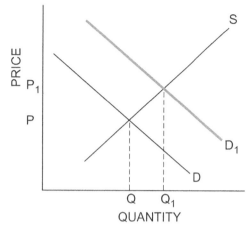

A. INCREASE IN DEMAND

D ↑

P ↑

Q ↑

B. DECREASE IN DEMAND

D

P

Q

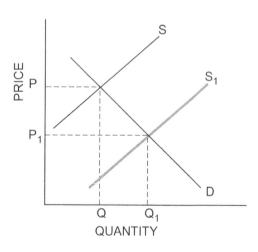

C. INCREASE IN SUPPLY

S ↑

P ↓

Q ↑

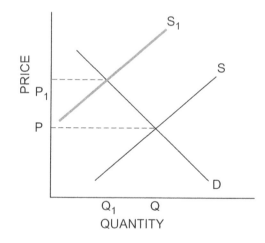

D. DECREASE IN SUPPLY

S

P

Q

Economic Systems

Introduction and Description

Each society must find a way to answer the three big economic questions of what to produce, how to produce it, and how to distribute what is produced. Different methods of answering these questions have evolved over time. In a *pure market economy*, the questions are answered through the interaction of buyers and sellers in the marketplace. Resources are privately owned, and the role of government is limited to providing laws that protect property rights. This system is sometimes called a *free enterprise system* or *capitalism*. In a *command economy*, the key economic questions are answered by the government, which owns or controls most of the country's resources. This system is also referred to as a *centrally planned economy*. In a *traditional system*, cultural traditions and religion strongly influence how the country addresses the three main economic questions. Most countries have a *mixed system*, which is a combination of the pure market and command systems. For example, the United States economy is a mixed system that relies primarily on markets but with a strong influence from government involvement.

Objectives

1. Explain the three main economic questions faced by each society: what to produce, how to produce it, and who gets what is produced.

2. Discuss the various types of economic systems and give examples of countries that illustrate these different models.

3. Ask students which model best enables a country to have economic growth.

4. Have students discuss the economic incentives provided by markets in each system. Ask them how the government affects those incentives.

Time Required

One class period or 45 minutes

Materials

Activity 1-10

Bell Ringer

In which country would consumers have a greater variety of goods and services available to them— one that has a pure market economy or one that has a command economy?

Teacher Alert: **Students need to weigh the benefits and costs of increased government involvement in a country's economic system.**

Procedure

1. State the three economic problems each society faces because of scarcity of resources.

2. Ask students how their country solves these questions.

3. Discuss the various types of economic systems that have developed over time. Have students identify countries that illustrate each type of economic system and explain their choices.

4. Have student complete Activity 1-10.

Marginal Analysis

Introduction and Description

When you get right down to it, economics is really about how much of something we should do. Because of scarcity, we cannot have everything we want. Therefore, we have to make decisions about how to allocate our time, money, and resources among the many different uses of these limited items. *Marginal analysis* is the tool economists use to make these allocation decisions. The idea of marginal analysis is quite simple: If the *marginal benefit* from another unit of some activity exceeds the *marginal cost* of that unit, you should undertake that extra unit of the activity. If the marginal benefit of the extra unit is less than the extra cost of that unit, do not take on the extra unit. (As a rule of thumb, if the marginal benefit and marginal cost of an extra unit are equal, economists say go ahead with that unit.) This lesson gives students some experience working with marginal analysis. Stress to students that they need to be clear in their answers about the difference between a "marginal" value (such as marginal benefit or marginal cost) and a "total" value (such as total benefit or total cost). This distinction makes a big difference in how well a student performs on the AP Microeconomics Exam.

Objectives

1. Understand why we all have to make decisions.

2. Define the terms marginal benefit, marginal cost, total benefit, and total cost.

3. Explain that economic decision making often focuses on a comparison of marginal benefit and marginal cost to determine how many units of an activity should be provided.

4. Emphasize the difference between marginal concepts and total concepts.

5. Explain that *the economic way of thinking* results in effective decisions being made.

Time Required

One class period or 45 minutes.

Materials

Activity 1-11

Bell Ringer

Will you do all you can to get an A on your next economics exam?

Teacher Alert: **Students must understand the difference between marginal concepts and total concepts. If students have this distinction clear in their minds early in the course, your job of teaching the material related to the firm and the factor markets will be easier and much more enjoyable!**

Procedure

1. Ask students, "Who will do all you can to earn an A on your next economics exam?" Count the many hands that will be waving. Ask them why they want an A. What is the benefit of an A over a B or a C? *(Answers will include a better report card, happier parents, and student satisfaction.)* Now ask them what they will have to give up to study the amount of time needed to make an A on their next exam. *(Answers will include time with friends, sleeping, gaming, working at a job, time with family, watching television, and, hopefully, studying for an exam in another course.)* Given the marginal cost of each extra hour devoted to studying for your exam, compared to the marginal benefit of receiving an A rather than a B or a C, ask students how many hours they are *really* willing to devote to your exam.

2. Here's another quick example to demonstrate marginal analysis. Ask which students have a one dollar bill with them. Pick one of those students to stand in the front of the room with you. Give that student an unsealed envelope with $0.85 in it but do not let the rest of the class know what is in the envelope. Ask the student if he/she will give you the dollar bill for what is in the envelope. Have the student look in the envelope and give you an answer. (The answer should be "No," of course.) Now quietly slip a quarter in the envelope so it contains $1.10. Ask the student a second time if he/she will give you the dollar bill for what is in the envelope. When the student accepts this offer, take the dollar bill and let the student keep the envelope and the $1.10. Now get the rest of the class involved. Ask the class why the student rejected the first offer; make them use the economic terms "marginal benefit" and "marginal cost." *(They will say because the marginal benefit was less than the marginal cost.)* Why did the student accept the second offer? *(Because the marginal benefit was greater than the marginal cost.)* Here is where they learn an important lesson on marginal analysis. Ask the volunteer student how much was in the envelope the first time: $0.85. When you ask the class what the volunteer's marginal benefit would have been if he/she had accepted the first offer, most students will say a loss of $0.15, or negative $0.15. But the correct answer is $0.85 because that is what the student would have received. The marginal cost to the volunteer of getting the envelope would have been $1.00.

Thus, because the marginal benefit of $0.85 was less than the marginal cost of $1.00, the volunteer wisely rejected the offer. But what is the economic name for the loss of $0.15? It is called the *net marginal benefit (NMB)* because it is the difference between marginal benefit (MB) and marginal cost (MC): NMB = MB – MC. If the NMB of an activity is negative, a person should not pursue that activity. For the second offer, the MB of $1.10 was greater than the MC of $1.00, so the volunteer agreed to the deal. The NMB of the exchange was +$0.10. If the NMB is positive, a person should say "Yes" to the activity. (This simple example can be used again when you take students into Unit 3 where a firm must decide how many units of output it should produce to maximize its total profit. That answer will come from marginal analysis as the firm compares the marginal revenue with the marginal cost of each extra unit of output. The net marginal benefit in that context will be called *marginal profit*.)

3. Have students complete Activity 1-11. Discuss the answers with them.

4. Ask students if marginal analysis means that they should do all they can to complete an assignment or an activity to the best of their abilities, regardless of the cost? *(They should compare the MB and the MC of each extra unit of the activity. If the MB is greater than [or equal to] the MC, they should undertake the next unit of the activity. If the MB is less than the MC, they should not undertake that unit.)*

MICROECONOMICS

Nature and Functions of Product Markets

Unit 2

12 class periods or 540 minutes
(16 percent of course time)

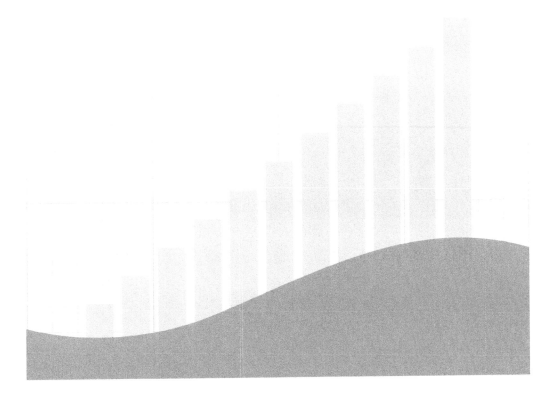

Unit 2 extends the basic framework of demand and supply that was covered in Unit 1. The material in Unit 2 accounts for 13–20 percent of the Advanced Placement (AP) Microeconomics Exam. Lesson 2 has students explore how competitive markets allocate society's scarce resources. They see how market prices serve to allocate these resources to their highest valued uses. The effects of changes in one market on the price and quantity in a related market are demonstrated. This lesson uses consumer theory based on marginal utility analysis to explain why the demand curve for a good or service is downward sloping. The concept of *consumer equilibrium* is used to illustrate how a consumer can maximize total utility from a given income by allocating that budget correctly between two products.

Lesson 3 of this unit gives students an understanding of elasticity, an important concept in a microeconomics course. Elasticity measures the strength of the response of one variable to a change in another variable. The price elasticity of demand for a product indicates how strongly the quantity demanded of a product changes in response to a change in the price of that product. Students learn how to calculate and interpret the value of the price elasticity of demand, and how it is related to total revenue. The lesson also discusses income elasticity of demand, cross-price elasticity of demand, and price elasticity of supply. The effect of an excise tax is examined as well.

Unit 2 concludes with Lessons 4 and 5, which provide a discussion of price floors and price ceilings, property rights, and deadweight loss. These topics are important on the AP Microeconomics Exam because they help students understand how society suffers a reduction in social welfare when the market produces an output level different from the one that would result from a perfectly competitive market free of outside influences.

Before you begin this unit, it would be a good idea to conduct a supply and demand simulation. By simulating market behavior, students better understand the behavior behind the demand and supply curves. There are many simulations available, including "A Market in Wheat" in CEE's *Economics in Action: 14 Greatest Hits for Teaching High School Economics*.

The Lesson Planner

Lesson 1   Resource Allocation; Activity 2-1

Lesson 2   Marginal Utility and the Law of Demand; Activity 2-2

Lesson 3   Elasticities; Activities 2-3, 2-4, 2-5, and 2-6, and Visuals 2-1, 2-2, and 2-3

Lesson 4   Price Floors and Ceilings; Activity 2-7 and Visuals 2-4 and 2-5

Lesson 5   Property Rights, Market Failure, and Deadweight Loss; Activities 2-8 and 2-9, and Visuals 2-6 and 2-7

Practice Free Response Questions (FRQs)

This is a partial list of FRQs that can be used with each unit of the *Advanced Placement Economics: Microeconomics* resource manual. These questions and grading rubrics are available at AP Central on the College Board Web site: http://apcentral.collegeboard.com

2012	Question 2, part (a): consumer equilibrium; marginal and total utility
2012	Question 2, part (b): income elasticity of demand
2012	Question 2, part (c): cross-price elasticity of demand
2011	Question 1, part (d): elasticity
2011 Form B	Question 2, part (b): price ceiling
2010	Question 1, part (b): elasticity
2010	Question 1, part (c): effect of increase in demand of one good on market of another good
2010	Question 3: consumer and producer surplus; deadweight loss
2010 Form B	Question 3: price elasticity of demand; perfectly inelastic supply; burden of an excise tax
2009	Question 1, part (c): spillover benefits
2009	Question 2: excise tax; price-elasticity of demand
2009 Form B	Question 2: maximize total utility
2008	Question 2: maximize total utility; price elasticity of demand; incidence of excise tax
2008	Question 3: competitive market with a price ceiling
2006	Question 3: land has alternate uses
2006 Form B	Question 2: price ceiling

Additional Resources

To download visuals for each lesson and to find related material, visit
http://www.councilforeconed.org/ap-economics

Resource Allocation

Introduction and Description

It is important for students to understand how society's scarce resources are allocated among their many possible uses. This lesson asks students to analyze the effects of a change in demand or supply in one market on the equilibrium position in a related market. Activity 2-1 assumes the product and resource markets are perfectly competitive.

Objectives

1. Explain that markets do not exist in isolation from other markets. A change in one market can have an effect on the demand and supply in another market. It is important that students recognize these *secondary effects* of the initial change.

2. Students should distinguish between a change in demand or supply and a change in quantity demanded or quantity supplied.

3. Point out the role played by price in a competitive market in the allocation of resources to higher value uses.

Time Required

One and a half class periods or 68 minutes

Materials

Activity 2-1

Bell Ringer

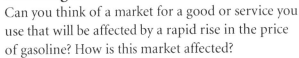

Can you think of a market for a good or service you use that will be affected by a rapid rise in the price of gasoline? How is this market affected?

Teacher Alert: **Students often miss questions that** **require them to know the difference between a shift of a demand or supply curve and a movement along the curve. This lesson gives them valuable practice developing this skill.**

Procedure

1. Have students brainstorm about markets that are somehow related to each other. Have them post these markets on the board and link them with arrows. Ask them if these are product markets or factor markets.

2. Ask students if they feel the allocation of resources through a pure market economy is better than the allocation of resources through a command economy. Be sure the discussion includes the role of prices in such an allocation. What information do consumers and sellers get from the price of a good in a competitive market that they would not receive in a command economy? *(Prices in a competitive market indicate the value consumers place on the items and the costs to sellers of producing the item.)*

3. Have students complete Activity 2-1. Discuss the results of their work.

Marginal Utility and the Law of Demand

Introduction and Description

This lesson engages students in an application of marginal analysis, which gives them a better understanding of the law of demand. Students need more than a superficial answer to the question of, "Why does a person buy more of a good when its price is reduced?" Activity 2-2 accomplishes two important goals. First, it shows the relationship between *total utility* and *marginal utility*. This "marginal–total" connection will be useful in future lessons as well. The activity helps students understand that people make decisions on the margin as they attempt to maximize a total concept such as total utility. Second, it shows students that having marginal utility data is not enough to maximize their total utility as they allocate a limited income between two goods. Students must determine the marginal utility per dollar to make that allocation correctly. (This skill will be used again by students in Unit 4 when they work with factor markets as firms allocate a given resource budget between different types of resources.) Lesson 2 also has the student determine the value of *consumer surplus* and distinguishes between the *substitution effect* and the *income effect* of a change in the price of a product.

Objectives

1. Explain the difference between a consumer's *total utility* and *marginal utility*.

2. Explain that as a person consumes additional units of an item, a positive marginal utility means total utility increased, a negative marginal utility means total utility decreased, and a marginal utility of zero means total utility did not change.

3. As a person consumes more of a good or service, eventually the consumer reaches a point where the marginal utility of an extra unit diminishes. Explain that because of *diminishing marginal utility*, a consumer will only buy more of a good if its price is reduced. This illustrates *the law of demand*.

4. To receive the greatest total utility from a given income, a consumer should allocate that income between two products in such a way that the *marginal utility per dollar* is the same for each product. This condition is called *consumer equilibrium* because the consumer has no incentive to change the allocation of income unless the price of a product changes.

5. When the price of a good changes, the consumer experiences a *substitution effect* and an *income effect*. These two effects usually support each other and explain the law of demand.

Time Required

One and a half class periods or 68 minutes

Materials

Activity 2-2

Bell Ringer

If you were at a party and there were plenty of free pizza, how many slices would you eat? How many slices would you eat if the host declared you would have to pay $2.00 for each slice? Why would you behave differently when the pizza is not free?

Teacher Alert: Students must understand *why* they need to calculate the marginal utility per dollar for both of the items they are purchasing. Simply comparing the marginal utility values from the two products will not lead them to an efficient allocation of their income between the two items.

Procedure

1. Define the terms total utility and marginal utility. Also, get students in the habit of saying "total utility" or "marginal utility" rather than just "utility." This is an important distinction.

2. Explain that a person's evaluation of her or his total satisfaction (total utility) from some amount of a good is subjective. Different people will receive different levels of total utility from a given number of units of a good. To keep things simple in this activity, we assume we can measure marginal utility in dollars to represent how much money a person is willing to spend to acquire an extra unit of the good. Total utility from a given amount of the good is the sum of the marginal utilities of the individual units.

3. Have students complete Table 2-2.1 in Activity 2-2. Check their answers to be sure everyone is on track.

4. Ask them why Dolores's marginal utility decreased for each good as she bought additional units. Ask if her diminishing marginal utility is related to the price of the good? *(It is not.)*

5. Have students explain the relationship between total utility and marginal utility. *(Marginal utility is the change in total utility when an extra unit is consumed. If total utility increases, then marginal utility from the extra unit is positive. If total utility decreases, then marginal utility from the extra unit is negative. If total utility does not change, then the marginal utility from the extra unit is zero.)*

6. Ask students if Dolores should stop consuming a good if the marginal utility from an extra unit is diminishing. *(Diminishing marginal utility is not a reason to stop consuming additional units of a good. Dolores must compare marginal utility per dollar for the two goods, and take income into account, as she decides when not to buy another unit of a good.)*

7. Have students plot the total utility and marginal utility data from Table 2-2.1 in Figure 2-2.1, and answer the questions based on the graphs. They should see that as long as marginal utility is positive, total utility is increasing. Diminishing marginal utility means the *increase* in total utility is less with each extra unit consumed.

Teacher Alert: **Some textbooks plot marginal utility** **values at the midpoint of two quantities of the good, while others plot the values at the higher of the two quantities. The latter approach is employed here. For example, the marginal utility of the second shirt is $40 and is plotted at 2 shirts rather than at 1.5 shirts.**

8. Part B of Activity 2-2 asks students how Dolores should allocate her budget between shirts and steaks. Note that the first example assumes the prices of shirts and steaks are equal. Be sure students can work an example in which the two prices are different. This shows students why they must compare the marginal utility per dollar for each good in deciding what the consumer should do. A condition called *consumer equilibrium* exists when the following equality holds true: $(MU/Price)_{Shirt} = (MU/Price)_{Steak}$. The condition of consumer equilibrium can also be expressed as: $(MU \text{ per } \$1)_{Shirt} = (MU \text{ per } \$1)_{Steak}$. Discuss this concept with students. They should understand why a consumer in a position of consumer equilibrium will not be better off if she moves $1 away from one good and spends it on the other good.

9. Have students complete Table 2-2.2, which has a consumer allocating her budget between units of gas and food, with the two products having different prices. Students should answer the questions based on this table.

10. Part C of Activity 2-2 deals with the topic of *consumer surplus*. Have students answer the questions based on Table 2-2.3.

11. Part D of Activity 2-2 introduces the *substitution and income effects* of a change in the price of a product. Explain these two effects and have students answer the questions in this section.

Elasticities

Introduction and Description

Now that students have mastered the foundation of demand and supply, it is time to have them move to the next level of market analysis. *Elasticity* is a measure of how strongly one variable responds to a change in another variable. In Lesson 3, students will learn about four economic elasticities. The most important one is *price elasticity of demand*, which measures the strength of the consumer response to a change in the price of a product. Both the price change and the resulting change in quantity demanded are measured as percentage changes. This is necessary because a comparison of the actual change in dollars and quantities does not indicate the relative size of the changes. (A $5 price increase is a large change if the product is a pizza but it is a small change if the product is a house.) The law of demand tells us that the value of the price elasticity of demand will be a negative number. When we interpret that value, we consider its absolute value.

Two other demand elasticities are *income elasticity of demand* and *cross-price elasticity of demand*. In the former, we measure how strongly consumers of a particular product respond to some percentage change in income. In the latter, the measurement is of how strongly consumers of one good respond to some percentage change in the price of a related good (a substitute or a complement). Students will work with one elasticity on the supply side of a market. The *price elasticity of supply* indicates how strongly producers of a good respond to a change in the price of that good. The law of supply tells us that the value of the price elasticity of supply will be a positive number.

A firm's *total revenue* is found by multiplying the quantity demanded by the price of the item. Since price and quantity demanded are the two variables involved in the calculation of the price elasticity of demand, students should recognize the relationship between total revenue and price elasticity of demand. Price elasticity of demand also affects the impact of an *excise tax* that the government may place on a good or service.

Objectives

1. Define price elasticity of demand.

2. Show students how to calculate the value of the price elasticity of demand. Explain why we expect price elasticity of demand to have a negative value and why we consider its absolute value when we interpret its value.

3. Explain what is meant by *elastic* demand, *inelastic* demand, and *unit* elastic demand.

4. Know why the slope of a demand curve and the price elasticity of demand are not the same thing.

5. Explain the relationship between total revenue and price elasticity of demand.

6. Explain the concepts of *perfectly elastic* demand and *perfectly inelastic* demand.

7. Discuss the determinants of price elasticity of demand.

8. Explain the other elasticities—income elasticity of demand, cross-price elasticity of demand, and price elasticity of supply.

9. Define and distinguish between *a normal good* and *an inferior good*.

10. Define and distinguish between *substitute goods* and *complementary goods*.

11. Analyze the effect of an excise tax.

Time Required

Three class periods or 135 minutes

Materials

1. Activities 2-3, 2-4, 2-5, and 2-6

2. Visuals 2-1, 2-2, and 2-3

 Bell Ringer

Would you respond more strongly to a 10 percent increase in the price of gasoline or a 10 percent increase in the price of hamburgers?

Teacher Alert: **Students will need to practice calculating and interpreting the value of price elasticity of demand. They should work to understand this material rather than memorize a formula.**

Procedure

1. Define the term price elasticity of demand.

2. Ask students why the value of price elasticity of demand is expected to be negative.

3. Have students focus on the nature of the consumer response to a price change. If the percentage change in quantity demanded is greater than the percentage change in price, then demand is elastic over that price range. If the consumer response is weak compared to the price change, demand is inelastic. If the two percentage changes happen to be equal, then demand is unit elastic (also called unitary elastic).

4. Do not let the fact that students have to calculate some percentage values on occasion distract them from the basic understanding of what the terms elastic, inelastic, and unit elastic mean.

5. Explain why economists use the midpoint or average value of price and quantity demanded when they calculate the percentage changes in these variables. (*Because the value of the price elasticity of demand is used for that specific part of the demand curve, they use the midpoint as*

their base value rather than one of the end point values.)

6. Have students work Parts A through E of Activity 2-3. This section has useful calculation examples for them. It also shows why the slope of a demand curve is different from price elasticity of demand.

7. Part F of Activity 2-3 illustrates the extreme examples of a perfectly elastic demand curve and one that is perfectly inelastic. Students sometimes think the terms "inelastic" and "perfectly inelastic" mean the same thing. Be sure to make the distinction between these two terms clear. Inelastic means consumers have a relatively weak response to a price change, while perfectly inelastic means they have no response at all to a price change.

8. The other three types of elasticities are discussed in Part G. Have students answer the questions in this section to show they understand the difference between a normal good and an inferior good and between substitute goods and complementary goods. They should also understand the difference between elastic supply and inelastic supply. On the AP Microeconomics Exam, it is highly unlikely that students will be asked to calculate the percentage changes for these three types of elasticities. Those calculations are reserved for examples involving price elasticity of demand.

9. Have student complete Activity 2-4, which discusses the determinants of price elasticity of demand. What are the factors that make the demand for one product more responsive to a price increase than another product?

10. Explain how a firm's total revenue is related to the price elasticity of demand. If the firm increases its price, two things affect its total revenue. First, it will receive a higher price for each unit sold, which will increase its total revenue. Second, because of the higher price,

it will sell fewer units, which will decrease its total revenue. What happens to its total revenue depends on which of these two effects is stronger. If demand is elastic, the decrease in quantity demanded (say, 10%) is greater than the price increase (say, 6%). Thus, total revenue will fall if price is increased while demand is elastic. If demand is inelastic, price and total revenue move in the same direction. For example, if price is increased by 6 percent and quantity demanded falls by only 2 percent, then total revenue will increase. Total revenue is unaffected by a price change if demand is unitary elastic.

11. Have students complete Activity 2-5 on the relationship between price elasticity of demand and total revenue.

12. Display Visuals 2-1 and 2-2 to provide a summary of price elasticity of demand.

13. Define an *excise tax* as a tax levied on a particular good or service. This tax typically is a per-unit tax, which means the seller must give the government a set amount of money for each unit sold. An example would be a tax of $0.50 placed on each gallon of gasoline sold.

The seller views the excise tax as an additional cost and will try to pass it on to consumers in the form of a higher price for the product. The supply curve will shift up vertically by the amount of the tax at all output levels. The price elasticity of demand for the good determines how much of the tax the consumers actually pay. If demand is highly elastic, then consumers will buy a lot less of the good if the price is increased so the incidence of the tax rests mainly on the seller. If demand is highly inelastic, the seller is able to raise the price by most of the tax and not lose many customers; the burden of the tax will be mainly on the consumer.

14. Assign Activity 2-6. This activity requires students to work with tables and graphs to analyze the impact of an excise tax.

15. Display Visual 2-3, which focuses on how price elasticity of demand affects the incidence of an excise tax. Ask students if consumers pay more of the tax if demand for the product is more elastic. *(Consumers will pay a smaller part of the tax if demand is more elastic.)*

Price Elasticity of Demand

(1) $\varepsilon_d = \dfrac{\text{percentage change in quantity demanded of Good X}}{\text{percentage change in price of Good X}} = \dfrac{\%\Delta Q_d}{\%\Delta P}.$

(2) The Midpoint or Arc Method:

$$\varepsilon_d = \frac{\left[\dfrac{\left(Q_2 - Q_1\right)}{\left(Q_2 + Q_1\right)/2}\right]}{\left[\dfrac{\left(P_2 - P_1\right)}{\left(P_2 + P_1\right)/2}\right]}.$$

Example: When price increases from \$9 to \$10, the quantity demanded decreases from 12 units to 10 units.

$$\varepsilon_d = \frac{\left[\dfrac{(10-12)}{(10+12)/2}\right]}{\left[\dfrac{(\$10-\$9)}{(\$10+\$9)/2}\right]} = \frac{\left(\dfrac{-2}{11}\right)}{\left(\dfrac{+\$1}{\$9.50}\right)} = \frac{-18.2\%}{+10.5\%} = -1.7.$$

As a result of the price rising by 10.5 percent, the quantity demanded fell by 18.2 percent. Since the absolute value of ε_d is greater than 1.0, the demand for the good is elastic over this price range.

(3) When price *increased*, total revenue *decreased* from \$108 to \$100. This means demand is elastic over this price range.

(4) Interpretation of the absolute value of the price elasticity of demand:

Absolute value of ε_d	Meaning
Greater than 1.0	Demand is *elastic* over this price range.
Equal to 1.0	Demand is *unit elastic* over this price range.
Less than 1.0	Demand is *inelastic* over this price range.

Advanced Placement Economics Microeconomics: Teacher Resource Manual © Council for Economic Education, New York, N.Y.

Summarizing Price Elasticity of Demand

Elasticity coefficient	Term	Description	Impact on total revenue of	
			Price increase	**Price decrease**
Greater than 1 $\lvert \varepsilon_d \rvert > 1$	Elastic	Quantity demanded changes by a larger percentage than does price.	Total revenue decreases.	Total revenue increases.
Equal to 1 $\lvert \varepsilon_d \rvert = 1$	Unit elastic	Quantity demanded changes by the same percentage as does price.	Total revenue is unchanged.	Total revenue is unchanged.
Less than 1 $\lvert \varepsilon_d \rvert < 1$	Inelastic	Quantity demanded changes by a smaller percentage than does price.	Total revenue increases.	Total revenue decreases.

Tax Incidence and Elasticity of Demand

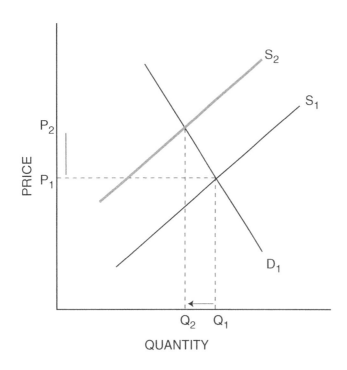

The more inelastic the demand for a good, the more the incidence of an excise tax can be shifted to the consumer.

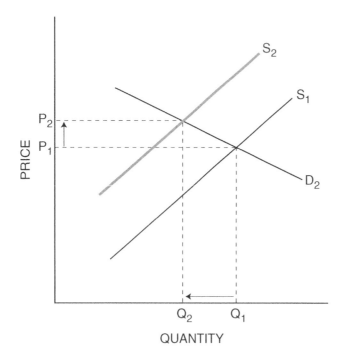

Price Floors and Ceilings

Introduction and Description

There are numerous examples of the government intervening in a competitive market to help either the consumers or the sellers of that particular good or service. Agricultural price supports for farmers and the minimum wage for lower income workers are examples of *price floors*. Such controls prevent the price of the product from falling below the stated price floor. To be effective (i.e., to have an impact) in the market, the price floor must be set above the equilibrium price, and it will result in a surplus of the item. The higher price increases the quantity supplied by sellers and decreases the quantity demanded by consumers. A price floor set below the equilibrium or market price has no effect. Rent controls are an example of a *price ceiling*. Such a control prevents the price of the item from rising above the price ceiling. To be effective, the price ceiling must be set below the equilibrium price, and it will result in a shortage of the item. The lower price increases the quantity demanded by consumers and decreases the quantity supplied by sellers. Because government price controls result in the market producing an output that is different from the socially optimal quantity, the controls result in a deadweight loss for society. While some individuals or groups benefit from the price floor or ceiling, overall there is a reduction in social welfare.

Objectives

1. Define price floors and price ceilings.

2. Explain how each control impacts a competitive market.

3. Identify the changes in consumer surplus and producer surplus that result from a price control.

4. Identify who gains and who loses from a price ceiling and from a price floor.

Time Required

One class period or 45 minutes

Materials

1. Activity 2-7

2. Visuals 2-4 and 2-5

Bell Ringer

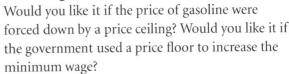

Would you like it if the price of gasoline were forced down by a price ceiling? Would you like it if the government used a price floor to increase the minimum wage?

Teacher Alert: **Students should understand why the government uses price controls and that there are winners and losers from such policies. Because they move the market quantity away from the socially optimal level, price controls reduce the sum of consumer surplus and producer surplus.**

Procedure

1. Define the terms price floor and price ceiling.

2. Ask students why the government sets such price controls. Whom is the government trying to assist with a price floor? (*It is trying to assist producers.*) What about with a price ceiling? (*It is trying to assist consumers.*)

3. Explain why the price ceiling is set below the market price and results in a shortage. (*Since the price ceiling is a limit on how high the price can go, it must be set below the market or equilibrium price. The reduced price increases the quantity demanded and decreases the quantity supplied, resulting in a shortage at the price ceiling.*)

4. Display Visual 2-4. Ask students these questions.

   (1) What are the equilibrium price and quantity in this market? *($3.00 and 1,000 units)*

   (2) If the government sets a price ceiling of $2.00 in this market, will there be a shortage or a surplus? *(There will be a shortage because the quantity demanded at that price is 1,400 units while the quantity supplied is only 600 units.)*

   (3) How many units will be exchanged at the price ceiling of $2.00? *(600 units. Even though consumers want to buy 1,400 units, sellers will only provide 600 units at a price of $2.00.)*

   (4) If the government sets a price ceiling of $4.00 in this market, will there be a shortage or a surplus? *(Neither. Since $4.00 is higher than the equilibrium price of $3.00, the price will not rise to $4.00.)*

5. Explain why the price floor is set above the market price and results in a surplus. *(Since the price floor is a limit on how low the price can go, it must be set above the market or equilibrium price. The increased price increases the quantity supplied and decreases the quantity demanded, resulting in a surplus at the price floor.)*

6. Display Visual 2-5. Ask students these questions.

   (1) What are the equilibrium price and quantity in this market? *($3.00 and 1,000 units)*

   (2) If the government sets a price floor of $5.00 in this market, will there be a shortage or a surplus? *(There will be a surplus because the quantity supplied at that price is 1,800 units while the quantity demanded is only 200 units.)*

   (3) How many units will be exchanged at the price floor of $5.00? *(200 units. Even though sellers want to sell 1,800 units, consumers will only buy 200 units at a price of $5.00.)*

   (4) If the government sets a price floor of $2.00 in this market, will there be a shortage or a surplus? *(Neither. Since $2.00 is lower than the equilibrium price of $3.00, the price will not fall to $2.00.)*

7. Have students work Activity 2-7 and discuss the results.

8. Ask students how the market output changed as a result of the price floor without a shift in either the demand or supply curve. *(The government policy stopped the market forces of demand and supply from moving the market to its equilibrium.)*

9. Discuss who gains and who loses under each type of price control. *(Under a price ceiling, those consumers who are able to buy the product at the reduced price gain. Some other consumers would like to buy the product at the lower price but are unable to do so because of the shortage. Under a price floor, those sellers who are able to sell the product at the increased price gain. Some other sellers would like to sell the product at the higher price but are unable to do so because of the surplus. Under each price control policy, because the quantity exchanged is less than the quantity in a free market, there is a deadweight loss to society.)*

10. Identify the changes in consumer surplus and producer surplus that result from price controls. *(The sum of consumer surplus and producer surplus is reduced when price controls are implemented.)*

A Price Ceiling

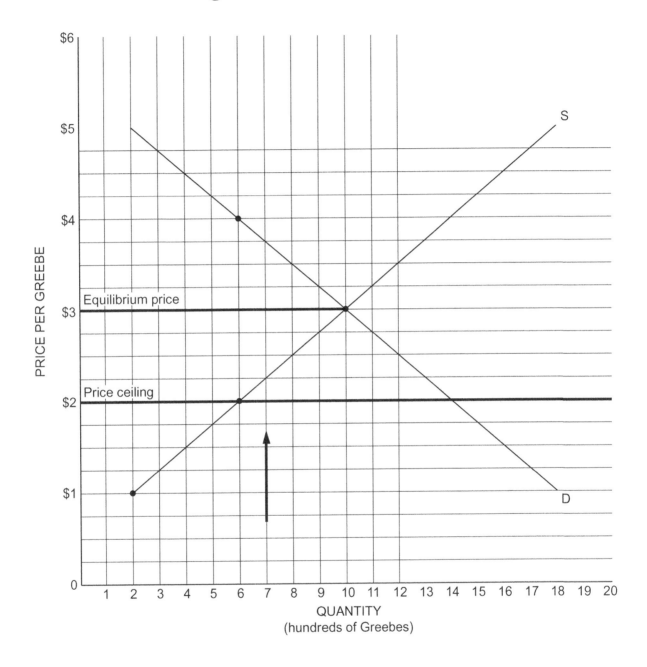

PRICE PER GREEBE

Equilibrium price

Price ceiling

S

D

QUANTITY
(hundreds of Greebes)

A Price Floor

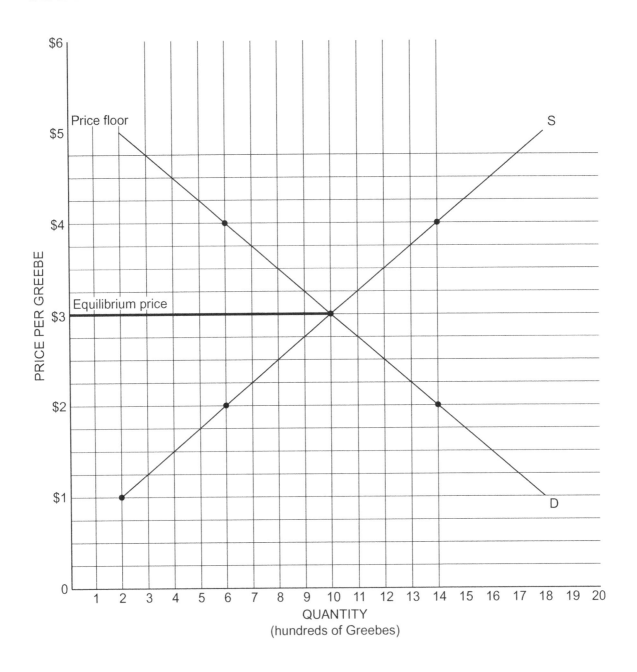

PRICE PER GREEBE

Price floor

Equilibrium price

S

D

QUANTITY
(hundreds of Greebes)

Property Rights, Market Failure, and Deadweight Loss

Introduction and Description

A cornerstone of an effective market economy is the presence of well-established *property rights*. When individuals own resources, they have incentives to allocate those resources to their most highly valued uses. This lesson shows students why property rights are important and how the absence of property rights can result in market failure and deadweight loss.

Society's optimal output in a particular market is where *marginal social benefit (MSB)* equals *marginal social cost (MSC)*. The market output is determined by *marginal private benefit (MPB)* being equal to *marginal private cost (MPC)*. The presence of an *externality* will result in the MSB being different from the MPB, or the MSC being different from the MPC. This means the quantity produced in the market will be different from the quantity society would like to have the market produce. This outcome is referred to as a *market failure*.

Objectives

1. Define property rights.

2. Explain how the absence of well-defined property rights can lead to market failure.

3. Understand the difference between MPB and MSB.

4. Understand the difference between MPC and MSC.

5. Define deadweight loss.

6. Analyze the impact of a market failure caused by a negative externality.

7. Explain how a price ceiling creates a deadweight loss in a market.

Time Required

Two class periods or 90 minutes

Materials

1. Activities 2-8 and 2-9

2. Visuals 2-6 and 2-7

Bell Ringer

Does a competitive market always produce the correct amount of a good or service?

Teacher Alert: Students know that the market 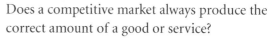 equilibrium quantity occurs where the demand and supply curves intersect. They need to know that a competitive market can fail to produce the socially optimal quantity because either the demand curve no longer represents both MSB and MPB or the supply curve no longer represents both MSC and MPC.

Procedure

1. Remind students that equilibrium quantity in a competitive market is determined by the intersection of the demand and supply curves.

2. Explain the concept of property rights. If the property rights to resources are not clearly defined, the market can produce a quantity that is different from the socially desired quantity.

3. Ask students why they see more litter along a country highway than they do in someone's front yard. *(Litterers feel that the marginal cost of littering on a desolate highway is less than it is in a well-populated neighborhood where someone will report their action.)*

4. Ask students whether a homeowner tends to take better care of her home than would someone who is renting a similar house. Have students discuss why this is the case. Decision makers respond to their marginal private benefits and marginal private costs. (*The homeowner finds it to be in her best interest to maintain her home, even if it costs time and money to do so. The renter may feel that she does not want to invest time and money maintaining a house that someone else owns.*)

5. Show Visual 2-6, which illustrates the market for paper. Assume the firms that make paper clean up all their waste products so there is no pollution. The MSC curve represents the MSC of paper production; it includes the paper companies' costs of materials, workers, energy, and pollution cleanup. If there is no pollution, the MSC curve is the same as the firms' MPC and is the market supply curve for paper. Now assume the paper companies begin to release their untreated wastes into a nearby river. This reduces the production costs for these paper companies. The new supply curve S represents the firms' MPC of production, but excludes the cost of cleaning up the pollution these firms are creating. Now the MPC is different from the MSC. The demand curve for paper represents both the MSB and the MPB from the consumption of paper. Only the consumers of paper receive benefits from the product. Ask students these questions based on Visual 2-6.

(A) How much paper is produced when there is no pollution? (*Q_1, the socially optimal quantity where MSB = MSC.*)

(B) What is the price of a unit of paper in the absence of pollution? (*P_2. This price covers all costs associated with paper production, including the cost of cleaning the waste products.*)

(C) Why does the MPC curve lie below the MSC curve when the paper companies pollute the river? (*The MPC curve shows the costs of the*

paper firms. Since these firms now avoid the cost of cleaning up their waste products, the MPC of producing paper is less than the true cost to society.)

(D) How much paper is produced when the paper companies dump their waste products into the river? (*Q_2 because that is where MPB = MPC.*)

(E) What is the price of a unit of paper when there is pollution? (*P_1. This price does not reflect the damage caused to other members of society by the pollution.*)

(F) How does society feel about the quantity produced by the polluting firms? (*At Q_2, MSB is less than MSC. From society's perspective, those paper units between Q_2 and Q_1 create more cost than benefit. This means society would like to see less paper produced.*)

6. Have students complete Activity 2-8. Discuss their answers.

7. Review the concepts of consumer surplus and producer surplus. Remind students that a perfectly competitive market, in the absence of outside interference, will maximize total welfare, which is the sum of consumer surplus and producer surplus.

8. Ask students to complete Part A of Activity 2-9. Discuss their answers.

9. Have students complete Part B of Activity 2-9. This assignment has students taking a slightly different approach to market analysis. They are told to graph the equations for linear (straight-line) demand and supply functions. While this particular calculation method will not be on the AP Microeconomics Exam, it is a useful activity to help students get a better picture of consumer surplus and producer surplus. Discuss their answers.

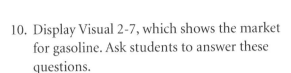

10. Display Visual 2-7, which shows the market for gasoline. Ask students to answer these questions.

   (A) What is the market price of a gallon of gasoline? *($5.00)*

   (B) What is the equilibrium quantity? *(400 million gallons)*

   (C) What is the value of consumer surplus? *($200 million = [0.5][400 million gallons] [$6.00 – $5.00].)*

   (D) What is the value of producer surplus? *($200 million = [0.5][400 million gallons] [$5.00 – $4.00]. Tell students that the values of consumer surplus and producer surplus do not have to be equal, as they happen to be in this graph.)*

   (E) What is the value of total welfare? *($400 million = consumer surplus + producer surplus.)*

   (F) Assume the government sets a price ceiling of $4.50 in the market. What will be the quantity demanded and the quantity supplied? *(The quantity demanded will be 600 million gallons, while the quantity supplied will be 200 million gallons. There will be a shortage of 400 million gallons.)*

   (G) What area of the graph shows the deadweight loss of the price ceiling? *(The deadweight loss is shown by the triangle bounded by the demand and supply curves between 400 million gallons and 200 million gallons.)*

The Effect of Pollution

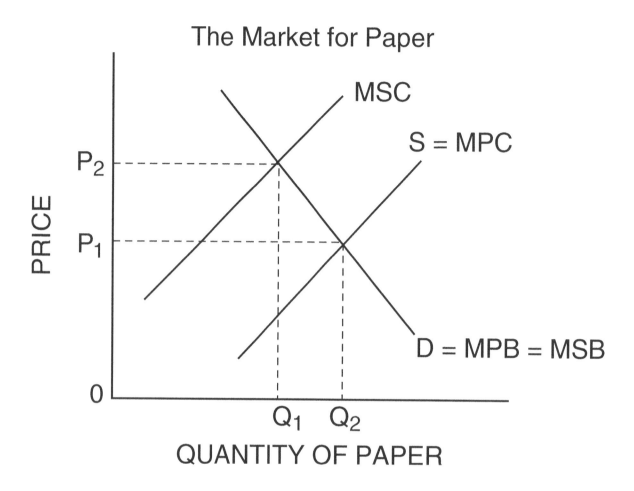

The Market for Paper

Deadweight Loss of a Price Ceiling

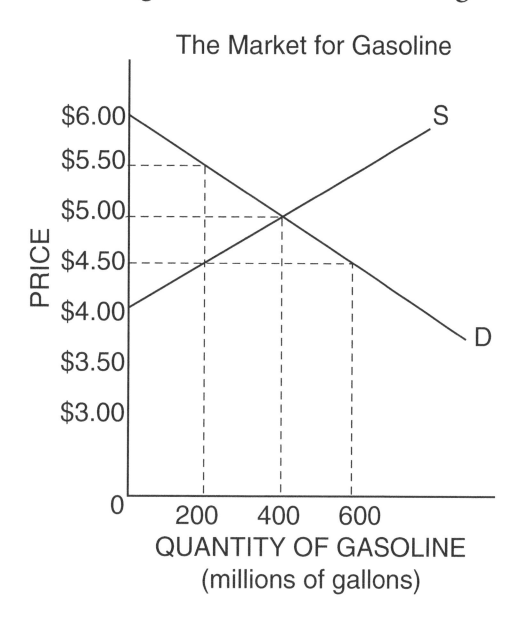

The Market for Gasoline

MICROECONOMICS

The Theory of the Firm

Unit 3

26 class periods or 1,170 minutes
(35 percent of course time)

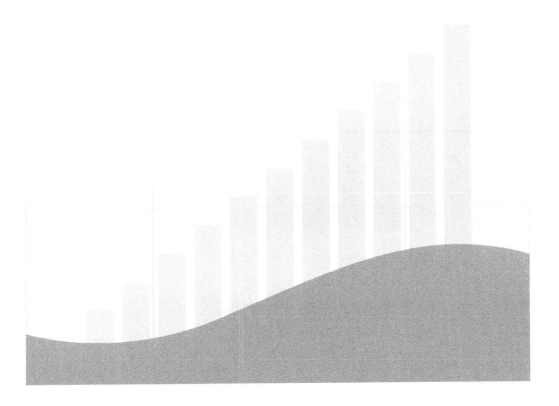

The theory of the firm is the heart of an Advanced Placement (AP) Microeconomics course. The content of this unit will account for 35–50 percent of the AP Microeconomics Exam.

This material is difficult for many students because it is abstract. This is why we have included exercises requiring students to plot cost curves and revenue curves before they interpret them. The risk in this approach is that students may get bogged down in details and miss the major theoretical conclusions. Before you begin this unit, you should give students an overview of what a firm does. It produces a good or service in an attempt to earn the largest possible total profit. To do so, the firm wants its resources to be highly productive. The firm must be efficient in its production because that will allow it to have lower costs and be competitive with other firms producing similar products. It will have to consider the demand for its product as it decides what price to charge. The firm itself is a consumer when it buys its resources in factor markets. Ultimately, to maximize its total profit a firm must decide on the optimal quantity to produce and price to charge. As you move through Unit 3, pause on occasion to remind students where they are in the examination of the firm—the production stage, the cost stage, the revenue stage, or the profit-maximization stage.

Students often feel there is an endless array of rules and restrictions to memorize in this key part of the course. To help students understand the material in Unit 3 rather than memorize it, share these three comforting facts with them.

1. The relationships that exist among marginal, average, and total measures will be the same in the areas of production, cost, revenue, and profit. When they master these relationships in the production section of this unit, they can apply them to the other areas as well. Here is an example:

    ■ If *marginal* physical product is less than *average* physical product, then *average* physical product will decrease.

    ■ If *marginal* cost is less than *average* total cost, then *average* total cost will decrease.

    ■ If *marginal* revenue is less than *average* revenue, then *average* revenue will decrease.

    ■ If *marginal* profit is less than *average* profit, then *average* profit will decrease.

2. The basic productivity and cost graphs will look the same for all firms. The difference between the profit-maximization graph of a perfectly competitive firm and that of a monopoly will be in the shapes of their demand and revenue curves. The cost curves will look the same in these two graphs.

3. The rules a firm follows to determine its profit-maximizing output and price will be the same for all firms.

After completing this unit, students should be able to differentiate between short-run and long-run equilibriums for both a profit-maximizing individual firm and for an industry. Students must understand the various measures of productivity, cost, revenue, and profit. They also must be able to compare a monopolist's price, level of output, and total profit with those of a perfectly competitive firm. They must know why competition is considered better than monopoly in terms of social welfare. This unit will help them evaluate government regulation of monopoly. Students must understand the kinds of market structures that exist between the models of monopoly and perfect competition, specifically oligopoly and monopolistic competition. Give students much practice on drawing graphs. On the AP Microeconomics Exam, they will have to draw graphs freehand and explain them.

Do what you can to have students relate to businesses and the decisions they must make. Bring in current events that illustrate competition among firms, efforts to increase productivity, and the impact of changes in government tax policies and regulations on businesses. Discuss stocks, bonds, and other financial instruments so students are familiar with them. This will make the cost and revenue curves in this unit more concrete. Most principles of economics books cover this material. Having said this, however, be careful not to spend too much time on current economic and social issues. You have too much material to cover for the AP Microeconomics Exam to devote significant time to these other topics.

There are several themes to keep in mind while students work their way through the Unit 3 material.

1. Firms should ignore sunk costs when making decisions. Why are marginal costs their primary consideration?

2. This material is based on the assumption that the objective of all firms is to maximize total economic profit. Is this assumption valid?

3. Firms maximize total profit where marginal revenue equals marginal cost. Why is this so?

4. When perfectly competitive firms maximize total profits, the general good is served. Why?

5. When monopolies maximize total profits, the general good is not served. Why?

6. Most U.S. markets can be classified as monopolistic competition or oligopoly. Why do we spend so much time on perfect competition and monopoly—forms of market structures that are not as common?

7. What type of antitrust policy should government pursue? Why?

It pays to give frequent quizzes in Unit 3. If students do not understand productivity, they will not understand cost. If they do not understand cost, they will not understand the logic of profit maximization. If they don't understand perfect competition, they will not understand monopoly. If they do not understand profit maximization in the product market, they will not understand profit maximization in the resource market. If this material is lost on students, they will have difficulty passing the AP Microeconomics Exam. On a much more positive note, for each of the topics above, if they do understand one stage of the unit, then they should understand the next stage! A sound foundation is critical for their success in your course and on the exam. As John Morton, economic educator extraordinaire, once said, "If a student understands the economic way of thinking, that student will have the flexibility to handle much of what is on an AP Economics Exam."

The Lesson Planner

Lesson 1 Introduction to Market Structures; Activity 3-1 and Visual 3-1

Lesson 2 Production and Cost; Activities 3-2, 3-3, and 3-4, and Visuals 3-2, 3-3, and 3-4

Lesson 3 Revenue, Profit, and Profit-Maximization Rules; Activity 3-5

Lesson 4   Perfect Competition in the Short Run and Long Run; Activities 3-6, 3-7, 3-8, and 3-9, and Visuals 3-5, 3-6, 3-7, 3-8, and 3-9

Lesson 5   Monopoly; Activities 3-10, 3-11, 3-12, 3-13, 3-14, and 3-15, and Visuals 3-10 and 3-11

Lesson 6   Monopolistic Competition and Oligopoly; Activities 3-16 and 3-17, and Visual 3-12

Practice Free Response Questions (FRQs)

This is a partial list of FRQs that can be used with each unit of the *Advanced Placement Economics: Microeconomics* resource manual. These questions and grading rubrics are available at AP Central on the College Board Web site: http://apcentral.collegeboard.com

2012	Question 1, parts (a) and (b): a monopoly with a loss
2011	Question 1, part (a)–(c): monopoly—profit maximization; allocative efficiency
2011	Question 1, part (e)–(f): regulation of monopoly
2011	Question 1, part (g): price discrimination
2011	Question 2: graph of a perfectly competitive firm
2011 Form B	Question 1: perfect competition; increasing cost; reaction to increase in market demand
2010	Question 1: perfectly competitive market
2010 Form B	Question 1: regulation of natural monopoly; accounting profit
2009	Question 1: monopoly—profit-maximization, allocative efficiency; regulation
2009	Question 3: game theory
2009 Form B	Question 1: a monopolistically competitive firm with a loss, then a profit
2009 Form B	Question 3: game theory
2008	Question 1: a perfectly competitive firm in long-run equilibrium
2008	Question 3: natural monopoly
2008 Form B	Question 1: monopoly graph; regulation; consumer surplus at allocatively efficient output
2007	Question 1: patent
2007	Question 3: game theory
2007 Form B	Question 1: graph of a monopolistically competitive firm

2007 Form B	Question 2: game theory
2006	Question 1: monopoly; accounting profits
2006	Question 3: questions about a perfectly competitive firm
2006 Form B	Question 1: monopoly graph; effect on total revenue if price is increased

Additional Resources

To download visuals for each lesson and to find related material, visit
http://www.councilforeconed.org/ap-economics

Introduction to Market Structures

Introduction and Description

This lesson introduces students to the kinds of *market structures* they will be studying during the next several weeks. Because most actual markets do not fit all the assumptions of the perfectly competitive market model, it is necessary to examine what happens when these assumptions are not met. Economists have developed models to explain how other market structures—monopoly, oligopoly, and monopolistic competition—can produce results that differ from those expected under purely competitive conditions.

Remind students that we are assuming firms want to maximize their total profit. Depending on the market structure of the industry, such behavior by firms has different effects on society and the economy. Stress that in Unit 3 students will use models and analytical skills to examine the behavior and effects of firms operating under different types of market structure. While there are some common rules that apply to all businesses, the results of the decisions made by firms can have different outcomes based on the nature of competition in the market.

Objectives

1. Describe the major characteristics of *perfect competition*, *monopolistic competition*, *oligopoly*, and *monopoly*.

2. Compare the results of the four market structures.

Time Required

One class period or 45 minutes

Materials

1. Activity 3-1

2. Visual 3-1

Bell Ringer

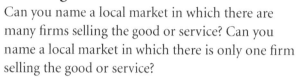

Can you name a local market in which there are many firms selling the good or service? Can you name a local market in which there is only one firm selling the good or service?

Teacher Alert: **Be sure students understand that even though the degree of competition among firms differs in the four market structures they will study, the basic rules of profit maximization will be the same for all firms.**

Procedure

1. Give a lecture on the characteristics of *perfect competition*, *monopolistic competition*, *oligopoly*, and *monopoly*.

2. Have students form groups to complete Activity 3-1. Allow them to use their textbooks.

3. Use Visual 3-1 as the answer key to discuss the answers to Table 3-1.1. Students may disagree on whether certain examples belong in one category or another. This may depend on how broadly they define the industry. For example, "canned food" might be monopolistic competition, while "canned corn" might be oligopolistic. They may also bring up examples not on Visual 3-1. Stress that sometimes it is difficult to determine the exact market structure of a particular industry.

4. Ask questions such as the following to reinforce students' understanding of the types of market structures:

(A) What is the difference between homogeneous and differentiated products? *(Homogeneous products are identical; differentiated products differ in quality and type. Raw cane sugar is homogeneous; candy bars are differentiated.)*

(B) What is the difference between perfect competition and monopolistic competition? *(Under monopolistic competition, products are differentiated, and competition takes place in terms of both price and product quality. In perfect competition, products are identical, and market forces set the price.)*

(C) Is monopolistic competition closer to monopoly or to perfect competition? *(It is closer to perfect competition because it has many firms and relatively easy entry. Also firms break even in the long run in both models.)*

(D) What are the main characteristics of oligopoly? *(There are only a few firms, firms have the ability to influence price, and there are some barriers to entry.)*

(E) What are some examples of barriers to entry? *(Examples include large advertising costs, patents, licenses, large capital investment, and control of key resources.)*

(F) What is the distinguishing characteristic of monopoly? *(There is only one supplier in an industry or in a particular geographic area.)*

Different Types of Market Structures

Characteristics

Market structure	Number of firms	Differentiated or homogeneous product	Ease of entry
Perfect competition	Very many	Homogeneous	Very easy
Monopolistic competition	Many	Differentiated	Relatively easy
Oligopoly	Few	Both are possible	Not easy
Monopoly	One	Only one product	Impossible

Results

Market structure	Price-setting power	Nonprice competition	Allocative and productive efficiency in long run	Long-run profits	Examples
Perfect competition	None (price taker)	None	Both	$0	None. Local agricultural markets come close.
Monopolistic competition	Some	Considerable	Neither	$0	Fast food, retail sales, cosmetics
Oligopoly	Limited	Considerable for a differentiated oligopoly	Neither	Positive	Cars, steel, soft drinks, computers
Monopoly	Absolute (price maker)	Some	Neither	Positive, possibly high	Small-town newspaper, rural gas station

Production and Cost

Introduction and Description

Lesson 2 helps students understand the relationship between the *productivity* and *cost* functions of a firm. There are three productivity measures and seven cost measures. Students should understand how productivity is the basis of cost. By increasing its productivity, a firm can reduce its cost. This lesson is critical if students are to grasp what follows. Although there are four types of market structure in which a firm can sell its output, the costs of the firm remain conceptually the same for a firm in any market structure. Unless students understand these cost concepts, they are likely to be confused when you begin discussing the steps by which a firm maximizes its total profit.

This lesson begins with a chart and a graph showing the three measures of a firm's productivity—*total product, average physical product*, and *marginal physical product*. This is followed by an explanation of the relationship between the productivity of a firm and its cost of production. Next, students learn the three different views of "profit"—*accounting profit, normal profit*, and *economic profit*. Be sure students know how these three measures of profit are related to each other and that we assume firms are trying to maximize their economic profit. Students learn the definitions of the seven short-run cost measures of a firm and how to calculate their values and show them graphically. Give them plenty of practice with graphs of the cost functions. Finally, the lesson explains the concept of a firm's *long-run average total cost* curve when all inputs are variable. The shape of this curve is determined by *economies and diseconomies of scale*. The topic of *returns to scale* also is discussed.

Objectives

1. Define the three measures of productivity.

2. Explain the relationships among marginal physical product, average physical product, and total product.

3. Show how to calculate values of the productivity measures and graph them.

4. Define the seven measures of short-run costs.

5. Explain the relationships among *total cost, total variable cost, total fixed cost, average total cost, average variable cost, average fixed cost,* and *marginal cost*.

6. Show how to calculate values of the cost measures and graph them.

7. Explain how marginal physical product is related to marginal cost.

8. Explain how average physical product is related to average variable cost.

9. Explain how *diminishing marginal productivity* determines the shape of a firm's marginal cost, average variable cost, and average total cost curves.

10. Define economic profit, accounting profit, and normal profit.

11. Use *explicit and implicit costs* to determine economic profit and loss.

12. Explain how the long-run average total cost curve is derived.

13. Explain how economies and diseconomies of scale determine the shape of the firm's long-run average total cost curve.

14. Discuss increasing, constant, and decreasing returns to scale.

Time Required

Four class periods or 180 minutes

Materials

1. Activities 3-2, 3-3, and 3-4

2. Visuals 3-2, 3-3, and 3-4

Bell Ringer

When you study for an exam, does it take you more time or less time to do the required studying if you focus on your notes and are not distracted by friends, television, or gaming activities? Does this increase in your productivity reduce your (opportunity) cost of studying for the exam?

Teacher Alert: Some textbooks plot marginal values (e.g., marginal physical product and marginal cost) at the midpoint between two units. The approach used in this publication is to plot marginal values at the higher of the two units. For example, if a firm's total output increases by 20 units when it increases labor from 5 units to 6 units, regard the +20 as the marginal physical product of the sixth labor unit and plot the +20 value in a chart or on a graph at 6 labor units rather than at 5.5 labor units.

Procedure

1. Start out with a simple discussion of revenue, cost, and profit. You might put up a simple income statement for a firm like this:

Total revenue (TR)	$10,000
Total fixed costs (TFC)	$2,000
Total variable costs (TVC)	$7,000
Total profit (TΠ)	$1,000

   You can then define total fixed cost and total variable cost, and explain that total revenue minus total cost equals total profit. This gives students an overview of a firm and sets the stage for you to move into material related to different measures of a firm's cost.

2. Explain that the more productive a firm is, the lower will be its costs of production. Point out that this will allow the firm to be more competitive with other firms in the product market as it tries to make a positive total profit.

3. Distinguish between the *short run* and the *long run* for a firm. In the short run, a key factor of

production (usually capital) is fixed in quantity while other inputs (often labor) are variable. In the long run, all resources are variable.

4. Define the three productivity measures of a firm: total product, average physical product, and marginal physical product. Define the law of diminishing marginal productivity. You can introduce these concepts with the following example of the productivity from different hours of study for an economics exam. In this example, diminishing marginal returns set in with the second hour of study. With the sixth hour of study, the student's total grade actually decreased, resulting in a negative marginal product for that hour.

Hours	Total points	Average points per hour	Marginal points per extra hour
0	–	–	–
1	40	40	+40
2	60	30	+20
3	75	25	+15
4	84	21	+9
5	90	18	+6
6	84	14	–6

5. Have students complete Part A of Activity 3-2. They will complete a productivity chart that shows how the three productivity measures of a firm are calculated and how they are related to each other. Then they will plot the productivity data in two graphs, one showing total output from labor and the other showing the marginal physical product and average physical product of labor. Students have questions to answer based on the firm's productivity measures. Be sure students understand the following productivity relationships as extra labor units are added to a fixed stock of capital:

   (A) If total output increases, then marginal physical product is positive.

(B) If total output decreases, then marginal physical product is negative.

(C) If total output is at its maximum, then marginal physical product is zero.

(D) If marginal physical product is greater than average physical product, then average physical product will increase.

(E) If marginal physical product is less than average physical product, then average physical product will decrease.

(F) If marginal physical product is equal to average physical product, then average physical product is at its maximum.

6. Define *marginal cost (MC)* and *average variable cost (AVC)*. Part B of Activity 3-2 shows how a firm's MC and AVC curves are mirror images of its *marginal physical product (MPP)* and *average physical product (APP)* curves, assuming the firm pays constant market prices for its inputs. Have students study these graphs and answer the questions based on the graphs. Stress that the curves and axes of the graphs must be labeled correctly.

7. Here are two ratios that connect the firm's productivity and cost measures.

(A) AVC of a unit of output = $\dfrac{\text{wage}}{\text{APP of a unit of labor}}$.

(B) MC of an extra unit of output = $\dfrac{\text{wage}}{\text{MPP of an extra unit of labor}}$.

8. Display Visual 3-2 to show how the productivity curves of a firm are related to its cost curves.

9. Explain to students that the two ratios in procedure 7 above lead to the following relationships, which are illustrated by Visual 3-2 and Figure 3-2.5:

(A) If the APP of labor increases, the AVC of producing output decreases.

(B) If the APP of labor decreases, the AVC of producing output increases.

(C) If the APP of labor is maximized, the AVC of producing output is minimized.

(D) If the MPP of labor increases, the MC of producing additional output decreases.

(E) If the MPP of labor decreases, the MC of producing additional output increases.

(F) If the MPP of labor is maximized, the MC of producing additional output is minimized.

10. If you have time, you may want to conduct a productivity simulation to show how diminishing marginal productivity affects a firm's output and costs. There are several examples in Council for Economic Education materials. A simulation could add a day to this unit but may make the abstract figures more concrete.

11. Move on to Activity 3-3, which has students identify three different views of profit and work with the seven short-run cost measures. Discuss the short story of Pat in Part A to illustrate the differences between accounting profit, normal profit, and economic profit.

12. Assign Part B for students to complete. It defines the seven measures of cost and has students complete a cost table. Get students in the habit of identifying each cost term as a

total, average, or marginal measure. There is a big difference between "total fixed cost" and "average fixed cost."

13. Next, have students plot the cost curves in Figures 3-3.1 and 3-3.2. Display Visuals 3-3 and 3-4. Discuss their answers to the questions based on these two graphs. Be sure students know how to draw these cost graphs and understand why each cost curve looks as it does. Figure 3-3.2, "The Firm's 'Marginal-Average' Cost Graph," is the same for all firms. In the next several lessons, students will add revenue curves to this important cost graph as they learn how a firm maximizes its total profit.

14. The last activity of Lesson 2 is Activity 3-4, in which the development of a firm's *long-run average total cost* (LRATC) curve is explained.

The downward-sloping portion of this curve is a result of *economies of scale*, with *diseconomies of scale* explaining why the curve eventually slopes upward. Explain how the LRATC curve is created from a series of short-run average total cost curves of a single firm. This activity also discusses *increasing, constant*, and *decreasing returns to scale* as special cases of economies and diseconomies of scale. Assign Activity 3-4 to students.

15. Update students on where they now stand in the search for a firm's profit-maximizing output and price. They have covered the productivity and cost aspects of a typical firm. The next stage of the course is to understand the revenue measures of a firm, add those measures to the cost measures just developed, and determine where total profit is maximized.

Marginal Physical Product and Marginal Cost
Average Physical Product and Average Variable Cost

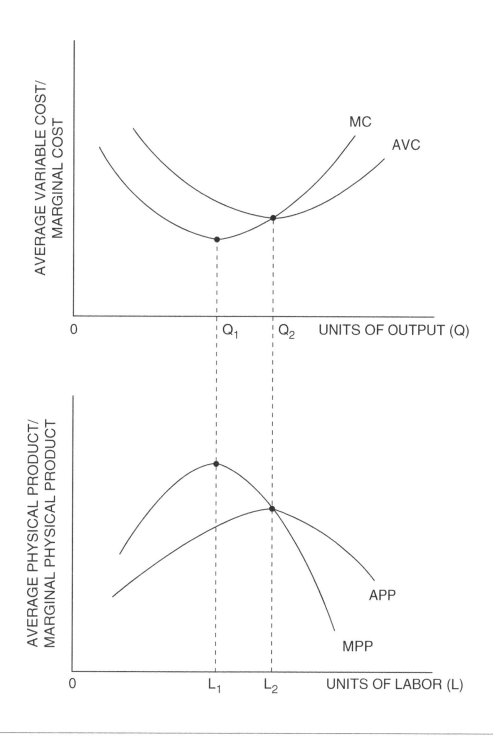

Total Cost (TC), Total Variable Cost (TVC), and Total Fixed Cost (TFC)

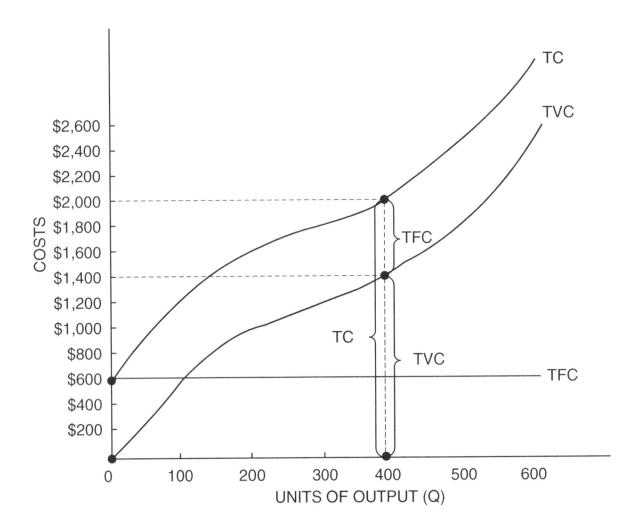

Average Total Cost (ATC), Average Variable Cost (AVC), and Average Fixed Cost (AFC)

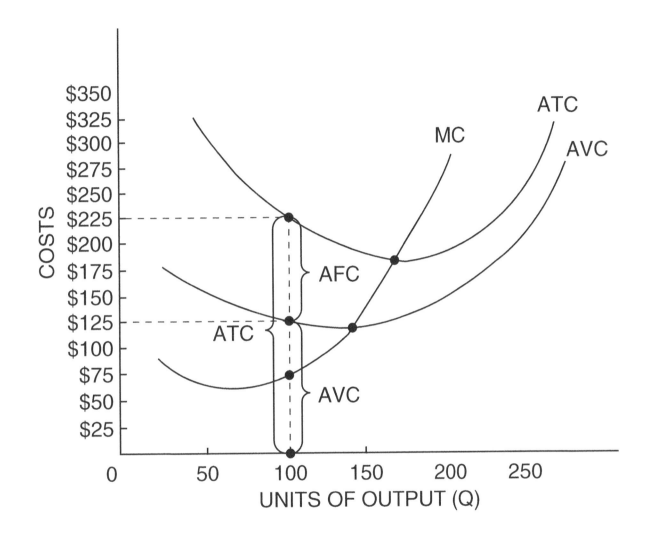

Revenue, Profit, and Profit-Maximization Rules

Introduction and Description

Now that students have a foundation in the cost structure of a typical firm, we turn to the revenue side of the operation. Lesson 3 explains to students the three measures of a firm's revenue—total revenue, average revenue, and marginal revenue. Although the shapes of the revenue curves will depend on the type of market in which the firm's product is sold, the definitions and calculations of the three revenue measures are the same for all firms. This lesson also introduces three similar measures of profit—*total profit*, *average profit*, and *marginal profit*. It concludes with a discussion of the key rules any firm follows to maximize its total economic profit.

Objectives

1. Define the three measures of revenue—total revenue, average revenue, and marginal revenue.

2. Show how to calculate the different measures of revenue.

3. Define the three measures of profit—total profit, average profit, and marginal profit.

4. Show how to calculate the different measures of profit.

5. State the key rules a firm should use to maximize its total profit.

Time Required

Two class periods or 90 minutes

Materials

Activity 3-5

Bell Ringer

Does an increase in a firm's total revenue resulting from selling more units of its product mean that its total profit also has increased?

Teacher Alert: **Don't let students confuse revenue and profit. Profit is revenue minus cost. The goal of the firm is to maximize its total profit. It is important that students understand why producing the output where marginal revenue (MR) = marginal cost (MC) will maximize a firm's total profit.**

Procedure

1. Tell students it is time to investigate the revenue side of a firm. This is the income the firm receives from selling its product. The total profit of a firm is the difference between its total revenue and its total cost.

2. Define the three measures of revenue—*total revenue*, *average revenue*, and *marginal revenue*. Have students study Part A of Activity 3-5. Discuss how students are to calculate the value of the three revenue measures.

3. Define the three measures of profit—*total profit*, *average profit*, and *marginal profit*. Have students study Part B of Activity 3-5. Discuss how students are to calculate the value of the three profit measures. Some textbooks do not use the concept of marginal profit. However, it is a useful tool for students to employ as they explore decision making by a firm.

4. Spend quality time on Part C of Activity 3-5. These three *rules for profit maximization* apply to firms in any of the four market structures:

   (A) Produce the output where MR = MC.

   (B) The optimal price is found on the demand curve at the optimal output.

   (C) Shut down (produce no output) if, at the optimal output, total revenue (TR) < total variable cost (TVC).

By mastering these rules now, students will be ready for future analysis as you take them through the ensuing units. Students should not memorize these principles; they need to understand why they work.

5. Assign the questions in Part D of Activity 3-5. Be certain students can answer these questions before taking them to the next activity.

Perfect Competition in the Short Run and Long Run

Introduction and Description

Lesson 4 is very important because it shows students how a firm in a perfectly competitive market maximizes its total profit in the short run and in the long run. The conditions under which a firm should shut down are discussed. The short-run supply curves of a perfectly competitive firm and industry are created. The lesson also examines a perfectly competitive industry in short-run and long-run equilibrium. Students are given practice drawing graphs of a perfectly competitive firm and a perfectly competitive industry in different profit situations. When students understand the decisions made by a firm in perfect competition, the extension of this material to that of a monopoly and a monopolistically competitive firm is much easier.

Objectives

1. Explain the rules a perfectly competitive firm uses to maximize its total profit.

2. Draw graphs of a perfectly competitive firm in four short-run profit scenarios: making a positive total profit, breaking even, making a loss but not shutting down, and making a loss and shutting down.

3. Explain how a perfectly competitive firm moves from a short-run equilibrium to a long-run equilibrium.

4. Know why a perfectly competitive firm's short-run supply curve is that portion of its marginal cost curve above its average variable cost curve.

5. Be able to create the market supply curve from the horizontal summation of the supply curves of the individual firms in the market.

6. Understand how an industry's long-run supply curve is derived from a series of industry long-run equilibriums.

Time Required

Six class periods or 270 minutes

Materials

1. Activities 3-6, 3-7, 3-8, and 3-9

2. Visuals 3-5, 3-6, 3-7, 3-8, and 3-9

Bell Ringer

What happens to price and quantity in a competitive market if all firms are earning positive total profit? What happens over time if most firms are making a loss?

Teacher Alert: Give students a lot of graphing practice in this lesson. Be sure they understand why MR = MC gives the firm's best output level and how to identify graphically the various profit, revenue, and cost measures at that output level. They need to understand how a perfectly competitive industry with profit in the short run moves to a long-run equilibrium and that all firms will break even in the long run.

Procedure

1. Discuss the characteristics of *a perfectly competitive market.* Tell students why each firm is a *price taker* and can sell all the output it wants at the market-determined price.

2. Have students complete Part A of Activity 3-6, which has them complete a table with the three revenue measures (TR, AR, and MR) of a perfectly competitive firm. Ask them why P = AR *(because AR = TR/Q = P)* and why P = MR *(because the firm does not have to lower its price to sell an extra unit)* for a perfectly competitive firm. Part A also has students plot the TR data in one graph and the AR and MR data in a second graph. Ask students why the

TR curve is an upward-sloping straight line beginning at the origin. *(If the firm sells no output, its TR is $0. The TR function is a straight line because the slope of the TR curve is ΔTR/ΔQ, which is MR, and we know MR is a constant value equal to the market price.)*

3. Ask students what happens to the firm's TR curve if the market price increases? *(The TR curve has a steeper slope because the firm's MR also has increased.)*

4. Why is the demand curve facing a perfectly competitive firm perfectly elastic? *(At the market price, the firm can sell all the product it wants. If it increases its price by even a tiny bit, it will sell no units because consumers will go to the many other firms charging the market price. Because this is the ultimate consumer response, it is called perfectly elastic.)*

5. Have students complete Part B of Activity 3-6. Students will calculate values of the seven cost measures and plot these values in two graphs, one with the total measures and the other with the average and marginal measures.

6. Have students complete Part C of Activity 3-6. Table 3-6.3 brings the revenue and cost data together. Students are asked to identify the output level that maximizes the total profit of a perfectly competitive firm. They also must add the revenue data to the two cost graphs in Part B. Students should understand that they can identify the firm's optimal quantity by using three rules:

(A) Produce the output where TR most exceeds TC.

(B) Produce the output where MR equals (or last exceeds) MC.

(C) Produce the output where MΠ equals (or last exceeds) $0.

7. Part D of Activity 3-6 covers *the shut down rule* of a firm. Be sure students understand the conditions under which a perfectly competitive firm is better off producing no output than producing the quantity where MR = MC. A firm should shut down if at the quantity where MR = MC, it finds TR is less than TVC, or AR is less than AVC, or P is less than AVC.

8. Activity 3-7 examines the four possible short-run profit positions of a perfectly competitive firm. The term *short-run equilibrium* means the firm is producing the output at which MR = MC. Discuss Table 3-7.1 with students.

9. Explain the information conveyed by a firm's supply curve. *(It shows how many units the firm will provide to the market at different prices.)* Have students complete the cost chart in Table 3-7.2 and plot the ATC, AVC, and MC data in Figure 3-7.1. Tell students to add the firm's marginal revenue curve to that graph for the four specified market prices. *(These will be horizontal MR lines at each of the four prices.)* They should complete Tables 3-7.3 and 3-7.4 as they derive the supply schedule for the perfectly competitive firm. They next must draw the firm's supply curve in Figure 3-7.2.

10. Ask students why the firm's supply curve is upward sloping. *(Because the firm's marginal costs increase as it produces more output, the firm must receive a higher price for extra units of output to be profitable.)*

11. Ask students why the firm will not produce any output if the market price drops below the firm's AVC curve. *(If price is less than AVC, the firm should produce no output; it should shut down for this production period.)*

12. Tell students to create the market supply curve by completing Part C of Activity 3-7. *(It is the horizontal summation of the supply curves of the individual firms.)*

13. Activity 3-8 explains how a perfectly competitive firm and market move from a short-run equilibrium to a long-run equilibrium in which each remaining firm breaks even (TΠ = $0). Compare the cost data given in Table 3-8.1 to the graphical representation of that same data presented in Figure 3-8.1. Ask students why the AVC and ATC curves decrease and then increase as the firm increases its level of output. *(The AVC and ATC curves fall as long as MC is below them, and they rise when MC is above them.)*

14. Tell students to complete Part A of Activity 3-8 to create the market for bricks shown in Figure 3-8.2. They should find the equilibrium price to be $40 and the equilibrium quantity to be 5,000 tons. When they add the D = AR = MR line for a perfectly competitive firm to the cost graph in Figure 3-8.1, students will discover the firm is earning a positive total profit at the market price of $40.

15. Display Visual 3-5, which has side-by-side graphs of a perfectly competitive industry and firm in short-run equilibrium. Because the D line is above the ATC curve, we know the firm is earning a positive total profit at the market price of $25. There is nothing in the industry graph that tells us the industry is generating positive total profits at a price of $25; that information comes from the firm's graph.

16. Ask students what will happen in the perfectly competitive market if firms are earning positive total profit. *(New firms will enter the market, the market supply will shift to the right, and the market price will decrease until it is equal to minimum value of the firm's ATC curve. Since all firms will be earning $0 in economic profit,*

outside firms no longer have an incentive to enter the market.)

17. Use Visual 3-6 to review the short-run equilibrium of a perfectly competitive firm at different market prices. *(At P_5 the firm earns a positive total profit by producing Q_5. At P_4 the firm will break even at Q_4. At P_3 it will have a loss at Q_3 but not want to shut down since price is above average variable cost. At P_2 the firm is indifferent between producing Q_2 and shutting down; its loss will be equal to its total fixed cost in either case. At P_1 the firm would prefer to shut down rather than produce Q_1.)*

18. Explain that a perfectly competitive firm in long-run equilibrium exhibits both productive efficiency and allocative efficiency. Display Visual 3-7 which shows a perfectly competitive firm in long-run equilibrium at a price of $18 and a quantity of 500 units.

    (A) *Productive efficiency* exists if the price charged by the firm is equal to the minimum value of its average total cost curve: $P = ATC_{min}$. This means consumers are getting the product at the lowest possible price.

    (B) *Allocative efficiency* exists if the price charged by the firm is equal to marginal cost: $P = MC$. This means the firm is producing the socially optimal quantity of its good or service.

19. Explain the difference between an industry's *long-run equilibrium* (LRE) and its *long-run supply* (LRS) curve. *(The LRE is the price and quantity combination at which there is zero profit, based on a given level of market demand for the product. The LRS curve is the collection of LREs, each of which is based on a different level of market demand.)*

20. Have students answer the questions in Part C of Activity 3-8 about a constant-cost, an increasing-cost, and a decreasing-cost industry. Discuss the shapes of the LRS curve in each of

these three cases. *(The LRS curve is horizontal for a constant-cost industry, upward sloping for an increasing-cost industry, and downward sloping for a decreasing-cost industry.)*

21. Display Visual 3-8 and assume the market price is $35 and that each firm breaks even at that price. The industry and the firm are in long-run equilibrium based on market demand D_1. Now assume the market demand increases to D_2. The market price increases to $40 and the firm's MR curve shifts up, creating a positive total profit at the higher price. The market supply curve will shift to the right as new firms enter the market, attracted by the presence of positive total profit. As supply increases, the market price decreases. If this is a constant-cost industry, the expansion of the industry continues until the supply curve becomes S_2 with the price back at its original level of $35. The firm's MR curve shifts back to its original position and the firm breaks even

again. The industry's long-run equilibrium based on D_1 is the combination of a price of $35 and a quantity of 60,000 units. The industry's long-run equilibrium based on D_2 is the combination of a price of $35 and a quantity of 70,000 units. If you connect these two LRE points, you will have the horizontal LRS curve, which characterizes a constant-cost industry. While the output of an individual firm is unchanged, the total industry output increased from 60,000 units to 70,000 units because of the increase in the number of firms.

22. Display Visual 3-9 and repeat the process in procedure 21 to show the effect of a decrease in the market demand for the product.

23. Assign Activity 3-9 for students to complete. This activity provides six pairs of graphs for students to complete for an industry and a firm in different profit scenarios. This graphing exercise is important.

A Perfectly Competitive Industry and Firm in Short-Run Equilibrium with Positive Total Profit

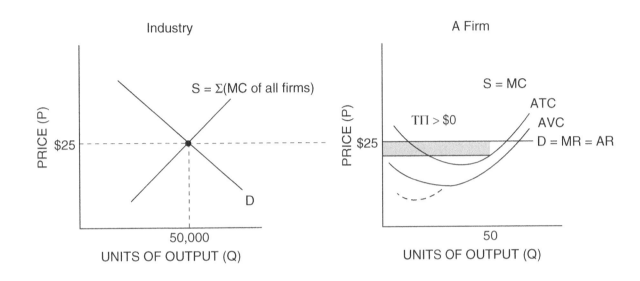

Different Profit Possibilities for a Perfectly Competitive Firm in Short-Run Equilibrium

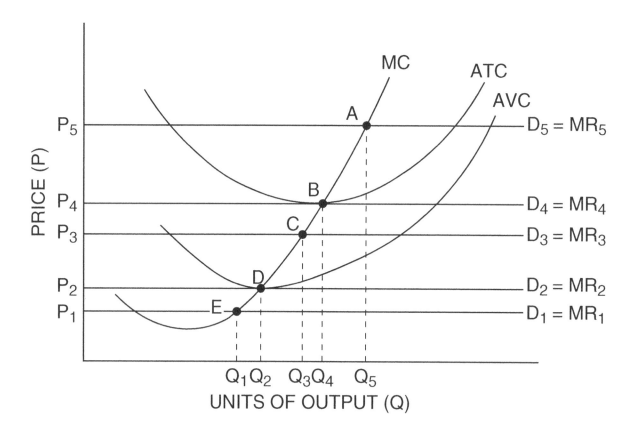

MR = MC at	The firm's total profit is
Point A	positive (P > ATC).
Point B	$0 (P = ATC).
Point C	negative (P < ATC) but the firm should not shut down (P > AVC). Loss < TFC.
Point D	negative (P < ATC) and the firm is indifferent about shutting down (P = AVC). Loss = TFC.
Point E	negative (P < ATC) and the firm should shut down (P < AVC). Loss > TFC.

A Perfectly Competitive Firm in Long-Run Equilibrium

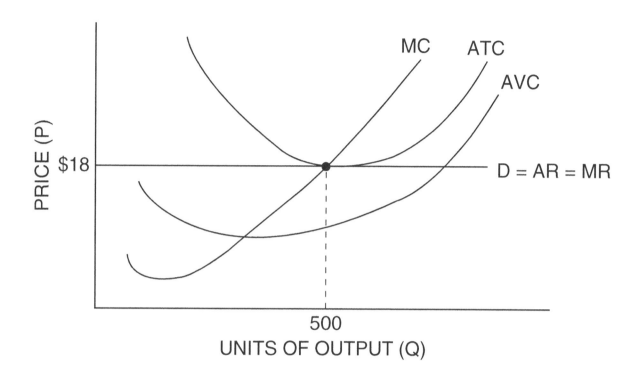

A perfectly competitive firm in long-run equilibrium is both productively and allocatively efficient:

(1) Productive efficiency $P = ATC_{minimum}$

(2) Allocative efficiency $P = MC$

How a Perfectly Competitive Industry and Firm Respond to an Increase in Demand

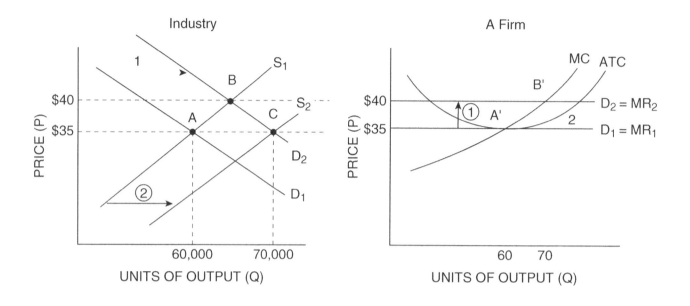

How a Perfectly Competitive Industry and Firm Respond to a Decrease in Demand

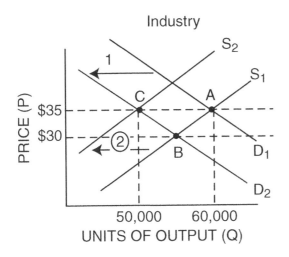

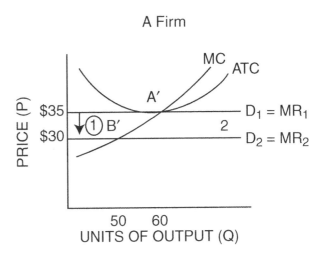

Monopoly

Introduction and Description

Lesson 5 extends the theory of the firm to the model of a *monopoly*. Students will see that the profit-maximization rules for the monopoly are the same as they were for a perfectly competitive firm. Because price (P) is greater than marginal revenue for a monopoly, however, the output will be smaller and the price higher than in a perfectly competitive market. It is in the monopoly's best interest to produce where MR = MC, not where P = MC. The monopoly will produce a smaller output than society would like it to produce. This results in the *total welfare* being smaller in a monopolistic market than in one that is perfectly competitive, thus creating a *deadweight loss* to society.

Objectives

1. Examine the demand, average revenue, marginal revenue, and total revenue functions of a monopoly.

2. Explain why price is greater than marginal revenue for a monopoly.

3. Explain the rules a monopoly uses to maximize its total profit.

4. Draw graphs of a monopoly and identify its optimal output, price, and total profit.

5. Discuss the barriers to entry that keep out other firms.

6. Compare monopoly to perfect competition in terms of output, price, total profit, consumer surplus, producer surplus, and total welfare.

7. Explain why *price discrimination* will increase the total profit of a monopoly.

8. Discuss three pricing plans for the *regulation of a natural monopoly*.

Time Required

Five class periods or 225 minutes

Materials

1. Activities 3-10, 3-11, 3-12, 3-13, 3-14, and 3-15

2. Visuals 3-10 and 3-11

Bell Ringer

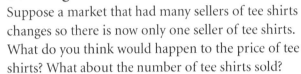

Suppose a market that had many sellers of tee shirts changes so there is now only one seller of tee shirts. What do you think would happen to the price of tee shirts? What about the number of tee shirts sold?

Teacher Alert: **Society would like the monopoly to produce the output at which P = MC, but the firm will produce the output where MR = MC. Students must understand these two different perspectives and why they result in a monopoly producing less output than society wants it to produce.**

Procedure

1. Discuss the characteristics of *a monopolistic market*.

2. Give examples of *barriers to entry* that keep other firms from competing with a monopoly. *(Examples include patents, control of key resources, economies of scale, and price discounts on purchases of large quantities of resources.)*

3. Tell students why a monopoly is a *price maker* and can set the price for its product. *(Because it is the only supplier, the monopoly faces the market demand curve.)*

4. Ask students why a monopolist must lower the price to sell more output. *(This is because the market demand curve is downward sloping.)*

5. Display Visual 3-10 and discuss the shapes of the TR, AR, and MR curves of a monopoly. Point out these facts for a monopoly that has a downward-sloping, straight-line demand curve:

   (A) The firm's MR curve is also downward sloping and linear and twice as steep as the demand curve.

   (B) The upper half (don't say upper "part") of the demand curve is elastic, the midpoint is unitary elastic, and the lower half is inelastic.

   (C) The firm's total revenue is maximized at the output level where MR = 0 (and where demand is unitary elastic).

   (D) The firm's total revenue curve is a symmetrical, bell-shaped curve.

6. Explain that the rules followed by a monopoly trying to maximize total profit are the same as those of a perfectly competitive firm:

   (A) Produce the output where MR = MC.

   (B) The optimal price is found on the demand curve at the optimal output.

   (C) Shut down (produce no output) if, at the optimal output, TR < TVC.

7. Assign Part A of Activity 3-11, which requires students to calculate values of revenue, cost, and profit variables of a monopoly. They also must plot the revenue and cost data on a graph and determine the monopoly's optimal output and price. Have students shade in the areas that represent total revenue, total cost, and total profit at that output level. (*Total revenue is the area of the rectangle drawn from a point on the AR curve at the optimal output level. Total cost is the area of the rectangle drawn from a point on the ATC curve at the optimal output level. Total profit is the area of the rectangle between the TR rectangle and the TC rectangle.*)

8. Use the questions in Part B of Activity 3-11 to explain why producing the output where MR = MC maximizes a monopoly's total profit. Table 3-11.2 is there just for that purpose. Do not be satisfied with students memorizing "MR = MC"; stress the need to understand why the rule works.

9. Use Visual 3-11 to review how a monopoly determines its profit-maximizing quantity and price. Tell students to calculate this monopoly's total profit. (*TΠ = $650 = 65 units × $100.*)

10. Assign Activity 3-12. After evaluating a perfectly competitive market, students are asked to evaluate that same market when it becomes a monopoly. They must compare price, quantity, and consumer surplus between the two different markets. They also must identify and calculate the value of the deadweight loss resulting from the market becoming monopolistic.

11. Now that you have examined the standard model of a monopoly, you will extend the analysis to two related topics. First, Activity 3-13 examines price discrimination. Next, Activity 3-14 covers government regulation of a natural monopoly.

12. Discuss the concept of *perfect price discrimination* (also called *first-degree price discrimination*). This means the monopolist is able to charge each individual consumer the highest price that particular consumer is willing to pay for a unit of the product. By doing so, the monopolist captures all of the consumer surplus and increases its total profit. In this model, the unique price paid by each individual consumer is the marginal revenue the firm receives from the extra unit. This means price is equal to marginal revenue, but note that the MR

curve will be the same as the downward-sloping demand curve. It also means that by producing the output at which MR = MC, the perfect price-discriminating monopoly is producing the socially optimal output where P = MC. This is the same output that would be produced if the market were perfectly competitive.

13. Assign Part A of Activity 3-13. Students calculate the total revenue and marginal revenue values for a standard monopolist and draw the market demand curve.

14. Now have students complete Part B of Activity 3-13. They will discover that by using perfect price discrimination, the monopolist has converted to profit all of the consumer surplus that existed in a perfectly competitive market. Because the output is the socially desired quantity, there is no deadweight loss if there is perfect price discrimination.

15. Before you assign Activity 3-14, you need to define the term *natural monopoly* and explain the three pricing plans that can be used by a government agency to *regulate* the natural monopoly.

    (A) A natural monopoly exists when a single firm's average total cost declines over a large range of output because of economies of scale.

    (B) The three pricing plans illustrated in this activity are:

       (1) *Monopoly pricing* – Let the firm do as it wishes. It will produce the quantity at which MR = MC and charge the price

on its demand curve at that output level. The firm will earn a positive total profit and produce less output than society wishes it would produce.

   (2) *Fair return pricing* – The government eliminates the firm's profit by having it charge a price equal to its average total cost (P = ATC). This output is where the demand curve intersects the average total cost curve. The output is more than under plan (1) but still less than the socially optimal quantity.

   (3) *Socially optimal pricing (also called efficiency pricing)* – The government tries to force the firm to produce the socially optimal quantity by telling it to set its price equal to its marginal cost (P = MC). This output is where the demand curve intersects the marginal cost curve. Because the firm will incur a loss under this plan (its price will be less than its average total cost), the firm will resist it unless provided a subsidy to offset its loss.

16. Assign Activity 3-14 to students. Discuss the results of their evaluation of the three pricing plans.

17. The last activity in Lesson 5 is Activity 3-15, which has students comparing the results of perfect competition with those of monopoly. By now they should be ready to complete this activity and discuss their answers.

The Revenue Graphs of a Monopoly

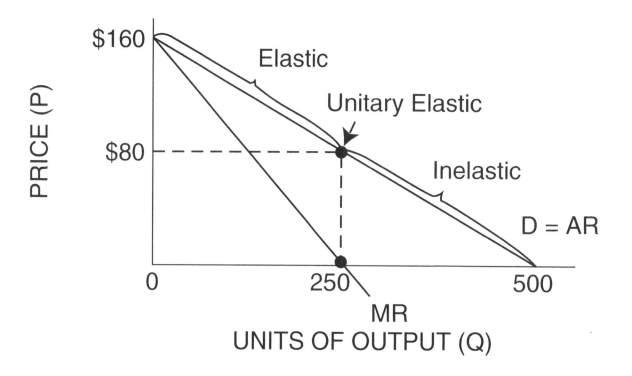

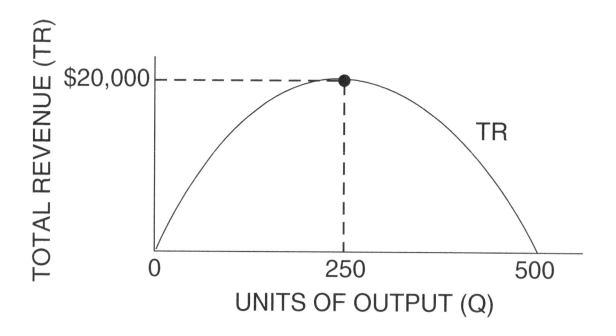

The Graph of a Profit-Maximizing Monopoly

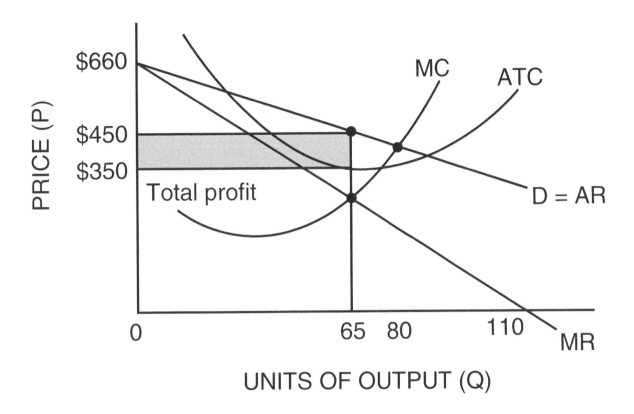

Output	Result	Rule
65 units	Monopoly maximizes total profit.	MR = MC
80 units	Monopoly produces socially optimal output.	P = MC
110 units	Monopoly maximizes total revenue.	MR = $0

Monopolistic Competition and Oligopoly

Introduction and Description

You have devoted a considerable amount of class time to perfect competition and monopoly, the two extreme models on the spectrum of market structure. Lesson 6 allows you to teach the more real-world models of *monopolistic competition* and *oligopoly*. Many retailing industries are conducted under conditions of monopolistic competition. Oligopoly exists in a number of manufacturing industries.

Monopolistic competition is indeed a mixture of perfect competition and monopoly. There are a large number of firms in active competition with each other, with the result being that they break even in long-run equilibrium. Because their products are not identical, the firms have some control over their prices and must reduce price to sell more units. This means the monopolistically competitive firm has a downward-sloping demand curve that lies above its downward-sloping marginal revenue curve. In fact, students will be pleased to learn that the graphs of a monopolistically competitive firm look virtually the same as those of a monopoly. Here are two key differences between these firms. First, the demand curve facing a monopolistically competitive firm is relatively more elastic than the demand curve facing a monopoly because the former has a number of competing firms. Second, because of barriers to entry, a monopoly can maintain a positive total profit in the long-run, whereas a monopolistically competitive firm will have to break even.

An oligopolistic industry is dominated by a few large firms that act interdependently in output and pricing decisions. Because there are so few firms, each one is aware of the actions taken by the other firms. If the firms decide to collude, they agree to restrict output so as to increase the price. Collusion is illegal in many countries, including the United States. The firms could decide to compete with each other, hoping to drive out competition and become a monopolist in complete control of the industry. One approach used to explain oligopolistic behavior is *game theory*. The movie, *A Beautiful Mind*, is based on the life of John Nash who won the Nobel Prize in economics for his contributions to the study of game theory. Game theory explains why collusion among oligopolists does not work in the long run.

Activity 3-16 explores the market structure of monopolistic competition. Game theory is demonstrated in Activity 3-17.

Objectives

1. Define and discuss the nature of monopolistic competition.

2. Given cost and revenue data, determine the output and price of a monopolistically competitive firm in the short run and the long run.

3. Explain how a monopolistically competitive firm moves from a short-run equilibrium with positive total profit to a long-run equilibrium where it breaks even.

4. Evaluate the efficiency of a monopolistically competitive firm in long-run equilibrium.

5. Define and discuss the nature of oligopoly.

6. Discuss the mutual interdependence of oligopolists and why they must monitor each other's actions.

7. Use game theory to evaluate a variety of oligopolistic situations.

Time Required

Two class periods or 90 minutes

Materials

1. Activities 3-16 and 3-17

2. Visual 3-12

Bell Ringer

How do you benefit from there being many stores where you can shop for clothes? Is there much nonprice competition among these stores?

Teacher Alert: Monopolistic competition should be relatively easy for students because its setup and graphs are so similar to those of a monopoly. Students need to be able to compare the results of this market structure with those of perfect competition and monopoly. Students often get confused by how to analyze the data in a game theory payoff matrix. Be certain they understand what the strategies and payoffs really mean as they work through the examples in Activity 3-17.

Procedure

1. Discuss the characteristics of a monopolistically competitive market.

2. Ask students for examples of industries that have these characteristics. *(Examples include retail clothing stores and restaurants.)*

3. Explain why the demand curve of a monopolistically competitive firm is downward sloping. *(It has to lower its price to attract more customers.)*

4. Explain why the firm's marginal revenue curve is below and steeper than the demand curve. *(As was true with the monopolist, price is greater than marginal revenue and the vertical gap between them grows as the firm sells more units.)*

5. Explain why the demand curve facing a monopolistically competitive firm is more elastic than the demand curve facing a monopolist. *(The monopolistically competitive firm has many competitors while the monopoly has none.)*

6. Demonstrate graphically that a monopolistically competitive firm can have four profit outcomes in the short run: earn a positive total profit, break even, make a loss but do not shut down, and make a loss and do shut down. *(These graphs will look very similar to the same graphs of a monopoly.)*

7. Explain why a monopolistically competitive firm must break even in long-run equilibrium. *(If there are profits in the industry, other firms enter. Each firm's share of the market demand is reduced. A firm's demand curve shifts left until it is tangent to its ATC curve and thus the firm breaks even. If firms are suffering losses, some firms leave the industry, causing the demand curve of a firm to shift right until it is tangent to its ATC, thus breaking even.)*

8. Display Visual 3-12 to illustrate the short-run and long-run positions of a monopolistically competitive firm.

9. Have students complete Activity 3-16 and discuss the answers with them.

10. Discuss the characteristics of an oligopolistic industry with students. Ask them for examples.

11. Give a lecture on game theory. Because Activity 3-17 can be challenging, be sure students understand the structure of a game theory example.

   (A) *Game theory* is used to explain the strategic behavior of oligopolistic firms. It is a way of explaining the effects of oligopolistic firms being highly interdependent.

   (B) Game theory is similar to a card game in which a player's *strategy* depends on the cards he or she is dealt and the actions of the other players.

   (C) A *dominant strategy* is one that is best for one player regardless of any strategy chosen by the other player.

(D) A *dominated strategy* is one whose outcome depends on the strategy chosen by the other player. It can be a good strategy if the player can predict the other player's move.

(E) A *Nash Equilibrium* is a combination of strategies that is the best response for a player given the other player's best response. It does not always provide the best result for society.

12. Ask students to read the introduction to Activity 3-17 and discuss the basics of game theory.

   (A) What is a payoff matrix? *(It is a table that shows the payoffs to each player from each possible strategy.)*

(B) What is a dominant strategy? *(It is a strategy that is best for one player regardless of what strategy is chosen by the other player.)*

(C) What is a Nash Equilibrium? *(It is any combination of strategies that is a best response for a player, given the other player's best response to this combination of strategies. It is an equilibrium because neither player has an incentive to change his or her strategy.)*

13. Have students complete Part A of Activity 3-17 and discuss the Coke-Pepsi exercise with them. This will show you where any confusion lies.

14. Assign the rest of Activity 3-17. Have students explain their decisions for each player in each example.

A Monopolistically Competitive Firm in Short-Run and Long-Run Equilibrium

Positive Total Profit in Short-Run Equilibrium

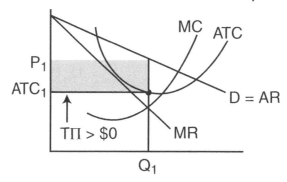

Negative Total Profit in Short-Run Equilibrium

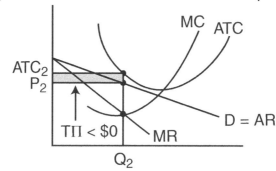

PRICE (P)

Breaking Even in Long-Run Equilibrium

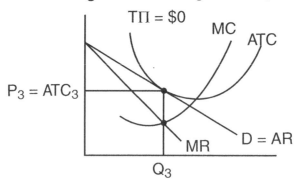

UNITS OF OUTPUT (Q)

MICROECONOMICS

Factor Markets

Unit 4

10 class periods or 450 minutes
(13 percent of course time)

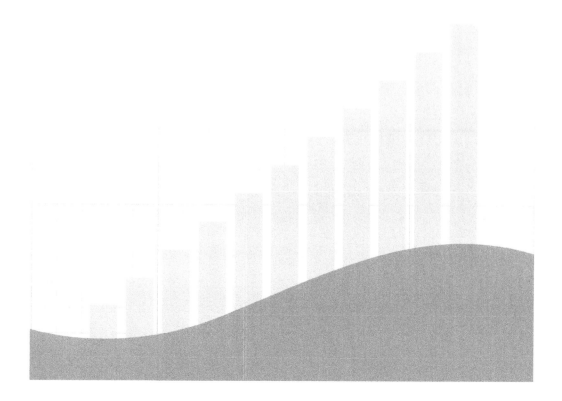

Unit 4 switches the roles of the household and business sectors of the economy. In the markets for resources, households are the suppliers and businesses are the demanders. The basic analytical framework for examining factor markets uses concepts similar to those used in the supply and demand units (Units 1 and 2) and the theory of the firm unit (Unit 3). The concepts of demand, supply, equilibrium, marginal analysis, and profit maximization are applied again in Unit 4. The difference is that they are applied to inputs rather than outputs. Students do not have to learn a lot of new concepts in this unit. Rather, they must apply to the factor or resource markets the concepts they already learned in studying product markets. The topics covered in Unit 4 account for 10–18 percent of the Advanced Placement (AP) Microeconomics Exam.

The demand for a resource is derived from the demand for the goods and services the resource can produce. This connection is important because some AP test questions involve examples relating the demand in the product market to the demand in the resource market.

A key concept in the study of factor markets is marginal productivity analysis, which is used to examine how the prices of resources (wage, rent, interest, and profit) are determined. Following the procedure used in most textbooks, this unit stresses wage determination for labor and uses it as an example to show how the factors of production are priced. The key point is that a firm will hire inputs until *marginal revenue product* equals *marginal resource cost*. The logic behind this rule is the same as that used to explain why a firm's profit-maximizing output is the one at which marginal revenue equals marginal cost.

Another part of Unit 4 compares how wages are determined in *a perfectly competitive labor market* and in *a monopsonistic labor market*. The unit analyzes the effects of government policies (e.g., minimum wage laws) and union activities using both competitive and monopsonistic models.

Although the major emphasis of the factor market portion of the AP Microeconomics Exam will be on labor markets, there may also be questions on the other factors of production: land, capital, and entrepreneurship. Be sure to have students focus on the key ideas related to any factor market.

Students should be familiar with several terms used to describe the change in a firm's total cost when it adds an extra unit of a resource. This unit uses the term *marginal resource cost*, but other common terms that mean the same thing include *marginal factor cost* and *marginal labor cost*.

The Lesson Planner

Lesson 1 How Resource Prices Are Determined; Activities 4-1, 4-2, 4-3, and 4-4, and Visuals 4-1, 4-2, and 4-3

Lesson 2 Competition versus Monopsony in Labor Markets; Activities 4-5 and 4-6, and Visuals 4-4 and 4-5

Lesson 3 Analyzing Factor Market Concepts; Activity 4-7 and Visual 4-6

Free Response Questions (FRQs)

This is a partial list of FRQs that can be used with each unit of the *Advanced Placement Economics: Microeconomics* resource manual. These questions and grading rubrics are available at AP Central on the College Board Web site: http://apcentral.collegeboard.com

2011	Question 2, Part (c): competitive labor market; D = MRP; wage and employment
2011 Form B	Question 3: monopsony and minimum wage
2010	Question 1, Part (d): increased demand for one good has effect on market of another good
2010	Question 2: market for rental machines; effect of fall in demand for good being produced
2010	Question 2, Part (c): cost-minimizing combination of inputs
2010 Form B	Question 2: diminishing marginal productivity and MRP chart; demand for labor
2008 Form B	Question 3: diminishing marginal productivity; MRP; number of workers to hire
2007	Question 2: draw labor supply curve; determine best number of workers and output
2006 Form B	Question 3: conditions for profit-maximizing amount of labor; draw firm's labor graph

Additional Resources

To download visuals for each lesson and to find related material, visit http://www.councilforeconed.org/ap-economics

How Resource Prices Are Determined

Introduction and Description

This lesson shows students how a firm determines the profit-maximizing quantity of resources and resource prices. Students see how the demand for a resource is dependent on the marginal productivity of the resource and on the demand for the goods and services that resource produces. They learn that the firm should employ a resource at the level where marginal revenue product equals marginal resource cost. The effect of a product market not being perfectly competitive is examined. The lesson compares the employment and resource price of a firm that hires a resource in a *perfectly competitive market* with those of a firm that acquires a resource in a *monopsonistic market*. Students work examples in which they must find the economically efficient and profit-maximizing combinations of resources.

Objectives

1. Explain the difference between a product market and a resource market.

2. Point out that the roles played by households and businesses are different in a resource market from what they are in a product market.

3. Define the terms *marginal revenue product (MRP)* and *marginal resource cost (MRC)*.

4. Explain why a firm maximizes its total profit by using the amount of a resource at which the MRP is equal to the MRC.

5. Explain why the demand for a resource is called a *derived demand*.

6. Explain why the supply of labor is perfectly elastic if the firm buys labor in a perfectly competitive factor market.

7. Show how the equilibrium wage and employment are affected by the product market not being perfectly competitive.

8. Define *monopsony*.

9. Explain why the monopsony's labor supply curve is upward sloping and why the MRC curve is above that labor supply curve.

10. Compare the equilibrium wage and employment in a monopsonistic labor market with those in a perfectly competitive labor market.

11. Understand the conditions necessary for a firm to have the economically efficient combination of resources.

12. Understand the conditions necessary for a firm to have the profit-maximizing combination of resources.

13. Know how resource markets are affected by changes in economic conditions, government policies, and union activity.

Time Required

Four class periods or 180 minutes

Materials

1. Activities 4-1, 4-2, 4-3, and 4-4

2. Visuals 4-1, 4-2, and 4-3

Bell Ringer

Why should an employer give you a job? What wage should the employer pay you? Would your salary be higher if there are many employers in your community or if there is only one employer?

Teacher Alert: Students will do better on this material if you reinforce the fact that the analysis of a resource market is similar to the analysis of a product market. Here are some connections you should stress:

(A) **Households represent the supply side of a resource market, whereas they represent** the demand side of a product market. Businesses represent the demand side of a resource market, whereas they represent the supply side of a product market.

(B) The laws of demand and supply hold true in factor markets just as they did in product markets. The demand curve is still downward sloping, and the supply curve is still upward sloping.

(C) A firm's supply of labor curve is perfectly elastic if it buys labor in a perfectly competitive factor market. A firm's output demand curve is perfectly elastic if it sells output in a perfectly competitive product market.

(D) A monopsonist's MRC curve is upward sloping and above its upward-sloping labor supply curve. A monopolist's marginal revenue (MR) curve is downward sloping and below its downward-sloping output demand curve.

(E) The profit-maximizing resource quantity is where MRP = MRC. The profit-maximizing output quantity for a firm is where MR = marginal cost (MC).

(F) The monopsonist finds its wage on the labor supply curve at the profit-maximizing amount of labor. A monopolist finds its price on the product demand curve at the profit-maximizing quantity of output.

Procedure

1. Discuss the similarities and differences between a factor market and a product market, including the dual roles of households and businesses.

2. Display Visual 4-1 to help you illustrate some of the points that follow.

3. Explain why the demand for labor is called a derived demand. (*This is because the demand*

for labor depends on the demand for the goods and services produced by labor.)

4. Define MRP and show how to calculate its value. (*MRP is the change in total revenue from adding an extra unit of labor. MRP = $\Delta TR/\Delta L$. If the product market is perfectly competitive, you can use MRP = (marginal physical product) (price of the good) = (MPP)(P).*)

5. Define MRC and show how to calculate its value. (*MRC is the change in total cost from adding an extra unit of labor. MRC = $\Delta TC/\Delta L$. If the labor market is perfectly competitive, you can use MRC = wage.*)

6. Explain that the profit-maximizing amount of a resource is where MRP = MRC. Remind students that this is similar to the MR = MC rule a firm uses to determine its profit-maximizing output.

7. Assign Part A of Activity 4-1, which has students calculate values of a firm's productivity and revenue from different amounts of labor. They plot the MRP values in a graph and add a horizontal labor supply curve because the firm buys labor in a perfectly competitive resource market. They determine the profit-maximizing quantity of labor at wages of $100, $75, and $50 and create the firm's demand schedule for labor. Point out that the firm will demand more labor at a low wage than at a high wage.

8. Display Visual 4-2 to illustrate how students calculate the value of MRP when the product market is perfectly competitive. (*[1] The firm will hire four units at a price of $45, five units at $35, and six units at $25. [2] The MRP falls because of diminishing marginal productivity as more resource units are added. [3] Yes. Because the resource market is perfectly competitive, the firm can hire all the units it wants at the market price of the resource: price of resource = marginal resource cost.*)

9. Explain why the downward-sloping portion of the firm's MRP curve is its demand curve for labor, *if* the labor market is perfectly competitive. *(Since MRC = wage if the labor market is perfectly competitive, the optimal labor amount is found where the horizontal labor supply curve [S = MRC] intersects the MRP curve. It is the downward-sloping portion of the MRP curve because if the firm stops at a point on the upward-sloping portion, it will miss some labor units that have MRP > MRC.)*

10. Assign Part B of Activity 4-1 to show students how an increase in the demand for the good will affect the demand for labor. *(The increase in the good's price causes an increase in labor's MRP, thus increasing the demand for labor.)*

11. In Part C of Activity 4-1, students are asked to explain the logic of hiring where MRP = MRC. *(Here is the logic. The firm wants to hire labor units for which MRP > MRC because those units have a positive marginal profit of labor [MΠL], which means they add to the firm's total profit. The labor unit where MRP = MRC does not change total profit [MΠL = $0]. But by stopping with the labor unit for which MRP = MCL, the firm does not hire units for which MRP < MCL. Those units would reduce total profit and have a negative marginal profit of labor [MΠL < $0]. By hiring the number of labor units where MRP = MCL, the firm hires all the profitable units and stops before hiring any units that would lower its total profit.)*

🛈 *Teacher Alert:* **If you use several college textbooks as references as you prepare for your AP Microeconomics course, you will notice that various concepts that include the word "efficiency" have different interpretations by different authors. The term "economic efficiency" is an example. Some textbooks use** the term to indicate society has allocated its resources to their highest valued uses. Others treat the term as an indication that a given output is produced at the lowest total cost. The latter interpretation is used in this context, but be sure students are aware of the different interpretations of "economic efficiency."

12. Before assigning Activity 4-2, tell students that in the long run the firm must decide on the best combination of all resources. In a simple model, the firm operates with labor and capital. This activity requires students to think about the best resource combination at two levels. First, what combination of labor and capital should the firm employ to be *economically efficient*? This means it produces a given output level at the lowest total cost, or it produces the most output possible from a given total cost. This requires the firm to have a resource combination such that the *marginal physical product per dollar* is the same for all resources. Second, what combination of resources will maximize the firm's total profit? This requires that MRP = MRC for each input. Economic efficiency is a necessary but not sufficient condition for profit maximization.

13. Assign Activity 4-2 and have students discuss their answers. Be sure they understand the difference between an economically efficient combination of resources and one that maximizes total profit.

14. The MRP of labor depends on the MPP of labor and the additional revenue the firm receives from that extra output. Activity 4-3 examines a firm that is a monopolist in the product market and hires labor in a perfectly competitive resource market. Because it must lower price to sell the output from an extra unit of labor, its

marginal revenue decreases as it hires more labor, thus making extra workers less valuable. Assign Activity 4-3 and discuss whether the firm's demand curve for labor is steeper because the product market is not perfectly competitive.

15. Display Visual 4-3 to show students how to calculate MRP when the product market is not perfectly competitive. (*[1] The firm will hire three units at a price of $45, four units at $35, and five units at $25. [2] The MRP falls because of diminishing marginal productivity as more resource units are added, and because of decreasing marginal revenue from extra units of output. [3] Yes. Because the resource market is perfectly competitive, the firm can* *hire all the units it wants at the market price of the resource: price of resource = marginal resource cost.*)

16. Assign Activity 4-4. Students determine the labor demand schedule for a firm that operates in perfectly competitive product and factor markets. They create the market demand for labor and determine the market wage and level of employment. They see that the market demand for labor increases when the market price of the good increases, increasing both the equilibrium wage and employment. An increase in the market wage reduces the quantity of labor a firm will hire.

Big Ideas about Factor (or Resource) Markets

1. The economic concepts are similar to those for product markets.

2. The demand for a factor of production is derived from the demand for the good or service produced from this resource.

3. A firm tries to hire additional units of a resource up to the point where the resource's marginal revenue product (MRP) is equal to its marginal resource cost (MRC).

4. In hiring labor, a perfectly competitive firm will do best if it hires up to the point where MRP = the wage rate. Wages are the marginal resource cost of labor if the labor market is perfectly competitive.

5. If you want a high wage:
   (A) Make something people will pay a lot for.
   (B) Work for a highly productive firm.
   (C) Be in relatively short supply.
   (D) Invest in your human capital.

6. Real wages depend on productivity.

7. Productivity depends on real or physical capital, human capital, labor quality, and technology.

The Demand for a Resource When the Product Market and Resource Market Are Perfectly Competitive

(1) Units of resource	(2) Total product (Q)	(3) Marginal physical product (MPP) = Δ(2)/Δ(1)	(4) Product price (P)	(5) Total revenue (TR) = (2)x(4)	(6) Marginal revenue product (MRP) = Δ(5)/Δ(1)
0	0	—	$5.00	$0.00	—
1	12	+12	$5.00	$60.00	+$60.00
2	26	+14	$5.00	$130.00	+$70.00
3	38	+12	$5.00	$190.00	+$60.00
4	48	+10	$5.00	$240.00	+$50.00
5	56	+8	$5.00	$280.00	+$40.00
6	62	+6	$5.00	$310.00	+$30.00
7	66	+4	$5.00	$330.00	+$20.00
8	68	+2	$5.00	$340.00	+$10.00

1. How many units of the resource would be hired at each of these perfectly competitive resource prices: $45, $35, and $25?

2. Why does the value of MRP decrease as more units of the resource are added by the firm?

3. Is the MRP curve the firm's demand curve for the resource?

The Demand for a Resource When the Product Market Is Imperfectly Competitive and the Resource Market Is Perfectly Competitive

(1) Units of resource	(2) Total product (Q)	(3) Marginal physical product (MPP) = Δ(2)/Δ(1)	(4) Product price (P)	(5) Total revenue (TR) = (2)x(4)	(6) Marginal revenue product (MRP) = Δ(5)/Δ(1)
0	0	—	$5.80	$0.00	—
1	12	+12	$5.60	$67.20	+$67.20
2	26	+14	$5.40	$140.40	+$73.20
3	38	+12	$5.20	$197.60	+$57.20
4	48	+10	$5.00	$240.00	+$42.40
5	56	+8	$4.80	$268.80	+$28.80
6	62	+6	$4.60	$285.20	+$16.40
7	66	+4	$4.40	$290.40	+$5.20
8	68	+2	$4.20	$285.60	−$4.80

1. How many units of the resource would be hired at each of these perfectly competitive resource prices: $45, $35, and $25?

2. Why does the value of MRP decrease as more units of the resource are added by the firm?

3. Is the MRP curve the firm's demand curve for the resource?

Competition versus Monopsony in Labor Markets

Introduction and Description

Lesson 2 asks students to compare a labor market that is perfectly competitive with one that is a monopsony. A *monopsony* is the sole buyer of labor and must offer a higher wage to attract more workers. The firm's marginal resource cost from adding another unit of labor is greater than the wage paid to that labor unit. Students work with graphs of perfectly competitive and monopsonistic labor markets to analyze the effects of changes in economic conditions, government policies, and union activities.

Objectives

1. Demonstrate the differences between a competitive labor market and a monopsonistic labor market.

2. Analyze the effect of a *minimum wage* in a perfectively competitive labor market and in a monopsonistic labor market.

3. Show graphically the impact of changes in economic conditions, government policies, and union activities.

Time Required

Two class periods or 90 minutes

Materials

1. Activities 4-5 and 4-6

2. Visuals 4-4 and 4-5

 Bell Ringer

What happens to the level of unemployment when the government establishes a minimum wage? Who benefits from such a policy? Who is harmed by it?

Teacher Alert: The basic hiring rule applies to any firm, regardless of whether it buys labor in a perfectly competitive or a monopsonistic labor market: Hire where MRP = MRC. Since the firm pays the market wage to all workers in a perfectly competitive labor market, that firm can also use the hiring rule of MRP = wage. A monopsony must stick with the MRP = MRC rule because the wage is less than the MRC for a monopsonist.

Procedure

1. Display Visual 4-4 as a review of how a firm is a "wage taker" if the labor market is perfectly competitive. Ask students why the market labor demand curve is downward sloping and why the market labor supply curve is upward sloping. Ask them why the labor supply to a firm is horizontal. *(The firm can hire all the labor it wants at the market wage; it does not have to raise the wage to attract more labor.)*

2. Display Visual 4-5 to illustrate the decisions made by a monopsony. The firm determines its profit-maximizing quantity of labor where MRP = MRC and its optimal wage comes from the labor supply curve at that quantity of labor.

3. Assign Activity 4-5.

    (A) What are the equilibrium wage and quantity of labor in the competitive labor market? *($8.00 and 4,000 hours of labor)*

    (B) What is the impact of a minimum wage placed in a competitive labor market? *(The wage rises and there is unemployment in the labor market.)*

(C) Why is the monopsony's labor supply curve upward sloping? *(It must raise the wage to attract more workers.)*

(D) Why is the monopsony's MRC curve above its labor supply curve? *(Because it pays the higher wage to all workers, the actual cost to the firm of an extra worker exceeds the wage paid to that worker.)*

(E) Is the MRP curve of a monopsony also the firm's demand curve for labor? *(No, because the wage is not equal to MRC.)*

4. Assign Activity 4-6 and have students explain their answers. This activity asks student to analyze the impact of changes in economic conditions, government policies, and union activities.

The Supply of and Demand for Labor in a Competitive Labor Market

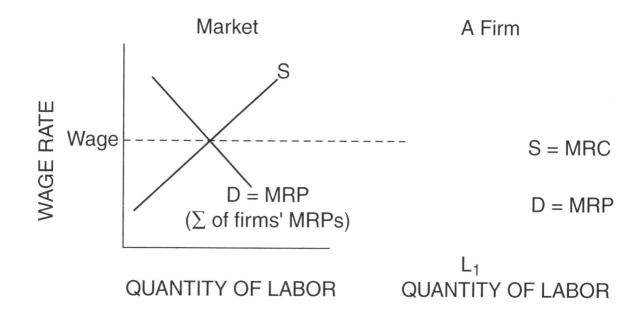

Market

A Firm

WAGE RATE

Wage

S

D = MRP
(Σ of firms' MRPs)

QUANTITY OF LABOR

S = MRC

D = MRP

L_1
QUANTITY OF LABOR

A Monopsonistic Labor Market

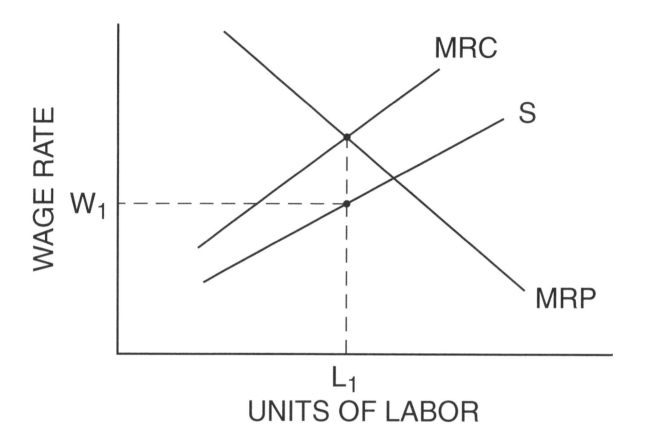

Analyzing Factor Market Concepts

Introduction and Description

In this lesson, students are given a variety of questions to see how well they have mastered the material on factor markets. If they do poorly on a particular question, they should review that material.

Objectives

1. Evaluate how well students understand factor markets.

2. Identify any problem areas and review those areas.

Time Required

One class period or 45 minutes

Materials

1. Activity 4-7

2. Visual 4-6

 Bell Ringer

How well do you understand resource markets? Here are some questions that put you to the test.

Teacher Alert: Use this lesson to identify problem areas and address them as time allows.

Procedure

1. Assign Activity 4-7. Go over the answers with students. If there are topics that students have not mastered, have them go back to the activities related to those topics for more practice.

2. Introduce the concept of *economic rent* and display Visual 4-6 to illustrate your discussion of this topic.

   (A) What is economic rent? (*It is the amount by which the price of a resource exceeds the minimum price necessary to make a resource available.*)

   (B) In Visual 4-6, the supply of land is shown as a vertical line because there is a fixed quantity available. It is assumed the initial price of the land is zero. The higher the demand for the fixed quantity of land, the greater is its economic rent.

   (C) Suppose a movie star earns $20 million a year making top-rated movies. If her best alternative occupation would earn her an annual income of $50,000, what is the value of her economic rent? (*$19,950,000*)

Economic Rent

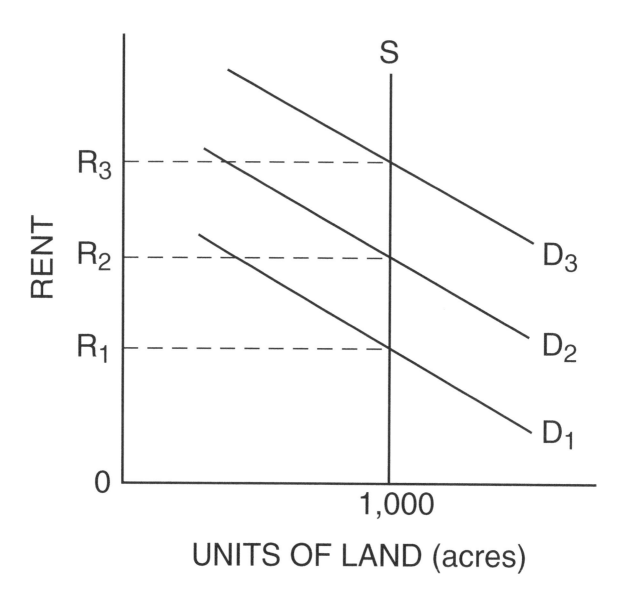

Economic rent is the amount by which the price of a resource exceeds the minimum level required to keep that resource in its current use. This graph assumes the quantity of land is fixed at 1,000 acres. The greater the demand for the land, the higher is the economic rent.

MICROECONOMICS

The Role of Government

Unit 5

11 class periods or 495 minutes
(15 percent of course time)

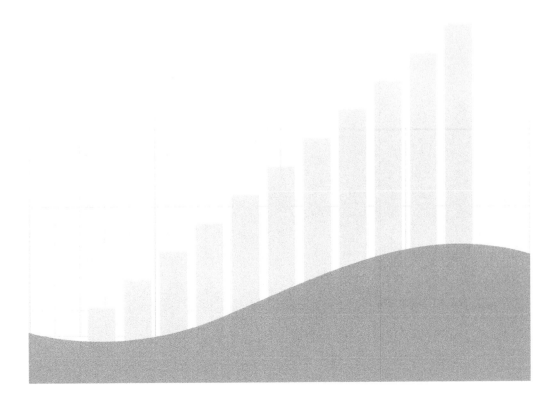

In this unit, students develop criteria to determine which activities government should undertake and to evaluate how well government performs these activities. Unit 5 accounts for 12–18 percent of the Advanced Placement (AP) Microeconomics Exam. It applies a variety of concepts students learned in previous units.

A distinction is made between private goods and public goods. Students learn that the government must provide public goods. Pure *public goods* must meet the criteria of *nonrivalry (shared consumption)* and *nonexclusion*.

The government attempts to correct *market failures*. A market failure occurs when the private market produces too much or too little of a good because of negative or positive *externalities*. Marginal analysis can be used to determine how much of a corrective action should be taken. For example, there is an optimal amount of pollution control that should be provided, rather than attempting to eliminate all pollution.

Finally, some people believe that government should make the distribution of income more equal. Government does this through taxation policies, although these policies do not always have the desired effects. The topic of income distribution is examined through the use of the *Lorenz curve* and the *Gini coefficient*.

The Lesson Planner

Lesson 1 Public Goods versus Private Goods; Activity 5-1 and Visual 5-1

Lesson 2 When Markets Fail; Activities 5-2, 5-3, and 5-4, and Visuals 5-2 and 5-3

Lesson 3 Efficiency, Equity, and Effects of Government Policies; Activities 5-5, 5-6, and 5-7

Practice Free Response Questions (FRQs)

This is a partial list of FRQs that can be used with each unit of the *Advanced Placement Economics: Microeconomics* resource manual. These questions and grading rubrics are available at AP Central on the College Board Web site: http://apcentral.collegeboard.com

2012	Question 1, parts (c) and (d): per unit and lump-sum subsidies; consumer surplus and deadweight loss
2012	Question 3, parts (b) and (c): effect of tariff on government tax revenue and consumer and producer surplus
2011	Question 3: negative externality; marginal private cost; marginal social cost
2011	Question 3, part (b): effect of a lump-sum tax on deadweight loss
2011 Form B	Question 2: college spillover benefits; government subsidy
2010	Question 3, parts (b) and (c): negative externality; government imposes a per-unit tax

2009   Question 1: government uses lump-sum subsidy

2008   Question 1: government uses lump-sum subsidy

2008 Form B   Question 2: vaccination has positive spillover benefits

2007   Question 1: government sets lump-sum tax; government sets a per-unit subsidy

2006   Question 1: government subsidizes a museum

2006   Question 3: negative externality: marginal private cost = marginal social cost?

Additional Resources

To download visuals for each lesson and to find related material, visit
http://www.councilforeconed.org/ap-economics

Public Goods versus Private Goods

Introduction and Description

This lesson makes the distinction between *private goods*, which are subject to exclusion and rivalry, and *public goods*, which are subject to *nonexclusion* and *nonrivalry*. Public goods cannot be excluded from people who do not pay for them. Also, someone using a public good does not prevent others from using it as well. Because of these characteristics, firms are unable to earn a positive profit by producing public goods and services. It has become the responsibility of government to provide them.

Objectives

1. Describe the major characteristics of *public goods* and *private goods*.

2. Explain why it is not profitable for the private market to produce public goods.

3. Explain why public goods are important for society and why the government provides them.

Time Required

One and a half class periods or 68 minutes

Materials

1. Activity 5-1

2. Visual 5-1

 Bell Ringer

Why do we rely on the government to provide national defense? How does the government pay for national defense?

Teacher Alert: Have students suggest additional examples of public goods. Ask them why profit-seeking firms would not be successful in producing these goods if they were not paid for by the government.

Procedure

1. Ask students to brainstorm jobs that government does. Have them list as many functions of local, state, and federal governments as they can.

2. Give a lecture on the economic role of government, using Visual 5-1.

3. Introduce the concept of a public good. Explain that a public good has the characteristics of shared consumption (nonrivalrous) and nonexclusion. You might ask students to classify some goods using:

   (A) Exclusion

   (B) Nonexclusion

   (C) Nonshared consumption (rival good)

   (D) Shared consumption (nonrival good)

4. Some possibilities are:

   (A) Hamburger: exclusion and rival

   (B) TV show: exclusion but nonrival

   (C) Park: exclusion but nonrival

   (D) Education: exclusion but nonrival

   (E) National defense: nonexclusion and shared consumption (nonrival)

5. Discuss the problem of *free riders* when people cannot be excluded from using goods. Ask what happens if a person does not contribute financial support for public television.

6. Discuss the answers to Table 5-1.1. There might be some discussion on shared consumption. For example, a private amusement park is shared consumption until it is full. Health care is shared consumption in some areas (public health) and not in others. This is a good opportunity to show these decisions are difficult.

7. Have students complete Table 5-1.2 and discuss their answers. These are students' opinions, but goods produced by government should meet the criteria of nonexclusion and shared consumption.

The Economic Functions of Government

1. Enforce laws and contracts.

2. Maintain competition.

3. Redistribute income. Provide an economic safety net.

4. Provide public goods:

   ■ Nonexclusion

   ■ Shared consumption

5. Correct market failures:

   ■ Provide market information.

   ■ Correct negative externalities.

   ■ Subsidize goods with positive externalities.

6. Stabilize the economy:

   ■ Fight unemployment.

   ■ Encourage price stability.

   ■ Promote economic growth.

When Markets Fail

Introduction and Description

The material discussed in Lesson 2 appears frequently on the AP Microeconomics Exam. Students need to understand the conditions under which a competitive market fails to produce the socially optimal quantity of a good or service. They also need to know what steps can be taken to remedy this situation. Some government intervention in the economy is designed to remedy problems arising from third-party costs and benefits of private activities or transactions. Students who understand *third-party effects*, often called *externalities*, can analyze the need for and effect of such government interventions. Activity 5-2 provides an overview of the externality problem.

When a government tries to correct a negative externality, it can choose to intervene in a number of ways, or the problem may be corrected by private negotiations, which is the basis for the *Coase Theorem* presented in Activity 5-3. When government does intervene, its objective should be to use marginal analysis so as to have the marginal social benefit of the last unit produced equal to that unit's marginal social cost. Activity 5-4 provides practice in doing this type of analysis as students must decide on the optimal amount of pollution cleanup.

Objectives

1. Explain how private market activities can cause externalities.

2. Define and give examples of *third-party costs* (also called *negative externalities* or *social spillover costs*).

3. Define and give examples of *third-party benefits* (also called *positive externalities* or *social spillover benefits*).

4. Analyze why positive and negative externalities cause underproduction or overproduction of goods and services in a competitive market.

5. Analyze the effectiveness of government policies designed to remedy problems caused by positive or negative externalities.

6. Explain the *Coase Theorem* and use it to analyze how negotiations among private property owners can resolve market allocation problems.

7. Analyze how marginal analysis can determine the optimum amount of pollution cleanup.

Time Required

Three and a half class periods or 158 minutes

Materials

1. Activities 5-2, 5-3, and 5-4

2. Visuals 5-2 and 5-3

Bell Ringer

You hear a neighbor say, "Pollution is nasty and stinks. We should do all we can to eliminate all pollution!" Do you agree with your neighbor?

Teacher Alert: **Have students be clear in their answers using the terms marginal social benefit (MSB), marginal social cost (MSC), marginal private benefit (MPB), and marginal private cost (MPC). Do not let them just say "marginal benefit" or "marginal cost."**

Procedure

1. Begin with a discussion on the external effects of production and consumption and some commonsense examples of positive and negative externalities.

   (A) Smoking creates external costs. The smoker is satisfied, and the tobacco company gains;

but third parties often have to cope with smell and litter, as well as the hazard to health from breathing secondary smoke.

(B) People who drive under the influence of alcohol are much more likely to cause accidents than other drivers. These accidents cause third parties to suffer personal injury and/or property damage.

(C) The productive work of maintaining one's house is an example of an external benefit provided by a consumer who also acts as a producer. If people landscape their yards and paint and maintain their houses, the whole neighborhood looks better. The houses are then worth more than houses in comparable neighborhoods where the owners do not maintain their houses to an equal extent.

(D) Education provides third-party benefits. On the whole, people's productivity increases with their level of education. A higher level of education also tends to be correlated with better health and a lower crime rate. Third parties benefit from this greater productivity through fewer demands on health care services and the lower burden on the police and judiciary.

(E) If you teach in a public school, ask students why taxpayers should pay for their education. One reason is the third-party benefits that education creates.

2. Now use graphical analysis to illustrate negative and positive externalities and how these externalities can be corrected.

(A) Use Visual 5-2 to illustrate the effects of a negative externality. (*The market will provide the output Q_1 where MPB = MPC, whereas the socially optimal output Q_2 is where MSB = MSC. The market*

overproduces this good or service as a result of the negative externality.)

(B) Use Visual 5-3 to illustrate the effects of a positive externality. (*The market will provide the output Q_1 where MPB = MPC, whereas the socially optimal output Q_2 is where MSB = MSC. The market underproduces this good or service as a result of the positive externality.*)

3. Have students read the opening section of Activity 5-2 and complete Part A. Discuss the answers to Part A. Note that not all textbooks handle the graphs of externalities the same way. Check out a couple of textbooks and see if you notice differences in how supply curves are used to represent MSC, MPC, and social spillover cost. Check out the demand curves in the textbooks as well with regard to how a positive externality is represented. The approach used in Activity 5-2 is to represent the *marginal external cost (MEC)* of an activity as the vertical distance between the MSC curve and the MPC curve. The *marginal external benefit (MEB)* of an activity is shown as the vertical distance between the MSB curve and the MPB curve.

4. Assign Parts B and C of Activity 5-2 and discuss the answers.

5. Part C of Activity 5-2 presents an important distinction between the effect of a per-unit tax and a lump-sum tax. (There is a parallel distinction between a per-unit subsidy and a lump-sum subsidy.) Because the per-unit policy affects a firm's marginal cost, it will change the firm's profit-maximizing output level where MR = MC. Because the lump-sum policy does not change the firm's marginal cost, that policy does not affect the firm's quantity. Be sure students are on the lookout for these two policies on the AP

Microeconomics Exam. A convenient way to incorporate a government per-unit subsidy to a firm is to reduce the firm's marginal cost by the amount of the subsidy; this will increase the quantity produced by the firm. Assign Parts C and D of Activity 5-2.

6. Discuss the Coase Theorem. Created by Ronald Coase, a Nobel Laureate in economics, this theory has many practical applications. The key is that resources can be allocated efficiently when private ownership rights are assigned and when there are no transaction costs. Most importantly, Coase maintained that no matter who receives the legal rights to ownership, the assignment will have no effect on the way economic resources are used.

7. Students may wonder why this is a big deal, particularly because all transactions do have costs. The excitement is that the Coase Theorem changes the way people look at economic problems. There is less need for government intervention. In any economic transaction, solutions that can benefit most parties can be achieved by negotiations. For example, environmental problems can be resolved if property rights are assigned rather than relying on government command and control.

8. Have students complete Activity 5-3 and go over the answers.

9. Now that we have established that markets can fail because of externalities, how should government address the problem? The environment is an important issue. Is it a good idea to clean up the environment as much as possible? This would ignore the opportunity cost of the cleanup. Therefore, the environment should be cleaned up to the point where the marginal social benefit of cleaning up equals the marginal social cost (MSB = MSC).

10. Before you assign Activity 5-4, note that the term "economic efficiency" in this example refers to using resources in a way that maximizes social welfare. This is a broader view of economic efficiency than the one used in Unit 4, where economic efficiency meant a given output was produced with the lowest cost combination of resources.

11. Have students complete Activity 5-4 and discuss the answers. Keep these points in mind as you discuss the answers:

Question 1(A). Correctly interpreted, it costs Firm 1 $160 to reduce pollution emissions by the first unit. The MSB from this emission reduction is $350. Thus, it clearly pays to reduce emissions by this first unit.

Question 1(B). Similarly, it costs Firm 1 $360 to reduce pollution emissions by the fifth unit, while the MSB from this damage reduction is only $150. Thus, it clearly does not pay to reduce emissions by this fifth unit of pollution.

Question 2(A). With MSC of $160 being less than MSB of $200, it pays for Firm 2 to reduce pollution emissions by the fourth unit.

Question 2(B). Because the MSC of $160 is greater than the MSB of $150, it does not pay Firm 2 to eliminate the fifth unit of foul sludge emissions.

12. The explanations for Questions 3 and 4 are shown on the answer key. Because the basic logic of "keep reducing pollution as long as MSB > MSC, and stop reducing when MSB < MSC" lends itself to graphical exposition—and because a graph also helps illustrate the socially optimum quantity of pollution control where MSB = MSC— two graphs of the numerical data in this problem are in the answer key for Activity 5-4.

13. Conduct a general discussion about why markets fail and how government attempts to correct these failures.

Illustrating a Negative Externality

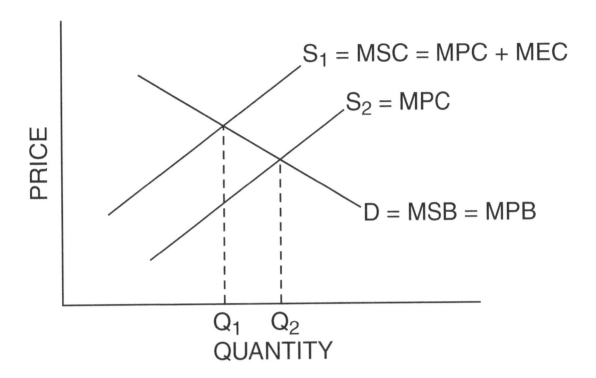

MSC = marginal social cost

MPC = marginal private cost

MEC = marginal external cost

MSB = marginal social benefit

MPB = marginal private benefit

Illustrating a Positive Externality

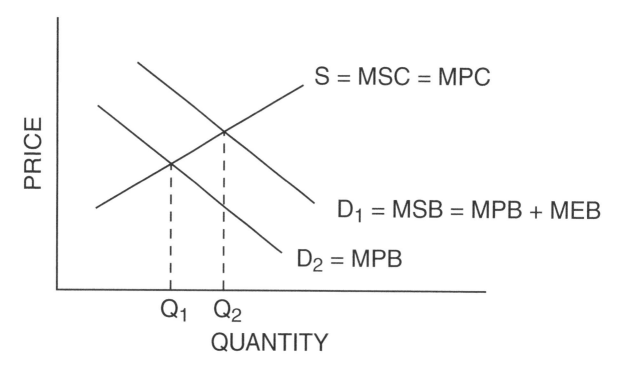

MSB = marginal social benefit

MPB = marginal private benefit

MEB = marginal external benefit

MSC = marginal social cost

MPC = marginal private cost

Efficiency, Equity, and Effects of Government Policies

Introduction and Description

Previous lessons have examined the role of government. This unit looks at the distribution of income and the effects of government policies to change that distribution. The controversy weighs *efficiency* against *equity*. Markets work. In a world of scarce resources, higher productivity is better than lower productivity. Markets create incentives that increase productivity and the size of the economic pie.

It also may be true that the poor are needier than the rich. Markets create inequalities, and governments use taxes and transfer payments to redistribute income. These very policies, however, may create disincentives that damage efficiency and shrink the size of overall output and income.

What should be the trade-off between efficiency and equity? Are there policies that can improve both?

Objectives

1. Define and differentiate between the *ability-to-pay* and the *benefits-received* theories of taxation.

2. Define and differentiate among *progressive*, *proportional*, and *regressive taxes*.

3. Describe the distribution of income in the United States. Use the *Lorenz curve* and *Gini coefficient* as measures of the equality of that distribution.

4. Describe who pays income taxes and which income earners bear the greatest burden of income taxes.

5. Analyze the effects of government redistribution policies.

Time Required

Three class periods or 135 minutes

Materials

Activities 5-5, 5-6, and 5-7

Bell Ringer

Should everyone pay the same percentage of their income in taxes?

Teacher Alert: **Make a distinction between the terms equity and efficiency.**

Procedure

1. Have students read Activity 5-5 until they reach the questions.

2. Give a lecture and/or start a discussion on tax equity that covers these points:
    (A) The difference between the *ability-to-pay* and the *benefits-received* theories of taxation
    (B) The difference between a *nominal* and an *effective tax rate*
    (C) The definitions of *progressive*, *proportional*, and *regressive taxes*

3. Be sure to make clear that the rate must be an effective rate applied against income. Students confuse an income-tax base with other tax bases, such as consumption or wealth. For example, they might incorrectly conclude that the sales tax is a proportional tax since the rate is the same for everyone. They might not distinguish between a consumption base and an income base.

4. Have students answer the questions in Activity 5-5 and discuss them.

5. Now bring up the question of whether the federal income tax is progressive, proportional, or regressive.

6. Have students complete Activity 5-6 and discuss the answers.

7. Be sure to make the point that the federal income tax is progressive. In 2009, the top 1 percent of taxpayers paid 36.7 percent of all income taxes. Their tax rate was 24.0 percent. The bottom 50 percent of taxpayers paid 2.3 percent of taxes. Their tax rate was 1.8 percent.

8. Discuss the following philosophical issues:

   (A) Why is efficiency important?

   (B) Why is equity important?

   (C) Do policies that redistribute income hurt efficiency, or are there policies that can improve both equity and efficiency?

9. Explain the concepts of the Lorenz curve and the Gini coefficient. What information does each measure provide?

10. Assign Activity 5-7. Have students discuss their answers.

Student Activities Solutions

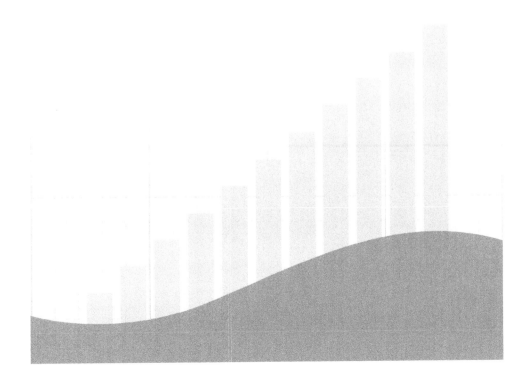

MICROECONOMICS

Basic Economic Concepts

Unit 1

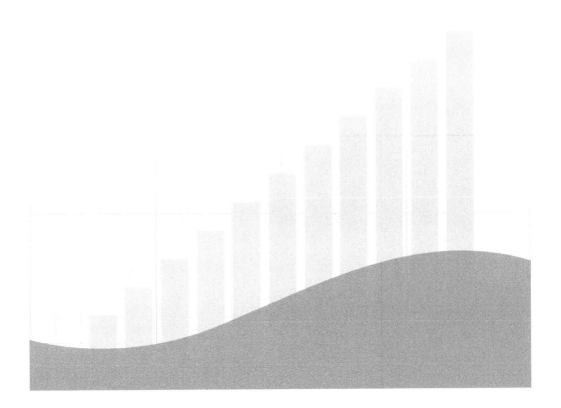

- Scarcity exists because we have limited resources and unlimited wants. No society has ever had enough resources to produce all the goods and services its members wanted.

- Goods and services are produced from resources. These resources—land, labor, capital, and entrepreneurship—are limited.

- Scarcity requires people to make choices. If we use scarce resources for one purpose, we cannot use them for another.

- Opportunity cost is the forgone benefit of the next best alternative when resources are used for one purpose rather than another.

- Because of scarcity, every decision has an opportunity cost.

- Economic costs take account of the opportunity cost of doing one thing rather than another.

- Economic costs include explicit costs and implicit costs. Explicit costs are expenditures for something. Implicit costs are the opportunity costs of using your own resources rather than selling them to someone else. Both implicit and explicit costs are opportunity costs.

- Using free goods does not involve opportunity cost because free goods are available in unlimited quantities.

- Economics is concerned with marginal decision making. In economics, "making decisions at the margin" is very important. Marginal choices involve the effects of additions and subtractions from the current situation. We compare the marginal benefit of an extra unit of an activity with that unit's marginal cost.

- A production possibilities curve can be used to illustrate scarcity, choice, and opportunity cost graphically.

- The slope of a production possibilities curve shows the opportunity cost of producing another unit of one good in terms of the amount of the other good that must be given up.

- Because resources are scarce, using them efficiently allows us to get the most from them. Efficiency is increased through specialization and trade. Economists use the concept of comparative advantage to explain why trade takes place between countries and between individuals. This concept is based on the differences in producers' opportunity costs of producing goods and services.

- Because of scarcity, people and societies use economic systems to determine what to produce, how to produce, and for whom to produce.

- Throughout history, nations have used tradition, command, and market systems to allocate resources.

- The law of comparative advantage shows how everyone can gain through trade.

- Economic theory is useful in analyzing and understanding the world around us.

- The test of an economic theory is its ability to predict correctly the future consequences of economic actions.

- The broad social goals of a society influence decisions about how best to use resources.

- A diagram of the circular flow of resources, goods and services, and money-income payments is a simplified way of illustrating how a market economy operates. Prices in the product market and prices in the factor, or resource, market are determined by the interaction of supply and demand. This diagram is also called the circular flow of income.

■ Markets bring together buyers and sellers of a good or service.

■ The law of demand states that buyers will want more of an item at a low price than at a high price, other things being equal.

■ The law of supply states that sellers will provide more of an item at a high price than at a low price, other things being equal.

■ The equilibrium price is the price at which the quantity demanded of an item equals the quantity supplied. That quantity is called the equilibrium quantity.

■ Shifts in the market demand and supply curves result in new values of the equilibrium price and quantity. Understanding what causes shifts in the demand and supply curves is an important part of knowing how a market operates.

Do You Think Like an Economist?

Circle T for *true* or F for *false* in the statements that follow.

T *F*   1. Because it is desirable, sunshine is scarce.

T *F*   2. Because it is limited, polio is scarce.

T *F*   3. Because water covers three-fourths of the earth's surface and is renewable, it cannot be considered scarce.

T (*F*)   4. The main cost of going to college is tuition, room, and board.

T (*F*)   5. If mass transportation fares are raised, almost everyone will take the trains anyway.

T (*F*)   6. You get what you pay for.

T (*F*)   7. If someone makes an economic gain, someone else loses.

T (*F*)   8. If one nation produces everything better than another nation, there is no economic reason for these two nations to trade.

T (*F*)   9. A nonregulated monopoly tends to charge the highest possible price.

T (*F*)   10. A business owner's decision to show more care for consumers is a decision to accept lower levels of profits.

Scarcity, Opportunity Cost, and Production Possibilities Curves

The primary economic problem facing all individuals, families, businesses, and nations is the scarcity of resources: There simply are not enough resources to satisfy the unlimited wants for goods and services. Scarcity necessitates choice. Consuming or producing more of one thing means consuming or producing less of something else. The opportunity cost of using scarce resources for one thing instead of something else is often represented in graphical form as a *production possibilities curve* (PPC). A nation's PPC shows how many units of two goods or services the nation can produce in one year if it uses its resources fully and efficiently. This activity uses the PPC to illustrate how scarcity requires choices and the opportunity cost of those choices.

Part A: Basic Production Possibilities Curves

Figure 1-2.1 shows a basic PPC for the production of Goods A and B. Use Figure 1-2.1 to answer the questions that follow.

 Figure 1-2.1
A Linear Production Possibilities Curve

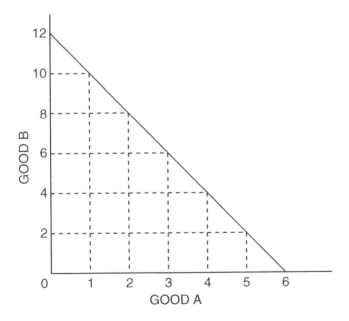

1. Assume the economy represented by Figure 1-2.1 is presently producing 12 units of Good B and 0 units of Good A:

   (A) The opportunity cost of increasing production of Good A from 0 units to 1 unit is the loss of _____2_____ unit(s) of Good B.

   (B) The opportunity cost of increasing production of Good A from 1 unit to 2 units is the loss of _____2_____ unit(s) of Good B.

   (C) The opportunity cost of increasing production of Good A from 2 units to 3 units is the loss of _____2_____ unit(s) of Good B.

   (D) This is an example of (***constant*** / *increasing* / *decreasing* / *zero*) opportunity cost per unit for Good A.

Figure 1-2.2 contains a typical PPC often used by economists. This PPC is concave to the origin; it gets steeper as the country moves out along its horizontal axis. Use Figure 1-2.2 to answer the questions below it.

Figure 1-2.2
A Concave Production Possibilities Curve

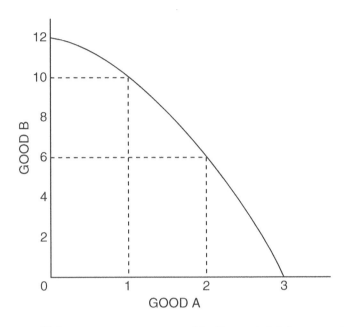

2. If the economy represented in Figure 1-2.2 is presently producing 12 units of Good B and 0 units of Good A:

   (A) The opportunity cost of increasing production of Good A from 0 units to 1 unit is the loss of ___*2*___ unit(s) of Good B.

   (B) The opportunity cost of increasing production of Good A from 1 unit to 2 units is the loss of ___*4*___ unit(s) of Good B.

   (C) The opportunity cost of increasing production of Good A from 2 units to 3 units is the loss of ___*6*___ unit(s) of Good B.

   (D) This is an example of (*constant* / ***increasing*** / *decreasing* / *zero*) opportunity cost per unit for Good A.

Part B: Understanding the Shape of a Concave PPC

The "law of increasing opportunity cost" explains why the typical PPC is concave to the origin (bowed outward). Figure 1-2.3 shows the PPC for the country of Costica. The country currently operates at point A and produces 75 million units of civilian goods and 2 million units of military goods. If the country decides to increase its military provision to 3 million units, it must give up only 5 million units in civilian goods because certain factories are easily converted from civilian production to military production. However, if Costica decides it must continue to increase its military production, the opportunity cost of doing so increases because now it is more difficult to convert other factories to military production. Resources are not equally well suited to the production of all goods. The opportunity cost of increasing military output from 6 million units to 7 million units (point C to point D) has increased to 15 million units in civilian goods. This increasing opportunity cost is reflected in the steeper slope of the PPC as the country produces more military goods and fewer civilian goods.

 Figure 1-2.3
Showing the Law of Increasing Opportunity Cost

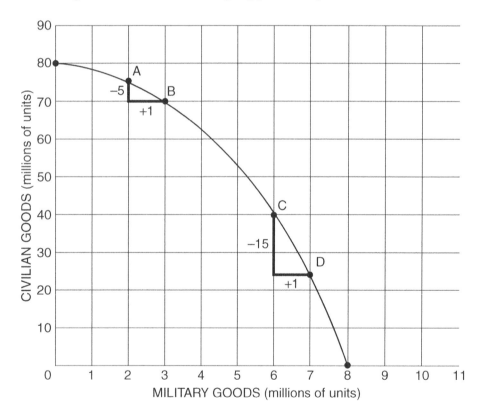

Part C: Drawing Various PPCs

Use the following axes to draw the type of curve that illustrates the label above each graph.

 Figure 1-2.4
Production Possibilities Curve 1:
Increasing Opportunity Cost per Unit
of Good B

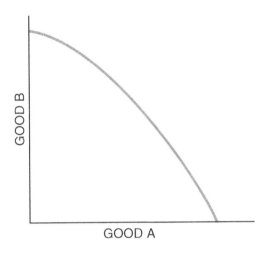

Figure 1-2.5
Production Possibilities Curve 2:
Zero Opportunity Cost per Unit of
Good B

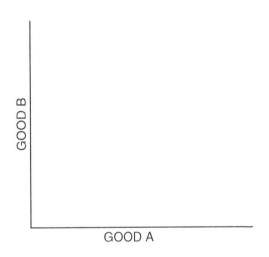

 Figure 1-2.6
Production Possibilities Curve 3:
Constant Opportunity Cost per Unit
of Good B

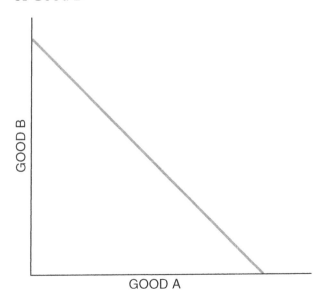

Part D: Economic Growth

Over time, most countries see an increase in their ability to produce goods and services. This "economic growth" is shown as an outward shift of the PPC and results from a variety of factors, including improved technology, better education, and the discovery of new resources. Use Figure 1-2.7 to answer the next five questions. Each question starts with Curve BE as a country's PPC.

Figure 1-2.7
Production Possibilities Curve: Capital Goods and Consumer Goods

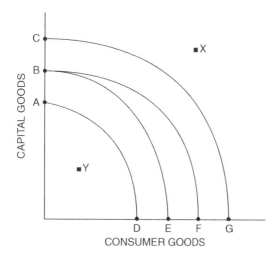

3. Suppose there is a major technological breakthrough in the consumer-goods industry, and the new technology is widely adopted. Which curve in the diagram would represent the new PPC? (Indicate the curve you choose with two letters.) ___**BF**___

4. Suppose a new government comes into power and forbids the use of automated machinery and modern production techniques in all industries. Which curve in the diagram would represent the new PPC? (Indicate the curve you choose with two letters.) ___**AD**___

5. Suppose massive new sources of oil and coal are found within the economy, and there are major technological innovations in both industries. Which curve in the diagram would represent the new PPC? (Indicate the curve you choose with two letters.) ___**CG**___

6. If BE represents a country's current PPC, what can you say about a point like X? (Write a brief statement.)
   It is impossible for this country to produce this combination of goods with its current resources and technology.

7. If BE represents a country's current PPC, what can you say about a point like Y? (Write a brief statement.)
   The country is producing beneath its potential because of unemployment and inefficient use of its resources.

Use Figure 1-2.8 to answer the next three questions.

Figure 1-2.8

Production Possibilities Curve: Economic Growth

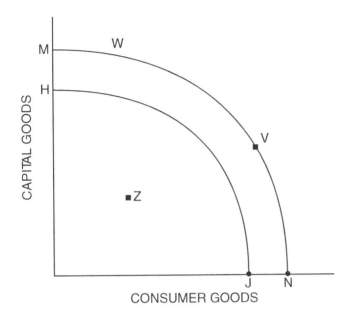

8. What change could cause the PPC to shift from the original curve (HJ) to the new curve (MN)?
   There are several possible reasons for this economic growth, including new technology, discovery of new resources, improved education.

9. Under what conditions might an economy be operating at Point Z?
   Resources are not fully employed or they are used inefficiently.

10. Why might a government implement a policy to move the economy from Point V to Point W?
    The government might want to encourage the production of more capital goods as a means of stimulating economic growth. This would result in the PPC shifting out faster in the future.

Determining Comparative Advantage

Voluntary trade between two individuals or two countries occurs if both parties feel that they will benefit. Producers have an incentive to make products for which they have a lower opportunity cost than other producers. When both producers specialize according to their *comparative advantage*, they increase the total amount of goods and services that are available for consumption. To determine who has a comparative advantage in producing a particular item, we need to calculate each producer's opportunity costs of creating the items. The way we calculate opportunity cost depends on how the productivity data are expressed.

There are two ways to measure productivity: the "input method" and the "output method." We can calculate the quantity of output produced from a given amount of inputs, or we can measure the amount of inputs necessary to create one unit of output. Examples of output are tons of wheat per acre, miles per gallon, words per minute, apples per tree, and televisions produced per hour. Examples of input are number of hours to do a job, number of gallons of paint to paint a house, and number of acres to feed a horse. We will work through an example that expresses productivity from the perspectives of an input measure and an output measure.

Part A: Two Approaches to Comparative Advantage

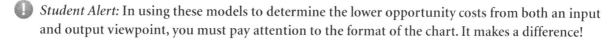 *Student Alert:* In using these models to determine the lower opportunity costs from both an input and output viewpoint, you must pay attention to the format of the chart. It makes a difference!

Input Method

The "input method" provides data on the amount of resources needed to produce one unit of output. Table 1-3.1 gives productivity information for Ted and Nancy.

 Table 1-3.1
Productivity Data Using the Input Method

	Time required to produce one radio	Time required to produce one bushel of wheat
Ted	20 minutes	5 minutes
Nancy	30 minutes	15 minutes

Ted has an *absolute advantage* in the production of both radios and wheat because he uses fewer resources (time) to produce each item than does Nancy. Even though this might suggest that Ted cannot benefit from trade with Nancy, our examination of the opportunity costs of production will show that is not the case.

Table 1-3.2 shows the opportunity costs for each producer. To find the opportunity cost of producing one radio, the amount of resources it takes to produce a radio goes *above* the amount of resources that it takes to produce a bushel of wheat.

 Table 1-3.2
Opportunity Cost of Producing Radios and Wheat

	Opportunity cost of producing one radio	Opportunity cost of producing one bushel of wheat
Ted	1 radio = $\dfrac{20 \text{ minutes}}{5 \text{ minutes}}$ = 4 bushels	1 wheat = $\dfrac{5 \text{ minutes}}{20 \text{ minutes}}$ = ¼ radio
Nancy	1 radio = $\dfrac{30 \text{ minutes}}{15 \text{ minutes}}$ = 2 bushels	1 wheat = $\dfrac{15 \text{ minutes}}{30 \text{ minutes}}$ = ½ radio

In the 20 minutes it takes Ted to produce one radio, he instead could have produced four bushels of wheat. Instead of producing one radio in 30 minutes, Nancy could have produced two bushels of wheat. The fact that Nancy has the lower opportunity cost of producing radios means she has the comparative advantage in radios.

In the five minutes he needs to produce one bushel of wheat, Ted could have made ¼ of a radio. Nancy's opportunity cost of producing one bushel of wheat is ½ of a radio. Because his sacrifice in producing one bushel of wheat is less than Nancy's, Ted has the comparative advantage in wheat production.

If Ted specializes in wheat production while Nancy specializes in radio production, their combined output of radios and wheat will be larger than it would be if each person produced both products.

Output Method

The "output method" gives data on the amount of output that can be produced with a given amount of an input. Now let's take this same set of productivity data and turn it into an output format. To do this, we ask how many units of an item the producers can create with a given amount of resources. Let's suppose that both producers have one hour to produce each product. Table 1-3.3 shows how many radios and how many bushels of wheat each producer can make in one hour. From this output viewpoint, you once again see that Ted has the absolute advantage in the production of both products. With the same amount of resources (one hour of labor), he can produce more radios and more wheat than Nancy.

 Table 1-3.3
Productivity Data Using the Output Method

	Radios produced per hour	Wheat produced per hour
Ted	$\dfrac{60 \text{ minutes}}{20 \text{ minutes}}$ = 3 radios	$\dfrac{60 \text{ minutes}}{5 \text{ minutes}}$ = 12 bushels
Nancy	$\dfrac{60 \text{ minutes}}{30 \text{ minutes}}$ = 2 radios	$\dfrac{60 \text{ minutes}}{15 \text{ minutes}}$ = 4 bushels

But what about the opportunity cost to produce each item? Check out Table 1-3.4, which shows how to calculate each producer's opportunity cost of the two items. To find Ted's opportunity cost of producing one radio, the number of radios he can produce in one hour goes *under* the number of bushels of wheat he can produce in that same time frame.

 Table 1-3.4

Opportunity Cost of Producing Radios and Wheat

	Opportunity cost of producing one radio	Opportunity cost of producing one bushel of wheat
Ted	3 radios = 1 hour = 12 bushels 1 radio = 12/3 = 4 bushels	12 bushels = 1 hour = 3 radios 1 bushel = 3/12 = ¼ radio
Nancy	2 radios = 1 hour = 4 bushels 1 radio = 4/2 = 2 bushels	4 bushels = 1 hour = 2 radios 1 bushel = 2/4 = ½ radio

Because Ted's cost per radio is four bushels of wheat, whereas Nancy's cost is only two bushels, we know Nancy has the comparative advantage in producing radios. Ted has the comparative advantage in wheat production since he has the lower opportunity cost of producing a bushel of wheat (¼ radio compared to Nancy's ½ radio). Does this sound familiar? This is the same result we reached using the input method.

The differences in opportunity costs define the limits of a trade in which both parties will benefit. If Nancy specializes in radio production, she will accept no less than two bushels of wheat for one radio. Ted will pay no more than four bushels of wheat per radio. Thus, the "terms of trade" acceptable to both producers must lie in the range between two bushels for one radio and four bushels for one radio. For example, suppose they agree to trade one radio for three bushels of wheat. By producing and trading one radio to Ted, Nancy will have a net gain of one bushel. Her opportunity cost of producing the radio is two bushels and she receives three bushels in return for the radio. Because his opportunity cost of producing one bushel is ¼ radio, Ted's opportunity cost of producing the three bushels, which he trades to Nancy, is ¾ radio. Thus, the trade gives Ted a net gain of ¼ radio. Both producers gain by specializing according to their comparative advantage.

When it comes to producing wheat, Ted would have to receive at least ¼ of a radio in trade for a bushel of wheat. Nancy would require at least ½ of a radio before she would trade a bushel of wheat. The acceptable terms of trade would be found between ¼ radio and ½ radio per bushel of wheat.

The output data in Table 1-3.3 can be used to create production possibility frontiers for Ted and Nancy to show the combinations of radios and wheat each can produce in one hour of work. See Figure 1-3.1.

Figure 1-3.1
Production Possibilities Curves for Ted and Nancy

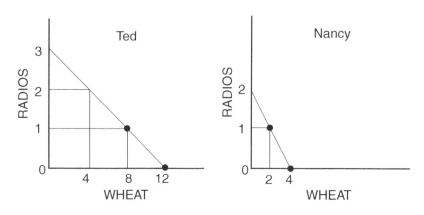

Part B: Comparative Advantage Exercises

For each of the following scenarios, answer the questions following the chart. The first problem is answered for you.

1. Anna and Barry can grow the following amounts of potatoes and cabbage with a week of labor.

	Potatoes per week	Cabbage per week
Anna	100 units	200 units
Barry	120 units	150 units

(A) Is this an example of an *input* problem or an *output* problem?
This is an output problem because it shows how much output each producer can create with a given amount of resources (one week of labor).

(B) What is the opportunity cost for each producer in making these products?

(1) Anna's opportunity cost of producing a unit of potatoes is ___*2*___ units of cabbage.

$$100 \text{ P} = 1 \text{ week} = 200 \text{ C}, \qquad \frac{100}{100} \text{ P} = \frac{200}{100} \text{C}, \qquad 1 \text{ P} = 2 \text{ C}.$$

(2) Barry's opportunity cost of producing a unit of potatoes is ___*1.25*___ units of cabbage.

$$120 \text{ P} = 1 \text{ week} = 150 \text{ C}, \qquad \frac{120}{120} \text{ P} = \frac{150}{120} \text{C}, \qquad 1 \text{ P} = 1¼ \text{ C} = 1.25 \text{ C}.$$

(3) Anna's opportunity cost of producing a unit of cabbage is   **0.5**   units of potatoes.

$$200 \text{ C} = 1 \text{ week} = 100 \text{ P}, \qquad \frac{200}{200} \text{ C} = \frac{100}{200} \text{ P}, \qquad 1 \text{ C} = \frac{1}{2} \text{ P} = 0.5 \text{ P}.$$

(4) Barry's opportunity cost of producing a unit of cabbage is   **0.8**   units of potatoes.

$$150 \text{ C} = 1 \text{ week} = 120 \text{ P}, \qquad \frac{150}{150} \text{ C} = \frac{120}{150} \text{ P}, \qquad 1 \text{ C} = \frac{4}{5} \text{ P} = 0.8 \text{ P}.$$

(C) Who has the comparative advantage in producing potatoes?   ***Barry***
   Barry has the comparative advantage in potatoes because his opportunity cost is lower than Anna's.

(D) Who has the comparative advantage in producing cabbage?   ***Anna***
   Anna has the comparative advantage in cabbage because her opportunity cost is lower than Barry's.

Note: In this example, each producer has the absolute advantage in producing one item: Barry in potatoes and Anna in cabbage. That might not be the case in the other examples.

2. Henry and John are fishermen who catch bass and catfish. This chart shows how many of each type of fish they can catch in one day.

	Bass	Catfish
Henry	4 bass	6 catfish
John	24 bass	12 catfish

(A) Is this an example of an *input* problem or an *output* problem?
   It is an output problem because it shows the daily output of each fisherman.

(B) What is the opportunity cost for each person in catching these fish?

   (1) Henry's opportunity cost of catching 1 bass is ____***1.5***____ catfish.
      4 bass = 6 catfish;1 bass = 1.5 catfish

   (2) John's opportunity cost of catching 1 bass is ____***0.5***____ catfish.
      24 bass = 12 catfish;1 bass = 0.5 catfish

   (3) Henry's opportunity cost of catching 1 catfish is ____***0.67***____ bass.
      6 catfish = 4 bass; 1 catfish = 0.67 bass

   (4) John's opportunity cost of catching 1 catfish is ____***2***____ bass.
      12 catfish = 24 bass; 1 catfish = 2 bass

(C) Who has the comparative advantage in catching bass? ____***John***____

(D) Who has the comparative advantage in catching catfish?   ***Henry***

3. This chart shows how many days it takes the ABC Corporation and the XYZ Corporation to produce one unit of cars and one unit of planes.

	Cars	Planes
ABC Corp.	8 days	10 days
XYZ Corp.	15 days	12 days

(A) Is this an example of an *input* problem or an *output* problem?

This is an input problem because you are told what resources (number of days) are needed to produce one unit of a good.

(B) What is the opportunity cost for each corporation in producing these goods?

(1) ABC's opportunity cost of producing a unit of cars is ___*0.8*___ units of planes.
1 car = 8 days = 0.8 planes

(2) XYZ's opportunity cost of producing a unit of cars is ___*1.25*___ units of planes.
1 car = 15 days = 1.25 planes

(3) ABC's opportunity cost of producing a unit of planes is ___*1.25*___ units of cars.
1 plane = 10 days = 1.25 cars

(4) XYZ's opportunity cost of producing a unit of planes is ___*0.8*___ units of cars.
1 plane = 12 days = 0.8 cars

(C) Who has the comparative advantage in producing cars? ___*ABC Corp.*___

(D) Who has the comparative advantage in producing planes? ___*XYZ Corp.*___

4. Here are the numbers of acres needed in India and China produce 100 bushels of corn or 100 bushels of rice each month.

	India	China
Corn	9 acres	8 acres
Rice	3 acres	2 acres

(A) Is this an example of an *input* problem or an *output* problem?

This is an input problem because you are told what resources (number of acres) are needed to produce a given amount of a good.

(B) What is the opportunity cost for each country in producing these goods?

(1) India's opportunity cost of growing 100 bushels of corn is ___*300*___ bushels of rice.
100 bushels of corn = 9 acres = 300 bushels of rice

(2) China's opportunity cost of growing 100 bushels of corn is ___*400*___ bushels of rice.
100 bushels of corn = 8 acres = 400 bushels of rice

(3) India's opportunity cost of growing 100 bushels of rice is ___*33.3*___ bushels of corn.
100 bushels of rice = 3 acres = 33.3 bushels of corn

(4) China's opportunity cost of growing 100 bushels of rice is ___*25*___ bushels of corn.
100 bushels of rice = 2 acres = 25 bushels of corn

(C) Who has the comparative advantage in growing corn? ___*India*___

(D) Who has the comparative advantage in growing rice? ___*China*___

5. This chart shows how many cans of olives and bottles of olive oil can be produced in Zaire and Colombia from one ton of olives.

	Zaire	Colombia
Olives	60 cans	24 cans
Olive oil	10 bottles	8 bottles

(A) Is this an example of an *input* problem or an *output* problem?
This is an output problem because the chart shows how much output can be produced from a given amount of resources.

(B) What is the opportunity cost for each country in producing these goods?

(1) Zaire's opportunity cost of producing 1 can of olives is ___*1/6*___ bottles of olive oil.
60 cans = 10 bottles; 1 can = 1/6 bottles

(2) Colombia's opportunity cost of producing 1 can of olives is ___*1/3*___ bottles of olive oil.
24 cans = 8 bottles; 1 can = 1/3 bottles

(3) Zaire's opportunity cost of producing 1 bottle of olive oil is ___*6*___ cans of olives.
10 bottles = 60 cans; 1 bottle = 6 cans

(4) Colombia's opportunity cost of producing 1 bottle of olive oil is ___*3*___ cans of olives.
8 bottles = 24 cans; 1 bottle = 3 cans

(C) Who has the comparative advantage in producing olives? *Zaire*

(D) Who has the comparative advantage in producing olive oil? *Colombia*

6. Here are the numbers of hours needed in Redland and Blueland to produce a unit of televisions and a unit of computers.

	Televisions	Computers
Redland	18 hours	6 hours
Blueland	16 hours	4 hours

(A) Is this an example of an *input* problem or an *output* problem?

This is an input problem because it states the amount of resources (hours of labor) needed to produce a unit of a good.

(B) What is the opportunity cost for each country in producing these goods?

   (1) Redland's opportunity cost of producing 1 unit of televisions is ___**3**___ units of computers.
   1 television = 18 hours = 3 computers

   (2) Blueland's opportunity cost of producing 1 unit of televisions is   **4**   units of computers.
   1 television = 16 hours = 4 computers

   (3) Redland's opportunity cost of producing 1 unit of computers is   **1/3**   units of televisions.
   1 computer = 6 hours = 1/3 television

   (4) Blueland's opportunity cost of producing 1 unit of computers is ___**1/4**___ units of televisions.
   1 computer = 4 hours = 1/4 television

(C) Who has the comparative advantage in producing televisions? ___**Redland**___

(D) Who has the comparative advantage in producing computers? ___**Blueland**___

Demand Curves, Movements along Demand Curves, and Shifts in Demand Curves

Part A: A Change in Demand versus a Change in Quantity Demanded

! *Student Alert:* The distinction between a "change in demand" and a "change in quantity demanded" is very important!

Table 1-4.1 shows the market demand for a hypothetical product: Greebes. Study the data and plot the demand for Greebes on the graph in Figure 1-4.1. Label the demand curve D, and answer the questions that follow.

 Table 1-4.1
Demand for Greebes

Price (per Greebe)	Quantity demanded per week (millions of Greebes)
$0.10	350
$0.15	300
$0.20	250
$0.25	200
$0.30	150
$0.35	100
$0.40	50
$0.45	0

 Figure 1-4.1
Demand for Greebes

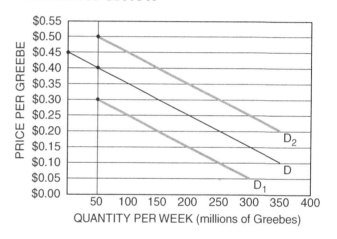

1. The data for demand curve D indicate that at a price of $0.30 per Greebe, buyers would be willing to buy ___*150*___ million Greebes. All other things held constant, if the price of Greebes increased to $0.40 per Greebe, buyers would be willing to buy ___*50*___ million Greebes. Such a change would be a decrease in (*demand* / ***quantity demanded***). All other things held constant, if the price of Greebes decreased to $0.20, buyers would be willing to buy ___*250*___ million Greebes. Such a change would be called an increase in (*demand* / ***quantity demanded***).

Now, let's suppose there is a change in federal income-tax rates that affects the disposable income of Greebe buyers. This change in the *ceteris paribus* (all else being equal) conditions underlying the original demand for Greebes will result in a new set of data, shown in Table 1-4.2. Study these new data, and add the new demand curve for Greebes to the graph in Figure 1-4.1. Label the new demand curve D_1 and answer the questions that follow.

 Table 1-4.2

New Demand for Greebes

Price (per Greebe)	Quantity demanded per week (millions of Greebes)
$0.05	300
$0.10	250
$0.15	200
$0.20	150
$0.25	100
$0.30	50

2. Comparing the new demand curve (D_1) with the original demand curve (D), we can say that the change in the demand for Greebes results in a shift of the demand curve to the (***left*** / *right*). Such a shift indicates that at each of the possible prices shown, buyers are now willing to buy a (***smaller*** / *larger*) quantity; and at each of the possible quantities shown, buyers are willing to offer a (*higher* / ***lower***) maximum price. The cause of this demand curve shift was a(n) (***increase*** / *decrease*) in tax rates that (*increased* / ***decreased***) the disposable income of Greebe buyers.

Now, let's suppose that there is a dramatic change in people's tastes and preferences for Greebes. This change in the *ceteris paribus* conditions underlying the original demand for Greebes will result in a new set of data, shown in Table 1-4.3. Study these new data, and add the new demand curve for Greebes to the graph in Figure 1-4.1. Label the new demand curve D_2 and answer the questions that follow.

 Table 1-4.3

New Demand for Greebes

Price (per Greebe)	Quantity demanded per week (millions of Greebes)
$0.20	350
$0.25	300
$0.30	250
$0.35	200
$0.40	150
$0.45	100
$0.50	50

3. Comparing the new demand curve (D_2) with the original demand curve (D), we can say that the change in the demand for Greebes results in a shift of the demand curve to the (*left* / **right**). Such a shift indicates that at each of the possible prices shown, buyers are now willing to buy a (*smaller* / **larger**) quantity; and at each of the possible quantities shown, buyers are willing to offer a (*lower* / **higher**) maximum price. The cause of this shift in the demand curve was a(n) (**increase** / *decrease*) in people's tastes and preferences for Greebes.

Part B: Do You Get It?

Now, to test your understanding, choose the answer you think is the best in each of the following multiple-choice questions.

4. All other things held constant, which of the following would *not* cause a change in the demand (shift in the demand curve) for motorcycles?

    (A) A decrease in consumer incomes

    (B) A decrease in the price of motorcycles. This will cause an increase in the "quantity demanded" of motorcycles.

    (C) An increase in the price of bicycles

    (D) An increase in people's tastes and preferences for motorcycles

5. "Rising oil prices have caused a sharp decrease in the demand for oil." Speaking precisely, and using terms as they are defined by economists, choose the statement that best describes this quotation.

    (A) The quotation is correct: an increase in price causes a decrease in demand.

    (B) The quotation is incorrect: an increase in price causes an increase in demand, not a decrease in demand.

    (C) The quotation is incorrect: an increase in price causes a decrease in the quantity demanded, not a decrease in demand.

    (D) The quotation is incorrect: an increase in price causes an increase in the quantity demanded, not a decrease in demand.

6. "As the price of domestic automobiles has risen, customers have found foreign autos to be a better bargain. Consequently, domestic auto sales have been decreasing, and foreign auto sales have been increasing." Using only the information in this quotation and assuming everything else remains constant, which of the following best describes this statement?

    (A) A shift in the demand curves for both domestic and foreign automobiles

    (B) A movement along the demand curves for both foreign and domestic automobiles

    (C) A movement along the demand curve for domestic autos, and a shift in the demand curve for foreign autos

    (D) A shift in the demand curve for domestic autos, and a movement along the demand curve for foreign autos

Part C: Consumer Surplus

Once we have the demand curve, we can define the concept of *consumer surplus*. Consumer surplus is the value a consumer receives from the purchase of a good in excess of the price paid for the good. Stated differently, consumer surplus is the difference between the amount a person is willing and able to pay for a unit of the good and the actual price paid for that unit. For example, if you are willing to pay $100 for a coat but are able to buy the coat for only $70, you have a consumer surplus of $30.

Refer again to the demand data from Table 1-4.1, and assume the price is $0.30. Some buyers will benefit because they are willing to pay prices higher than $0.30 for this good. Note that each time the price is reduced by $0.05, consumers will buy an additional 50 million units. Table 1-4.4 shows how to calculate the consumer surplus resulting from the price of $0.30.

 Table 1-4.4
Finding the Consumer Surplus When the Price Is $0.30

Price willing to pay	Quantity demanded	Consumer surplus from the increments of 50 million units if P = $0.30
$0.40	50 million units	($0.10)(50 million units) = $5.0 million
$0.35	100 million units	($0.05)(50 million units) = $2.5 million
$0.30	150 million units	($0.00)(50 million units) = $0.0 million

For those consumers willing to buy 50 million units at a price of $0.40, the consumer surplus for each unit is $0.10 (= $0.40 – $0.30), making the consumer surplus for all these units equal to $5.0 million. If the price is reduced from $0.40 to $0.35, there are consumers willing to buy another 50 million units; the consumer surplus for these buyers is $0.05 per unit ($0.35 – $0.30) or a total of $2.5 million for all 50 million units. If the price is lowered another $0.05 to $0.30, an extra 50 million units will be demanded; the consumer surplus for these units is $0.00 since $0.30 is the highest price these consumers are willing to pay. Thus, if the price is $0.30, a total of 150 million units are demanded and the total consumer surplus is $7.5 million.

An approximation of the total consumer surplus from a given number of units of a good can be shown graphically as the area below the demand curve and above the price paid for those units. In Figure 1-4.2, redraw the demand curve (D) from the data in Table 1-4.1. We see that if the price is $0.30, the quantity demanded is 150 million units. Consumer surplus from these 150 million units is the shaded area between the demand curve D and the horizontal price line at $0.30. We can find the area of this triangle using the familiar rule of (½) × base × height.

Figure 1-4.2
Consumer Surplus

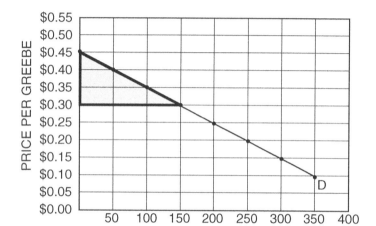

7. What is the value of consumer surplus in this market if the price is $0.30? ***$11.25 million or $11,250,000*** Show how you calculated the value of the area of the triangle representing consumer surplus.
   Consumer surplus = (0.5)(150 million)($0.45 − $0.30) = $11.25 million.

8. Answer these questions based on the discussion of Figure 1-4.2.

   (A) If the price is increased from $0.30 to $0.35, consumer surplus will (*increase* / ***decrease***). Why?
   Consumers will buy fewer units because of the higher price, and the consumer surplus of the units they buy will be smaller.

   (B) If the price is decreased from $0.30 to $0.25, consumer surplus will (***increase*** / *decrease*). Why?
   Consumers will buy more units because of the lower price, and the consumer surplus of the units they buy will be larger.

Reasons for Changes in Demand

Part A: Does the Demand Curve Shift?

Read the eight newspaper headlines in Table 1-5.1, and use the table to record the impact of each event on the demand for U.S.-made autos. In the second column, indicate whether the event in the headline will cause consumers to buy more or less U.S.-made autos. Use the third column to indicate whether there is a change in demand (ΔD) or a change in quantity demanded (ΔQd) for U.S.-made autos. In the third column, decide whether the demand curve shifts to the right or left or does not shift. Finally, indicate the letter for the new demand curve. Use Figure 1-5.1 to help you. **Always start at curve B**, and move only one curve at a time.

 Table 1-5.1
Impact of Events on Demand for U.S.-Made Autos

Headline	Will consumers buy more or less U.S. autos?	Is there a change in demand (ΔD) or a change in quantity demanded (ΔQd)?	Does the demand curve for U.S. autos shift to the right or left or not shift?	What is the new demand curve for U.S. autos?
1. Consumers' Income Drops	More / **(Less)**	**(ΔD)** / ΔQd	*Right* / **Left** / *No Shift*	**A** / B / C
2. Millions of Immigrants Enter the U.S.	**(More)** / Less	**(ΔD)** / ΔQd	**Right** / *Left* / *No Shift*	A / B / **C**
3. Price of Foreign Autos Drop	More / **(Less)**	**(ΔD)** / ΔQd	*Right* / **Left** / *No Shift*	**A** / B / C
4. Major Cities Add Inexpensive Bus Lines	More / **(Less)**	**(ΔD)** / ΔQd	*Right* / **Left** / *No Shift*	**A** / B / C
5. Price of U.S. Autos Rises	More / **(Less)**	ΔD / **(ΔQd)**	*Right* / *Left* / **No Shift**	A / **B** / C
6. Price of U.S. Autos Expected to Rise Soon	**(More)** / Less	**(ΔD)** / ΔQd	**Right** / *Left* / *No Shift*	A / B / **C**
7. Families Look Forward to Summer Vacations	**(More)** / Less	**(ΔD)** / ΔQd	**Right** / *Left* / *No Shift*	A / B / **C**
8. U.S. Auto Firms Launch Effective Ad Campaigns	**(More)** / Less	**(ΔD)** / ΔQd	**Right** / *Left* / *No Shift*	A / B / **C**

Figure 1-5.1
Demand for U.S.-Made Autos

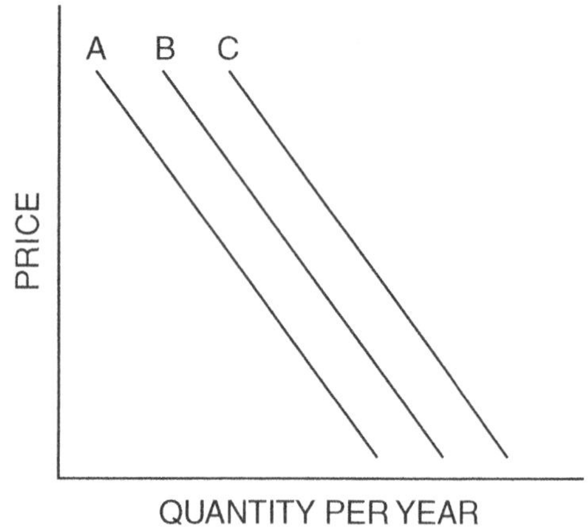

Part B: Why Does the Demand Curve Shift?

Categorize each change in demand in Part A according to the reason why demand changed. A given demand curve assumes that consumer expectations, consumer tastes, the number of consumers in the market, the income of consumers, and the prices of substitutes and complements are unchanged. In Table 1-5.2, place an X next to the reason that the event described in the headline caused a change in demand. One headline will have no answer because it will result in a change in quantity demanded rather than a change in demand.

Table 1-5.2
Reasons for a Change in Demand for U.S.-Made Autos

	Headline number							
Reason	1	2	3	4	5	6	7	8
9. A change in consumer expectations						X	X	
10. A change in consumer taste								X
11. A change in the number of consumer in the market		X						
12. A change in income	X							
13. A change in the price of a substitute good			X	X				
14. A change in the price of a complementary good								

Supply Curves, Movements along Supply Curves, and Shifts in Supply Curves

In this activity, we will assume that the supply curve of Greebes is upward sloping.

Part A: A Change in Supply versus a Change in Quantity Supplied

 Student Alert: The distinction between a "change in supply" and a "change in quantity supplied" is very important!

Study the data in Table 1-6.1 and plot the supply of Greebes on the graph in Figure 1-6.1. Label the supply curve S and answer the questions that follow.

Table 1-6.1
Supply of Greebes

Price (per Greebe)	Quantity supplied per week (millions of Greebes)
$0.05	0
$0.10	50
$0.15	100
$0.20	150
$0.25	200
$0.30	250
$0.35	300
$0.40	350

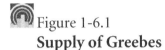 Figure 1-6.1
Supply of Greebes

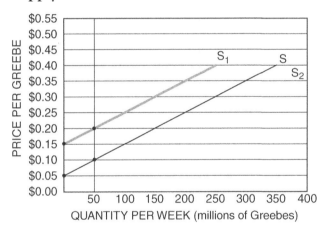

1. The data for supply curve S indicate that at a price of $0.25 per Greebe, suppliers would be willing to offer ___**200**___ million Greebes. All other things held constant, if the price of Greebes increased to $0.30 per Greebe, suppliers would be willing to offer ___**250**___ million Greebes. Such a change would be an increase in (*supply* / ***quantity supplied***). All other things held constant, if the price of Greebes decreased to $0.20 per Greebe, suppliers would be willing to offer **150** million Greebes. Such a change would be called a decrease in (*supply* / ***quantity supplied***).

Now, let's suppose that there is a change in the price of several of the raw materials used in making Greebes. This change in the *ceteris paribus* conditions underlying the original supply of Greebes will result in a new set of data, such as that shown in Table 1-6.2. Study the data, and plot this supply of Greebes on the graph in Figure 1-6.1. Label the new supply curve S_1 and answer the questions that follow.

 Table 1-6.2
New Supply of Greebes

Price (per Greebe)	Quantity supplied per week (millions of Greebes)
$0.15	0
$0.20	50
$0.25	100
$0.30	150
$0.35	200
$0.40	250

2. Comparing the new supply curve (S_1) with the original supply curve (S), we can say that the change in the supply of Greebes results in a shift of the supply curve to the (***left*** / right). Such a shift indicates that at each of the possible prices shown, suppliers are now willing to offer a (***smaller*** / larger) quantity; and at each of the possible quantities shown, suppliers are willing to accept a (***higher*** / lower) minimum price. The cause of this supply curve shift was a(n) (***increase*** / decrease) in prices of several of the raw materials used in making Greebes.

Now, let's suppose that there is a dramatic change in the price of Silopanna, a resource used in the production of Greebes. This change in the *ceteris paribus* conditions underlying the original supply of Greebes will result in a new set of data shown in Table 1-6.3. Study the data, and plot this supply of Greebes on the graph in Figure 1-6.1. Label the new supply curve S_2 and answer the questions that follow.

 Table 1-6.3
New Supply of Greebes

Price (per Greebe)	Quantity supplied per week (millions of Greebes)
$0.10	150
$0.15	200
$0.20	250
$0.25	300
$0.30	350
$0.35	400

3. Comparing the new supply curve (S_2) with the original supply curve (S), we can say that the change in the supply of Greebes results in a shift of the supply curve to the (*left* / ***right***). Such a shift indicates that at each of the possible prices shown, suppliers are now willing to offer a (*smaller* / ***larger***) quantity; and at each of the possible quantities shown, suppliers are willing to accept a (***lower*** / *higher*) minimum price. The cause of this supply curve shift is a(n) (*increase* / ***decrease***) in the price of Silopanna, a resource used in the production of Greebes.

Part B: Do You Get It?

Now, to check your understanding, choose the answer you think is the one best alternative in each of the following multiple-choice questions.

4. All other things held constant, which of the following would *not* cause a change in the supply of beef?

   (A) A decrease in the price of beef (This will cause a decrease in the quantity supplied of beef.)

   (B) A decrease in the price of cattle feed

   (C) An increase in the price of cattle feed

   (D) An increase in the cost of transporting cattle to market

5. "Falling oil prices have caused a sharp decrease in the supply of oil." Speaking precisely, and using terms as they are defined by economists, choose the statement that best describes this quotation.

(A) The quotation is correct: decrease in price causes a decrease in supply.

(B) The quotation is incorrect: decrease in price causes an increase in supply, not a decrease in supply.

(C) The quotation is incorrect: decrease in price causes an increase in the quantity supplied, not a decrease in supply.

(D) *The quotation is incorrect: a decrease in price causes a decrease in the quantity supplied, not a decrease in supply.*

6. You overhear a fellow student say, "Economic markets are confusing. If supply increases, then price decreases; but if price decreases, then supply also will decrease. If supply falls, price will rise; but if price rises, supply also will rise." Dispel your friend's obvious confusion (in no more than one short paragraph) below.

My friend does not understand the difference between a change in supply, which will cause a change in price, and a change in quantity supplied, which is the result of a change in price. If supply increases, then price will decrease. However, a decrease in price will lead to a decrease in quantity supplied, not a decrease in supply. If supply falls, then price will increase. If however, there is an increase in price, it will result in an increase in quantity supplied.

Part C: Producer Surplus

Once we have the supply curve, we can define the concept of *producer surplus*. Producer surplus is the value a producer receives from the sale of a good in excess of the marginal cost of producing the good. Stated differently, producer surplus is the difference between the price a seller receives for a unit of the good and the cost to the seller of producing that unit. For example, if your cost of producing a coat is $50 but you are able to sell the coat for $70, you have a producer surplus of $20.

Refer again to the supply curve data from Table 1-6.1, and assume the price is $0.25. Some sellers will benefit because based on their low marginal costs of production, they are willing to accept prices lower than $0.25 for this good. Note that each time the price is increased by $0.05, sellers will provide an additional 50 million units. Table 1-6.4 shows how to calculate the producer surplus resulting from the price of $0.25.

 Table 1-6.4
Finding the Producer Surplus When the Price Is $0.25

Price willing to accept	Quantity supplied	Producer surplus from the increments of 50 million units if P = $0.25
$0.10	50 million units	($0.15)(50 million units) = $7.5 million
$0.15	100 million units	($0.10)(50 million units) = $5.0 million
$0.20	150 million units	($0.05)(50 million units) = $2.5 million
$0.25	200 million units	($0.00)(50 million units) = $0.0 million

For those producers willing to sell 50 million units at a price of $0.10, the producer surplus for each unit is $0.15 (= $0.25 – $0.10), making the producer surplus for all these units equal to $7.5 million. There are other producers who will put an extra 50 million units on the market if the price is $0.15. The producer surplus for these sellers is $0.10 per unit (= $0.25 – $0.15) or a total of $5.0 million for all 50 million units. If the price is raised another $0.05 to $0.20, an extra 50 million units will be supplied; the producer surplus for these units is $2.5 million, or $0.05 per unit (= $0.25 – $0.20). If the price is $0.25, another 50 million units will be supplied. The producer surplus for these units, however, is $0.00 since $0.25 is the lowest price these producers are willing to accept. Thus, if the price is $0.25, a total of 200 million units are supplied and the total producer surplus is $15.0 million.

An approximation of the total producer surplus from a given number of units of a good can be shown graphically as the area above the supply curve and below the price paid for those units. In Figure 1-6.2, redraw the supply curve (S) from the data in Table 1-6.1. We see that if the price is $0.25, the quantity supplied is 200 million units. Consumer surplus from these 200 million units is the shaded area between the supply curve S and the horizontal price line at $0.25. We can find the area of this triangle using the familiar rule of (½) × base × height.

 Figure 1-6.2
Producer Surplus

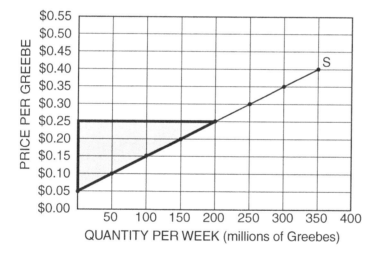

7. What is the value of producer surplus in this market if the price is $0.25? ***$20.0 million***
   Show how you calculated the value of the area of the triangle representing producer surplus.
   PS = (0.5)(200 million)($0.25 – $0.05) = $20.0 million

---

8. Answer these questions based on the discussion of Figure 1-6.2.

   (A) If the price is increased from $0.25 to $0.30, producer surplus will (***increase*** / *decrease*). Why?
   Producers are putting more units on the market and receiving a higher price.

   (B) If the price is decreased from $0.25 to $0.20, producer surplus will (*increase* / ***decrease***). Why?
   Producers are putting fewer units on the market and receiving a lower price.

Reasons for Changes in Supply

Part A: Does the Supply Curve Shift?

Read the eight newspaper headlines in Table 1-7.1, and use the table to record the impact of each event on the supply of cars from U.S. auto producers. In the second column, indicate whether the event in the headline will cause American auto producers to provide more or less cars. Use the third column to indicate whether there is a change in supply (ΔS) or a change in quantity supplied (ΔQs) of cars. In the third column, decide whether the supply curve shifts to the right or left or does not shift. Finally, indicate the letter for the new supply curve. Use Figure 1-7.1 to help you. **Always start at curve B**, and move only one curve at a time.

 Table 1-7.1
Impact of Events on Supply of U.S.-Made Autos

Headline	Should U.S. auto firms produce more or less?	Is there a change in supply (ΔS) or a change in quantity supplied (ΔQs)?	Does the supply curve of cars shift to the right or left or not shift?	What is the new supply curve for cars?
1. Auto Workers' Union Agrees to Wage Cuts	**(More)** / Less	**(ΔS)** / ΔQs	**Right** / Left / No Shift	A / B / **C**
2. New Robot Technology Increases Efficiency	**(More)** / Less	**(ΔS)** / ΔQs	**Right** / Left / No Shift	A / B / **C**
3. Price of U.S. Cars Increases	**(More)** / Less	ΔS / **(ΔQs)**	Right / Left / **No Shift**	A / **B** / C
4. Nationwide Auto Workers Strike Begins	More / **(Less)**	**(ΔS)** / ΔQs	Right / **Left** / No Shift	**A** / B / C
5. Cost of Steel Decreases	**(More)** / Less	**(ΔS)** / ΔQs	**Right** / Left / No Shift	A / B / **C**
6. Major Auto Producer Goes Out of Business	More / **(Less)**	**(ΔS)** / ΔQs	Right / **Left** / No Shift	**A** / B / C
7. Buyers Reject New Car Models	More / **(Less)**	ΔS / **(ΔQs)**	Right / Left / **No Shift**	A / **B** / C
8. Government Gives Car Producers a Subsidy	**(More)** / Less	**(ΔS)** / ΔQs	**Right** / Left / No Shift	A / B / **C**

Figure 1-7.1
Supply of U.S.-Made Cars

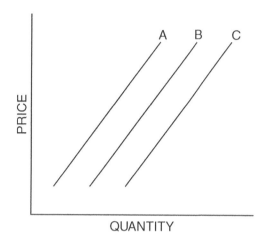

Part B: Why Does the Supply Curve Shift?

Categorize each change in supply in Part A according to the reason why supply changed. In Table 1-7.2, place an X next to the reason that the headline indicated a change in supply. In some cases, more than one headline could be matched to a reason. It is possible a headline does not indicate a shift in supply because it will result in a change in quantity supplied rather than a change in supply.

 Table 1-7.2
Impact of Events on Supply of U.S.-Made Autos

Reason	Headline number							
	1	2	3	4	5	6	7	8
9. A change in costs of inputs to production process	X			X	X			
10. A change in technology		X						
11. A change in the number of producers in the market						X		
12. Government policies								X

Equilibrium Price and Equilibrium Quantity

Table 1-8.1 below shows the demand for Greebes and the supply of Greebes. Plot these data on the graph in Figure 1-8.1. Label the demand curve D and label the supply curve S. Then answer the questions that follow.

 Student Alert: A "change in demand" or a "change in supply" results in a change in price, while a "change in quantity demanded" or a "change in quantity supplied" is the result of a change in price.

 Table 1-8.1
Demand for and Supply of Greebes

Price (per Greebe)	Quantity demanded (millions of Greebes)	Quantity supplied (millions of Greebes)
$0.05	400	0
$0.10	350	50
$0.15	300	100
$0.20	250	150
$0.25	200	200
$0.30	150	250
$0.35	100	300
$0.40	50	350
$0.45	0	400

Figure 1-8.1
Demand for and Supply of Greebes

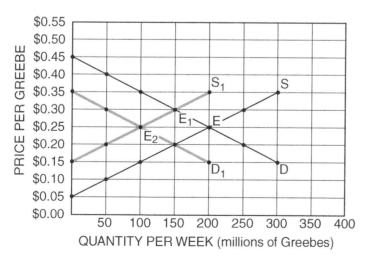

1. Under these conditions, competitive market forces would tend to establish an equilibrium price of **$0.25** per Greebe and an equilibrium quantity of **200** million Greebes.

2. If the price currently prevailing in the market is $0.30 per Greebe, buyers would want to buy **150** million Greebes and sellers would want to sell **250** million Greebes. Under these conditions, there would be a (*shortage* / **surplus**) of **100** million Greebes. Competitive market forces would cause the price to (*increase* / **decrease**) to a price of **$0.25** per Greebe. At this new price, buyers would now want to buy **200** million Greebes, and sellers now want to sell **200** million Greebes. Because of this change in (**price** / *underlying conditions*), the (*demand* / **quantity demanded**) (**increased** / *decreased*) by **50** million Greebes, and the (*supply* / **quantity supplied**) (*increased* / **decreased**) by **50** million Greebes.

3. If the price currently prevailing in the market is $0.20 per Greebe, buyers would want to buy **250** million Greebes, and sellers would want to sell **150** million Greebes. Under these conditions, there would be a (**shortage** / *surplus*) of **100** million Greebes. Competitive market forces would cause the price to (**increase** / *decrease*) to a price of **$0.25** per Greebe. At this new price, buyers would now want to buy **200** million Greebes, and sellers now want to sell **200** million Greebes. Because of this change in (**price** / *underlying conditions*), the (*demand* / **quantity demanded**) (*increased* / **decreased**) by **50** million Greebes, and the (*supply* / **quantity supplied**) (**increased** / *decreased*) by **50** million Greebes.

4. At equilibrium, is each of the following true or false? Explain.

   (A) The quantity demanded is equal to the quantity supplied.
   True. The point on the demand and supply curves is the same, so the quantity demanded equals the quantity supplied at the equilibrium price. Quantities refer to points on the graph.

   (B) Demand equals supply.
   False. Demand refers to the entire demand curve and supply refers to the entire supply curve. The two curves are different, therefore supply does not equal demand. At the equilibrium price, the quantity demanded equals the quantity supplied.

5. Now, suppose a mysterious blight causes the supply schedule for Greebes to change as shown in Table 1-8.2:

 Table 1-8.2
New Supply of Greebes

Price (per Greebe)	Quantity supplied (millions of Greebes)
$0.15	0
$0.20	50
$0.25	100
$0.30	150
$0.35	200

Plot the new supply schedule on the axes in Figure 1-8.1 and label it S_1. Label the new equilibrium E_1. Under these conditions, competitive market forces would tend to establish an equilibrium price of __*$0.30*__ per Greebe and an equilibrium quantity of *150* million Greebes.

Compared with the equilibrium price in Question 1, we say that because of this change in (*price* / ***underlying conditions***), the (***supply*** / *quantity supplied*) changed; and both the equilibrium price and the equilibrium quantity changed. The equilibrium price (***increased*** / *decreased*), and the equilibrium quantity (*increased* / ***decreased***).

Compared with the consumer and producer surpluses in Question 4, consumer surplus has (*increased* / ***decreased***), and producer surplus has (*increased* / ***decreased***).

6. Now, with the supply schedule at S_1, suppose further that a sharp drop in people's incomes as the result of a prolonged recession causes the demand schedule to change as shown in Table 1-8.3.

 Table 1-8.3
New Demand for Greebes

Price (per Greebe)	Quantity demanded (millions of Greebes)
$0.15	200
$0.20	150
$0.25	100
$0.30	50
$0.35	0

Plot the new demand schedule on the axes in Figure 1-8.1 and label it D_1. Label the new equilibrium E_2. Under these conditions, with the supply schedule at S_1, competitive market forces would establish an equilibrium price of **$0.25** per Greebe and an equilibrium quantity of **100** million Greebes. Compared with the equilibrium price in Question 5, because of this change in (*price* / **underlying conditions**), the (**demand** / *quantity demanded*) changed. The equilibrium price (*increased* / **decreased**), and the equilibrium quantity (*increased* / **decreased**).

Shifts in Supply and Demand

Part A: The Market for Jelly Beans

Fill in the blanks with the letter of the graph that illustrates each situation. You may use a graph more than once.

 Figure 1-9.1
The Supply and Demand for Jelly Beans

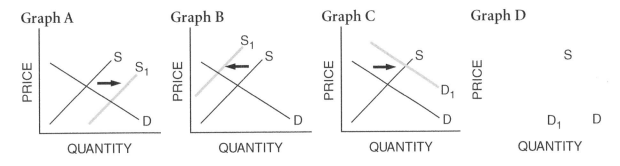

1. The price of sugar, a key ingredient in producing jelly beans, increases.   ***B***

2. The price of bubble gum, a close substitute for jelly beans, increases.   ***C***

3. A machine is invented that makes jelly beans at a lower cost. _____***A***_____

4. The government places a tax on foreign jelly beans, which have a considerable share of the market. _____***B***_____

5. The price of soda, a complementary good for jelly beans, increases.   ***D***

6. Widespread prosperity allows people to buy more jelly beans.   ***C***

Part B: Apples, Pears, and Pies

Connecticut ships large amounts of apples to all parts of the United States by rail. Circle the words that show the effects on price and quantity for each situation, and complete the graphs below, showing how a hurricane that destroys apples before they are picked in Connecticut might affect the price and quantity of each commodity. Then provide your reasoning.

7. **Apples in Boston**

   Price: **Rises** / *Unchanged* / *Falls*

   Quantity: *Rises* / *Unchanged* / **Falls**

   Reason: **A hurricane destroyed the apples.**

   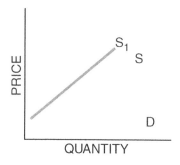

8. **Land devoted to apple orchards in the state of Washington**

   Price: (Rises) / *Unchanged* / *Falls*

   Quantity: (Rises) / *Unchanged* / *Falls*

   Reason: **Washington farmers grow more apples because the price is higher. To do this, they must buy more land.**

   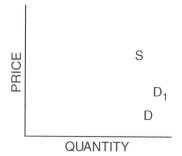

9. **Apples grown in the state of Washington**

   Price: (Rises) / *Unchanged* / *Falls*

   Quantity: (Rises) / *Unchanged* / *Falls*

   Reason: **Consumers substitute Washington apples for Connecticut apples.**

   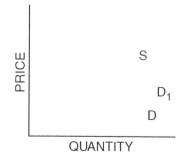

10. **Pears**

Price: *Rises* / *Unchanged* / *Falls*

Quantity: *Rises* / *Unchanged* / *Falls*

Reason: *Consumers substitute pears for apples.*

PRICE

S

D_1

D

QUANTITY

11. **Apple pies**

Price: *Rises* / *Unchanged* / *Falls*

Quantity: *Rises* / *Unchanged* / *Falls*

Reason: *Apples are used to bake pies. Higher-priced apples increase the cost of producing pies.*

S_1

S

PRICE

D

QUANTITY

Economic Systems

Read the following description of economic systems, answer the review questions, and then complete the table.

It's a fact: our needs and wants are always greater than the available resources necessary to satisfy us. We all face scarcity, which forces us to choose how best to use the limited resources that are available. Ultimately, society has to make three very important economic decisions: what do we produce, how do we produce, and for whom do we produce? To answer these three questions, a society develops an economic system, or organized way of answering the three questions. Because people do not all share the same values, beliefs, geographic circumstances, and climates, different societies have developed very different economic systems to deal with scarcity. Figure 1-10.1 shows a continuum of the economic systems that have been developed throughout history based on the amount of freedom individuals have to answer the three economic questions.

 Figure 1-10.1
Economic Systems

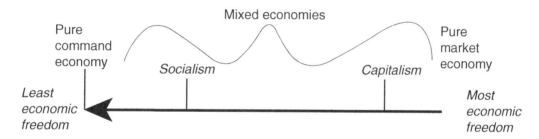

In a pure command economy, all economic decisions are made by the government or even a single leader. Ancient Egypt under the pharaohs and present-day North Korea are close, if not perfect, examples of pure command economies. The leaders decide what is to be produced, how it is produced, and for whom it is produced. Private property is nonexistent in the pure command model, and only the needs of the government are addressed.

In a pure market economy, all economic decisions are left to the individuals in the society. These individuals, motivated by their own self-interest and their desire for private property, answer the three economic questions. To get what they need or want, individuals come together in markets and trade for mutual benefit.

Although pure market economies are nonexistent, something close to the pure market model called *capitalism* does exist. The United States and a number of other countries can be described as capitalistic economies. Capitalism is an example of a mixed economy. Mixed economies are the reality of today's world. In a mixed economy, both individuals and government answer the three basic economic questions. If most decisions and property are under the control of individuals in the society, then the system can be described as capitalistic. If most decisions and property are under state control, then the system can be described as socialist.

1. What three basic questions must all societies answer?
   The questions are:
   (1) What goods and services should be produced?
   (2) How should those goods and services be produced?
   (3) For whom are the goods and services produced?

2. Define economic system.
   An economic system is an organized way society answers the three basic economic questions.

3. What is a market?
   A market is where sellers and buyers of a good or service come together to trade.

4. Complete the following table:

	Pure command economy	Mixed economy	Pure market economy
Who answers the three basic economic questions?	*Government*	*Government and individuals*	*Individuals*
What degree of economic freedom exists for individuals?	*None*	*Some*	*Most*
Under which type of economic system would you prefer to live and why? Be prepared to discuss your answers with your classmates.	*Answers may vary.*	*Answers may vary.*	*Answers may vary.*

Anything Worth Doing Is Not Necessarily Worth Doing Well

Student Alert: Should you do all you can to earn a perfect grade of 100 on your next economics exam?

Bartlett's Familiar Quotations contains wisdom from writers separated by more than a millennium. Whose wisdom best fits today's world?

> ***Always take the short cut; and that is the rational one. Therefore say and do everything according to soundest reason.***
>
> > *Meditations iv.51*
> > Marcus Aurelius
> > A.D. 120 to 181

> ***Whatever is worth doing at all is worth doing well.***
>
> > Philip Dormer Stanhope
> > Earl of Chesterfield
> > 1694 to 1773

Between these two extremes, one discovers the economic way of thinking. We know that productive resources are limited, so we cannot have everything we want. We must economize by choosing among alternatives.

We may want the very best product available, but we settle on a product with fewer features or less durability because the extra benefit of the product we would most like to have is simply not worth the extra cost. Resources that aren't devoted to making a good product perfect can be allocated to making other products.

Few choices we make in life are all-or-nothing decisions. We decide on the number of assigned chapters to read today based on alternative uses of our time. We frequently adjust the number of hours we study for each subject because of tests and nonschool uses of our day. Epidemic doses of "senioritis"—severely curtailing work for grades after college-acceptance letters are received—may suggest that the majority of students agree with Marcus Aurelius rather than the Earl of Chesterfield. Even the most severe victims of senioritis may admit that they are incurring a very different cost: the lost opportunities to learn the cultural and scientific knowledge that will be required in college.

An excellent academic record in high school expands the array of college choices for the graduating high school senior. "A" grades are preferred to "C" grades for reasons that don't warrant an explanation: the extra benefits of the explanation are not worth the extra costs of reading it.

This comparison of additional, or marginal, benefits and costs applies to production decisions, too. Of course, auto companies can make cars that work for a quarter century, but would the extra manufacturing cost be worthwhile over the product lifetime? Technical advances frequently lead to superior products at lower cost. Because of blindingly rapid changes in computer technology, the concept of an "old" computer is measured in months; so building a computer case that lasts for 50 years would be wasteful. Can you suggest services or products that are satisfactory, but not superior?

Thinking about the future requires that we acknowledge what we have and then make incremental changes so the marginal benefits of the changes exceed the marginal costs. Mechanical equipment in an aircraft must meet higher quality standards than the same product in a car. If the alternator fails in a car, one typically has enough time to pull off the road before the car stops. In an airplane, safe landing options are fewer than those available to the motorist. Both quality decisions are correct because the added benefits from avoiding failure in a plane greatly exceed the marginal benefits from avoiding mechanical failure in a car.

1. After reading in *Bartlett's Familiar Quotations* that "knowledge is power," a student decides to be as knowledgeable as possible by devoting the next 20 years, without interruption, to college. From the hypothetical data below, would you advise this person to reconsider a career as a professional student? Answer the questions that follow.

 Table 1-11.1

Degree Earned and Expected Lifetime Earnings and Costs

Highest degree earned	Expected lifetime earnings (total benefit) by degree	Marginal benefit of additional degree	Expected lifetime costs (total cost) by degree	Marginal cost of additional degree
High school	$600,000	+$600,000	$0	+$0
Associate	$1,200,000	*+$600,000*	$200,000	*+$200,000*
Bachelor's	$1,700,000	*+$500,000*	$500,000	+$300,000
Master's	$2,100,000	+$400,000	$900,000	*+$400,000*
Doctorate	$2,400,000	*+$300,000*	$2,400,000	*+$1,500,000*

(A) Complete Table 1-11.1 with the missing values of the marginal benefit and marginal cost of earning an additional degree.

(B) Would a master's degree and a doctorate degree increase the human capital of the student? (**_Yes_** / No)

(C) In the process of building knowledge, would the doctorate degree be the best example of doing a job well? (**_Yes_** / No)

(D) Assuming that inflation and interest rates have been taken into account in these data, what is the optimal degree for this person to earn?

Comparing the values of marginal benefit and marginal cost, the optimal degree for the person is the Master's degree. For this degree the marginal benefit equals the marginal cost. The marginal benefit of earning the doctorate degree is less than the marginal cost.

(E) Which criterion did you use to determine the optimal degree this person should obtain?

*Total Benefit = Total Cost / **Marginal Benefit = Marginal Cost***

(F) Since inflation is already factored into the data, what is the most likely reason that the costs of a doctorate degree rise to such a high level?

A person seeking a doctorate degree already has acquired enough education to have high income earning skills. The opportunity cost of the additional time needed to earn the doctorate degree is the sacrifice of high earnings during this time.

2. Wrapping garbage neatly before taking it to the trash can, raking leaves on a windy day, hand-drying dishes after they have been run through a dishwasher's dry cycle, and similar tasks seem to push the credibility of any value in doing a job well. Give examples of jobs with highly diminishing marginal benefits.

Answers will vary. Ironing blue jeans and cleaning up every speck of dust are examples of such jobs.

3. Consider an electronic item that you have thought about buying. Do you always choose the highest-priced good? Explain your answer.

People frequently don't purchase the highest-priced goods because the marginal benefit of the highest quality is not worth the additional cost.

4. If you wanted to eliminate "senioritis," how would you change the college acceptance process and/or the incentives offered by high school instructors?

You could make college acceptance conditional on work during the entire senior year. This would raise the cost of senioritis and provide an incentive for seniors to study harder.

MICROECONOMICS

The Nature and Functions of Product Markets

Unit 2

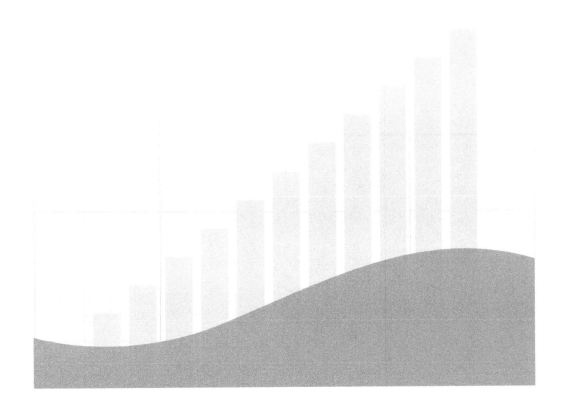

■ Demand is the relationship between price and the amount of a good or service that consumers are willing and able to purchase at various prices in a given period of time. The law of demand states that consumers buy more at lower prices and less at higher prices, all other things being equal.

■ There is a difference between a "change in demand" and a "change in quantity demanded." A change in the quantity demanded of Good X can be caused only by a change in the price of Good X. It is a movement along the demand curve. At a lower price, a greater quantity is demanded.

■ The reason the price of Good X is treated differently from the other factors which influence consumers is that the price of Good X is on the vertical axis of the graph.

■ A change in demand means that more or less is demanded at every price; it is caused by changes in preferences, incomes, expectations, population, and the prices of complementary or substitute goods.

■ The income effect, the substitution effect, and the law of diminishing marginal utility explain why a demand curve is downward sloping.

■ The law of diminishing marginal utility states that as more of a good or service is consumed in a given period of time, the additional benefit or satisfaction from an extra unit declines.

■ Supply is the relationship between price and the amount of a good or service that producers are willing and able to sell at various prices in a given period of time. Producers are willing to sell more at higher prices and less at lower prices, all other things being equal.

■ There is a difference between a "change in supply" and a "change in quantity supplied."

A change in the quantity supplied of Good X can be caused only by a change in the price of Good X. It is a movement along the supply curve. A change in supply is a shift of the curve where more or less is supplied at every price. Changes in technology, production costs, taxes, subsidies, and expectations will cause a shift in supply.

■ In competitive markets, supply and demand constitute the sum of many individual decisions to sell and to buy. The interaction of supply and demand determines the price and quantity that will clear the market. The price where quantity supplied and quantity demanded are equal is called the equilibrium or market-clearing price.

■ At a price higher than equilibrium, there is a surplus and pressure on sellers to lower their prices. At a price lower than equilibrium, there is a shortage and pressure on buyers to offer higher prices.

■ An administered maximum price is called a price ceiling. A price ceiling below the equilibrium price causes a shortage. A price ceiling set at or above the equilibrium price has no effect on the market.

■ An administered minimum price is called a price floor. A price floor above the equilibrium price causes a surplus. A price floor set at or below the equilibrium price has no effect on the market.

■ Market prices promote economic progress because at the equilibrium price there is both consumer surplus and producer surplus. In other words, buyers and sellers are both better off at the equilibrium price.

■ Consumer surplus is the difference between the highest price consumers are willing to pay for a good or service and the price that they actually have to pay.

■ Producer surplus is the difference between the lowest price businesses would be willing to accept for a good or service and the price they actually receive.

■ Price elasticity of demand refers to how strongly the quantity demanded changes in response to a given change in price. If the percentage change in quantity demanded is greater than the percentage change in price, the demand for the good is considered elastic. If the percentage change in quantity demanded is less than the percentage change in price, the demand for the good is considered inelastic. If the percentage change in price is equal to the percentage change in quantity demanded, the demand for the good is considered unit elastic.

■ Luxuries have a more elastic demand than necessities. High-priced goods have a more elastic demand than low-priced goods. Goods that are habit-forming tend to have an inelastic demand. Demand is more elastic in the long run than in the short run.

■ Price elasticity of demand can be determined by comparing the value of total revenue before and after the price change and by using the arc method to calculate the percentage changes in price and quantity demanded.

■ Price elasticity of supply refers to how strongly quantity supplied changes in relation to a change in price. Supply is more elastic in the long run than in the short run.

■ In a market economy, prices provide information to buyers and sellers, allocate resources, and act as rationing devices. It is important to know how to illustrate a wide range of situations with supply and demand graphs.

■ When property rights are not established, a market will fail to provide an efficient allocation of resources.

■ The presence of an externality results in a market failure with the market output not being the socially efficient level.

How Markets Allocate Resources

Markets use prices as signals to allocate resources to their highest valued uses. Consumers will pay higher prices for goods and services that they value more highly. Producers will devote more resources to the production of goods and services that have higher prices, other things being equal. And other things being equal, workers will provide more hours of labor to jobs that pay higher salaries.

This allocation principle applies both to product markets for items such as cars, houses, and haircuts and to resource markets for items such as labor, land, and equipment. Households play two important roles in an economy—they demand goods and services and supply resources. Businesses also have dual roles—they supply goods and services and demand resources. The interaction of demand and supply in product and resource markets generates prices that serve to allocate items to their highest valued alternatives. Factors that interfere with the workings of a competitive market result in an inefficient allocation of resources, causing a reduction in society's overall well-being.

Figures 2-1.1 and 2-1.2 illustrate how markets can be interrelated. Assume the markets are perfectly competitive and that the supply and demand model is completely applicable. The graphs show the supply and demand in each market *before* the assumed change occurs. Trace through the effects of the assumed change, all other things held constant. Work your way from left to right. Shift no more than one curve in each market. In each market graph, show any shift in the demand or supply curve, labeling each new curve D_1 or S_1. Then circle the correct symbol under each graph ($\uparrow$ for increase, — for unchanged, and $\downarrow$ for decrease).

1. Assume that a new fertilizer dramatically increases the number of potatoes that can be harvested with no additional labor or machinery. Also assume that this fertilizer does not affect wheat farming and that people are satisfied to eat either potatoes or bread made from wheat flour.

 Figure 2-1.1
Effects of a New Fertilizer

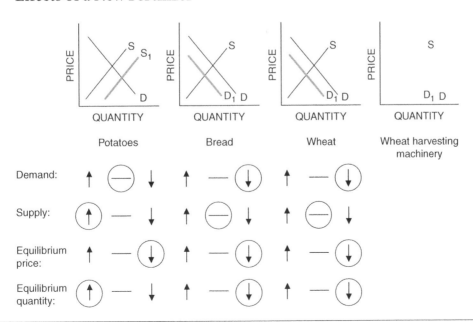

2. Assume new studies show that coffee is worse for people's health than tea and that more people use cream in coffee than in tea.

 Figure 2-1.2

Effects of New Health Studies

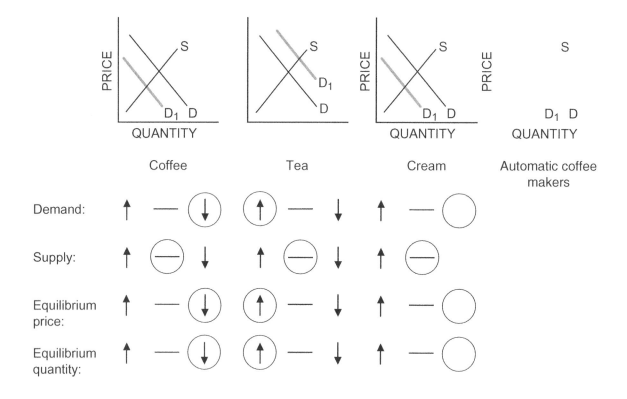

Advanced Placement Economics Microeconomics: Teacher Resource Manual © Council for Economic Education, New York, N.Y.

3. Examine Figure 2-1.3, which shows an increase in demand in the housing market in the country of Pajotte.

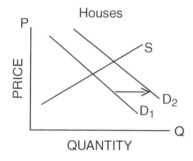 Figure 2-1.3

Increase in Housing Demand in Pajotte

(A) Which of the following factors would cause an increase in the demand for houses in Pajotte?

(1) *An increase in the annual income of many Pajottians*

(2) A reduced rate of immigration into Pajotte

(3) *Lower interest rates on loans to buy houses*

(B) The demand for lumber in Pajotte would (***increase*** / *decrease*), which would result in (***higher*** / *lower*) lumber prices.

(C) Employment of workers who build houses would (***increase*** / *decrease*) and their wages would (***increase*** / *decrease*).

Why Is a Demand Curve Downward Sloping?

To most people, the law of demand is obvious: consumers buy more of a good at a lower price and less at a higher price. Economics goes beyond describing the combined demand of all consumers in a market. To explain why a demand curve is downward sloping, or negatively sloped, economists focus on the demand curve of a single consumer.

The total utility of a quantity of goods and services to a consumer can be represented by the maximum amount of money he or she is willing to give in exchange for that quantity. The marginal utility of a good or service to a consumer (measured in monetary terms) is the maximum amount of money he or she is willing to pay for one more unit of the good or service. With these definitions, we can now state a simple idea about consumer tastes: the more of a good a consumer has, the less will be the marginal utility of an additional unit.

Part A: Total Utility and Marginal Utility

Table 2-2.1 presents data on Dolores's evaluation of different quantities of polo shirts and different quantities of steak.

1. Use the data to compute the marginal utility of each polo shirt and each steak. The total utility numbers in the figure represent the total satisfaction in dollars Dolores receives from a given quantity of shirts or steaks. The marginal utility numbers represent the amount of dollars Dolores is willing to pay for an additional shirt or steak.

 Table 2-2.1

Marginal Utility of Polo Shirts and Steaks

Number of polo shirts	Total utility	Marginal utility	Number of steaks	Total utility	Marginal utility
0	$0		0	$0	
1	$60	$60	1	$20	$20
2	$100	$40	2	$36	$16
3	$130	*$30*	3	$51	*$15*
4	$150	*$20*	4	$65	*$14*
5	$165	*$15*	5	$78	*$13*
6	$175	*$10*	6	$90	*$12*

2. Using Figure 2-2.1, plot Dolores's total utility and marginal utility for polo shirts and steaks. Each graph has two points to get you started.

Figure 2-2.1
Total and Marginal Utility of Polo Shirts and Steaks

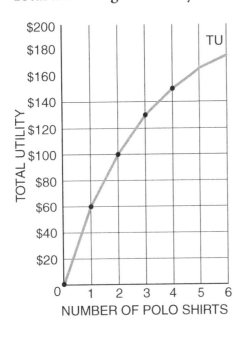

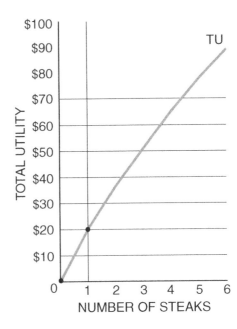

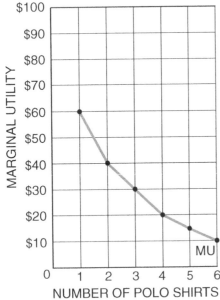

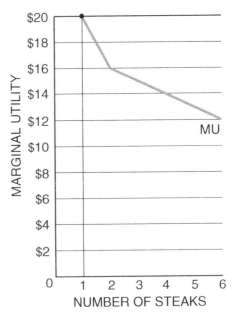

Advanced Placement Economics Microeconomics: Teacher Resource Manual © Council for Economic Education, New York, N.Y.

3. Looking at the table and graphs, you can conclude for both goods that as she consumes more units:

(A) total utility is always (***increasing*** / *decreasing*).

(B) marginal utility always (*increases* / ***decreases***).

Because your graphs show that Dolores receives less and less marginal utility, you have demonstrated the law of *diminishing marginal utility*.

Part B: The Marginal Utility per Dollar

Student Alert: In spending your income wisely, it is the marginal utility per dollar (MU per $1) that matters, and not the marginal utility (MU) by itself.

If Dolores has a given budget and must choose between polo shirts and steaks, she will make her choice so that the marginal utility per dollar spent of each good is the same. Using the data in Table 2-2.1 and assuming that the price of both goods is $30, let's see what happens if Dolores spends her entire budget of $150 dollars and buys five polo shirts and zero steaks. Her marginal utility from the fifth polo shirt is $15, and her marginal utility from the first steak is $20. So if she buys only four polo shirts and one steak, her total utility drops by $15 on the polo shirt, but it increases by $20 on the steak. Dolores is better off because her total utility has increased by $5 and her total budget is unchanged.

Suppose Dolores spends her $150 and buys four polo shirts and one steak. Her marginal utility from the fourth polo shirt is $20, and her marginal utility from the first steak is also $20. She will not want to switch. To buy the next steak gives her an increase in total utility of $16, but she would have to give up a polo shirt, which would reduce her utility by $20. Conversely, to buy an additional polo shirt would increase her total utility by $15, but she would lose $20 from giving up the steak. Dolores should not change her purchases. Note that this example assumes both the shirt and steak have the same price.

If the prices (P) of the two goods differ, then Dolores will adjust her consumption until the MU of the two goods, *per dollar spent,* are equal. Or, stated in another way,

$$\frac{MU_x}{P_x} = \frac{MU_y}{P_y}.$$

4. Use the information in Table 2-2.2 to analyze Callie's choice between gasoline and food.

Callie has an income of $55, the price of a unit of gasoline is $5, and the price of a unit of food is $10. Complete the table.

 Table 2-2.2

Callie Buys Gasoline and Food

Gasoline (G)	MU_G	MU_G/P_G	Food (F)	MU_F	MU_F/P_F
1 unit	+$60	*+12.0*	1 unit	+$120	*+12.0*
2 units	+$30	*+6.0*	2 units	+$80	+8.0
3 units	+$15	+3.0	3 units	+$60	*+6.0*
4 units	+$5	*+1.0*	4 units	+$30	+3.0
5 units	+$3	+0.6	5 units	+$10	*+1.0*
6 units	+$1	*+0.2*	6 units	+$5	+0.5

(A) What is the meaning of the value "+3" when Callie consumes the fourth unit of food?
It means she receives $3 in additional utility for each dollar spent on that fourth unit.

(B) How much income would Callie have to spend to purchase the combination of 1 G and 5 F?
$55 = (1G)($5) + (5F)($10).

(C) Will the combination of 1 G and 5 F maximize Callie's total utility? Why?
No, because the MU per $1 from gas (+12) is greater than the MU per $1 from food (+1).

(D) If the combination of 1 G and 5 F will not maximize her total utility from her income of $55, Callie should

(1) buy more units of G and fewer units of F.

(2) buy more units of F and fewer units of G.

(E) Callie will maximize her total utility from her budget of $55 if she buys **3** units of G and **4** units of F. This combination will give her a total utility of $**395**.
The MU per $1 is the same for the third unit of G and the fourth unit of F.
TU = sum of the MUs = $60 + $30 + $15 + $120 + $80 + $60 + $30 = $395.

Advanced Placement Economics Microeconomics: Teacher Resource Manual © Council for Economic Education, New York, N.Y.

Part C: Consumer Surplus

Assume you go into a store to buy a bottle of water. The bottle of water costs you $1. You would have been willing to pay $2. The difference between what you paid and what you would have been willing to pay is *consumer surplus.*

We can calculate Dolores's consumer surplus from buying steak by looking at her demand curve. Refer back to Table 2-2.1 and look at her marginal utility values for steak. If she has two steaks, Dolores is willing to pay $15 for one more steak; if she has three steaks, she is willing to pay $14 for a fourth steak. Dolores will buy steak until the point where the price is equal to the marginal utility of the last steak. Dolores will pay the same price for each of the steaks she buys. Thus, if the price of steak is $14, she will buy four steaks; the marginal utility of the fourth steak is $14. Dolores would have been willing to pay more for the first three steaks. She has gotten a bargain buying four steaks at $14 apiece for a total expenditure of $56. She would have been willing to pay $20 for the first steak, $16 for the second, $15 for the third, and $14 for the fourth, for a total outlay of $65. The consumer surplus is the difference between what she was willing to pay ($65) and what she actually paid ($56). Her total consumer surplus from buying four steaks at a price of $14 is $9.

Consider the information in Table 2-2.3 on Joel's total utility for CD purchases, and then answer the questions that follow.

 Table 2-2.3
Total Utility of CDs

Number of CDs	Total utility
1	$25
2	$45
3	$63
4	$78
5	$90
6	$100
7	$106
8	$110

5. What marginal utility is associated with the purchase of the third CD?

   (A) $18   (B) $21   (C) $45   (D) $63

   His TU increases from $45 to $63 when he buys the third CD.

6. What is Joel's consumer surplus if he purchases three CDs at $11 apiece?

   (A) $30   (B) $33   (C) $63   (D) $96

   His consumer surplus is the difference between what he was willing to pay for the three CDs and what he actually did pay. What he was willing to pay is found by adding the MUs for the three CDs: $25 + $20 + $18 = $63. This is his TU from three CDs. He paid a total of $33 (3 × $11) so his consumer surplus is $30.

7. What would happen to Joel's consumer surplus if he purchased an additional CD at $11?

   (A) Consumer surplus declines by $11.

   (B) Consumer surplus increases by $11.

   (C) Consumer surplus increases by $15.

   (D) Consumer surplus increases by $4.

   Since his MU from the fourth CD is $15, his consumer surplus from that extra CD is $15 – $11 = +$4.

8. How many CDs should Joel buy when they cost $11 apiece?

   (A) 0   (B) 3   *(C) 5*   (D) 7

   The MU from the fifth CD ($12) is greater than the price of $11, but the MU from the sixth CD ($10) is less than $11. He will not be willing to buy the sixth CD.

9. What is Joel's consumer surplus at the optimal number of CD purchases at the price of $11?

   (A) $35   (B) $55   (C) $79   (D) $100

   His TU from five CDs is $90 and he paid only $55 for them.

10. If CDs go on sale and their price drops to $8, how many CDs do you expect Joel to buy?

    (A) 5   *(B) 6*   (C) 7   (D) 8

    At a price of $8, the sixth CD is worth buying because its MU ($10) now is greater than the price. Since the MU of the seventh CD is only $6, he would not be willing to pay $8 for it.

11. Why is consumer surplus important? How does it help explain the law of demand?
    Consumer surplus is an indication that consumers are able to buy the product at a price which is lower than the price they are willing to pay. Consumers will buy more of a product when its price drops below the marginal utility of additional units. Because the lower price creates consumer surplus for these additional units, consumers will purchase more of the product.

Part D: Income and Substitution Effects

Another way of explaining the downward sloping demand curve is through the *income* and *substitution effects*.

Income effect: When the price of a good falls, consumers experience an increase in purchasing power from a given income level. When the price of a good increases, consumers experience a decrease in purchasing power.

Substitution effect: When the price of a good falls, consumers will substitute toward that good and away from other goods.

Here's an example. Suppose you go to your favorite burger place. The price of a burger has increased, but the price of the chicken sandwich stays the same. Over the course of a week, you generally buy both burgers and chicken sandwiches.

12. How will the increase in the price of a burger affect your purchase of burgers? Explain.
    You will buy fewer burgers because they are relatively more expensive than chicken sandwiches.

13. Describe how the substitution effect changes your purchases of hamburgers and chicken sandwiches.
    Because the price of burgers increased, chicken sandwiches are relatively less expensive. Therefore, you substitute chicken sandwiches for burgers and buy more chicken sandwiches and fewer burgers.

14. Describe how the income effect changes your purchases.
    The increase in the price of burgers is the same as if you had a decrease in real income or purchasing power. Therefore, you would buy fewer burgers.

Elasticity: An Introduction

🔵 *Student Alert:* Elasticity measures the ***strength*** of your response to a change in a variable.

In many circumstances, it is not enough for an economist, policymaker, firm, or consumer to simply know the direction in which a variable will be moving. For example, if I am a producer, the law of demand tells me that if I increase the price of my good, the quantity demanded by consumers will decrease. The law of demand tells me the *direction* of the consumer response to the price change, but it does not tell me the *strength* of the consumer response. The law of demand doesn't tell me what will happen to my total revenue (the price of the good times the number of units sold). Whether total revenue increases or decreases depends on how responsive the quantity demanded is to the price change. Will total revenue increase or decrease by a little or a lot? Throughout the discipline of economics, in fact, the responsiveness of one variable to changes in another variable is an important piece of information. In general, *elasticity* is a measurement of how responsive one variable is to a change in another variable, *ceteris paribus* (holding all other variables constant).

Because elasticity measures responsiveness, changes in the variables are measured relative to some base or starting point. Each variable's change is measured as a percentage change. Consider the following elasticity measurements:

The price elasticity of demand, ε_d

$$\varepsilon_d = \frac{\text{percentage change in quantity demanded of Good X}}{\text{percentage change in price of Good X}}.$$

The income elasticity of demand, ε_I

$$\varepsilon_I = \frac{\text{percentage change in quantity demanded of Good X}}{\text{percentage change in income}}.$$

The cross-price elasticity of demand, ε_{CP}

$$\varepsilon_{CP} = \frac{\text{percentage change in quantity demanded of Good X}}{\text{percentage change in price of Good W}}.$$

The price elasticity of supply, ε_S

$$\varepsilon_S = \frac{\text{percentage change in quantity supplied of Good X}}{\text{percentage change in price of Good X}}.$$

Part A: Bonus Pay at Work

1. You have a job stocking items on the shelves at the local home improvement store. To increase productivity, your boss says a bonus will be paid based on how many items you put on the shelves each hour. Write the equation of the "elasticity of productivity" for this situation:

$$\varepsilon_{productivity} = \frac{percentage\ change\ in\ \textbf{number\ of\ items\ stocked}}{percentage\ change\ in\ \textbf{pay}}.$$

2. Assume your boss wants you to double your output, which would be a 100 percent increase in the number of items you shelve each hour. Underline the correct answer in each of these statements.

   (A) If your productivity is very responsive to a pay increase, then a given increase in your pay results in a large increase in your hourly output. In this case, your boss will need to increase the bonus pay by (*more than* / ***less than*** / *exactly*) 100 percent.

   (B) If your productivity is not very responsive to a pay increase, then a given increase in your pay results in a small increase in your hourly output. In this case, your boss will need to increase the bonus pay by (***more than*** / *less than* / *exactly*) 100 percent.

Part B: The Price Elasticity of Demand

It's easy to imagine that there are many applications for the elasticity concept. Here we will concentrate on the price elasticity of demand for goods and services. For convenience, the measure is repeated here:

$$\varepsilon_d = \frac{percentage\ change\ in\ quantity\ demanded\ of\ Good\ X}{percentage\ change\ in\ price\ of\ Good\ X}.$$

Note the following points:

■ Price elasticity of demand is always measured *along* a demand curve. When measuring the responsiveness of quantity demanded to a change in price, all other variables must be held constant.

■ Because of the law of demand, which states that price and quantity demanded move in opposite directions, when you calculate the value of the price elasticity of demand, expect it to be a negative number. When we interpret that value, we consider the absolute value of ε_d.

■ Along a linear, downward sloping demand curve, there are price ranges over which demand is elastic, unit elastic, and inelastic.

Table 2-3.1
Relationship between Changes in Quantity Demanded and Price

%ΔQd compared to %ΔP	Absolute value of ε_d	Interpretation
%ΔQd > %ΔP	> 1	Elastic
%ΔQd = %ΔP	= 1	Unit elastic
%ΔQd < %ΔP	< 1	Inelastic

Part C: Calculating the Arc Elasticity Coefficient

The arc elasticity calculation method is obtained when the midpoint or average price and quantity are used in the calculation. This is reflected in the formula below.

$$\varepsilon_d = \frac{\text{percentage change in quantity demanded}}{\text{percentage change in price}} = \frac{\left(\dfrac{Q_2 - Q_1}{(Q_2 + Q_1)/2}\right)}{\left(\dfrac{P_2 - P_1}{(P_2 + P_1)/2}\right)} = \frac{\left(\dfrac{\Delta Q}{(Q_2 + Q_1)/2}\right)}{\left(\dfrac{\Delta P}{(P_2 + P_1)/2}\right)}.$$

$$\varepsilon_d = \frac{\left(\dfrac{\text{the actual change in Q}}{\text{the average value of Q}}\right)}{\left(\dfrac{\text{the actual change in P}}{\text{the average value of P}}\right)}.$$

Suppose in Figure 2-3.1 that price is decreased from P_1 to P_2 and so quantity demanded increases from Q_1 to Q_2.

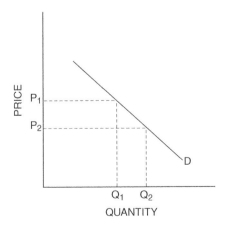
Figure 2-3.1
Calculating the Arc Elasticity Coefficient

Because price decreased, our calculations will show the percentage change in price is negative. Because quantity demanded increased, the percentage change in quantity demanded is positive. The ratio of the two percentage changes thus will have a negative value. When we interpret the calculated value of ε_d, we consider its absolute value in deciding whether demand over this price range is elastic, unit elastic, or inelastic. Note that we have used the average of the two prices and the two quantities. We have done this so that the elasticity measured will be the same whether we are moving from Q_1 to Q_2 or the other way around.

Part D: Coffee Problems

Suppose Moonbucks, a national coffee-house franchise, finally moves into the little town of Middleofnowhere. Moonbucks is the only supplier of coffee in town and faces the weekly demand schedule as shown in Table 2-3.2. Answer the questions that follow.

 Table 2-3.2

Cups of Coffee Demanded per Week

Price (per cup)	Quantity demanded	Price (per cup)	Quantity demanded
$10	0	$4	120
$9	20	$3	140
$8	40	$2	160
$7	60	$1	180
$6	80	$0	200
$5	100		

3. What is the arc price elasticity of demand when the price changes from $1 to $2? **−0.18**

$$\varepsilon_d = \frac{\left(\dfrac{(160-180)}{(160+180)/2}\right)}{\left(\dfrac{(\$2.00-\$1.00)}{(\$2.00+\$1.00)/2}\right)} = \frac{\dfrac{-20}{170}}{\dfrac{+\$1.00}{\$1.50}} = \frac{-11.8\%}{+66.7\%} = -0.18.$$

So, over this range of prices, demand is (*elastic* / *unit elastic* / ***inelastic***).

4. What is the arc price elasticity of demand when the price changes from $5 to $6? **−1.22**

$$\varepsilon_d = \frac{\left(\dfrac{(80-100)}{(80+100)/2}\right)}{\left(\dfrac{(\$6.00-\$5.00)}{(\$6.00+\$5.00)/2}\right)} = \frac{\dfrac{-20}{90}}{\dfrac{+\$1.00}{\$5.50}} = \frac{-22.2\%}{+18.2\%} = -1.22.$$

So, over this range of prices, demand is (***elastic*** / *unit elastic* / *inelastic*).

Advanced Placement Economics Microeconomics: Teacher Resource Manual © Council for Economic Education, New York, N.Y.

Part E: Comparing Slope and Price Elasticity of Demand

Now, consider Figure 2-3.2, which graphs the demand schedule given in Table 2-3.2.

Recall that the slope of a line is measured by the rise over the run: slope = rise / run = $\Delta P / \Delta Q$.

Figure 2-3.2
Elasticity of Demand for Coffee

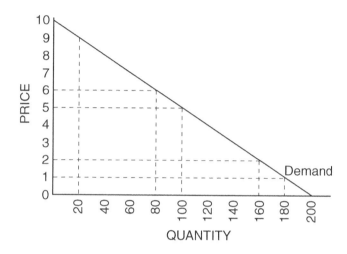

5. Using your calculations of ΔP and ΔQ from Question 3, calculate the slope of the demand curve between the prices of $1 and $2.

$$Slope = \frac{\Delta P}{\Delta Q} = \frac{\$2 - \$1}{160 - 180} = \frac{+\$1}{-20} = -0.05.$$

6. Using your calculations of ΔP and ΔQ from Question 4, calculate the slope of the demand curve between the prices of $5 and $6.

$$Slope = \frac{\Delta P}{\Delta Q} = \frac{\$6 - \$5}{80 - 100} = \frac{+\$1}{-20} = -0.05.$$

7. The law of demand tells us that an increase in price results in a decrease in the quantity demanded. Questions 5 and 6 remind us that the slope of a straight line is *constant everywhere along the line*. Anywhere along this demand curve, a change in price of $1 generates a change in quantity demanded of 20 cups of coffee a week.

You've now shown mathematically that while the slope of the demand curve is related to the price elasticity of demand, the two concepts are not the same thing. Briefly discuss the relationship between where you are along the demand curve and the price elasticity of demand. How does this tie into the notion of *responsiveness*?

The unit change in Q in response to a given dollar change in P will be the same all along a downward-sloping, straight-line demand curve because the curve has constant slope. You saw above that each $1 increase in P results in a 20-unit decrease in Q, no matter where you are on the demand curve. However, elasticity is quite different. How large a percentage change in P results from a $1 increase in P depends on where you are on the demand curve. If the initial P is a small value (like $1), *then a $1 increase is a larger percentage change in P. If the initial P is a large value (like $5), then a $1 increase is a smaller percentage change in P. The same is true for a 20-unit decrease in Q. If the initial Q is large (like 180), then you have a smaller percentage change in Q. But if the initial Q is small (like 100), then you have larger percentage change in Q. You will find that the value of ε_d varies all along the length of a downward-sloping, linear demand curve. At a high price, a given percentage change in P results in a larger percentage in Q. At a low price, that same percentage change in P results in a smaller percentage change in Q. If the demand curve is a downward-sloping straight line, the upper half of the demand curve is elastic, the lower half is inelastic, and the midpoint is unitary elastic.*

Part F: Two Extreme Cases of Price Elasticity of Demand

8. A horizontal demand curve is *perfectly elastic* because consumers will completely stop buying the good if the price is increased even by a small amount. This extreme case is shown by the demand curve facing a perfectly competitive firm. Such a firm can sell all it wants at the current market price (P_1), but if it raises its price it will lose all of its customers to other firms selling the same product at price P_1.

 Figure 2-3.3
Perfectly Elastic Demand

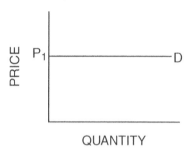

9. A vertical demand curve is *perfectly inelastic* because consumers want to buy the same amount (Q_1) of the good, no matter what the price. If the price increases, there is no response by consumers. This extreme case is approximated by the demand for a life-saving drug for which there are no acceptable substitutes.

 Figure 2-3.4
Perfectly Inelastic Demand

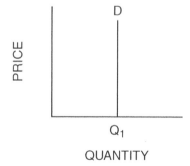

Part G: Other Types of Elasticities

While the concept of price elasticity of demand captures most of the attention, an economist can create a measure of the elasticity that exists between any two variables. Three other elasticities that merit examination are income elasticity of demand, cross-price elasticity of demand, and price elasticity of supply.

The *income elasticity of demand* shows how responsive consumers are to a change in their income.

$$\varepsilon_I = \frac{\text{percentage change in quantity demanded of Good X}}{\text{percentage change in income}}.$$

Table 2-3.3 shows how economists interpret the value of ε_I:

 Table 2-3.3

Income Elasticity of Demand

Value of ε_I	Interpretation
$\varepsilon_I > 0$	Good X is a normal (superior) good.
$\varepsilon_I < 0$	Good X is an inferior good.

A *normal good* is one for which income and demand move in the same direction. If income and demand move in opposite directions, the good is an *inferior good*.

10. Example: When income increases by 5 percent, the amount demanded of Tasty Cola increases by 3 percent and the amount demanded of Crusty Cola decreases by 2 percent. Answer these questions:

(A) The value of ε_I for Tasty Cola is __+0.6__.

$$\varepsilon_I = \frac{+3\%}{+5\%} = +0.6$$

(B) The value of ε_I for Crusty Cola is __−0.4__.

$$\varepsilon_I = \frac{-2\%}{+5\%} = -0.4$$

(C) Tasty Cola is considered a(n) (***normal*** / *inferior*) good.

(D) Crusty Cola is considered a(n) (*normal* / ***inferior***) good.

The *cross-price elasticity of demand* shows how responsive consumers of Good X are to a change in the price of some other good.

$$\varepsilon_{CP} = \frac{\text{percentage change in quantity demanded of Good X}}{\text{percentage change in price of Good W}}.$$

Table 2-3.4 shows how economists interpret the value of ε_{CP}:

 Table 2-3.4
Cross-Price Elasticity of Demand

Value of ε_{CP}	Interpretation
$\varepsilon_{CP} > 0$	X and W are substitute goods.
$\varepsilon_{CP} = 0$	X and W are unrelated goods.
$\varepsilon_{CP} < 0$	X and W are complementary goods.

Hamburgers and pizzas are *substitute goods*; if the price of pizza rises, the amount of hamburgers demanded also rises. Ice cream and ice cream cones are *complementary goods*; if the price of ice cream falls, the amount of cones demanded rises.

11. Example: When the price of Good W increases by 4 percent, the amount demanded of Good A increases by 3 percent, the amount demanded of Good B falls by 2 percent, and the amount demanded of Good C is unchanged. Answer these questions:

(A) The value of ε_{CP} between Good A and Good W is __+0.75__ .

$$\varepsilon_{CP} = \frac{+3\%}{+4\%} = +0.75$$

(B) The value of ε_{CP} between Good B and Good W is __−0.50__ .

$$\varepsilon_{CP} = \frac{-2\%}{+4\%} = -0.50$$

(C) The value of ε_{CP} between Good C and Good W is __+0.00__ .

$$\varepsilon_{CP} = \frac{+0\%}{+4\%} = +0.00$$

(D) Good A and Good W are (***substitute*** / *unrelated* / *complementary*) goods.

(E) Good B and Good W are (*substitute* / *unrelated* / ***complementary***) goods.

(F) Good C and Good W are (*substitute* / ***unrelated*** / *complementary*) goods.

The *price elasticity of supply* shows how responsive producers of Good X are to a change in the price of Good X. The law of supply tells us that the sign of ε_S will be positive because price and quantity supplied move in the same direction.

$$\varepsilon_S = \frac{\text{percentage change in quantity supplied of Good X}}{\text{percentage change in price of Good X}}.$$

Table 2-3.5 shows how economists interpret the value of ε_S:

 Table 2-3.5

Price Elasticity of Supply

Value of ε_S	Interpretation
$\varepsilon_S > 1$	Supply is elastic over this price range.
$\varepsilon_S = 1$	Supply is unit elastic over this price range.
$\varepsilon_S < 1$	Supply is inelastic over this price range.

12. Example: Assume the price of bookcases increases by 5 percent.

(A) If the quantity supplied of bookcases increases by 8 percent, the value of ε_S is   *+1.6* and the supply is (*__elastic__* / *unit elastic* / *inelastic*) over this price range.

$$\varepsilon_s = \frac{+8\%}{+5\%} = +1.6$$

(B) If the quantity supplied of bookcases increases by 5 percent, the value of ε_S is   *+1.0* and the supply is (*elastic* / *__unit elastic__* / *inelastic*) over this price range.

$$\varepsilon_s = \frac{+5\%}{+5\%} = +1.0$$

(C) If the quantity supplied of bookcases increases by 3 percent, the value of ε_S is   *+0.6* and the supply is (*elastic* / *unit elastic* / *__inelastic__*) over this price range.

$$\varepsilon_s = \frac{+3\%}{+5\%} = +0.6$$

The Determinants of Price Elasticity of Demand

Suppose we don't know the precise demand schedule for electricity and there is a 20 percent increase in the price of a kilowatt hour of electricity. We know that quantity demanded will decrease, but will it be by less than 20 percent (inelastic demand), exactly 20 percent (unit elastic demand), or more than 20 percent (elastic demand)? What factors influence the price elasticity of demand? (Remember, *ceteris paribus*!)

Part A: Presence of a Substitute Good or Service

Consider the following representative households in our market for electricity: Household A uses electricity for lighting, appliances, and heating. Household B uses electricity for lighting, appliances, and heating. It also has a heating system that can be switched to burn natural gas.

1. Household ___**B**___ will have the more elastic demand for electricity because of the presence of a ___**substitute**___ good.

2. Because Household A has no available substitutes, should we assume that the quantity demanded of electricity will remain unchanged given the increase in price?   ***No***

   Do you think Household A's response will be relatively more elastic or inelastic than that of Household B? ___***Inelastic***___

3. Rate the following items in terms of their price elasticity of demand. Put a 1 in front of the good with the most elastic demand, a 3 in front of the item with the least elastic demand, and a 2 in front of the other good. Explain your reasoning.

   ___**3**___ Demand for insulin

   ___**1**___ Demand for Granny Smith apples

   ___**2**___ Demand for running shoes

   Rationale:
   The smaller the number of substitute goods, the less elastic is the demand for that good. Insulin has no substitutes. There are more substitutes for Granny Smith apples than for running shoes because Granny Smith is a particular type of apple, and running shoes include all running shoes. This is why the demand for Granny Smith apples is most elastic.

4. To summarize: demand is (***more*** / less) elastic for goods with many available substitutes.

Part B: Proportion of Income Spent on a Good or Service

Consider the following representative households in the electricity market: Household A has income of $1,200 per month and spends $300 a month on electricity. Household B has income of $3,600 per month and spends $300 a month on electricity.

5. Household ___*A*___ will have the more elastic demand for electricity because the expenditures on this good account for a (*smaller* / ***larger***) proportion of its income.

6. Illustrate your understanding of price elasticity of demand by placing a 1, 2, or 3 by each item below, denoting the most elastic (1) to the least elastic (3). Explain your reasoning.

   ___*3*___ Demand for chewing gum

   ___*1*___ Demand for automobiles

   ___*2*___ Demand for clothing

   Rationale:
   Autos take the largest proportion of income, then clothing, then chewing gum.

7. To summarize: goods that command a (*small* / ***large***) proportion of a consumer's income tend to be more price elastic.

Part C: Nature of the Good or Service

We expect that the price elasticity of demand will also vary with the nature of the good being considered. Is it a necessity? Is it a durable good? Are we considering the short run or the long run? Consider the following alternatives, and choose the option that correctly completes each statement.

8. The price elasticity of demand for cigarettes: a product that is considered to be a necessity will have a relatively price (*elastic* / ***inelastic***) demand.

9. The price elasticity of demand for automobiles: in the short run, consumers can postpone the purchase of durable goods, and so the demand for such goods will be relatively (***more*** / *less*) price elastic.

10. Briefly summarize how the nature of the good—necessity, durable good, or luxury good—and the time frame over which demand is measured affect the price elasticity of demand for a good or a service.

    Demand is more inelastic for items that are necessities and more elastic for items that are durable or luxuries. The longer the time frame, the more elastic is the demand for a good or a service.

Part D: Income Elasticity of Demand

Now, suppose that prices in the market for electricity remain constant, but consumers' income increases by 30 percent. Even though we may not know the precise demand schedule, we are able to use the concept of income elasticity of demand to speculate about what will happen to demand.

Recall the income elasticity of demand, ε_I:

$$\varepsilon_I = \frac{\text{percentage change in quantity demanded}}{\text{percentage change in income}}.$$

Note in this case, income and quantity demanded are the relevant variables. All other variables, including the price of electricity, are held constant.

11. In measurements of income elasticity, if income and quantity demanded move in opposite directions—that is, if one increases while the other decreases—then the income elasticity coefficient will be (*positive* / ***negative***).

12. Remember that if income increases, the demand for a normal good increases and the demand for an inferior good decreases. If the good is a normal good, income elasticity will be (*negative* / ***positive***). If it is an inferior good, income elasticity will be (***negative*** / *positive*).

Elasticity and Total Revenue

The income a firm receives from selling its good or services is called its *total revenue*. It also can be thought of as total consumer expenditure on that good or service.

Total revenue (TR) = Price (P) × quantity demanded (Qd).

Since price and quantity demanded were involved in our discussion of price elasticity of demand, it makes sense that total revenue somehow is related to the demand elasticity of the good or service the firm is selling. How strongly quantity demanded responds to a change in price will determine whether that price change leads to an increase or decrease in the firm's total revenue.

The law of demand tells us that a price increase will result in a decrease in quantity demanded. By itself, the higher price increases total revenue because the firm gets a higher price for each unit sold. But total revenue also is decreased because the firm will sell fewer units at the higher price. What happens to total revenue when price increases is determined by whether the effect of the higher price dominates the effect of the lower quantity demanded. Knowing the price elasticity of demand allows us to answer this important question. Table 2-5.1 presents the "total revenue test" related to the price elasticity of demand.

 Table 2-5.1
Price Elasticity of Demand and Total Revenue

Category of price elasticity of demand	Relationship between price and total revenue
Elastic	P and TR move in opposite directions.
Inelastic	P and TR move in the same direction.
Unit elastic	TR is unaffected by a change in P.

1. Choose the correct answers in Table 2-5.2 to test your understanding of the "total revenue test."

 Table 2-5.2

Price Elasticity of Demand and Total Revenue

	%ΔP	%ΔQd	Over this price range, demand is:	As a result of the ΔP, TR will:
(A)	+5%	−2%	elastic / unit elastic / **inelastic**	**rise** / fall / not change
(B)	+5%	−5%	elastic / **unit elastic** / inelastic	rise / fall / **not change**
(C)	+5%	−8%	**elastic** / unit elastic / inelastic	rise / **fall** / not change
(D)	−4%	+6%	**elastic** / unit elastic / inelastic	**rise** / fall / not change
(E)	−4%	+3%	elastic / unit elastic / **inelastic**	rise / **fall** / not change
(F)	−4%	+4%	elastic / **unit elastic** / inelastic	rise / fall / **not change**

You can use the total revenue test to determine the nature of price elasticity of demand without using percentage change values or calculating the value of the price elasticity of demand. Suppose when the price of calculators is increased from $15 to $17, the quantity demanded decreases from 10 million to 6 million calculators.

2. Complete Table 2-5.3 by determining the value of TR before and after the price change, then answer the questions that follow.

 Table 2-5.3

Using Changes in TR to Identify Elasticity

	P	Qd	TR
(A) Old value	$15	10 million	**$150** million
(B) New value	$17	6 million	**$102** million

(C) How did TR change when P increased?

TR decreased when P increased over this price range.

(D) This indicates that demand over this price range is (***elastic*** / unit elastic / inelastic).

Note: The total revenue test in Table 2-5.1 is based on the price elasticity of demand. It is not related to the price elasticity of supply because if suppliers produce a lot more of their product when its price increases, that does not tell us how much of the product consumers are buying.

Excise Taxes

Table 2-6.1 and Figure 2-6.1 show the current supply of Greebes.

 Table 2-6.1
Supply Schedule of Greebes

Quantity (millions)	Supply price before tax (per Greebe)	Supply price after tax (per Greebe)
50	$0.10	*$0.25*
100	$0.15	*$0.30*
150	$0.20	*$0.35*
200	$0.25	*$0.40*
250	$0.30	*$0.45*
300	$0.35	*$0.50*

 Figure 2-6.1
Current Supply Schedule of Greebes

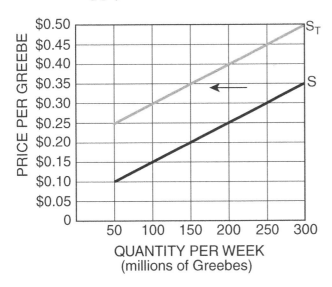

Now, suppose that in order to raise revenue for higher education, the government enacts an excise (sales) tax on sellers of $0.15 per Greebe. *This tax will result in a new supply curve for Greebes.* Since sellers will view this tax as an additional cost to them, there will be a decrease in supply. To determine where this new supply curve lies, reason as follows. Firms will try to pass the tax on to consumers through a higher price. If before the tax, firms were willing to supply 50 million Greebes at a price of $0.10, they would now be willing to supply 50 million Greebes only if the price were $0.25. (Remember: $0.15 of the price of each Greebe sold is now going to go to the government. So, if the price is $0.25 and the government is getting $0.15 of this price, then the seller is receiving the remaining $0.10.)

1. Fill in the blank spaces in Table 2-6.1. In Figure 2-6.1 draw the new supply curve that results from the tax. Label the new supply curve S_T.

What will be the result of this excise tax on the equilibrium quantity of Greebes? On the equilibrium price paid by buyers? On the equilibrium price received by sellers? On the tax revenue received by the government? On the revenue kept by sellers after they give the government its tax revenue?

The answers to these important questions will depend on the price elasticity of demand for Greebes. The next section of this activity will help you determine the effects of a $0.15 per unit excise tax on Greebes under four different demand conditions.

Part A: Relatively Elastic and Relatively Inelastic Demand

Compare the demand curves in Figures 2-6.2 and 2-6.3. Demand curve D_1 is relatively more inelastic than demand curve D_2. Put another way, D_2 is relatively more elastic than D_1.

Figure 2-6.2
Relatively Inelastic Demand for Greebes

Figure 2-6.3
Relatively Elastic Demand for Greebes

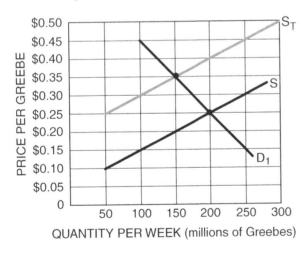

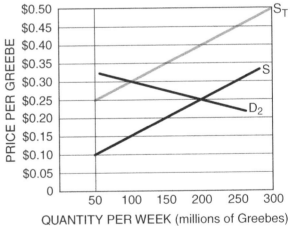

2. Complete Table 2-6.2, which compares conditions before the tax and after the tax based on demand curves D_1 and D_2. Remember, the government is placing a $0.15 per unit excise tax on the sellers of the good. You will need to add the new supply curve S_T to Figures 2-6.2 and 2-6.3.

Table 2-6.2

Comparing Effects of Tax Based on Price Elasticity of Demand

	Relatively inelastic demand D_1 Figure 2-6.2		Relatively elastic demand D_2 Figure 2-6.3	
	Before tax	After tax	Before tax	After tax
Equilibrium quantity	200 million	*150 million*	*200 million*	100 million
Equilibrium price	$0.25	*$0.35*	*$0.25*	$0.30
Total expenditure by consumers	*$50.0 million*	$52.5 million	$50.0 million	*$30.0 million*
Total revenue sellers get to keep	$50.0 million	*$30.0 million*	*$50.0 million*	$15.0 million
Total tax revenue to government	$0.0 million	*$22.5 million*	$0.0 million	*$15.0 million*

The incidence or burden of the excise tax refers to how the $0.15 per unit excise tax is shared between the buyers and the sellers. The incidence on the consumer is the increase in the equilibrium price resulting from the tax. The seller's incidence is that part of the tax not paid by consumers.

3. Under demand curve D_1, the incidence of the tax is ___*$0.10*___ per unit on consumers and ___*$0.05*___ per unit on sellers. Remember, these two values must add up to the per unit excise tax of $0.15.

4. Under demand curve D_2, the incidence of the tax is ___*$0.05*___ per unit on consumers and ___*$0.10*___ per unit on sellers. Remember, these two values must add up to the per unit excise tax of $0.15.

5. The incidence of the tax is greater on buyers if demand is relatively (***more*** / *less*) inelastic.

6. The incidence of the tax is greater on sellers if demand is relatively (*more* / ***less***) inelastic.

Part B: Perfectly Elastic and Perfectly Inelastic Demand

 Figure 2-6.4
Perfectly Inelastic Demand for Greebes

Figure 2-6.5
Perfectly Elastic Demand for Greebes

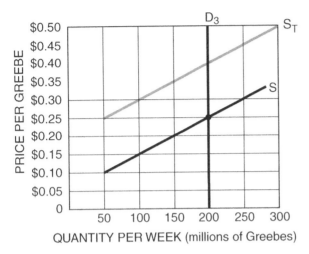

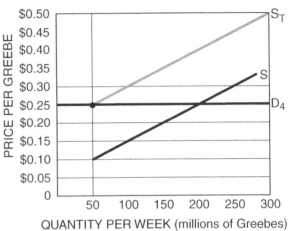

7. In the extreme cases of perfectly inelastic or perfectly elastic demand, the burden of the excise tax is not shared by consumers and sellers—one party will pay the entire tax. Compare Figures 2-6.4 and 2-6.5 and complete Table 2-6.3. Then answer the questions following the table. Remember, the government is placing a $0.15 per unit excise tax on the sellers of the good. You will need to add the new supply curve S_T to Figures 2-6.4 and 2-6.5.

 Table 2-6.3
Comparing Effects of Tax Based on Perfectly Inelastic or Perfectly Elastic Demand

	Perfectly inelastic demand D_3 Figure 2-6.4		Perfectly elastic demand D_4 Figure 2-6.5	
	Before tax	After tax	Before tax	After tax
Equilibrium quantity	200 million	*200 million*	*200 million*	50 million
Equilibrium price	$0.25	*$0.40*	*$0.25*	$0.25
Total expenditure by consumers	*$50.0 million*	$80.0 million	$50.0 million	*$12.5 million*
Total revenue sellers get to keep	$50.0 million	*$50.0 million*	*$50.0 million*	$5.0 million
Total tax revenue to government	$0.0 million	*$30.0 million*	$0.0 million	*$7.5 million*

8. Under demand curve D$_3$, the incidence of the tax is **$0.15** per unit on consumers and **$0.00** per unit on sellers. Remember, these two values must add up to the per unit excise tax of $0.15.

9. Under demand curve D$_4$, the incidence of the tax is **$0.00** per unit on consumers and **$0.15** per unit on sellers. Remember, these two values must add up to the per unit excise tax of $0.15.

10. The incidence of the tax is totally on buyers if demand is perfectly (*elastic* / ***inelastic***).

11. The incidence of the tax is totally on sellers if demand is perfectly (***elastic*** / *inelastic*).

Part C: Excise Tax Examples

12. A famous Supreme Court justice once said, "The power to tax is the power to destroy." This is more likely to be true regarding sellers if the demand for the product taxed is relatively (***elastic*** / *inelastic*).

13. If you were a government revenue agent interested in getting the most tax revenue possible, you would suggest putting excise taxes on goods whose demand is (*elastic* / *unit elastic* / ***inelastic***).

14. Think of some real-world goods on which the government places excise taxes: liquor, cigarettes, gasoline. Do you think that the demand for these goods is relatively elastic or relatively inelastic? How does this affect the amount of tax revenue the government receives from taxes on these goods? *The demand for these goods is relatively inelastic. No good substitutes are available for people who are heavily dependent on these goods. Because the demand for these goods is inelastic, taxes on them generate a lot of tax revenue for government.*

Maximum and Minimum Price Controls

Prices send signals and provide incentives to buyers and sellers. When supply or demand changes, market prices adjust, affecting incentives. High prices induce extra production while they discourage consumption.

In this exercise, we discover how the imposition of price controls (maximum or minimum prices) interrupts the process that matches production with consumption. *Price ceilings* (maximum prices) sometimes appear in the form of rent control, utility prices, and other caps on upward price pressure. *Price floors* (minimum prices) occur in the form of agricultural price supports and minimum wages.

When the government imposes price controls, citizens should understand that some people gain and some people lose from every policy change. By understanding the consequences of legal price regulations, citizens are able to weigh the costs and benefits of the change.

As a general rule, price floors create a *surplus* of goods or services, or *excess supply*, since the quantity demanded of goods is less than the quantity supplied. Conversely, price ceilings generate *excess quantity demanded*, causing *shortages*.

 Figure 2-7.1
Price Floors and Ceilings

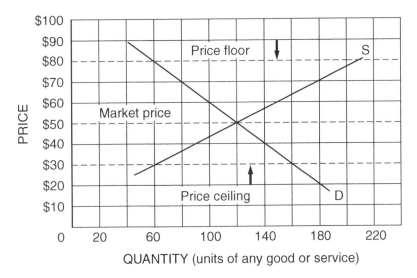

Price floors and ceilings can be plotted with supply and demand curves. Use Figure 2-7.1 to answer the questions.

1. What is the market price? __$50__

2. What quantity is demanded and what quantity is supplied at the market price?

   (A) Quantity demanded   *120 units*

   (B) Quantity supplied   *120 units*

3. What quantity is demanded and what quantity is supplied if the government passes a law requiring the price to be no higher than $30 (a price ceiling)?

   (A) Quantity demanded   *160 units*

   (B) Quantity supplied   *60 units*

   (C) There is a (***shortage*** / *surplus*) of   *100 units*   .

4. What quantity is demanded and what quantity is supplied if the government passes a law requiring the price to be no lower than $80 (a price floor)?

   (A) Quantity demanded   *60 units*

   (B) Quantity supplied   *210 units*

   (C) There is a (*shortage* / ***surplus***) of   *150 units*

   (D) What happens to total consumer surplus?   *Consumer surplus decreases.*

   (E) Is society better or worse off after the price floor is imposed?   *Society is worse off.*

   (F) Who gains from the price floor?   *Producers gain who are able to sell their product at the price floor.*

Property Rights and Market Failure

A key requirement of a well-functioning market economy is the establishment and enforcement of well-defined property rights. When individuals, rather than central governments, own the land and physical capital, many important economic incentives are created. When a person owns property, he or she has the right to use, sell, or trade with another person for mutual gain. For example, a homeowner has an incentive to keep that home in nice condition whether he wants to continue to live in the home or if he thinks that the home might eventually be sold. If the person living in that home doesn't own the home, he may not have a very strong incentive to keep the home in tip-top condition.

If the owner of a restaurant owns the capital used by the firm, she has a profit incentive to produce a high-quality product that is demanded by consumers. After all, if the firm is not profitable, the firm will go bankrupt and the owner's physical capital may be lost.

In the case of the homeowner and the restaurateur, property rights allow for the housing and restaurant markets to exist and to function reasonably well. This of course begs the question: what would happen to a market if property rights were not very well established or were absent altogether?

Many cities and towns are located along a river for two reasons: the river proved to be an excellent source of water for residential and industrial usage, and it was an excellent way of disposing of residential and industrial wastes. A river is an example of a nation's natural resources, but it is owned by nobody. As a result of the absence of property rights to the water (either for consumption or for disposal purposes), it tends to be overused and polluted. We can see this with another example of a negative externality.

Suppose that many chemical companies are located on the banks of the lovely Bohio River. The Bohio is a source of drinking water for many cities, it is a source of recreation for swimmers and boaters, a fishing industry exists on the Bohio, and the river serves a pivotal role in the ecosystem throughout the watershed.

Like all firms, these companies incur marginal production costs for each ton of chemicals that is produced. These marginal costs that accrue to the chemical companies are referred to as *marginal private costs* (*MPC*) of production and are assumed to increase as more tons of chemicals are produced. In fact, it is the marginal private cost curve that represents the market supply of chemicals. Suppose that the chemical companies can discharge toxic waste into the Bohio River, a common resource that is critical to everyone but owned by no one. This toxic waste requires cities to install additional water purification equipment, causes swimmers to develop skin rashes, hurts the profitability of the firms in the fishing industry, and threatens the viability of the ecosystem. These negative by-products of producing another ton of chemicals are additional *external costs* to society. When we add the marginal private cost to the external cost of producing chemicals, we get a higher dollar amount, the *marginal social cost* (*MSC*). Figure 2-8.1 shows both the MSC and MPC curves in the market for chemicals. The vertical distance between the two represents the external costs, or negative externality, imposed upon society because nobody owns the Bohio River.

The graph also shows the downward sloping *marginal social benefit* (*MSB*) curve that represents the demand for chemicals in this market. Assuming that all the benefits of the chemicals are received by the buyers of the chemicals, the demand curve also represents the *marginal private benefit* (*MPB*) curve.

1. The market for chemicals will ignore the external costs to society. Businesses seeking to maximize their total profit will produce the output level where their marginal private benefit equals their marginal private cost (MPB = MPC). In Figure 2-8.1, label the market equilibrium quantity of chemicals and the equilibrium price of chemicals as Q_M and P_M.
Because the market will ignore the external costs to society, the market equilibrium (Q_M and P_M) is at the intersection of the MPC (supply) and MPB (demand) curves.

Figure 2-8.1
The Market for Chemicals

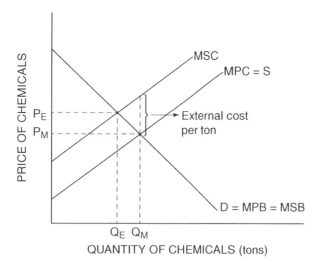

2. From society's perspective, the optimal or socially efficient output level of chemicals is the one where marginal social benefit equals marginal social cost (MSB = MSC). In the graph, label the socially efficient quantity of chemicals and socially efficient price of chemicals as Q_E and P_E.
The true costs to society of producing chemicals is reflected in the MSC curve so the socially efficient outcome (Q_E and P_E) is where the MSC curve intersects the MSB curve.

3. Which output level is greater: the one produced by firms in the market or the one desired by society? Does this indicate that the negative externality caused by pollution results in an over-allocation or an under-allocation of society's scarce resources to the chemical market? Explain.
The market output Q_M is greater than the socially efficient output Q_E. This outcome means that the negative externality creates an over-allocation of resources to the chemical market. Because the external costs are not recognized by the market, too many of society's scarce resources are allocated to chemical production. Economists would say that too many tons of chemicals are being produced in this competitive market.

4. What impact did the absence of property rights for the Bohio River have on the outcome of the chemical market?
The absence of property rights resulted in too many units of chemicals being produced from society's perspective. By responding only to private benefits and costs, the market allocated too many of society's scarce resources to the production of chemicals.

Deadweight Loss

When a market transaction is made between a buyer and a seller, both parties expect to benefit from that transaction: Buyers will receive consumer surplus, and sellers will receive producer surplus. If the market is competitive and free of externalities, the equilibrium price and quantity are such that the sum of consumer surplus and producer surplus (total surplus or total welfare) is maximized. There is no other outcome that can generate more total welfare than the competitive outcome. However, when something prevents the market from reaching that equilibrium outcome, total welfare falls, and the decline in total welfare is called *deadweight loss*. Deadweight loss really just represents the value of transactions that *could have* been made, but are not made. In the activities below you will see deadweight loss can emerge in a couple of different ways but common sources of deadweight loss include: price and quantity controls, excise taxes, monopoly power, and externalities.

Part A: The Market for Hamburgers

Table 2-9.1 shows the demand and supply schedules for hamburgers, a good that is currently exchanged in a competitive market. We can see that consumers have diminishing marginal benefit from hamburgers as more are consumed. We can also see that suppliers have increasing marginal cost of producing hamburgers as more are produced. Use the table to answer the questions that follow.

 Table 2-9.1
The Market for Hamburgers

Demand			Supply		
Quantity of hamburgers demanded	Marginal benefit from a hamburger	Consumer surplus (CS)	Quantity of hamburgers supplied	Marginal cost of a hamburger	Producer surplus (PS)
1	$10	$4	1	$2	*$4*
2	$9	*$3*	2	$3	$3
3	$8	*$2*	3	$4	*$2*
4	$7	*$1*	4	$5	*$1*
5	$6	*$0*	5	$6	*$0*
6	$5	−*$1*	6	$7	−*$1*
7	$4	−*$2*	7	$8	−*$2*
8	$3	−*$3*	8	$9	−*$3*
9	$2	−$4	9	$10	−*$4*
10	$1	−*$5*	10	$11	−$5

1. What is the equilibrium quantity of hamburgers exchanged in the market, and what is the equilibrium price in the market?
   Equilibrium quantity is where the diminishing marginal benefit (the demand curve) intersects the increasing marginal cost (the supply curve) and this occurs at the quantity of five hamburgers and a price of $6.

2. At the equilibrium quantity, complete the columns of consumer and producer surplus. Remember that each hamburger is sold at the equilibrium price.
   Consumer surplus (CS) is the difference between the marginal benefit of a hamburger to a consumer and the price the consumer paid for that hamburger. For the first hamburger, a consumer would have received $10 of marginal benefit but only had to pay $6 for it, leaving him with $4 of consumer surplus. Producer surplus (PS) is the difference between the price a seller receives for the hamburger and the marginal cost of producing it. For the first hamburger, a seller received $6 from the sale of the hamburger and it cost her $2 to produce it, creating $4 of producer surplus for her. The rest of the table is completed by making quick subtractions and using the equilibrium price of $6:
   CS = Marginal Benefit – Price Paid ($6).
   PS = Price Received ($6) – Marginal Cost.

3. What is the total welfare generated by the competitive equilibrium in the hamburger market?
   Total welfare (TW) is the sum of all consumer and producer surplus for the units that are bought and sold.

   $$TW = CS + PS = (\$4 + \$3 + \$2 + \$1 + \$0) + (\$4 + \$3 + \$2 + \$1 + \$0) = \$20.$$

4. Now suppose the government decides that too many hamburgers are being exchanged in the competitive market and requires that only three hamburgers be bought and sold at the equilibrium price found in Question 1. How does this regulation affect total welfare?
   If only three hamburgers can be bought and sold at the market price of $6, total welfare is

   $$TW = CS + PS = (\$4 + \$3 + \$2) + (\$4 + \$3 + \$2) = \$18.$$

   Since total welfare fell from $20 in the unregulated market to $18, a deadweight loss of $2 has been created. These dollars represent the unearned consumer and producer surplus from the fourth and fifth hamburgers that would have been exchanged in the absence of government intervention in the market.

Part B: The Market for Textbooks

This activity will use a little bit of algebra and graphical analysis to see how deadweight loss is created with a price ceiling.

Suppose that the market for textbooks can be described with the following demand and supply equations.

$$\text{Market Demand: } P = 300 - Q_d$$

$$\text{Market Supply: } P = 100 + Q_s$$

5. Sketch a graph of this market and solve for the equilibrium price and quantity.
   These equations give us straight lines for the demand and supply curves. The graph should show that the demand curve hits the vertical price axis at $300 and the supply curve has a price axis intercept at $100. The demand curve would hit the horizontal quantity axis at 300 units.

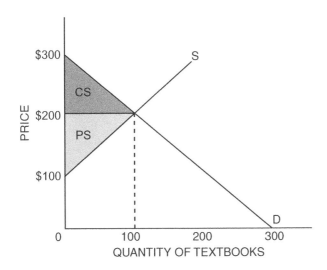

Figure 2-9.1
The Market for Textbooks

Market equilibrium is described in one of two ways: it is the only price where quantity demanded is equal to quantity supplied, or it is the only quantity where the buyer's price is equal to the seller's price. Using algebra, equilibrium is found by setting the following price equations equal to each other and solving for quantity (at equilibrium there is no distinction between Q_d and Q_s):
$300 - Q = 100 + Q$ $200 = 2Q$ $Q = 100$ units
   Equilibrium price is found by putting this quantity into either of the following equations:
Demand: $P = 300 - 100 = \$200$, or Supply: $P = 100 + 100 = \$200$.

6. Show the area of CS and PS in the graph.
   Because CS is the difference between the highest price a buyer would have paid and the price she actually paid, consumer surplus is the area below the demand curve and above the price for the 100 textbooks bought. Because PS is the difference between the price the seller received and the lowest price he would have accepted, producer surplus is the area above the supply curve and below the price for the 100 textbooks sold.

7. Compute the dollar value of CS and PS.
   The areas of CS and PS are the areas of the triangles equal to: ½ (base)(height).

$$CS = ½ (100 \text{ units})(\$100) = \$5,000.$$

$$PS = ½ (100 \text{ units})(\$100) = \$5,000.$$

Note: there is no rule that says that the areas of CS and PS must always be the same size. That result here is due to the specific equations given at the beginning of the exercise.

8. Now suppose a benevolent college president has decided that the price of textbooks is "too high" and successfully imposes a price ceiling of $150. Show the impact of a price ceiling in the graph.
A price ceiling is a maximum price set below the equilibrium price. This will create a permanent shortage of textbooks because, at the price ceiling, there are 150 textbooks demanded and only 50 supplied. The price ceiling (P_c) is illustrated in Figure 2-9.2.

Figure 2-9.2
Deadweight Loss of a Price Ceiling

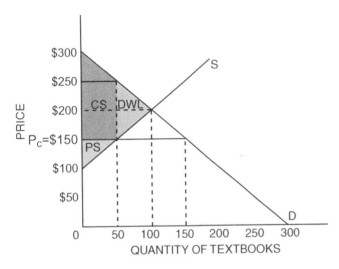

9. Recalculate the CS and PS and determine the amount of deadweight loss (DWL) that is created by this policy.
Rather than 100 textbooks being exchanged at a price of $200, there are now only 50 books being exchanged at a price of $150. The area of consumer surplus is still found below the demand curve and above the price, but it is no longer a triangle, it is a trapezoid (a triangle and a rectangle). The area of producer surplus is still a triangle, but a much smaller one than before.

CS = ½ (50 units)($50) + (50 units)($100) = $1,250 + $5,000 = $6,250.

PS = ½ (50 units)($50) = $1,250.

TW = CS + PS = $7,500.

Note: CS can also be found using the formula for the area of a trapezoid:

Area = height × [(sum of sides)/2] = 50 × [(150 + 100)/2] = $6,250.

Before the price ceiling, a total welfare of $10,000 was earned in the textbook market. With the price ceiling, only $7,500 was earned. The missing $2,500 is the deadweight loss. The deadweight loss emerges because there are 50 additional textbooks that could have been exchanged but the price control didn't allow it. Because those 50 textbooks could not be exchanged, the value of those mutually beneficial transactions between sellers and buyers goes unrealized. The area of DWL is also shown in Figure 2-9.2.

MICROECONOMICS

The Theory of the Firm

Unit 3

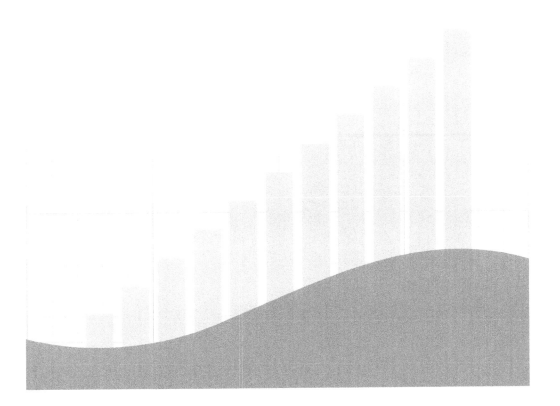

■ All firms have costs. It is important to be able to define and plot graphically these costs.

■ Explicit costs are monetary payments a firm must make to an outsider to obtain a resource.

■ Implicit costs are income a firm sacrifices when it employs a resource it owns to produce a product instead of selling the resource to someone else.

■ Total fixed costs do not change with a change in output. There are fixed costs only in the short run. The long run is defined as a period in which there are no fixed costs, and firms are free to allocate their resources as they please.

■ Total variable costs change with a change in output. Total costs equal total fixed costs plus total variable costs. Marginal cost is the additional cost of producing an additional unit of output. Marginal cost is very important in determining at what price and output a firm will operate.

■ Marginal cost eventually rises because of the law of diminishing marginal returns. The law of diminishing marginal returns is based on evidence that marginal product eventually declines when equal amounts of a variable factor of production are added to fixed factors of production.

■ Average total cost and average variable cost are total cost and total variable cost divided by output.

■ Average total cost and average variable cost fall when marginal cost is below them and rise when marginal cost is above them.

■ The marginal cost curve crosses the average variable cost curve and the average total cost curve at their lowest points.

■ If a firm has total revenue that just covers its total cost, it breaks even.

■ An economist views total cost as the sum of explicit cost and implicit cost.

■ If a firm has more total revenue than total costs, it makes a positive economic profit.

■ If a firm has more total costs than total revenue, it operates at an economic loss.

■ In the long run, a firm must cover all its implicit and explicit costs, including a normal rate of profit.

■ A normal profit represents the opportunity cost of an entrepreneur using her/his own resources in the firm. It is the return needed to keep those resources in their current use.

■ In the short run, a firm can operate at a loss as long as its total revenue covers its total variable costs.

■ Economic profits are profits over and above the normal rate of profit at which a firm just covers its total costs. A firm makes an accounting profit when its total revenue exceeds its explicit costs.

■ A firm makes an economic profit if its total revenue is greater than the sum of its explicit and implicit costs.

■ The objective of a firm is to maximize total economic profit or minimize loss.

■ Firms maximize total profit when they produce the level of output where marginal revenue equals marginal cost.

■ Perfect competition exists when there are many small producers and many small consumers of a homogeneous product.

■ For a perfectly competitive firm, marginal revenue is equal to price. A perfectly competitive firm produces where price equals marginal cost. A perfectly competitive firm breaks even in the long run and earns a normal profit.

■ Other things being constant, the most efficient allocation of resources occurs when a firm produces at the level of output where price is equal to marginal cost.

■ A monopoly occurs when one firm controls the market. It faces the market demand for the good or service it is selling.

■ Barriers to entry allow a monopoly to keep out competing firms and maintain a positive economic profit in the long run.

■ Allocative efficiency means a firm operates at the point where price equals marginal cost. Productive efficiency means a firm operates at the point where price equals the minimum value of average total cost.

■ A perfectly competitive firm is allocatively and productively efficient in the long run.

■ For a monopoly firm or any other firm under imperfect competition, marginal revenue is less than price.

■ A monopoly firm maximizes profits by producing at the quantity where marginal revenue equals marginal cost and by setting price according to the demand curve at that quantity.

■ A monopoly firm can make economic profits in the long run. However, a long-run economic profit is not guaranteed.

■ In the long run, a monopoly firm charges a higher price and produces at a lower output than a perfectly competitive market with the same cost curves.

■ A monopoly firm will operate where price is greater than marginal cost, causing it to produce too little of its good or service from society's perspective.

■ A monopoly is neither productively efficient nor allocatively efficient.

■ Oligopoly occurs when a few large firms control the market.

■ Monopolistic competition is close to pure or perfect competition except that there is product differentiation.

■ A monopolistically competitive firm will break even in the long run. It will be neither productively efficient nor allocatively efficient.

Different Types of Market Structures

Firms sell goods and services in an attempt to maximize their total economic profit. It is important to understand the nature of the four types of product markets in which a firm can sell its good or service. At one end of the spectrum is a perfectly competitive market in which there are many small firms selling the identical product. At the other end of the market spectrum is a monopoly in which only one firm supplies the product. In between these two market formats are monopolistic competition and oligopoly. Although all firms have the common goal of profit maximization, the characteristics of the product markets influence a firm's decisions about how much output to produce and what price to charge.

After you have learned about the four types of market structures, complete Table 3-1.1.

 Table 3-1.1
Market Structures

Characteristics			
Market structure	Number of firms	Differentiated or homogeneous product	Ease of entry
Perfect competition	*Very many*	*Homogeneous*	*Very easy*
Monopolistic competition	*Many*	*Differentiated*	*Relatively easy*
Oligopoly	*Few*	*Homogeneous or differentiated*	*Not easy*
Monopoly	*One*	*Only product of its kind (no close substitutes)*	*Impossible*

Results					
Market structure	Price-setting power	Nonprice competition	Allocative and productive efficiency in long run	Long-run profits	Examples
Perfect competition	*None (price taker)*	*None*	*Both*	*$0*	*None. Agriculture is close.*
Monopolistic competition	*Some*	*Considerable*	*Neither*	*$0*	*Fast food, retail sales, cosmetics*
Oligopoly	*Limited*	*Considerable for a differentiated oligopoly*	*Neither*	*Positive*	*Cars, steel, soft drinks, computers*
Monopoly	*Absolute (price maker)*	*Some*	*Neither*	*Positive, possibly high*	*Small-town newspaper, rural gas station*

Mirror Images: Marginal Product and Marginal Cost

Most of the activities in this unit concern a firm's costs of production. You will learn about a firm's costs of producing a given amount of its product—*total fixed cost (TFC)*, *total variable cost (TVC)*, and *total cost (TC)*. You also will work with the firm's costs of a typical (average) unit of output—*average fixed cost (AFC)*, *average variable cost (AVC)*, and *average total cost (ATC)*. The most important measure of a firm's cost is *marginal cost (MC)* because it shows the change in the firm's total cost when it produces one more unit of output. You will not be surprised to find that the cost of producing output is based on the productivity of the firm. If a firm is highly productive, that means it is producing a lot of output from a given amount of resources, thus reducing its costs of production. Firms that are inefficient will have high production costs and be at a competitive disadvantage. Because high productivity implies low cost, economists treat a firm's cost measures as mirror images of its productivity measures.

A firm makes production decisions in two time horizons. The "short run" is a period of time in which the amount of some key factor of production, often capital, is fixed. Other factors, such as labor, are variable because the firm can increase or decrease the amount of these resources in the short run. In the "long run," all resources are variable and can be increased or decreased by the firm.

There are three measures of the productivity of a firm.

1. The firm's *total physical product* or *total output* (Q) is how many units of its good or service the firm produces in a specified period of time. If a firm produces 100 units per week, we express this as Q = 100.

2. The firm's *average physical product* (APP) shows how many units of output are produced by an average unit of labor (the variable resource). If the firm uses five units of labor (L) to produce 100 units of output each week, we say APP = Q/L = 100/5 = 20 units of output.

3. The firm's *marginal physical product* (MPP) tells us the change in total product when the firm adds an extra unit of labor to its fixed stock of capital. If, as a result of adding a sixth unit of labor, the firm's total output increases from 100 units to 114 units, then the MPP of the sixth labor unit is +14 units: MPP = $\Delta Q / \Delta L$ = +14/+1 = +14.

❗ *Student Alert*: The terms *average physical product* and *average product* mean the same thing. Also, *marginal physical product* is the same as *marginal product*. Some textbooks use APP and MPP, while others use AP and MP. But you cannot use "average" terms interchangeably with "marginal" terms!

The key productivity principle in the short run is the "law of diminishing marginal productivity" (also called the law of diminishing marginal returns). Assume a firm operates in the short run with a fixed amount of capital and with labor as its variable resource. The law of diminishing marginal productivity states that as the firm adds more labor units to its fixed stock of capital, eventually the MPP from an extra unit of labor will diminish.

Part A: The Productivity Measures of a Firm

Table 3-2.1 is a short-run production chart showing how the productivity of the firm changes as it adds additional units of labor to its fixed stock of capital. Assume the data refer to the firm's productivity in a one-week period.

1. Complete Table 3-2.1. Some data are already included in the chart. Put the values of MPP at the new labor level. For example, when the firm increases its labor from one to two units per week, its total output increases by 15 units. Write "+15" at L = 2 in the MPP column.

 Table 3-2.1

The Three Productivity Measures of a Firm

L	Q	MPP = ΔQ/ΔL	APP = Q/L
0	0	–	–
1	10	*+10*	10.0
2	25	+15	*12.5*
3	36	*+11*	*12.0*
4	46	*+10*	11.5
5	55	+9	*11.0*
6	63	*+8*	*10.5*
7	63	*+0*	9.0
8	60	–3	*7.5*

2. When you have completed Table 3-2.1, plot the L and Q data in Figure 3-2.1. (The first two combinations are plotted for you already.) This Q curve shows how much total output the firm produces with different amounts of labor. Note that the firm's total product increases as it adds more labor, but eventually the total product declines if the firm adds too many labor units on its limited amount of equipment.

 Figure 3-2.1
Total Product

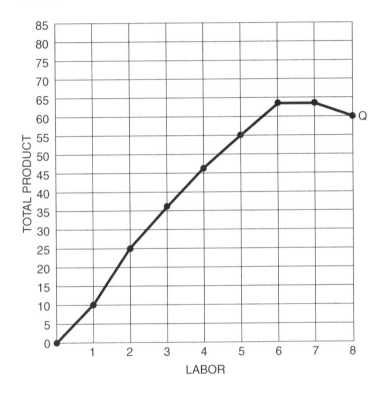

3. Now plot the L, MPP, and APP data in Figure 3-2.2. You can connect the MPP points with a solid line and the APP points with a dotted line. (Some combinations are plotted for you already.) Plot the values of MPP at the new labor level. For example, put a dot on the graph at the combination of L = 2 and MPP = +15 since the MPP resulting from adding the second labor unit is 15 units of output. Note that both MPP and APP increase initially but then decrease as the firm adds more units of labor.

 Figure 3-2.2

Marginal Physical Product and Average Physical Product

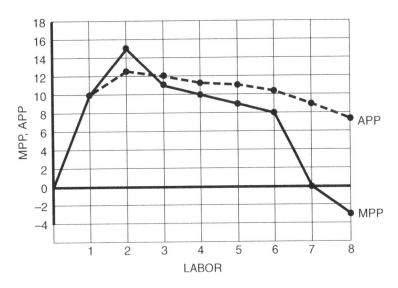

4. Diminishing marginal productivity sets in with the addition of the __*third*__ labor unit.

5. The average physical product continues to increase as long as the marginal physical product is (**_greater than_** / *equal to* / *less than*) the average physical product.

6. Can the average physical product of labor be negative? Why?
   APP cannot be negative because it is the ratio Q/L and neither Q nor L can be negative.

7. Can the marginal physical product of labor be negative? Why?
   Yes, because MPP shows the change in Q when an extra labor unit is added. If Q decreases when labor is increased, then MPP will be negative.

8. Total product increases as the firm adds units of labor as long as the marginal physical product is (***positive*** / *zero* / *negative*).

9. Although our graphs have no information about the price of the good or the price of labor, we can conclude that the firm will not want to hire a unit of labor for which marginal physical product is (*diminishing* / ***negative***). Explain your answer.
   As long as MPP is positive, Q is increasing. This is true even if MPP is diminishing. It is possible that the extra unit of labor adds more to the firm's total revenue than to its total cost. But if MPP is negative, that means Q decreased when an extra unit of labor was hired. A firm will not want to pay for an extra worker if its total output decreases; its total profit will decrease if it does.

10. What is the relationship between marginal physical product and total product?
    The relationship between MPP and Q can be expressed as follows:

    (1) If MPP is positive, Q will increase.

    (2) If MPP is zero, Q will not change as Q is at its maximum value.

    (3) If MPP is negative, Q will decrease.

11. What is the relationship between marginal physical product and average physical product?
    The relationship between MPP and APP can be expressed as follows:

    (1) If MPP is greater than APP, APP will increase.

    (2) If MPP is equal to APP, APP will not change as APP is at its maximum value.

    (3) If MPP is less than APP, APP will decrease.

Part B: Productivity and Cost: A Mirror View of Each Other

As you work with productivity and cost graphs, note how the axes are labeled. The productivity graphs typically have L on the horizontal axis because that is the variable resource that the firm changes in order to alter its level of total output. The vertical axis has some measure of productivity (such as Q or APP). There are no dollar signs on a productivity graph because such graphs are not dealing with revenue or cost. The cost graphs always have total output or total physical product (Q) on the horizontal axis because costs are expressed in relation to the Q of the firm. Cost graphs always have a dollar-measured concept on the vertical axis (such as total cost [TC]or marginal cost [MC]).

Figure 3-2.3 shows the relationship between a firm's MPP and APP. The graph assumes MPP initially increases as the firm adds labor units due to specialization of labor on the firm's equipment. Eventually diminishing marginal productivity sets in, which means that at some point APP also will decline as more labor units are added.

Figure 3-2.3

Marginal Physical Product and Average Physical Product

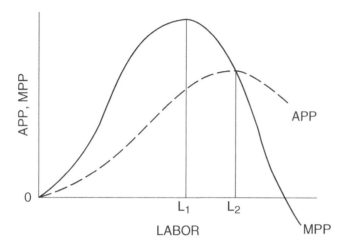

12. Diminishing marginal productivity sets in at ($\underline{L_1}$ / L_2) labor units.

13. APP increases as long as MPP is (***greater than*** / *equal to* / *less than*) APP.

14. APP decreases as long as MPP is (*greater than* / *equal to* / ***less than***) APP.

15. Why is APP maximized at L_2 labor units?
    APP is maximized at L_2 labor units because that is where MPP = APP. Before that quantity of labor, MPP is greater than APP so APP is increasing. Beyond that quantity of labor, MPP is less than APP so APP is decreasing.

16. "If MPP is diminishing, then APP must also be diminishing." Is this a correct statement? Why?
    This is an incorrect statement. There is a range of labor of units for which MPP is diminishing but APP is increasing because MPP is still greater than APP. In Figure 3-2.3, this is between L_1 and L_2 labor units.

Figure 3-2.4 shows the relationship between a firm's MC and AVC: AVC = TVC/Q. If the firm has L as its only variable resource, then AVC represents the labor cost per unit of output. Suppose a firm pays each of its 10 workers a daily wage of $80 and produces a Q of 400 units. Its TVC is $800 = (10)($80), and its AVC is $2 = $800/400. Each of its 400 units has a labor cost component of $2.

Figure 3-2.4
Marginal Cost and Average Variable Cost

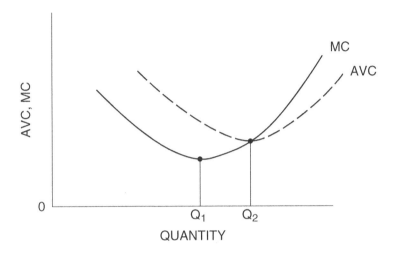

17. AVC decreases as long as MC is (*greater than / equal to / **less than***) AVC.

18. AVC increases as long as MC is (***greater than*** */ equal to / less than*) AVC.

19. Why is AVC minimized at Q_2 units of output?
    AVC is minimized at Q_2 units because that is where MC = AVC. Before that quantity of output, MC is less than AVC so AVC is decreasing. Beyond that quantity of output, MC is greater than AVC so AVC is increasing.

20. "If MC is increasing, then AVC must also be increasing." Is this a correct statement? Why?
    This is an incorrect statement. There is a range of output units for which MC is increasing but AVC is decreasing because MC is still less than AVC. In Figure 3-2.4, this is between Q_1 and Q_2 output units.

Figure 3-2.5

Mirror Image of Productivity and Cost Measures

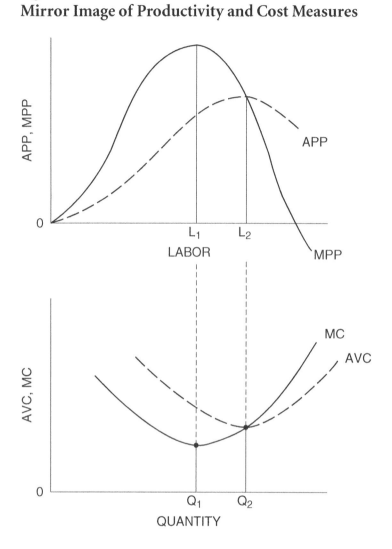

The productivity of a firm is the basis of its cost. A firm wants to be highly productive in order to keep its costs low. Refer to Figure 3-2.5 to answer the following questions based on a firm's productivity and cost measures. Assume outputs Q_1 and Q_2 are produced by this firm when it uses L_1 and L_2 labor units, respectively.

21. As long as the MPP of labor is increasing, the MC of producing extra units of output will (*increase* / *not change* / ***decrease***).

22. As long as the MPP of labor is decreasing, the MC of producing extra units of output will (**increase** / *not change* / *decrease*).

23. The MC of producing extra units of output will be minimized when the MPP of labor is **maximized at L_1 labor units and Q_1 output units.**

24. As long as the APP of labor is increasing, the AVC of producing output will (*increase* / *not change* / **decrease**).

25. As long as the APP of labor is decreasing, the AVC of producing output will (**increase** / *not change* / *decrease*).

26. The AVC of producing output will be minimized when the APP of labor is **maximized at L_2 labor units and Q_2 output units.**

Understanding the Different Cost Measures of a Firm

Part A: Different Meanings of the Word "Profit"

Economists assume the goal of a firm is to maximize its total profit. This sounds like an easy goal to understand, but the economist's view of profit is different from that of an accountant. Let's use a short story about Pat to illustrate the differences. First, we must define two categories of cost. An *explicit cost* is an expenditure by the firm; it could be a payment for items such as wages, rent, or advertising. An *implicit cost* is the opportunity cost of an entrepreneur using his/her own resource in the company.

An economic short story: Pat is a banker who earned an annual salary of $50,000 last year. She invested a total of $100,000 of her own money in various savings assets, which gave her interest income of $6,000. Pat also owns a small building, which she leased to someone last year for $14,000. But now Pat decides she wants to leave banking and set up her own landscaping company. Rather than borrowing money to buy new equipment, she uses her $100,000 in savings to buy it. She also decides to stop leasing her building so she can use it for her new enterprise. In her first year of landscaping, Pat brings in total revenue of $300,000. She spends $220,000 for such things as her equipment, workers, supplies, and insurance.

1. An accountant defines total profit to be total revenue minus explicit costs. Pat's *accounting profit* from her landscaping company is $**80,000** this year.

   Accounting profit = total revenue – explicit costs = $300,000 – $220,000 = $80,000.

2. In addition to explicit costs, an economist considers implicit costs as well. This year, Pat's *economic profit* from her landscaping business is $**10,000**.

   Economic profit = total revenue – (explicit costs + implicit costs)

   $$= \$300,000 - (\$220,000 + \$50,000 + \$6,000 + \$14,000)$$

   $$= \$300,000 - \$290,000 = \$10,000.$$

3. Another type of profit is called *normal profit*. It recognizes that Pat should "pay herself" for using her resources in her own company. Her normal profit, which is equal to her implicit costs, indicates the income Pat's resources would have earned had they been used in their best alternative occupations. Pat's normal profit is $**70,000**.

   Normal profit = $50,000 + $6,000 + $14,000 = $70,000.

4. If Pat's total revenue from her landscaping business is only $280,000, what would be the values of the different measures of profit?

   (A) Accounting profit = $**60,000** *(Accounting profit = $280,000 – $220,000.)*

   (B) Economic profit = $**–10,000** *(Economic profit = $280,000 – $290,000.)*

   (C) Normal profit = $**70,000**

Part B: The Seven Measures of a Firm's Short-Run Costs

The Morton Boat Company produces the very popular Jazzy Johnboat, which is desired by many fishermen and fisherwomen. Assume the firm operates in the short run with a fixed amount of equipment (capital) and views labor as its only variable resource. If it wants to produce more output, it will add more units of labor to its stock of equipment. Of course, the firm will have to pay its workers and also the owners of its capital, which means its total cost will increase as it produces more boats. Table 3-3.1 defines the seven cost measures the Morton Boat Company must consider.

 Table 3-3.1

The Seven Short-Run Cost Measures of a Firm

Cost measure	What it means	How to calculate it
Total fixed cost (TFC)	All costs that do not change when output changes. TFC is a constant amount at all Q levels.	TFC = total cost of all fixed factors of production TFC = Q × AFC
Total variable cost (TVC)	All costs that do change when output changes. TVC gets bigger as Q increases because the firm needs more labor to make more output.	TVC = total cost of all variable factors of production TVC = Q × AVC
Total cost (TC)	All costs at a given output level. TC is the sum of TFC and TVC. TC increases as the level of output increases.	TC = TFC + TVC TC = Q × ATC
Average fixed cost (AFC)	Fixed cost (capital cost) per unit of output. AFC always falls as Q rises since TFC is a constant value.	AFC = TFC/Q
Average variable cost (AVC)	Variable cost (labor cost) per unit of output. AVC falls at first, and then rises as Q increases.	AVC = TVC/Q
Average total cost (ATC)	Total cost per unit of output. It is the sum of AFC and AVC. ATC falls at first, and then rises as Q increases.	ATC = TC/Q ATC = AFC + AVC
Marginal cost (MC)	Change in the firm's TC when it produces another unit of output. Also shows change in TVC from an extra unit of output. MC falls at first, and then rises as Q increases.	MC = ΔTC/ΔQ MC = ΔTVC/ΔQ because the only part of TC that changes when more Q is produced is TVC.

Reminder: The AVC curve is U-shaped (falls, then rises as Q increases) because its shape is the mirror image of the APP curve as shown in Activity 3-2. The MC curve also is U-shaped because it is the mirror image of the MPP curve. Refer back to Figure 3-2.5.

Table 3-3.2 is the cost spreadsheet for the Morton Boat Company. It has information on all seven short-run cost measures based on different Q levels of the firm.

5. Complete Table 3-3.2. Some of the data have been posted for you already.

Table 3-3.2

The Seven Short-Run Cost Measures of the Morton Boat Company (daily data)

Q boats per day	(1) TFC	(2) TVC	(3) TC = TFC + TVC	(4) AFC = TFC/Q	(5) AVC = TVC/Q	(6) ATC = TC/Q = AFC + AVC	(7) MC = ΔTC/ΔQ = ΔTVC/ΔQ
0	*$300*	*$0*	*$300*	–	–	–	–
1	$300	*$700*	$1,000	*$300*	*$700*	*$1,000*	*$700*
2	*$300*	*$1,300*	*$1,600*	*$150*	$650	*$800*	$600
3	*$300*	$1,800	*$2,100*	*$100*	*$600*	*$700*	*$500*
4	*$300*	*$2,400*	*$2,700*	$75	*$600*	*$675*	$600
5	$300	*$3,100*	*$3,400*	*$60*	$620	$680	*$700*
6	*$300*	*$3,840*	*$4,140*	*$50*	*$640*	*$690*	$740

6. What trend do you observe in the value of TFC as the level of Q is increased? How do you explain this trend?
   TFC does not change as Q increases. TFC represents costs that do not depend on Q.

7. What trend do you observe in the value of TVC as the level of Q is increased? How do you explain this trend?
   TVC increases as Q increases. TVC represents costs of variable resources such as labor. Because the firm must add more variable resources to produce more output, TVC increases as Q increases. The changing slope of TVC reflects increasing marginal productivity (the slope of the TVC curve deceases) and diminishing marginal productivity (the slope of the TVC curve increases) of the variable resources.

8. Compare the ATC value at any Q level with the MC value at the next Q level. What relationship do you see between ATC and MC?
   The relationship between ATC and MC can be expressed as follows:

   (1) If MC is greater than ATC, then ATC will increase.

   (2) If MC is equal to ATC, then ATC does not change and is at its minimum value.

   (3) If MC is less than ATC, then ATC will decrease.

9. Compare the AVC value at any Q level with the MC value at the next Q level. What relationship do you see between AVC and MC?

The relationship between AVC and MC can be expressed as follows:

(1) If MC is greater than AVC, then AVC will increase.

(2) If MC is equal to AVC, then AVC does not change and is at its minimum value.

(3) If MC is less than AVC, then AVC will decrease.

10. Compare the AFC value at any Q level with the MC value at the next Q level. What relationship do you see between AFC and MC?

Because TFC does not change as Q increases, AFC always decreases as Q increases. There is no relationship between AFC and MC.

Part C: Graphing the Cost Functions of a Firm

The relationships that exist among the firm's cost functions can be illustrated by plotting the data in Table 3-3.1 in cost graphs. Figure 3-3.1 is the "total" cost graph because it contains information about the firm's TC, TVC, and TFC functions. Figure 3-3.2 is the "marginal-average" cost graph because it shows the data for the firm's MC, ATC, AVC, and AFC functions.

11. Plot the data from Table 3-3.1 in the appropriate graphs. Two observations of TC and AVC have already been plotted for you.

12. Plot the values of MC at the new output level. For example, put a dot on the graph at the combination of Q = 4 and MC = $600 since the MC resulting from producing the fourth boat is $600. Connect the MC dots in your graph with a dotted line.

Figure 3-3.1
The Firm's "Total" Cost Graph

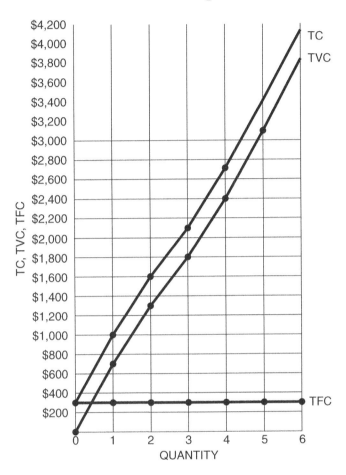

13. Why is the vertical gap between the TC and TVC curves the same at all Q levels?
    That vertical gap is TFC, which has the same value at all Q levels.

14. The slope of the TC curve can be expressed as rise/run = $\Delta TC/\Delta Q$. Do you know another cost function that is found using the ratio $\Delta TC/\Delta Q$?
    The slope of the TC curve is equal to MC.

15. Why do both the TC and TVC curves keep climbing higher and higher as the Morton Boat
Company increases the number of boats it produces?
To produce more output, the firm must add more variable resources which means TVC increases
as Q increases. Since TC = TVC + TFC, this means TC also increases as Q increases.

16. Why does the TC curve not begin at the origin?
When the firm produces no output, it still has TFC. The TC curve intersects the vertical axis at
the level of TFC.

Figure 3-3.2
The Firm's "Marginal-Average" Cost Graph

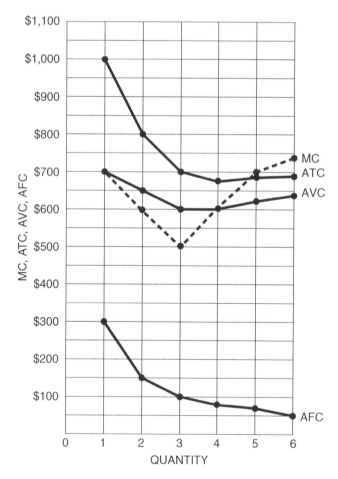

17. AVC continues to decrease as long as MC is (*greater than* / *equal to* / ***less than***) AVC.

18. AVC continues to increase as long as MC is (***greater than*** / *equal to* / *less than*) AVC.

19. ATC continues to decrease as long as MC is (*greater than* / *equal to* / ***less than***) ATC.

20. ATC continues to increase as long as MC is (***greater than*** / *equal to* / *less than*) ATC.

21. Mr. Burpin, your AP teacher, asks you to explain the following statement: "Average fixed cost falls as long as marginal cost is less than average fixed cost." What is your response?
    AFC is not affected by whether MC is greater than or less than AFC. AFC always decreases as the firm produces more output.

22. Do you agree with the following statement? "Average variable cost is minimized at the output level where marginal cost is equal to average variable cost." Explain.
    Yes. When MC is below AVC, AVC decreases. When MC is above AVC, AVC increases. When MC is equal to AVC, AVC is at its minimum value.

23. What do you say to someone who says, "Fixed cost is the same at all output levels"?
    I would tell that person to be accurate when referring to fixed cost. TFC is the same at all output levels, but AFC decreases as Q increases.

24. Can you tell from Table 3-3.1 how many boats the Morton Boat Company should produce to maximize its total profit? Explain.
    No. We have no information about the revenue the firm receives from the sale of its boats. We will need revenue and cost data to determine the profit-maximizing number of boats.

A Firm's Long-Run Average Total Cost Curve

The cost curves that we used in previous activities were the short-run cost curves of a firm. In the short run, a firm can vary its output by changing its variable resources, but it cannot change its plant capacity. In this activity we turn to the long run, defined as a time period in which all resources, including plant capacity, can be changed. In the short run, the shapes of the firm's average total cost (ATC) and marginal cost (MC) curves result from the principle of diminishing marginal productivity of resources. In the long run, the shape of the firm's long-run average total cost (LRATC) curve results from *economies of scale* and *diseconomies of scale*. Economies of scale explain why the firm's ATC decreases as it expands its scale of operations. Sources of economies of scale include specialization of resources, more efficient use of equipment, a reduction in per-unit costs of factor inputs, an effective use of production by-products, and an increase in shared facilities. Diseconomies of scale explain why the firm's ATC can increase as it increases its level of production. Sources of diseconomies of scale include limitations on effective management decision making and competition for factor inputs.

Part A: A Firm's Long-Run Average Total Cost Curve

A firm's LRATC curve shows the lowest ATC at which a firm can produce different levels of output when all inputs are variable. The LRATC is derived from a set of the firm's short-run average total cost (SRATC) curves. Figure 3-4.1 shows four SRATC curves for the Goodman Company, which is considering which of four different plant sizes it should use to produce various levels of output. Each SRATC curve represents the ATC of the firm as it produces output in the short run with a fixed plant size. As the firm increases its level of output, at some point it will need to increase its plant size. As it does so, we see that its SRATC falls as it moves from Plant Size 1 to Plant Size 2, and it falls again as it moves to Plant Size 3. As it moves to the larger Plant Size 4 to produce even larger output levels, its SRATC curve shifts upward. Note that the graph shows four SRATC curves of one firm, not one SRATC for each of four different firms.

Figure 3-4.1
A Firm's Long-Run Average Total Cost Curve

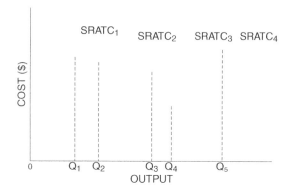

1. What does each of the SRATC curves represent?
   Each SRATC represents the firm's short-run ATC based on a given plant size. Decisions made by the firm when it has a fixed plant size are short-run decisions. When all inputs, including plant size, are variable, the firm is making long-run decisions.

2. At what output level in the long run will the firm minimize its ATC? Does this mean the firm will maximize its total profit if it produces this output level? Why?
   Q_4 *is the output that will minimize the firm's average total cost in the long-run. Since we have no information about the firm's revenue, we cannot determine its profit-maximizing Q level.*

3. The Goodman Company can produce output Q_1 with either Plant Size 1 or Plant Size 2. If the demand facing the firm is for this level of output, which plant size should the firm use? Why?
   It should produce Q_1 with Plant Size 1 since the ATC of that output is less with Plant Size 1 than with Plant Size 2.

4. As the long-run demand for the company's product increases, it must decide which plant size is best as it tries to produce an output level at the lowest possible ATC. In the following chart, circle the firm's best plant size for these output levels.

Output level	Optimal plant size
Q_1	(1) 2 3 4
Q_2	1 (2) 3 4
Q_3	1 2 (3) 4
Q_5	1 2 3 (4)

5. Since the LRATC curve shows the lowest ATC at which different output levels can be produced, we can show it on Figure 3-4.1. Mark heavily the portions of each SRATC curve that will minimize the firm's ATC as the firm increases it scale of production. Label this heavily shaded curve as "LRATC."

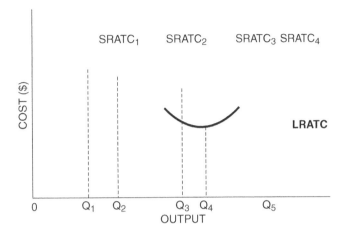

Part B: Economies and Diseconomies of Scale

The opening section of this activity explained the concepts of economies and diseconomies of scale. They explain why the firm's LRATC curve slopes downward and then upward as the firm increases the scale of its production.

6. In Figure 3-4.1, as the firm increases its level of output from 0 to Q_4, it is experiencing (***economies of scale*** / *diseconomies of scale*).

7. As the firm increases its production level beyond Q_4, it is experiencing (*economies of scale* / ***diseconomies of scale***).

Part C: Returns to Scale

There are three concepts that are special cases of economies and diseconomies of scale where a firm increases all its inputs by the same percentage. A firm has *increasing returns to scale* if a proportionate increase in all resources results in an increase in output that is larger than the increase in resources. For example, if a firm increases all of its resources by 10 percent, and output increases by 14 percent, the firm experiences increasing returns to scale. *Decreasing returns to scale* are present if the increase in output is less than the proportionate increase in all resources. If output increases by only 7 percent when all inputs are increased by 10 percent, the firm has decreasing returns to scale. If output increases by the same proportion as all inputs were increased, the firm has *constant returns to scale*.

If we know the nature of the firm's returns to scale, we can determine what happens to the firm's ATC in the long run when it increases all resources by the same proportion. Since ATC = TC/Q, whether the firm's ATC increases, decreases, or stays the same depends on the resulting increase in output.

8. Assume the Goodman Company increases all of its inputs by 15 percent.

   (A) Its total cost will increase by (*more than* / ***exactly*** / *less than*) 15 percent.
     If all inputs are increased by 15 percent, then its expenditures on all inputs also will increase by 15 percent.

   (B) If it has increasing returns to scale, its output will increase by (***more than*** / *exactly* / *less than*) 15 percent, and its ATC will (*increase* / *not change* / ***decrease***).
     Since Q is increasing by more than 15 percent while TC increases by 15 percent, the firm's ATC will decrease if it has increasing returns to scale.

   (C) If it has decreasing returns to scale, its output will increase by (*more than* / *exactly* / ***less than***) 15 percent, and its ATC will (***increase*** / *not change* / *decrease*).
     Since Q is increasing by less than 15 percent while TC increases by 15 percent, the firm's ATC will increase if it has decreasing returns to scale.

   (D) If it has constant returns to scale, its output will increase by (*more than* / ***exactly*** / *less than*) 15 percent, and its ATC will (*increase* / ***not change*** / *decrease*).
     Since Q is increasing by 15 percent while TC also increases by 15 percent, the firm's ATC will not change if it has constant returns to scale.

9. In Figure 3-4.2, draw the LRATC curve for a firm that experiences increasing returns to scale between output levels Q_1 and Q_2, constant returns to scale between Q_2 and Q_3, and decreasing returns to scale between Q_3 and Q_4. Label the curve as "LRATC." Be sure to label the axes.

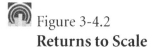 Figure 3-4.2
Returns to Scale

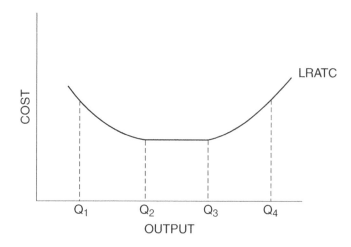

Revenue, Profit, and Rules to Maximize Total Profit

Now that you have explored the productivity and cost functions of a firm, you are ready to learn about its revenue and profit functions. It is important to note that the productivity and cost graphs look the same for any firm, regardless of whether the firm sells its output in a perfectly competitive, monopolistic, monopolistically competitive, or oligopolistic product market. Think of it this way: suppose you run a firm that produces computers. The productivity of your workers in your factory will determine your cost of producing computers. But now you are ready to take your computers from the factory and transport them to the product market to sell them. As we will see in subsequent activities, the shapes of your revenue functions will depend on how much competition you face in the product market. So although your productivity and cost functions are not affected by the product market, your revenue and profit functions will be. (We will see in Unit 4 that the factor markets for your resources will affect the prices you pay for inputs and thus will affect your cost functions.)

Part A: Revenue Terms

 *Student Alert:* The distinction between total, marginal, and average measures is important!

There are three revenue terms you need to understand before you can answer questions about profit maximization. When a firm sells its product, the revenue it receives can be described in the three ways shown in Table 3-5.1.

Table 3-5.1
Three Measures of Revenue

Measure of revenue	Meaning	How to calculate
Total revenue (TR)	The total income the firm receives from selling a given level of output (Q) at a particular price (P)	$TR = P \times Q$
Average revenue (AR)	The revenue the firm receives from one unit at a given level of output	$AR = TR/Q$
Marginal revenue (MR)	The change in total revenue resulting from the firm selling one more unit of output	$MR = \Delta TR/\Delta Q$

The shapes of these revenue functions will depend on the type of product market in which a firm sells its good or service. The key point to watch for is whether a firm has to lower its price to sell more of its product. You will calculate values of these revenue measures and draw graphs of them in other activities where the type of product market is specified.

Part B: Profit Terms

In Activity 3-3 you learned the difference between accounting profit and economic profit. Since this book is preparing you to succeed on the AP Microeconomics Exam, it is time to focus on how a firm maximizes its total *economic* profit. A good habit to learn now is always to use the correct adjective in front of the word "profit": total, average, or marginal. Accuracy counts when you are answering exam questions. (The same habit also should be applied to measures of productivity, cost, and revenue!)

There are three profit (Π) terms you need to master so you will understand the decisions made by a firm as it tries to maximize its *total* profit. When a firm sells its product, the profit (or loss) it receives can be described in the three ways shown in Table 3-5.2.

 Table 3-5.2
Three Measures of (Economic) Profit

Measure of profit	Meaning	How to calculate
Total profit (TΠ)	The difference between the firm's total revenue (TR) and total cost (TC) at a given level of output (Q)	$T\Pi = TR - TC$ $T\Pi = Q \times A\Pi$
Average profit (AΠ)	The profit the firm receives from one unit at a given level of output (= per-unit profit)	$A\Pi = T\Pi/Q$ $A\Pi = AR - ATC$ $A\Pi = P - ATC$
Marginal profit (MΠ)	The change in total profit resulting from the firm selling one more unit of output	$M\Pi = \Delta T\Pi/\Delta Q$ $M\Pi = MR - MC$

Note: While some college textbooks do not introduce the concept of marginal profit, it is a useful concept as you explain why a firm should (or should not) sell an extra unit of output.

Here's another useful hint: Be careful about mixing "totals," "averages," and "marginals." Look again at the three basic ways to calculate the measures of profit:

■ Total profit = *total* revenue – *total* cost.

■ Average profit = *average* revenue – *average* total cost.

■ Marginal profit = *marginal* revenue – *marginal* cost.

Part C: Key Rules for Any Firm to Follow

Economists assume firms try to maximize their total profit. This means a firm must decide how many units of its good or service to produce and what price to charge for that product. Fortunately, there are several basic rules that apply to any firm as it makes these decisions. At this point, we will give a general overview of the rules. You will work in detail with each rule as you move through other activities for firms in different types of product markets. Although the basic rules apply to all firms, the different levels of competition in the various markets will require that you stay focused to help the firm make the correct decisions.

Rule 1: A firm should produce the output level at which MR = MC.

This rule sounds so simple, but many students never really understand it (although many memorize it). How can producing a unit for which MR = MC maximize total profit? After all, doesn't MΠ = $0 for that unit? Yes, and ironically, that is why the rule works. Look at Table 3-5.3 which has information about the Sosin Company.

 Table 3-5.3
The Sosin Company

Output units	MR compared to MC	MΠ	TΠ
1–499	MR > MC	MΠ > $0	TΠ increases.
500	MR = MC	MΠ = $0	TΠ has reached its peak.
501 and beyond	MR < MC	MΠ < $0	TΠ decreases.

If MR > MC for the first 499 units, the firm certainly wants to produce all of them. These units create positive MΠ, which means TΠ increases with each additional unit. What does the 500th unit do for the firm's TΠ? Nothing at all. The MΠ of the 500th unit is $0 because its MR is equal to its MC. But check out units beyond 500. Each of these units adds less to TR than it adds to TC (or, MR < MC). If the Sosin Company produces these units, each unit will have a negative MΠ, which means TΠ will decrease, and the firm does not want that to happen.

So what is so special about the 500th unit where MR = MC? The answer is surprisingly simple. If the firm produces 500 units, it has produced all the units that increased its TΠ (MΠ > $0) and stopped before it produced any units that would decrease its TΠ (MΠ < $0). The 500th unit itself had no effect on TΠ, but economists like the simple "MR = MC" rule as an efficient way to locate the output level that will maximize a firm's TΠ.

Rule 2: A firm should charge the price on the demand curve for its optimal output level.

Suppose your boss offers you a $5 per hour pay raise. Are you going to decline that offer? Of course not! You want to get the highest pay you can for your labor. A firm is no different. Once it decides on the optimal number of units of its product (where MR = MC), it wants to receive the highest possible price for that output level. And that is exactly the information the firm gets from its demand curve. Basically, it will go up to the demand curve at its optimal output level and hang a direct left to the vertical price axis.

Rule 3: A firm should shut down and produce zero output if TR is less than total variable cost (TVC).

Unfortunately, there are times when a firm cannot earn a positive total profit. Perhaps the high prices of resources have made the firm's production costs unprofitably high. Or perhaps a downturn in the economy has so reduced demand that the firm cannot get a profitable price for its product. When a firm earns a negative total profit at its best output level, it has two choices in the short-run: It can go ahead and produce that output and accept the loss, or it can produce no output at all (shut down).

Here is the rule the firm should follow: If its TR is greater than its TVC, it should produce its optimal output (where MR = MC) rather than shut down.

Here's the logic behind this rule:

■ If the firm shuts down (Q = 0), it will have no TR or TVC, but it will still have its total fixed cost (TFC). Thus, by shutting down, the firm is committed to a loss equal to its TFC (loss = TFC).

■ If the firm produces its best output and has *TR that is less than TVC*, then the firm will make a loss on its variable resources and still have all of its TFC. Its loss will be larger if it produces than if it shuts down (loss > TFC).

■ If the firm produces its best output and has *TR that exceeds TVC*, then after it pays all its TVC the firm has some leftover TR to apply toward its TFC. This will makes its loss less than its TFC (loss < TFC).

Part D: Do You Get It?

Here are some questions to see if you understand the revenue and profit terms and the three key rules to maximize total profit. Circle "T" if you feel the statement is true and "F" if you think it is false. Explain your answer for each statement.

T (F) 1.   If a firm sells 200 units of its product at a price of $8, its total profit will be $1,600.
   The firm's total revenue will be $1,600. To find its total profit, we would need information about the firm's total cost of producing 200 units.

(T) F   2.   If the average revenue from 150 units is $20, the firm's total revenue is $3,000.
   Total revenue can be calculated by multiplying the number of units by the average revenue per unit. TR = (Q)(AR) = (150)($20) = $3,000.

T F 3. If the marginal revenue from the twenty-first unit is $30, then the total revenue from 22 units is $30 greater than the total revenue from 21 units.
Marginal revenue is the change in total revenue resulting from the firm selling one more unit of output. The increase in TR is $30 when the firm increased Q from 20 to 21 units, not from 21 to 22 units.

T F 4. As long as MR is greater than MC, a firm's TΠ will increase if it increases its level of output.
If MR is greater than MC, an extra unit of output will add more to TR than it adds to TC so the firm's TΠ will increase.

T (F) 5. When MΠ is $0, we know TΠ also is $0.
TΠ is maximized when MΠ = $0. TΠ is $0 when TR = TC.

(T) F 6. If MΠ is negative, a firm's TΠ will increase if the firm produces fewer units of output.
If MΠ is negative, that means MR is less than MC for the last unit produced. By reducing its output, the firm will increase its TΠ.

T (F) 7. At its current output level, the Placone Firm has AR = $12 and MC = $10, which means its AΠ = $2.
AΠ = AR – ATC. Since MC is not the same thing as ATC, this statement is false.

T (F) 8. A firm determines it will maximize its total profit by producing 800 units per week because at that output both MR and MC are $600. The price the firm should charge for its output also is $600.
This question anticipates topics to be covered in later activities in this unit. If the firm sells its product in a perfectly competitive market, this statement would be true because price would be equal to MR. But in an imperfectly competitive market, the statement would be false because price would be greater than MR.

Answer Questions 9 and 10 based on this information: The Wright Company estimates the following values at its optimal level of output: TR = $20,000, TVC = $18,000, and TFC = $5,000.

T (F) 9. This firm should shut down rather than produce its optimal level of output.
Even though the firm will suffer a loss of $3,000 by producing its optimal output, it should do so. If it shuts down, it will have a larger loss of $5,000 equal to its TFC. As long as TR is greater than TVC, the firm is better off producing its optimal output than shutting down. In this example, the firm has enough TR to cover all its TVC and contribute $2,000 toward its TFC.

(T) F 10. If its optimal output is 5,000 units, the price it charges for its good is $4.00.
Since TR = (P)(Q) and we know TR = $20,000, the firm's price must be $4.00 if it is selling 5,000 units.

Profit Maximization by a Perfectly Competitive Firm

A perfectly competitive firm will maximize its total profit by producing the output level at which marginal revenue equals marginal cost. You need to understand how economists find these two important "marginal" measures.

Part A: Revenue Measures of a Perfectly Competitive Firm

A perfectly competitive firm is a "price taker." This means it has no control over price and will charge the market-determined price for its product. In fact, because it is such a small participant in the market, a perfectly competitive firm can sell all the output it wants at the market price. It does not have to reduce its price to sell additional units. This makes the revenue measures of a perfectly competitive firm easy to calculate and to graph.

1. Assume the market for yo-yos is perfectly competitive and that the market price currently is $17 per box of yo-yos. Complete Table 3-6.1, which has the three revenue measures of a typical firm in this market. Put the MR values at the new output level. For example, when the firm increases output from four to five units, its total revenue increases by $17, so put "+$17" in the MR column for Q = 5.

 Table 3-6.1
Revenue Measures of a Perfectly Competitive Firm

(1) Output (Q) [boxes of yo-yos]	(2) Price (P) [per box]	(3) Total revenue TR = P × Q	(4) Marginal revenue MR = ΔTR/ΔQ	(5) Average revenue AR = TR/Q
0	$17	*$0*	–	–
1	$17	*+$17*	*+$17*	*$17*
2	$17	*+$34*	*+$17*	$17
3	$17	$51	*+$17*	*$17*
4	$17	*+$68*	*+$17*	*$17*
5	$17	*+$85*	+$17	*$17*
6	$17	*+$102*	*+$17*	*$17*
7	$17	*+$119*	*+$17*	$17
8	$17	$136	*+$17*	*$17*
9	$17	*+$153*	*+$17*	*$17*
10	$17	*+$170*	*+$17*	*$17*

2. What happens to the value of MR as more output is sold? Why?

MR is a constant value because the firm does not have to lower price to sell an extra unit. Thus, the change in total revenue for an extra unit is equal to the market price.

3. What is the relationship between MR and AR at every output level? Why?

The two measures are equal because the firm does not have to lower price to sell an extra unit of output.

4. What happens to the value of TR each time the firm sells one more unit of its good? Why?

TR increases by an amount equal to the market price. Since it does not have to reduce price, TR increases by the same amount with each new unit of output. This increase in TR is the firm's MR.

5. Why is P equal to $17 at every level of Q?

Because the firm is a price taker, it can sell all it wants at the market price of $17.

6. What is the relationship between P, MR, and AR? Why?

For a perfectly competitive firm, these three measures are equal to each other because the firm does not have to lower price to sell more output.

7. Plot the firm's total revenue data in Figure 3-6.1.

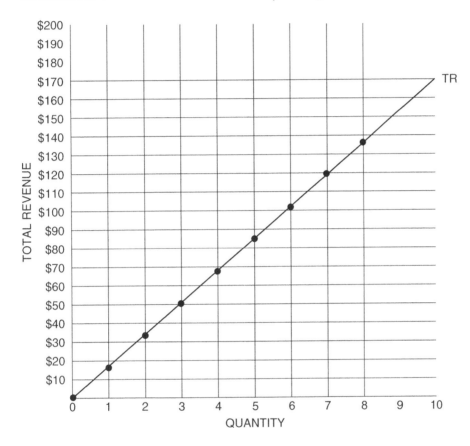

Figure 3-6.1

Total Revenue Function of a Perfectly Competitive Firm

8. The slope of the total revenue function is ΔTR/ΔQ. What economic function does this ratio represent? Why is the TR curve a straight line?
   The slope of the TR function is MR. For a perfectly competitive firm, the TR function is a straight line because MR is a constant value.

9. If the market price increases, what will happen to the slope of the firm's TR curve? Will the TR curve still begin at the origin?
   The TR function will be steeper because MR will be larger. The TR curve will still begin at the origin.

10. Plot the firm's marginal revenue, average revenue, and demand data in Figure 3-6.2.

Figure 3-6.2

Marginal Revenue, Average Revenue, and Demand Functions of a Perfectly Competitive Firm

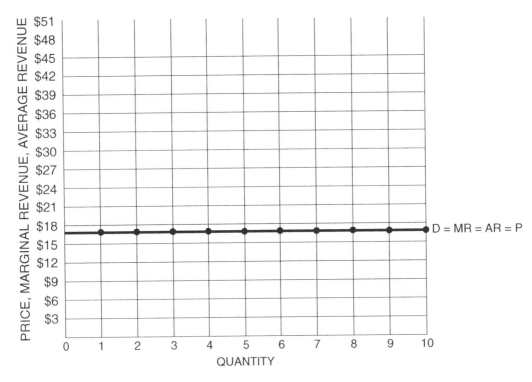

11. Does the demand curve D represent the firm's demand for something, such as inputs?
    No, it is the demand of consumers for the product of the firm.

12. Why is the demand function horizontal?
    It is horizontal because the firm does not have to reduce its price to sell more output. It can sell all it wants at the market price of $17.

13. What would happen to the quantity demanded of the firm's product if it increased the price above the market price of $17? What does this tell you about the price elasticity of demand for the firm's product?
    The quantity demanded would drop to zero because consumers would buy yo-yos from other firms at the market price. This means the demand facing a perfectly competitive firm is perfectly elastic—a slight price increase moves the firm from being able to sell all it wants to selling no units at all.

14. Would you recommend that this firm lower its price below the market price of $17? Why?
No. It can sell all it wants at the market price, so why reduce the price?

15. What do you note about the relationship between price and marginal revenue for a perfectly competitive firm? What about between price and average revenue?
P = MR and P = AR for a perfectly competitive firm.

Part B: Cost Measures of a Perfectly Competitive Firm

The short-run cost curves of a perfectly competitive firm give you values of the various cost measures at different output levels.

16. Complete Table 3-6.2, which has the seven cost measures of a typical firm in this market. Put the MC values at the new output level. For example, when the firm increases output from four to five units, its total cost increases by $4, so put "+$4" in the MC column for Q = 5. Some of the cost values are provided for you.

 Table 3-6.2
Cost Measures of a Perfectly Competitive Firm

(1) Output (Q) [boxes]	(2) Total fixed cost (TFC)	(3) Total variable cost (TVC)	(4) Total cost (TC)	(5) Marginal cost (MC) = ΔTC/ΔQ	(6) Average fixed cost (AFC) = TFC/Q	(7) Average variable cost (AVC) = TVC/Q	(8) Average total cost (ATC) = TC/Q
0	*$40.00*	*$0.00*	$40.00	–	–	–	–
1	*$40.00*	$10.00	*$50.00*	+$10.00	*$40.00*	*$10.00*	*$50.00*
2	$40.00	*$16.00*	*$56.00*	+$6.00	*$20.00*	*$8.00*	*$28.00*
3	*$40.00*	*$21.00*	*$61.00*	+$5.00	*$13.33*	$7.00	*$20.33*
4	*$40.00*	*$26.00*	*$66.00*	+$5.00	*$10.00*	*$6.50*	$16.50
5	*$40.00*	$30.00	*$70.00*	+$4.00	*$8.00*	*$6.00*	*$14.00*
6	*$40.00*	*$36.00*	*$76.00*	+$6.00	*$6.67*	$6.00	*$12.67*
7	*$40.00*	*$45.50*	$85.50	+$9.50	$5.71	*$6.50*	*$12.21*
8	$40.00	*$56.00*	*$96.00*	+$10.50	*$5.00*	*$7.00*	$12.00
9	*$40.00*	$72.00	*$112.00*	+$16.00	*$4.44*	*$8.00*	*$12.44*
10	$40.00	*$90.00*	*$130.00*	+$18.00	*$4.00*	*$9.00*	*$13.00*

17. What happens to the value of AFC as Q rises? Why?

    AFC always decreases as Q rises because AFC = TFC/Q. Since TFC is constant, an increase in Q must reduce AFC.

18. What happens to the value of AVC as Q increases? Why?

    AVC decreases, then increases as the firm increases its level of output. Initially, MC is less than AVC which makes AVC decrease. When MC eventually rises above AVC, AVC will increase.

19. What happens to the value of MC as Q increases? Is this trend related to the marginal physical productivity of the firm's variable resources? Explain.

    MC decreases, then increases as the firm increases output. Yes, the shape of the MC curve is inversely related to the shape of the MPP curve. When MPP increases, MC decreases. When MPP decreases, MC increases. When MPP is maximized, MC is minimized.

20. Is the value of MC the same whether it is computed as a change in TC or as a change in TVC? Why?

    Yes, the only change in a firm's TC is the change in its TVC. So MC is the same using a change in either TC or TVC when an extra unit of output is produced.

21. Why does the value of TVC continue to get larger as the firm produces more Q?

    In the short run, the only way the firm can produce more output is by adding more units of its variable resource (labor). Thus, its total outlay on labor must increase as the firm makes more output.

22. The slope of the TC curve is $\Delta TC/\Delta Q$. Do you recognize this ratio as the expression of some other important economic function?

    Yes, the slope of the TC curve is MC.

23. Plot the firm's TC, TVC, and TFC data in Figure 3-6.3.

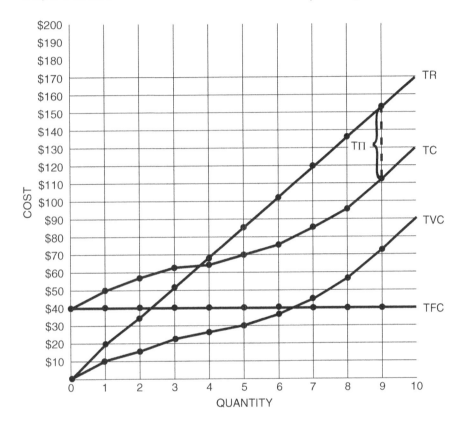

Figure 3-6.3
TC, TVC, and TFC Functions of a Perfectly Competitive Firm

24. What does the vertical gap between the TC and TVC represent? What happens to the size of this gap as the firm increases its level of production?
    The gap represents TFC which does not change with output. The TFC gap is the same at all output levels.

25. Why does the TC cost curve not begin at the origin?
    Because even if it produces no output, the firm still has TFC. The TC curve begins at the level of TFC.

26. Why does the TVC curve have the same slope as the TC curve?
    Both the TVC and TC curves have slope equal to MC. MC = $\Delta TC/\Delta Q$ = $\Delta TVC/\Delta Q$.

27. Plot the firm's ATC, AVC, AFC, and MC data in Figure 3-6.4 and answer the questions that follow the graph. Connect the MC values with a dotted line in your graph.

Figure 3-6.4

ATC, AVC, AFC, and MC Functions of a Perfectly Competitive Firm

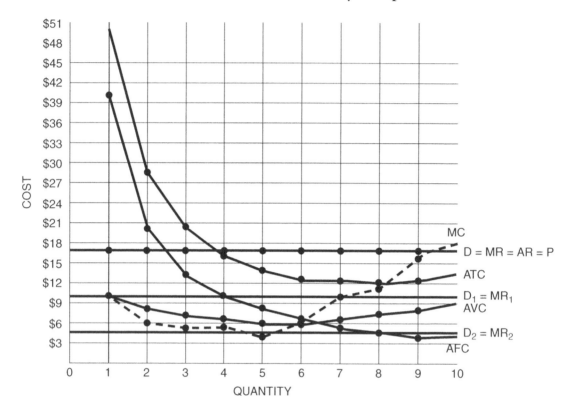

28. Why does the vertical gap between the ATC and AVC curves get smaller as the firm increases its Q?
    That gap is AFC which decreases as the level of output increases.

29. At what unique point does the MC curve intersect both the AVC curve and the ATC curve? Why?
    The MC curve intersects the AVC and ATC curves at their minimum points. When MC is below these average curves, they decrease. When MC is above them, they increase.

30. Between Q = 6 and Q = 8, AVC is rising while ATC is falling. How can this be?
    This is because over this output range, the decrease in AFC is greater than the increase in AVC. As a result, ATC continues to fall.

Part C: Profit Maximization by a Perfectly Competitive Firm

Now that you have mastered the revenue and cost terms for a perfectly competitive firm, you can bring them together to determine how many units of output the firm should produce to maximize its total profit.

31. Complete Table 3-6.3 using your data from Tables 3-6.1 and 3-6.2. Some data have been entered for you.

 Table 3-6.3

A Perfectly Competitive Firm Maximizes Total Profit

Q	TR	TC	TΠ	MR	MC	MΠ
0	*$0.00*	$40.00	−$40.00	–	–	–
1	*$17.00*	*$50.00*	*−$33.00*	*+$17.00*	+$10.00	*+$7.00*
2	$34.00	*$56.00*	*−$22.00*	+$17.00	*+$6.00*	*+$11.00*
3	*$51.00*	*$61.00*	−$10.00	*+$17.00*	*+$5.00*	+$12.00
4	*$68.00*	$66.00	*$2.00*	*+$17.00*	+$5.00	*+$12.00*
5	*$85.00*	*$70.00*	*$15.00*	+$17.00	*+$4.00*	*+$13.00*
6	$102.00	*$76.00*	*$26.00*	*+$17.00*	*+$6.00*	+$11.00
7	*$119.00*	*$85.50*	$33.50	*+$17.00*	*+$9.50*	*+$7.50*
8	*$136.00*	$96.00	*$40.00*	*+$17.00*	+$10.50	*+$6.50*
9	*$153.00*	*$112.00*	*$41.00*	+$17.00	*+16.00*	+$1.00
10	$170.00	*$130.00*	*$40.00*	*+$17.00*	+$18.00	*−$1.00*

32. The value of TΠ is greatest at Q = __*9*__ units. The maximum TΠ = *$41.00* .

33. The firm should produce each unit for which MR > MC. The last unit with MR > MC is the __*ninth*__ unit, which has MΠ = *$+1.00* .

34. Should the firm produce the tenth unit of Q? Why?
    No, because that unit has MR < MC which means it has a negative MΠ. If the firm sold that unit, TΠ would fall by $1.00.

35. MΠ has its greatest value at Q = **5** units. Should this be the Q level the firm decides to produce? Why?
No, because the sixth through the ninth units each have positive MΠ (MR > MC) which means they will increase the firm's TΠ.

36. Go back to Figure 3-6.3 and draw the firm's TR function. (You can get it from Figure 3-6.1). Label the function "TR."

37. What do we call the vertical gap between the TR and TC curves?
That vertical gap is total profit (TΠ).

38. We saw in Table 3-6.3 that this firm should produce Q = **9** units to maximize its TΠ. Indicate the part of Figure 3-6.3 that represents this maximum TΠ.

39. Go back to Figure 3-6.4 and draw the firm's D, MR, and AR functions at the current market price of $17. (You can get these from Figure 3-6.2). Label the functions.

40. The last unit of output for which MR > MC is the ___*ninth*___ unit. This is the last unit the firm should produce in order to maximize its TΠ.

41. What does the vertical gap between the MR and MC curves represent?
That vertical gap is marginal profit (MΠ). As long as the gap is positive, the firm should keep producing more units of output.

Part D: When Is a Firm's Best Just Not Good Enough?

You proved this firm can earn a positive total profit if the market price is $17. But what if the market price drops? Since a perfectly competitive firm is a price taker, it will have to sell its product at the lower market price, which will reduce its total profit.

42. Assuming all its costs are unchanged, what will happen to the perfectly competitive firm if the market price drops to $10? In Figure 3-6.4, draw a new "$D_1 = MR_1$" line at the price of $10.

    (A) Based on a comparison of MR and MC, the firm's optimal Q level is   *7*   units.

    (B) Its TR will be (*greater than* / *equal to* / ***less than***) its TC at this Q level.

    (C) Its TR will be (***greater than*** / *equal to* / *less than*) its TVC.

    (D) What should the firm do? Choose one of these decisions:

    (1) It should produce its optimal Q even though it will make a loss.

    (2) It should shut down and produce no Q this period.

43. Assuming all its costs are unchanged, what will happen to the perfectly competitive firm if the market price drops to $5? In Figure 3-6.4, draw a new "$D_2 = MR_2$" line at the price of $5.

    (A) Based on a comparison of MR and MC, the firm's optimal Q level is   *5*   units.

    (B) Its TR will be (*greater than* / *equal to* / ***less than***) its TC at this Q level.

    (C) Its TR will be (*greater than* / *equal to* / ***less than***) its TVC.

    (D) What should the firm do? Choose one of these decisions:

    (1) It should produce its optimal Q even though it will make a loss.

    (2) It should shut down and produce no Q this period.

Note: Even though economists chant, "Produce where MR = MC," in a discrete case with a limited number of Q levels being considered, there might not be a level of Q where MR = MC. In such a case, the firm should produce units for which MR > MC and stop before it produces units for which MR < MC. That's what you did in this example.

44. A puzzle for you! Economists say a perfectly competitive firm can sell at the Q it wants at the going market price. So why doesn't a single firm decide to produce all the Q that is demanded in the market?
    It will only produce more output as long as MR is greater than or equal to MC. Once the firm's MC rises about its MR, the firm will decide not to produce any more units.

Short-Run Equilibrium and Short-Run Supply in Perfect Competition

The word "equilibrium" refers to being in a state of rest or balance. You know the meaning of this term in the context of a competitive market: the equilibrium price is the one at which the quantity demanded is equal to the quantity supplied. Neither the buyers nor the sellers have reason to move from this spot, unless factors cause the demand or supply curve to shift.

Part A: Short-Run Equilibrium for a Perfectly Competitive Firm

A perfectly competitive firm is in a *short-run equilibrium* position when it produces the output level Q^* at which marginal revenue (MR) is equal to marginal cost (MC). The firm will stay at this output level unless something causes a change in its MR curve or MC curve. In its short-run equilibrium position, the firm could be in any of four profit scenarios as shown in Table 3-7.1.

1. In the last column, circle what you feel the firm should do in each of these cases—produce or shut down.

 Table 3-7.1

Four Possible Total Profit Positions of a Firm in Short-Run Equilibrium

Total profit (TΠ) at Q^* where MR = MC	Total revenue (TR) compared to total cost (TC) and total variable cost (TVC) at Q^*	What should the firm do?
1. TΠ > \$0	TR > TC	**_Produce Q*_** / *shut down*
2. TΠ = \$0	TR = TC	**_Produce Q*_** / *shut down*
3. TΠ < \$0	TVC < TR < TC	**_Produce Q*_** / *shut down*
4. TΠ < \$0	TR < TVC < TC	*Produce Q** / **shut down**

Note: You will see in Activity 3-8 how a perfectly competitive firm moves from a position of short-run equilibrium to one of long-run equilibrium where it must break even (total profit = \$0).

Part B: Short-Run Supply Curve of a Perfectly Competitive Firm

A market supply curve tells you how many units of a good or service producers will provide at different prices, other things being constant. The typical market supply curve is upward sloping because producers will put more units on the market at a higher price. A perfectly competitive firm also has a supply curve that is upward sloping. The basis of its short-run supply curve is its marginal cost curve as shown in the following exercise. Table 3-7.2 has information about some of the daily cost functions of the Fiasco Company, which sells its product in a perfectly competitive market.

2. Fill in the missing cost values in Table 3-7.2.

 Table 3-7.2

Cost Functions of a Perfectly Competitive Firm

Q	TC	TVC	MC	Average total cost (ATC)	Average variable cost (AVC)
0	$12.00	$0.00	–	–	–
1	$16.00	$4.00	+$4.00	$16.00	$4.00
2	$19.00	$7.00	+$3.00	$9.50	$3.50
3	$21.00	$9.00	+$2.00	$7.00	$3.00
4	$24.00	$12.00	+$3.00	$6.00	$3.00
5	$30.00	$18.00	+$6.00	$6.00	$3.60
6	$39.00	$27.00	+$9.00	$6.50	$4.50
7	$49.00	$37.00	+$10.00	$7.00	$5.29
8	$61.00	$49.00	+$12.00	$7.63	$6.13
9	$75.00	$63.00	+$14.00	$8.33	$7.00
10	$91.00	$79.00	+$16.00	$9.10	$7.90

3. In Figure 3-7.1, plot and label the ATC, AVC, and MC curves of the firm. Plot the MC values at the higher of the two output levels. For example, when the firm increases output from 5 units to 6 units, its TC increases by $9, so plot the MC = $9 value at Q = 6. Use a dotted line to draw the MC curve.

Figure 3-7.1
Cost Curves of the Fiasco Company

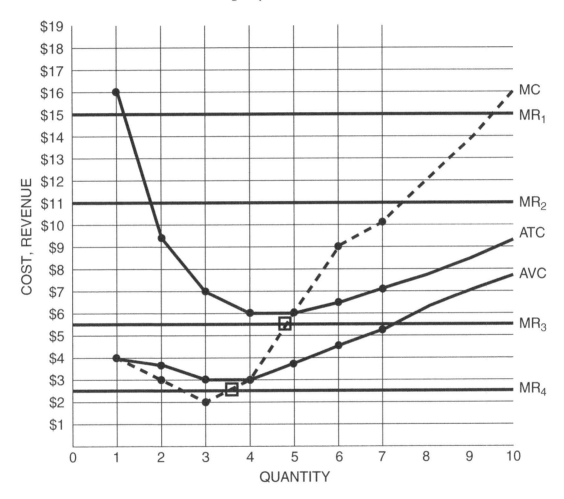

How many units of Q should the firm produce to maximize its total profit? Given its cost functions, the answer depends on the market price that the perfectly competitive firm must charge for its product. Consider these four possible market prices: $15.00, $11.00, $5.50, and $2.50.

4. In Figure 3-7.1, draw the appropriate marginal revenue curve for each of these prices (P) and label them as follows: MR_1 (for P = $15.00), MR_2 (for P = $11.00), MR_3 (for P = $5.50), and MR_4 (for P = $2.50).

5. Using Figure 3-7.1 and Table 3-7.2, complete Table 3-7.3 and determine how many units of Q the firm should produce at each of the four market prices.

Table 3-7.3

Optimal Output Level for the Fiasco Firm at Different Market Prices

(1) P	(2) Q* (units)	(3) TR	(4) TVC	(5) TFC	(6) TΠ
$15.00	*9 units*	*$135.00*	*$63.00*	*$12.00*	*$60.00*
$11.00	*7 units*	*$77.00*	*$37.00*	*$12.00*	*$28.00*
$5.50	*4 units*	*$22.00*	*$12.00*	*$12.00*	*−$2.00*
$2.50	*3 units*	*$7.50*	*$9.00*	*$12.00*	*−$13.50*

6. What rule did you use to determine the Q level that would maximize the firm's TΠ if P were $15.00? Why?
The rule to use is MR = MC. At the price of $15.00, you can see how many units had MR greater than or equal to MC. This gives 9 units.

7. Did you use this same rule to find the profit-maximizing Q level at P of $11.00? Why?
Yes. The first 7 units had MR greater than MC. Since the MR of the eighth unit was less than its MC, the eighth unit is not profitable at a price of $11.00.

8. Should the firm shut down if P is $5.50? What if P is $2.50? Explain.
At both of these prices the firm will make a loss because P < ATC. However, P > AVC at a price of $5.50, so the firm should use the MR = MC rule to produce 4 units at a smaller loss than it would have if it shut down. At a price of $2.50, P < AVC, so the firm is better off shutting down and having a loss equal to its TFC.

9. Complete Table 3-7.4, which is the supply schedule for the Fiasco Firm. It shows how many units the firm will provide to the market at different prices.

Table 3-7.4

Supply Schedule for the Fiasco Firm

P	Q supplied (units)
$15.00	*9 units*
$11.00	*7 units*
$5.50	*4 units*
$2.50	*0 units*

10. Plot the supply curve of the Fiasco Firm in Figure 3-7.2. Label the curve as "S."

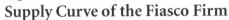 Figure 3-7.2

Supply Curve of the Fiasco Firm

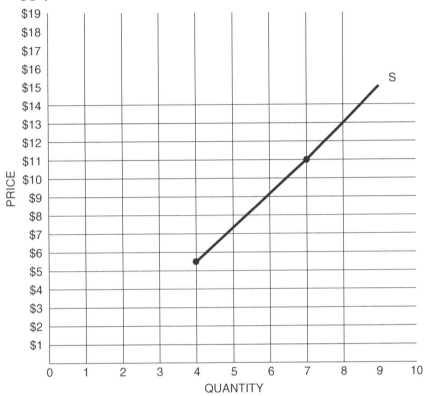

11. To create the supply curve of this perfectly competitive firm, you used two important rules of profit maximization:

(A) The firm's optimal Q level is the one where __MR__ = __MC__.

(B) The firm should shut down if at its best Q level, __TR < TVC or P < AVC__.

12. In general, the supply curve of a perfectly competitive firm is that part of its __marginal__ cost curve that lies above its __average variable__ cost curve.
Refer back to Figure 3-7.1 to see where you went at each of the four prices to find the best Q level for the firm.

13. What is the connection between a perfectly competitive firm having diminishing marginal productivity and its short-run supply curve being upward sloping?
The short-run supply curve of a perfectly competitive firm is that portion of its MC curve above its AVC curve. The reason the MC curve is upward sloping is that the MPP of extra units of labor (the variable resource) is diminishing. The firm must receive a higher price to cover its higher MC if it is to produce additional units of output.

Part C : Short-Run Supply Curve of a Perfectly Competitive Industry

The industry (or market) supply curve tells you how many units will be supplied by all firms at each possible price. To get the industry supply, you add the quantity supplied by each firm at each price. Economists call this *adding horizontally* because you add the quantity supplied (measured on the horizontal axis) at each price. Assume the Fiasco Firm is a typical firm in a perfectly competitive industry with 800 firms.

14. Complete Table 3-7.5. Refer to Table 3-7.4 for how many units a typical firm supplies at each price.

 Table 3-7.5
Supply Schedule for the Industry (800 firms)

P	Q supplied (units)
$15.00	**7,200 units**
$11.00	**5,600 units**
$5.50	**3,200 units**
$2.50	**0 units**

15. Plot the data from Table 3-7.5 in Figure 3-7.3. Is the market supply curve upward sloping? Why?
   The market supply curve is upward sloping because it is the summation of the upward-sloping supply curves of all the firms in the industry.

 Figure 3-7.3
Market Supply Curve

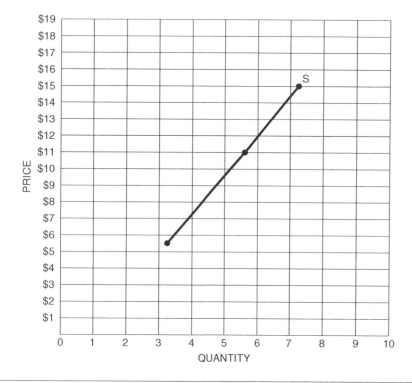

Long-Run Equilibrium and Long-Run Supply in Perfect Competition

A firm is in a *short-run equilibrium (SRE)* position when it maximizes its total profit by producing the output level where marginal revenue equals marginal cost: MR = MC. When firms in short-run equilibrium in a perfectly competitive market are earning positive total profits, other firms will enter the market. If firms are making a loss in their short-run equilibrium position, over time some of the firms will exit the market. Eventually the perfectly competitive market reaches a *long-run equilibrium* (LRE) where all of the firms in the industry are earning zero total profits, based on the current market demand. Firms in other industries thus have no incentive to enter this market. And firms in this market have no incentive to leave it because they are earning their normal profit. An industry's *long-run supply* (LRS) curve is the set of LREs where each LRE is based on a different level of market demand. The shape of the LRS curve depends on how the production costs of firms change as the industry expands. The three cases to consider are *constant-cost*, *increasing-cost*, and *decreasing-cost industries*.

Part A: Movement from Short-Run Equilibrium to Long-Run Equilibrium

Table 3-8.1 presents some cost data for a typical firm in the perfectly competitive market for bricks. These cost data are shown in Figure 3-8.1.

 Table 3-8.1

Cost Data for a Typical Perfectly Competitive Firm

Output (Q) (tons)	Average total cost (ATC)	Average variable cost (AVC)	MC
0	–	–	–
1	$50.00	$40.00	+$40.00
2	$40.00	$35.00	+$30.00
3	$33.33	$30.00	+$20.00
4	$32.50	$30.00	+$30.00
5	$34.00	$32.00	+$40.00
6	$36.67	$35.00	+$50.00
7	$40.00	$38.57	+$60.00
8	$43.75	$42.50	+$70.00

Figure 3-8.1
Cost Functions of a Typical Firm

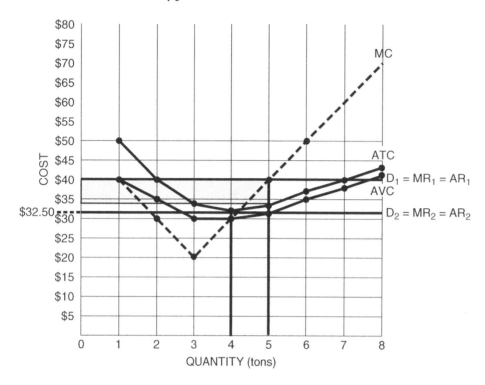

1. Complete Table 3-8.2, which shows how many units a firm will make available at different prices. Assume a firm cannot produce fractions of a unit.

 Table 3-8.2
Supply Schedule of a Typical Firm

Price (P)	Quantity supplied (Q_s) (tons)
$70	8
$60	7
$50	6
$40	5
$30	4
$20	0
$10	0

2. Assume there are 1,000 firms in the brick industry. Complete Table 3-8.3, which shows the market supply schedule. Information about the market demand schedule is included in Table 3-8.3.

 Table 3-8.3
Market Supply and Demand Schedules

P	Q_s (tons)	Quantity demanded (Q_d) (tons)
$70	**8,000**	2,000
$60	**7,000**	3,000
$50	**6,000**	4,000
$40	**5,000**	5,000
$30	**4,000**	6,000
$20	**0**	7,000
$10	**0**	8,000

3. Figure 3-8.2 shows the market demand curve D_1. Draw the market supply curve S_1 from Table 3-8.3. What is the equilibrium price of bricks? What is the equilibrium quantity? Label the SRE intersection of D_1 and S_1 as "SRE."
   The equilibrium price of a ton of bricks is $40 and the equilibrium quantity is 5,000 tons.

 Figure 3-8.2
The Market for Bricks

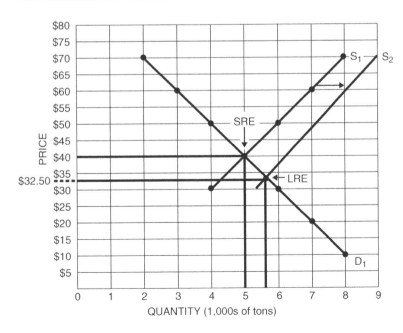

4. In Figure 3-8.1, draw the marginal revenue (MR$_1$), average revenue (AR$_1$), and demand (D$_1$) curves of a firm at the equilibrium price. How many units will the firm produce to maximize its total profit? (Assume the firm cannot produce fractions of a unit.) Does this number agree with your work in Table 3-8.2?
   The perfectly competitive firm will produce 5 tons of bricks. Yes, it agrees.

5. What is the value of the firm's average profit? What is the value of its total profit? In Figure 3-8.1, shade in the area representing its total profit.
   AΠ = AR – ATC = \$40.00 – \$34.00 = \$6.00.
   TΠ = Q × AR = 5 × \$6.00 = \$30.00.

6. Is the industry in a position of LRE? How do you know?
   No, because firms are earning positive total profit.

7. Why will other firms want to enter this industry? Assume the cost curves of a typical firm in the industry do not change as new firms enter.
   Other firms will enter the industry because firms are earning positive total economic profits.

8. As more firms enter the industry, the market supply curve shifts to the (**right** / left), which makes the market price (increase / **decrease**).

9. The industry is in a position of LRE when all firms break even based on the current level of market demand D$_1$. What is the LRE price? Why?
   More firms will enter the market until the price falls to the minimum value of a firm's ATC curve. As seen in Table 3-8.1, this is \$32.50.

10. In Figure 3-8.2, draw the new market S curve (label it S$_2$) that will result in this LRE price. Do not change the existing market demand curve D$_1$. Label the LRE point as "LRE."

11. In Figure 3-8.1, draw the firm's MR_2, AR_2, and D_2 curves at the LRE price. How many units will the typical firm produce at this price? What is the total profit of a firm in this LRE position?
    The typical firm will produce 4 units and earn a total economic profit of $0.

12. If all firms in the market earn $0 in economic profit, will other firms still want to enter the market? Will some firms want to exit the market? Why?
    No other firms will want to enter the market because there are no economic profits. Firms now in the market will have no incentive to leave because they are earning their normal profits.

Part B: Long-Run Equilibrium for a Perfectly Competitive Firm

Let's leave the brick market and move to some other perfectly competitive market. Figure 3-8.3 shows a perfectly competitive firm in LRE, selling 640 units at a price of $18.

Figure 3-8.3

A Perfectly Competitive Firm in Long-Run Equilibrium

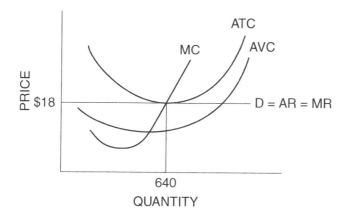

13. What does it mean for a firm to be productively efficient? Is this firm productively efficient? How do you know?
    A firm is productively efficient if its price is equal to the minimum value of its average total cost. This firm does exhibit productive efficiency. Consumers are getting the product at the lowest possible price.

14. What does it mean for a firm to be allocatively efficient? Is this firm allocatively efficient? How do you know?
    A firm is allocatively efficient if its price is equal to marginal cost. This firm is allocatively efficient. It is producing the output level society wants it to produce. If there are no externalities (effects on other parties), then price measures the marginal social benefit (MSB) and MC measures the marginal social cost (MSC) of the last unit. Because MSB = MSC, the correct amount of society's scarce resources are being allocated to the production of this firm's product.

Part C: Long-Run Supply for a Perfectly Competitive Industry

The industry shown in Figure 3-8.4 is in LRE at point A with supply curve S_1 and demand curve D_1. The market price is $20, and the equilibrium quantity is 500 units. Now the demand for the industry's product increases to D_2. The price increases to $27 and quantity increases to 620 units. Because this boost in the market price results in positive total profits for firms in the industry, point B is considered a *short-run equilibrium (SRE)*. How the industry moves to its new LRE in response to this increase in demand depends on whether it is a constant-cost, increasing-cost, or decreasing-cost industry.

Figure 3-8.4
A Perfectly Competitive Industry

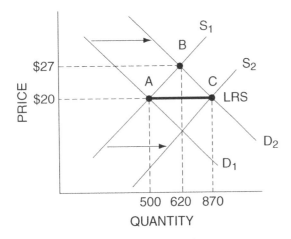

15. Assume the industry is a constant-cost industry. Explain how the industry moves to its new LRE. Show changes in supply and/or demand in Figure 3-8.4 and indicate the new LRE as point C.
Because of profits in the industry, other firms will enter. This makes the market supply curve shift to the right which reduces the market price. Since this is a constant-cost industry, the average total cost of production does not change as the industry expands. Thus, the supply curve will shift to the right to S_2 where it intersects D_2 at point C at the price of $20. Firms will break even at this price as they did at point A. Point C is the long-run equilibrium based on demand curve D_2.

16. Is the new LRE price greater than, equal to, or less than $20? Why?
The new LRE price is equal to $20 because the average total cost of firms did not change as the industry expanded. The firms will break even at the original LRE price of $20. The industry quantity has increased due to the inflow of new firms.

17. The industry's LRS curve is the collection of LREs where each LRE is based on a different market demand curve. Draw a line connecting point A and point C, and label this line as "LRS." Is the LRS curve of a constant-cost industry upward sloping, horizontal, or downward sloping? What does this tell you about how price and quantity change as the industry expands in response to increases in demand?
The LRS curve of a constant-cost industry is horizontal. As the industry expands, the market price will not change as the market output increases.

18. Now assume the industry is an increasing-cost industry. In Figure 3-8.5, the industry is in LRE at point A. When demand increases to D₂, the industry moves to SRE at point B, where firms enjoy positive total profit. Explain how the industry moves to its new LRE. Show changes in supply and/or demand in Figure 3-8.5 and indicate the new LRE as point C.

Because of profits in the industry, other firms will enter. Two things happen to eliminate profits in the market. First, the market supply curve shifts to the right which reduces the market price. Second, since this is an increasing-cost industry, the average total cost of production increases as the industry expands. Thus, the supply curve will shift to the right to S₂ where it intersects with D₂ at point C at a price higher than $20, say $24. Firms will break even at this price as they did at point A. Point C is the long-run equilibrium based on demand curve D₂.

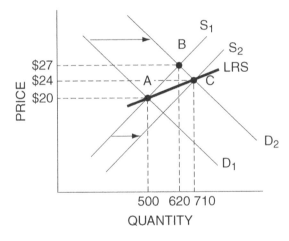

Figure 3-8.5
A Perfectly Competitive Industry

19. Is the new LRE price greater than, equal to, or less than $20? Why?

The new LRE is greater than $20 because this is an increasing-cost industry. As the industry expanded, firms competing for needed resources drove up the prices of those resources, thus increasing the average total cost of production. This means the price will fall from $27 but will not fall all the way back to $20. Firms will break even at some price above $20, say $24.

20. Draw a line connecting point A and point C, and label this line as "LRS" for long-run supply. Is the LRS curve of an increasing-cost industry upward sloping, horizontal, or downward sloping? What does this tell you about how price and quantity change as the industry expands in response to increases in demand?

The LRS curve of an increasing-cost industry is upward sloping. As the industry expands, both the market price and output will increase.

21. If the industry were a decreasing-cost industry, what would happen to the market price and quantity as the industry expanded? What would be the shape of the industry LRS curve?

In a decreasing-cost industry, the market price will decrease and output increase as the industry expands. The LRS curve will be downward sloping.

Graphing Perfect Competition

Figures 3-9.1 through 3-9.6 show side-by-side graphs of perfectly competitive industries and firms. Each pair of graphs illustrates the specific situation that is given.

(A) For the industry's graph, draw the supply (S) and demand (D) curves. Indicate by P* and Q* the equilibrium price and quantity.

(B) For the firm's graph, draw the average total cost (ATC), average variable cost (AVC), average revenue (AR), and demand (D) curves. Indicate by P* and Q* the firm's optimal price and output.

(C) Explain the reasoning for your graphs in each situation.

1. A firm earning positive total profit in the short run.

 Figure 3-9.1
Short-Run Economic Profit

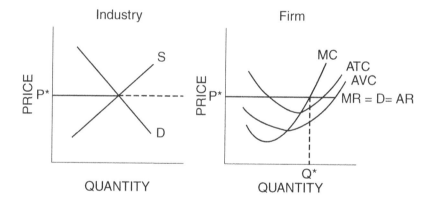

Explanation: ***The firm produces Q* where MR = MC. Because the market price P* is greater than ATC, the firm earns positive total profit.***

2. A firm operating with an economic loss but not wanting to shut down in the short run.

 Figure 3-9.2
Short-Run Economic Loss but Not Shutting Down

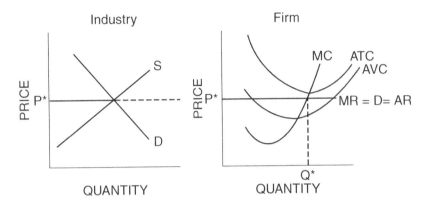

Explanation: *The firm's optimal output is Q* where MR = MC. Even though it will make a loss because the market price P* is less than ATC, the firm will not shut down because P* is greater than AVC. The firm is able to pay all its TVC and part of its TFC.*

3. A firm in a classic shutdown position in the short run.

 Figure 3-9.3
Classic Shutdown Position

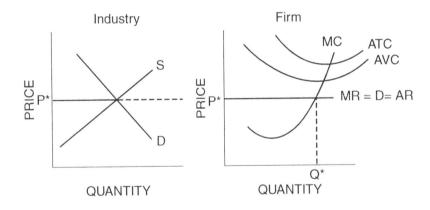

Explanation: *At Q*, where MR = MC, the market price P* is less than AVC. The firm will shut down rather than produce Q*. By shutting down, the firm's loss will be equal to its TFC. If it produces Q* it will have a loss which is greater than its TFC.*

4. LRE for a firm and the industry.

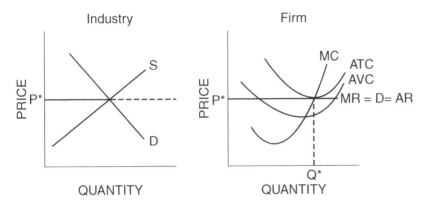

Figure 3-9.4
Long-Run Equilibrium

Explanation: *The firm will break even with output Q*, where MR = MC, because the market price P* is equal to ATC at the minimum point on the ATC curve. The industry is in LRE: firms will neither enter nor leave the industry because the firms in the industry are earning a normal profit but no economic profit.*

5. Illustrate how economic profits will disappear in the long run.

Figure 3-9.5
From Short-Run Profit to Long-Run Equilibrium

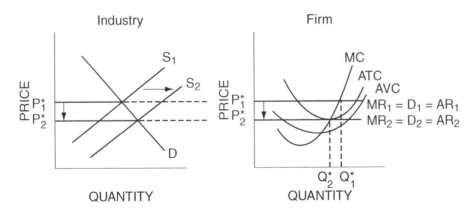

Explanation: *With supply S_1, the typical firm is earning a positive total profit at Q_1^* because the market price P_1^* is greater than ATC. As new firms enter the industry, attracted by the presence of profits, the market supply curve shifts to the right until it becomes S_2 which creates the market price P_2^*. At P_2^*, each firm breaks even because P_2^* is equal to ATC at the minimum point on the ATC curve. The industry is in long-run equilibrium. A firm produces Q_2^* and charges P_2^*.*

6. Illustrate how economic losses will disappear in the long run.

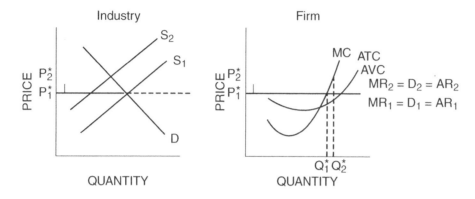

Figure 3-9.6
From Short-Run Loss to Long-Run Equilibrium

Explanation: *With supply S_1, the typical firm is earning a negative total profit at Q_1^* because the market price P_1^* is less than ATC. As some firms leave the industry because of losses, the market supply curve shifts to the left until it becomes S_2 which creates the market price P_2^*. At P_2^*, each firm breaks even because P_2^* is equal to ATC at the minimum point on the ATC curve. The industry is in long-run equilibrium. A firm produces Q_2^* and charges P_2^*.*

The Revenue Functions of a Monopoly

At the opposite end of the market spectrum from perfect competition is monopoly. A monopoly exists when only one firm sells the good or service. This means the monopolist faces the market demand curve since it has no competition from other firms. If the monopolist wants to sell more of its product, it will have to lower its price. As a result, the price (P) at which an extra unit of output (Q) is sold will be greater than the marginal revenue (MR) from that unit.

🛈 *Student Alert:* **P is greater than MR for a monopolist.**

1. Table 3-10.1 has information about the demand and revenue functions of the Moonglow Monopoly Company. Complete the table. Assume the monopoly charges each buyer the same P (i.e., there is no price discrimination). Enter the MR values at the higher of the two Q levels. For example, since total revenue (TR) increases by $37.50 when the firm increases Q from two to three units, put "+$37.50" in the MR column for Q = 3.

 Table 3-10.1

The Moonglow Monopoly Company

Q	P	TR	MR	Average revenue (AR)
0	$100.00	*$0.00*	–	–
1	*$87.50*	*$87.50*	*+$87.50*	$87.50
2	*$75.00*	$150.00	*+$62.50*	*$75.00*
3	$62.50	*$187.50*	+$37.50	*$62.50*
4	*$50.00*	*$200.00*	*+$12.50*	$50.00
5	*$37.50*	$187.50	*–$12.50*	*$37.50*
6	$25.00	*$150.00*	*–$37.50*	*$25.00*
7	*$12.50*	*$87.50*	–$62.50	*$12.50*
8	*$0.00*	$0.00	*–$87.50*	*$0.00*

2. Draw the demand (D), AR, and MR curves in Figure 3-10.1. Plot the MR values at the higher of the two Q levels.

Figure 3-10.1

Monopoly's Demand, Average Revenue, and Marginal Revenue Curves

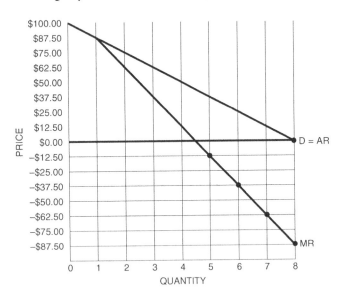

3. Plot the firm's TR curve in Figure 3-10.2.

 Figure 3-10.2

Monopoly's Total Revenue Curve

4. We see in Table 3-10.1 that the price at which the firm can sell three units is $62.50. Yet the MR from the third unit is only $37.50. How do you explain this difference?

When the firm lowers its price from $75.00 to $62.50 to increase sales from 2 units to 3 units, two things happen to total revenue:

(1) It receives $62.50 in new total revenue from the sale of the third unit.

(2) It has a loss in total revenue of $25.00 from the first two units this period: (2)($75.00 − $62.50) = $25.00. The marginal revenue of the third unit is the sum of these two effects = +$62.50 − $25.00 = +$37.50. Because the firm cannot sell 3 units at the same price at which it sold 2 units, the price of the third unit is greater than the marginal revenue from that unit.

Advanced Placement Economics Microeconomics: Teacher Resource Manual © Council for Economic Education, New York, N.Y.

5. Why does the vertical gap between the firm's D curve and MR curve get larger as the firm sells more output?

This is because the loss in total revenue from the first units resulting from lowering the price to sell one more unit gets larger as the firm's total output increases. In other words, the value in Part (2) of the solution to Question 4 gets bigger as the firm's output gets bigger.

Table 3-10.1 is an example of a *discrete* case because it has a small number of observations (output varies from zero to eight units). Figure 3-10.3 is an example of a *continuous* case because it is based on a large number of observations. Answer Questions 6–8 based on Figure 3-10.3.

Figure 3-10.3

A Continuous Example of a Monopoly's Revenue Curves

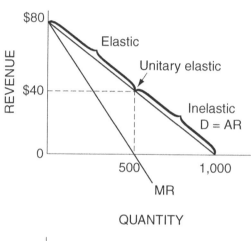

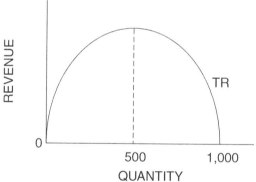

6. Indicate clearly in the top graph of Figure 3-10.3 the elastic, unitary elastic, and inelastic portions of the D curve. Explain your answer.

Based on the total revenue test, we know demand is elastic if total revenue rises when price is reduced. Total revenue does not change if demand is unitary elastic. Demand is inelastic if total revenue falls when price is lowered. If the demand curve is linear and downward sloping, then the upper half of the demand curve is elastic, the midpoint is unitary elastic, and the lower half is inelastic.

7. Marginal revenue is found using the ratio MR = ΔTR/ΔQ. This is also the formula for the slope of the TR curve. Thus, MR = slope of the TR curve.

   (A) Over what range of output is the slope of the TR curve positive? Over what range of output is the firm's MR positive?
   Over the first 499 units

   (B) Over what range of output is the firm's MR negative? Over what range of output is the slope of the TR curve negative?
   Over those units from 501 to 1,000

   (C) Over what range of output is the slope of the TR curve equal to zero? Over what range of output is the firm's MR equal to zero?
   At the 500th unit

8. What is the maximum dollar value of TR this firm can receive?
   $500 \times \$40 = \$20,000.$

Bonus Question!

9. When the Galaxy Firm lowers its price from $60 to $57, the number of units it sells increases from 36 to 39. What is the value of MR? How should you interpret this value?
   As a result of selling three extra units, the firm's total revenue increases by $63 ($2,160 to $2,223). Since marginal revenue refers to the extra revenue from one more unit of output, you need to use the MR formula: MR = ΔTR/ΔQ = +$63/+3 units = +$21. The interpretation of this MR value is that the firm's total revenue increases by $21 for each of the three extra units.

Profit Maximization by a Monopoly

The profit-maximizing monopolist works with the same key rules as any firm:

1. The optimal output level (Q^*) is the one where marginal revenue equals marginal cost (MR = MC).

2. The optimal price (P^*) is found on the demand curve at output Q^*.

3. The firm should shut down if at Q^* it finds its total revenue is less than its total variable cost (TR < TVC).

Because price (P) and MR were equal for a perfectly competitive firm, that firm could also find its Q^* by setting P = MC. But that is not the case for a monopoly since P and MR will be different. The monopolist will find its profit-maximizing output (Q) where MR = MC, not where P = MC. This activity shows how a monopolist finds the output at which it will maximize its total profit and the price it should charge for that output.

Part A: Determining the Optimal Output and Price for a Monopoly

Table 3-11.1 provides some revenue, cost, and profit data for a monopoly.

1. Complete Table 3-11.1. Enter the MR and MC values at the higher of the two output levels. For example, the MR value of $300 is placed at Q = 4 rather than at Q = 3.

   Be sure to distinguish between total profit (TΠ), average profit (AΠ), and marginal profit (MΠ):

   (A) $TΠ = TR - TC = (Q)(AΠ)$

   (B) $AΠ = AR - ATC = TΠ/Q$

   (C) $MΠ = MR - MC = ΔTΠ/ΔQ$

 Table 3-11.1
Revenue, Cost, and Profit Values for a Monopoly

Q	P	TR	TC	TΠ	AR	ATC	AΠ	MR	MC	MΠ
0	$1,350	*$0*	$100	−*$100*	–	–	–	–	–	–
1	*$1,200*	*$1,200*	*$900*	$300	$1,200	$900	*$300*	+$1,200	+$800	+$400
2	*$1,050*	$2,100	$1,600	*$500*	*$1,050*	*$800*	$250	+$900	+$700	+$200
3	$900	*$2,700*	*$2,100*	$600	*$900*	*$700*	$200	+$600	+$500	+$100
4	*$750*	*$3,000*	*$2,400*	*$600*	$750	*$600*	$150	+$300	+$300	*$0*
5	$600	*$3,000*	$2,800	*$200*	*$600*	*$560*	*$40*	*$0*	+$400	−$400
6	*$450*	$2,700	*$3,600*	−*$900*	*$450*	$600	−*$150*	−$300	+$800	−$1,100

2. In Figure 3-11.1, draw the monopolist's D, AR, MR, and ATC curves using the data from Table 3-11.1. Plot the MR and MC values at the higher of the two output levels rather than at the midpoint between the two levels. Use dotted lines for the MR and MC curves in your graph. Label each curve.

Figure 3-11.1
Revenue and Cost Curves of a Monopolist

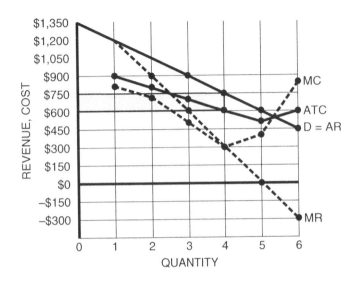

3. To maximize its total profit, this monopolist should produce ___4___ units.
   The first three units have MR > MC. The fourth unit has MR = MC. Subsequent units have MR < MC and should not be produced.

4. What price should the monopolist charge for each of these units?
   The highest price the firm can charge for four units is $750. This price is found on the D curve.

5. What is the total profit this firm will earn? ___$600___ Shade in the total profit area in Figure 3-11.1.
   The AΠ for four units is $150: AΠ = AR − ATC = $750 − $600.

   TΠ = (Q)(AΠ) = (4)($150) = $600.

Part B: Other Monopoly Examples

6. Suppose a monopolist can sell an extra unit of its good at a price of $50 and the MR of that unit is $44. If the MC of producing the extra unit is $46, the firm's total profit would (*increase* / **decrease**) by ___$2___ if the firm sells that unit. Should the firm produce this additional unit of output? Explain your answer.
   The firm should not produce the extra unit because its MR is less than its MC. This unit has a marginal profit of −$2 which means the firm's total profit would decrease by $2 if it sold that unit. The firm compares MR to MC, not P to MC, to decide if an extra unit should be produced.

7. Figure 3-11.2 shows the MR and MC curves of a monopolist. Economists claim that the firm will maximize its total profit by producing 800 units where MR = MC. Show your understanding of this rule by circling the correct answer in each cell of Table 3-11.2.

Figure 3-11.2

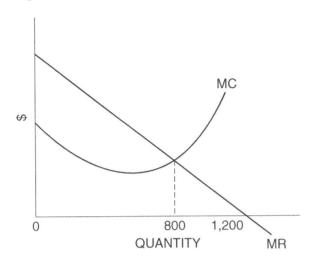

Table 3-11.2
The Logic behind the "MR = MC" Rule

Units of Q	For each extra unit of output in this range:		
1–799	MR is (⊘/ = / <) MC.	MΠ is (⊘/ = / <) $0.	TΠ will (**rise** / fall / not change).
800	MR is (> /⊜/ <) MC.	MΠ is (> /⊜/ <) $0.	TΠ will (rise / fall / **not change**).
801–1200	MR is (> / = /⊘) MC.	MΠ is (> / = /⊘) $0.	TΠ will (rise / **fall** / not change).

8. The firm illustrated in Figure 3-11.2 will maximize its total revenue if it produces 1,200 units. So why does it not want to produce those units between 800 and 1,200?
Each of the units between 800 and 1200 has MR < MC which means the firm's total profit will be decreased if these units are produced.

9. The monopolist's profit-maximizing output level will be in the (*elastic* / *unitary elastic* / *inelastic*) range of its demand curve. Explain.
The output level where MR = MC must be in the elastic range because MC is always a positive value, which means MR must also be a positive value. MR is only positive in the elastic range of the demand curve.

Here's a more interesting answer to Question 9. Assume the firm is producing an output level in the inelastic range. If the firm increases its price, three things will happen:

(1) Total revenue will increase because an increase in price when demand is inelastic increases total revenue.

(2) Total cost will decrease because the firm will need fewer resources since it will be selling fewer units of output because of the higher price.

(3) Total profit will increase because total revenue increases and total cost decreases when price is increased in the inelastic range of the demand curve. [See (1) and (2).]

Thus, if the firm is operating in the inelastic range of its demand curve, it should keep increasing its price (and its total profit) until it backs into the elastic range where it eventually hits the output level where MR = MC.

Advanced Placement Economics Microeconomics: Teacher Resource Manual © Council for Economic Education, New York, N.Y.

Equilibrium in a Monopolistic Market

Part A: Equilibrium in a Perfectly Competitive Market

Consider Figure 3-12.1, which shows a perfectly competitive market. The market supply curve S is the horizontal summation of the marginal cost (MC) curves of all the firms in the market. Use Figure 3-12.1 to answer the questions that follow the graph.

Figure 3-12.1

Equilibrium in a Perfectly Competitive Market

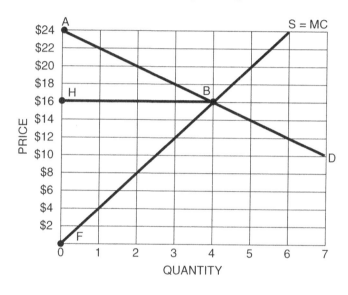

1. What is the equilibrium quantity in the market?
   4 units

2. What is the equilibrium price?
   $16

3. What area of the graph represents consumer surplus in the market? Calculate the dollar value of consumer surplus.
   CS is represented by area ABH. CS = (0.5)(4)($24 − $16) = $16.

4. What area of the graph represents producer surplus in the market? Calculate the dollar value of producer surplus.
   PS is represented by area BHF. PS = (0.5)(4)($16 − $0) = $32.

5. What area of the graph represents total surplus (also called social welfare or total welfare)? Calculate the dollar value of total surplus.
   TS is represented by area ABF. TS = CS + PS = $48.

Part B: Equilibrium in a Monopolistic Market

Now consider the same demand and cost curves, but assume the market is a monopoly. Because the monopoly faces the downward sloping market demand curve, it must reduce its price to sell more output, which means price will be greater than marginal revenue (MR). We add the firm's MR curve below its demand curve in Figure 3-12.2, as well as the monopolist's MC curve. Use Figure 3-12.2 to answer the questions that follow the graph.

 Figure 3-12.2
Equilibrium in a Monopolistic Market

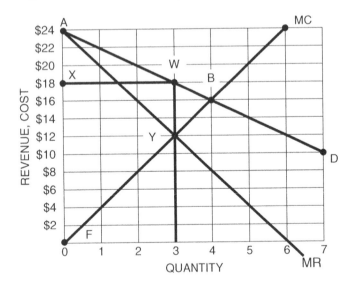

6. What output level will the monopolist produce? Why?
   It will produce 3 units where MR = MC.

7. What price will the monopolist charge for this output? Why?
   The monopolist will charge a price of $18 because, based on the demand curve, that is the highest price consumers will pay for 3 units.

8. What area of the graph represents consumer surplus in the market? Calculate the dollar value of consumer surplus.
   CS is represented by area AWX. CS = (0.5)(3)($24 – $18) = $9.

9. What area of the graph represents producer surplus? Calculate the dollar value of producer surplus.
   PS is represented by area FXWY. To calculate the value of PS, break the FXWY area into a triangle and a rectangle.

   PS = (0.5)(3)($12 – $0) + (3)($18 – $12) = $18 + $18 = $36.

10. What area of the graph represents total surplus? Calculate the dollar value of total surplus.
    TS is represented by area AWYF. TS = CS = PS = $45.

Part C: Comparing Equilibrium in the Two Markets

11. How do the price and output of a monopolist differ from those in the perfectly competitive market?
    The monopolist has a higher price and a lower output than a perfectly competitive market.

12. What is the dollar value of the portion of consumer surplus in the competitive market that is transferred to the firm's producer surplus in the monopoly situation?
    Note that CS drops from $16 in perfect competition to $9 in monopoly. What happens to the $7 reduction in CS when the market becomes a monopoly?

    (1) Some of it is captured by the monopoly as PS = (3)($18 – $16) = $6.

    (2) The other part is lost because output was reduced by one unit because of the monopoly. This is called a deadweight loss (DWL) to society. In this example, the DWL in terms of CS is equal to $1: (0.5)(4 –3)($18 – $16) = $1.

13. How does a monopoly affect consumer surplus? Is this good or bad from the perspective of consumers?
    Consumer surplus is reduced when a perfectly competitive market becomes a monopoly. This is bad news for consumers.

14. What area of Figure 3-12.2 represents the deadweight loss resulting from the market being a monopoly? Calculate the dollar value of the deadweight loss.
    Deadweight loss results from the market output being reduced by 1 unit (from 4 units to 3 units) when the market changes from perfect competition to monopoly. The DWL is represented by the area BWY.

    DWL = (0.50)(1)($18 – $16) + (0.5)(1)($16 – $12) = $1 + $2 = $3.

    The value of DWL also can be found as the reduction in TS when a perfectly competitive market becomes a monopoly: ΔTS = $48 – $45 = $3.

Price Discrimination

When producers have market power and sell a good or service that cannot be resold, the possibility of price discrimination arises. *Price discrimination* exists when a producer charges different prices to different customers for the same item, for reasons other than differences in cost. The seller needs to be able to divide the total market for the good into separate submarkets, each with a different demand for the good. There also must be no possibility of resale of the product between the submarkets; otherwise the different submarkets will collapse into a single market.

Part A: Regular Monopoly with No Price Discrimination

Pat's Patriotic Tattoos is the only tattoo parlor in town. Pat provides only one tattoo—the American flag. There are 10 consumers in town who are willing to buy one tattoo, and they vary in their willingness to pay. One consumer is willing to pay $20 for a tattoo, another is willing to pay $18, and so forth, down to the tenth consumer who is willing to pay only $2. Table 3-13.1 shows the demand schedule for Pat's flag tattoo.

1. Complete Table 3-13.1 assuming the firm can only charge one price for its service. (There is no price discrimination yet.) If Pat wants to sell three units, she will sell all three units at a price of $16, so her TR is $48. Put each MR value at the higher of the two output levels.

 Table 3-13.1
Demand Schedule for Pat's Tattoo

Price	Quantity	Total revenue (TR)	Marginal revenue (MR)
$20	1	*$20*	+$20
$18	2	*$36*	*+$16*
$16	3	$48	*+$12*
$14	4	*$56*	*+$8*
$12	5	*$60*	+$4
$10	6	*$60*	*+$0*
$8	7	*$56*	*–$4*
$6	8	*$48*	*–$8*
$4	9	$36	–$12
$2	10	*$20*	*–$16*

2. What is the total consumer surplus if Pat sells three units at a price of $16?
CS is the difference between the highest price a consumer is willing to pay and the price he or she actually does pay. CS= ($20 – $16) + ($18 – $16) + ($16 – $16) = $4 + $2 + $0 = $6.

3. What is the total consumer surplus if she sells five units at a price of $12?
CS = ($20 – $12) + ($18 – $12) + ($16 – $12) + ($14 – $12) + ($12 – $12)
    = $8 + $6 + $4 + $2 + $0
    = $20.

4. In Figure 3-13.1, draw the demand curve for Pat's tattoos.

Figure 3-13.1
Demand for Pat's Tattoos

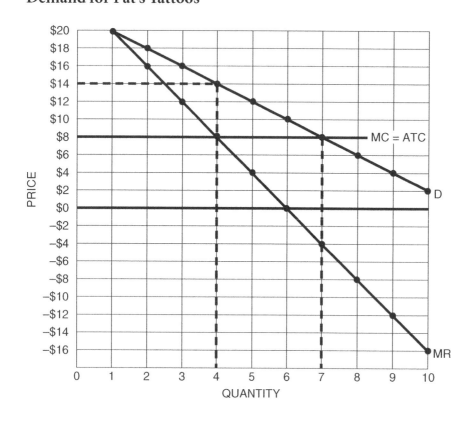

Advanced Placement Economics Microeconomics: Teacher Resource Manual © Council for Economic Education, New York, N.Y.

Part B: Perfect Price Discrimination (Also Called First-Degree Price Discrimination)

Perfect price discrimination is a monopolist's dream because it means that the firm can charge each individual consumer the highest price that he or she is willing to pay for the firm's product. As we will see in this activity, perfect price discrimination eliminates all consumer surplus and increases the monopolist's total profit above what it would if the firm sold all output at one price. For the questions in this section, assume that Pat's average total cost and marginal cost are constant and equal to $8 (ATC = MC = $8).

5. In Figure 3-13.1, draw the firm's ATC=MC curves as a horizontal line at $8.

6. If this were a perfectly competitive market, the MC curve would represent the supply of the product. If Pat produces the perfectly competitive quantity and charges the perfectly competitive price:

    (A) How many tattoos will she supply? Why?
    She will produce 7 units because that is where P = MC. In perfect competition, a firm can sell all it wants at the current price, so P and MR are the same value. Since we assume MC = $8, she will produce 7 units.

    (B) What price will she charge for each tattoo? Why?
    Her price will be $8 because she will operate where P= MC.

    (C) What is the amount of consumer surplus? Why?
    CS = ($20 − $8) + ($18 − $8) + ($16 − $8) + ($14 − $8) + ($12 − $8) + ($10 − $8) + ($8 − $8)
    = $12 + $10 + $8 + $6 +$4 + $2 + $0
    = $42.

7. If Pat produces the monopoly quantity and charges the monopoly price:

    (A) Draw her marginal revenue (MR) curve in Figure 3-13.1.

    (B) How many tattoos will she supply? Why?
    She will produce 4 units because that is where MR = MC. The monopolist compares MR to MC, not P to MC.

    (C) What price will she charge for each tattoo? Why?
    She will charge $14 for each of the 4 units because in the demand schedule we see that is the highest price consumers will pay for 4 units.

    (D) What is the amount of consumer surplus? Why?
    CS= ($20 − $14) + ($18 − $14) + ($16 − $14) + ($14 − $14) = $6 + $4 + $2 + $0 = $12.

8. Now assume Pat knows the tastes and preferences of all consumers and the conditions necessary for first-degree price discrimination apply.

   (A) Does the MR curve for the non-discriminating monopolist still apply? Why?
   No. She is able to charge each consumer a unique price so her demand curve is also her marginal revenue curve because it shows the increase in her total revenue from each extra unit she sells.

   (B) How many tattoos will she supply? Why?
   She will supply 7 tattoos because that is where MR = MC. In this case, you also can say that is where P = MC.

   (C) Complete Table 3-13.2, which shows what price she will charge each individual consumer for her/his tattoo.

 Table 3-13.2

Prices Charged by a Perfectly Discriminating Monopsonist

Consumer	1st	2nd	3rd	4th	5th	6th	7th	8th	9th	10th
Price	*$20*	*$18*	*$16*	*$14*	*$12*	*$10*	*$8*	*$6*	*$4*	*$2*

   (D) What is the amount of consumer surplus?
   There is no consumer surplus because Pat charged each consumer the highest price he or she was willing to pay for a tattoo.

9. In Table 3-13.3, show Pat's total profit under each of the three market structures. Remember our assumption that ATC = MC = $8.

 Table 3-13.3

Profit in Each Market Structure

Type of market	Pat's total profit
Perfect competition	*$0*
Regular monopoly	*$24*
Perfect price discrimination monopoly	*$42*

Perfect competition: TΠ = TR − TC = (Q)(P) − (Q)(ATC) = (7)($8) − (7)($8) = $0.
Regular monopoly: TΠ = TR − TC = (Q)(P) − (Q)(ATC) = (4)($14) − (4)($8) = $24.
Discriminating monopoly: TΠ = TR − TC = (sum of prices) − (Q)(ATC)
                                 = ($20 + $18 + $16 + $14 +$12 + $10 + $8) − (7)($8) = $98 − $56
                                 = $42.

10. How does the total profit of the perfectly discriminating monopolist compare to the consumer surplus that existed in the perfectly competitive market? [See Question 6 (C).] Why?

They are equal because the perfectly discriminating monopolist was able to capture all the consumer surplus from each individual consumer.

11. Is the total profit for a regular monopolist different from the total profit of a monopolist that is able to practice perfect price discrimination? Why?

Yes. The total profit of a nondiscriminating monopolist is smaller than that of the monopolist who can practice perfect price discrimination. The latter captures all the consumer surplus because it does not have to sell its output at one price.

12. Is the output the same for perfect competition and perfect price discrimination? Why?

Yes. In these two examples, price is equal to marginal revenue. The perfectly competitive firm can sell all the output it wants at the market price, so it has P = MR. Even though the perfectly discriminating monopolist must reduce its price to sell more output, it also has P = MR because it can charge a unique price to each consumer. Because each firm faces the same MC, the output in each market structure will be the same where P = MC.

13. Is there a deadweight loss resulting from the non-discriminating monopolist? What about from the monopolist with first-degree price discrimination?

There is a deadweight loss from the nondiscriminating monopolist because the output is less than the socially optimal output which would occur in the perfectly competitive model. There is no deadweight loss from the discriminating monopolist, however, because the output is the same as in the perfectly competitive model.

14. If an orange sells in Nebraska for $1.00 and the same quality orange sells in Florida for only $0.50, is this clear evidence of price discrimination? Why?

No. The price difference could reflect the cost of transporting the orange from Florida (where it was produced) to Nebraska.

15. What is an example of price discrimination that works in favor of students?

Students often receive a lower price for movie tickets than do "regular" people. Because it is the same service at the same cost of production, this is an example of price discrimination.

Regulating a Monopoly

There are some firms that have decreasing marginal costs over a large range of output. As long as marginal cost (MC) is below average total cost (ATC), the firm also will experience decreasing ATC. Such firms are called *natural monopolies* and are often regulated by a governmental agency that allows the firm to be the only provider of the service. This is an attempt to take advantage of the low average total cost of the firm. This activity lets you explore several regulation plans and their effects on the firm and the market.

Suppose you are the manager of a local natural monopoly. Figure 3-14.1 illustrates the revenue and cost functions of your monopoly.

 Figure 3-14.1
Revenue and Cost Functions

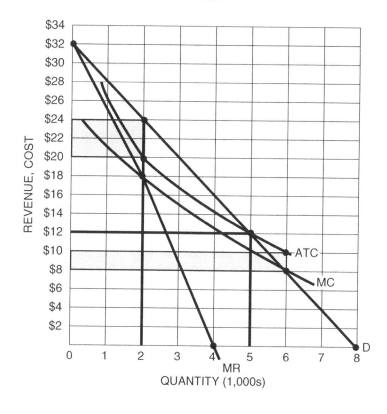

1. Complete Table 3-14.1, which examines three possible pricing plans for the monopoly.

Table 3-14.1
Three Pricing Regulation Plans

	Output (Q)	Price (P)	Total revenue (TR)	Total cost (TC)	Average profit (AΠ)	Total profit (TΠ)
Unregulated monopoly	2,000	$24	$48,000	$40,000	$4	$8,000
Fair return pricing	5,000	$12	$60,000	$60,000	$0	$0
Socially optimal pricing	6,000	$8	$48,000	$60,000	–$2	–$12,000

2. In Figure 3-14.1, shade in the area representing your firm's total profit under each of the three regulation plans.
   For the unregulated monopoly, the shaded rectangle at 2,000 units of output shows a positive total profit of $8,000. For the fair return pricing plan, there is no area to shade because the firm breaks even. Under the socially optimal pricing scheme, the firm's loss of $12,000 is shown as the shaded rectangle at 6,000 units of output.

3. As the manager of this firm, which of the three regulation plans would you prefer? Why?
   I would prefer the unregulated monopoly plan because it allows my firm to earn positive total profit.

4. As the manager of the firm, which plan would you totally oppose? Why? What could the government do to make this plan acceptable to you?
   I would not accept the socially optimal pricing plan because it forces me to accept a price which is below my average total cost and make a loss. Since the goal of this plan is to have my firm produce the output level society desires, the government could give me a subsidy to keep my firm from making a loss.

5. Which plan would society like to see the government agency apply to your firm? Why?
   Society would prefer the socially optimal output level. That plan has the firm producing the output level at which P = MC. This is the allocatively optimal output level society desires.

6. Under the fair return pricing plan, does your firm earn an economic profit? Does it earn a normal profit?

No, it does not earn an economic profit; it breaks even. Yes, it does earn a normal profit because its implicit costs are included in the economic costs.

7. Each of the three plans has its own rule for deciding how many units of output your firm will provide. State those rules.

   (1) Unregulated monopoly: produce the quantity at which MR = MC.

   (2) Fair return pricing: produce the quantity at which P = ATC.

   (3) Socially optimal pricing: produce the quantity where P = MC.

Comparing Perfect Competition and Monopoly

The productivity and cost curves of a firm are the same regardless of the degree of competition the firm faces in the product market. The shapes of the productivity and cost curves depend on the productivity of resources and the prices the firm pays to acquire those resources. It is on the revenue side of the firm that we find the impact of the type of product market in which the firm sells its good or service.

Part A: A Comparison of Firms

Answer the following questions based on Figure 3-15.1, which shows the revenue and cost functions of a monopoly and a perfectly competitive firm. Assume the monopoly will charge only one price for output (i.e., it does not price discriminate).

Figure 3-15.1
Revenue and Cost Functions for a Monopoly and a Perfectly Competitive Firm

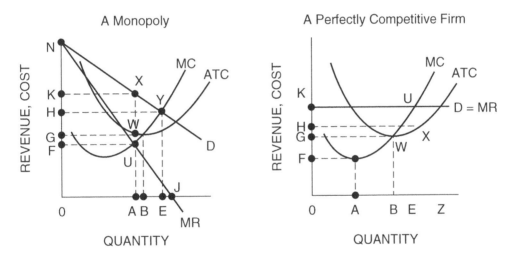

Note: The values of coordinates are not the same in both graphs. For example, the value of 0K is greater in the monopoly graph than is the value of 0K in the graph of the competitive firm.

1. The monopoly will maximize its total profit by producing _____ units of output.

   (A) 0A   (B) 0B   (C) 0E   (D) 0J

2. The perfectly competitive firm will maximize its total profit by producing _____ units of output.

   (A) 0A   (B) 0B   *(C) 0E*   (D) 0Z

3. The profit-maximizing price for the monopoly is

   (A) 0F.   (B) 0G.   (C) 0H.   *(D) 0K.*

4. The profit-maximizing price for the perfectly competitive firm is

   (A) 0F. (B) 0G. (C) 0H. **(D) 0K.**

5. The maximum total profit of the monopoly is shown by the coordinates

   (A) AX. (B) UX. **(C) GWXK.** (D) 0AXK.

6. The maximum total profit of the perfectly competitive firm is shown by the coordinates

   (A) EU. (B) UX. (C) 0EUK. **(D) HXUK.**

7. The maximum average profit of the perfectly competitive firm is at output

   (A) 0A. **(B) 0B.** (C) 0E. (D) 0Z.

8. The marginal profit of the monopoly is $0 at output

   (A) 0A. (B) 0B. (C) 0E. (D) 0J.

9. The marginal profit of the perfectly competitive firm is $0 at output

   (A) 0A. (B) 0B. **(C) 0E.** (D) 0Z.

10. The marginal profit of the perfectly competitive firm is maximized at output

    (A) 0A. (B) 0B. (C) 0E. (D) 0Z.

11. At output 0A, the total cost of the monopoly is shown by the coordinates

    (A) AU. (B) AW. (C) 0AUF. **(D) 0AWG.**

12. The monopolist will maximize its total revenue at output

    (A) 0A. (B) 0B. (C) 0E. **(D) 0J.**

13. What price will the perfectly competitive firm charge when it is in long-run equilibrium?

    (A) 0F **(B) 0G** (C) 0H (D) 0K

14. What area represents consumer surplus when the monopoly maximizes its total profit?

    (A) KXN (B) 0AXN (C) GWXN (D) HYN

15. The profit-maximizing output of the monopoly is _____ the output society would like the firm to produce.

    (A) greater than (B) equal to **(C) less than**

16. The profit-maximizing output of the perfectly competitive firm is _____ the output society would like the firm to produce.

    (A) greater than **(B) equal to** (C) less than

17. Is the perfectly competitive firm in a position of long-run equilibrium?

    (A) Yes **(B) No** (C) We need more information.

18. Which firm will operate at the minimum point of its ATC curve in long-run equilibrium?

   (A) Only the perfectly competitive firm

   (B) Only the monopolistic firm

   (C) Both firms

   (D) Neither firm

Part B: A Comparison of Markets

Figure 3-15.2 shows a perfectly competitive market with demand curve D and supply curve S. The equilibrium output is Q_2, and the equilibrium price is 0F. If the market were to become a monopoly, the firm would restrict output to some smaller output such as Q_1. Answer the questions below Figure 3-15.2.

 Figure 3-15.2
Comparing Perfect Competition and Monopoly

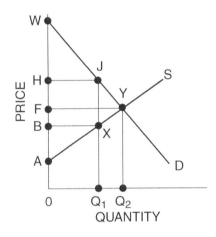

19. Complete Table 3-15.1 with the coordinates of the variables under each type of market.

 Table 3-15.1
Comparing Perfect Competition and Monopoly

Market type	Consumer surplus	Producer surplus	Total surplus*
Perfect competition	*FYW*	*AFY*	*AWY*
Monopoly	*HWJ*	*AHJX*	*AWJX*
*Total surplus is also called total welfare and social welfare.			

20. Explain what the triangle JXY represents.
   This shows the deadweight loss to society from the perfectly competitive market becoming a monopoly. Society loses the total surplus from those units between Q_1 and Q_2 because those units will not be produced if the market is a monopoly.

Monopolistic Competition

Monopolistic competition is an appropriate name for this important market structure. There is competition because there is a large number of firms producing similar but not identical products. Each firm has some monopoly power over price because its product is different from others with which it is competing. Each monopolistically competitive firm faces a downward sloping demand (D) curve so it has to reduce its price to have consumers buy more of its product. This means it has a downward sloping marginal revenue (MR) curve that lies below its D curve. In fact, the revenue graph of a monopolistically competitive firm looks like the revenue graph of a monopoly.

A monopolistically competitive firm is similar to a perfectly competitive firm because while it can earn a positive total profit in its short-run equilibrium, it will break even in its long-run equilibrium. It is different from a monopoly in this regard because a monopoly can maintain a positive total profit in the long run as long as it has barriers to entry that prevent other firms from coming into the market.

Part A: Short-Run Equilibrium of a Monopolistically Competitive Firm

A monopolistically competitive firm is in short-run equilibrium when it produces the output where marginal revenue equals marginal cost (MR = MC). Its optimal price is found on its demand curve at this output level. Like other firms, the firm will shut down if at its best output level, its total revenue is less than its total variable cost. Figure 3-16.1 shows a monopolistically competitive firm in short-run equilibrium with an output of 600 units per period. Answer the questions that follow the graph.

 Figure 3-16.1
A Monopolistically Competitive Firm in Short-Run Equilibrium

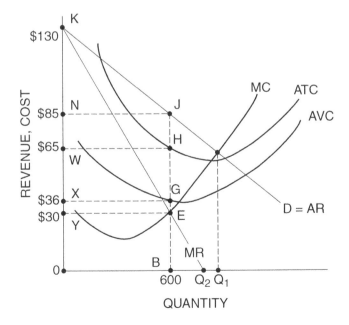

1. What price will the firm charge for its profit-maximizing output?
   $85

2. What are the dollar values and coordinates of these items at the output of 600 units?

   (A) Total revenue *($85)(600) = $51,000, OBJN*

   (B) Total cost *($65)(600) = $39,000, OBHW*

   (C) Total profit *($20)(600) = $12,000, WHJN*

   (D) Average profit *($85 – $65) = $20, HJ*

   (E) Marginal profit *($30 – $30) = $0, no gap between MR and MC curves at 600*

3. What is the value of the firm's total fixed cost at 600 units? What is the value of its total fixed cost at 0 units?
   At Q = 600, TFC = (600)($65 – $36) = $17,400. This is the value of TFC at all output levels including Q = 0.

4. Should this firm shut down? Why?
   No. It is earning a positive total profit. It would only shut down if it were making a loss and TR were less than TVC.

5. On the horizontal axis, indicate by Q_1 the output level society would like this firm to produce. Why does the firm not want to produce Q_1?
   Q_1 is the output level at which P = MC, or where the D curve intersects the MC curve. The monopolistically competitive firm does not want to produce Q_1 because those units between 600 and Q_1 have MR < MC which means they will reduce the firm's total profit.

6. On the horizontal axis, indicate by Q_2 the output level at which this firm would maximize its total revenue. Why does the firm not want to produce Q_2?
   Q_2 is the output level at which MR = 0. The monopolistically competitive firm does not want to produce Q_2 because those units between 600 and Q_2 have MR < MC which means they will reduce the firm's total profit.

7. What are the dollar value and the coordinates of consumer surplus when the firm maximizes its total profit?
   CS = (0.5)(600)($130 – $85) = $13,500
   CS = triangle NJK

Part B: Movement from Short-Run Equilibrium to Long-Run Equilibrium

If firms in a monopolistically competitive market are earning positive economic profits, other firms have an incentive to enter this market. As they do so, each firm's share of the total market demand gets smaller and smaller. This means the demand curve facing a monopolistically competitive firm shifts to the left. This process continues until all firms remaining in the industry break even. Outside firms then will no longer have an incentive to enter the market, and existing firms will have no reason to leave because they are receiving their normal profit. Figure 3-16.2 shows the demand and average total cost curves for a typical firm in the monopolistically competitive market for sport shirts.

 Figure 3-16.2

Movement of a Monopolistically Competitive Firm to Long-Run Equilibrium

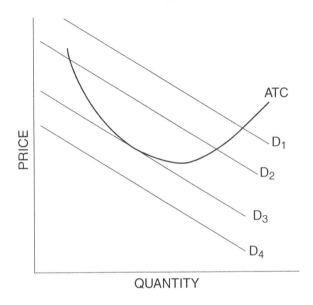

8. If the demand curve for this firm is D_1, is the firm earning positive total profit? If so, will other firms enter the market? What will this do to this firm's share of the market demand?
   Yes, the firm is earning positive total profit because demand (average revenue) is greater than average total cost. Other firms will enter the industry and this firm's share of the market demand will decrease.

9. If this firm's demand decreases from D_1 to D_2, will the firm earn a positive total profit? What will happen to this firm's share of the market demand?
   Yes, the firm is earning positive total profit because demand (average revenue) is greater than average total cost. Other firms will enter the industry and this firm's share of the market demand will decrease.

10. Assume the demand facing the firm drops from D_2 to D_4. Will it earn a positive total profit? If some other firms in the industry are in a similar situation, what will happen to the number of firms in the industry? What will happen to this firm's share of the market demand?
No, the firm will earn a loss because demand (average revenue) is less than average total cost. Some firms will leave the industry over time and this will increase this firm's share of the market demand.

11. Suppose this firm's demand shifts from D_4 to D_3. Is this firm making a positive total profit or a loss? If this is the condition for other firms as well, will firms enter or leave the market?
The firm is breaking even because demand (average revenue) is equal to average total cost. If all firms are breaking even, the industry is in long-run equilibrium and firms will neither enter nor exit the market.

Part C: Evaluation of a Monopolistically Competitive Firm in Long-Run Equilibrium

When a monopolistically competitive firm is in long-run equilibrium, it will break even or earn $0 in total economic profit. Because it is receiving its normal profit, it is doing as well with its resources here as it would in its best alternative. Thus, the firm has no incentive to leave the industry. Figure 3-16.3 illustrates a monopolistically competitive firm in long-run equilibrium with quantity Q^* and price P^*.

Figure 3-16.3

A Monopolistically Competitive Firm in Long-Run Equilibrium

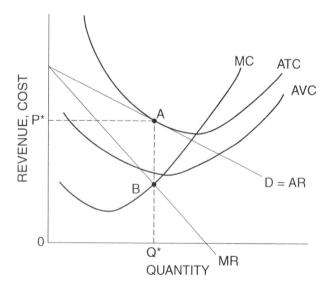

12. If you were asked to draw a graph of a monopolistically competitive firm in a position of long-run equilibrium, there are two conditions you must show with your graph at the profit-maximizing output.

    (A) At Q*, the firm's average revenue (or price) must be (*greater than* / **equal to** / *less than*) its average total cost. This is shown by drawing the demand curve tangent to the ATC curve at point A.

    (B) At Q*, the firm's marginal revenue must be (*greater than* / **equal to** / *less than*) its marginal cost. This is shown by drawing your MR curve through the MC curve at Q* at point B.

13. Is a monopolistically competitive firm productively efficient when it is in long-run equilibrium? Explain.
    No, because its price is greater than the minimum value on its average total cost curve. Consumers are not getting the product at the lowest possible price.

14. Is a monopolistically competitive firm allocatively efficient when it is in long-run equilibrium? Explain.
    No, because its price is greater than its marginal cost. Society would like the firm to produce more output.

15. Is the demand curve facing a monopolistically competitive firm more or less elastic than the demand curve facing a monopoly? Why?
    It is more elastic because the monopolistically competitive firm has many substitute products available in the market.

16. What are the characteristics of a monopolistically competitive market? What are two examples of such a market?
    There are many firms producing similar but not identical products. Entry and exit in the market are relatively easy. Each firm has some control over its price because its product is not identical to other firms' products. Advertising is important in such a market. Examples would include retail clothing stores and restaurants.

Game Theory

Strategic thinking is the art of outdoing an adversary, knowing that the adversary is trying to do the same to you. Dixit and Nalebuff[*]

Game theory is used to explain how two or more players make decisions or choose actions when their actions (or strategies) affect each participant. Each player determines his or her best response to the possible actions of every other player. According to game theory, a player's choice of strategy depends on the strategy the player thinks other players will choose. In some cases, these strategies reinforce each other, but in other cases they do not. When the chosen strategies reinforce each other, the game achieves what is called a *Nash Equilibrium*. The Nash Equilibrium is named after John F. Nash, Jr., who was co-winner of the 1994 Nobel Prize in Economics for his work in this area and the subject of the 2001 movie, *A Beautiful Mind*.

Game theory provides insights into how business and government decisions are made and has numerous real-world applications. For example, game theory has helped economists analyze antitrust policy, tariff wars, and auctioning behavior. This lesson is an introduction to the basic elements of game theory. As you do the math, think about the implications of the results.

Part A: The Basic Elements of Game Theory

The three basic elements of a game are

(A) the players,

(B) the strategies available to each player,

(C) the payoffs each player receives.

These three elements are summarized in a table called a *payoff matrix*. A payoff matrix describes the payoffs to each player for combinations of given strategies. Here is an example of a payoff matrix:

		Coke	
		Advertise	Don't Advertise
Pepsi	Advertise	80, 80	120, 45
	Don't Advertise	45, 120	100, 100

The first number in each square refers to the payoff for the row (horizontal) player, here Pepsi. The second number in each square refers to the payoff for the column (vertical) player, here Coke. The numbers represent the profit (in $ millions) for Pepsi and Coke.

---

[*]Avinash K. Dixit and Barry J. Nalebuff, *Thinking Strategically: The Competitive Edge in Business, Politics, and Everyday Life* (New York: W.W. Norton, 1991), p. 409.

In this game:

(A) The players are Pepsi and Coke.

(B) Here are the strategies available to each player:

- Pepsi, as the row player, can choose either Advertise or Don't Advertise.

- Coke, as the column player, can choose either Advertise or Don't Advertise.

(C) The payoffs each player receives:

- If Pepsi chooses Advertise and Coke chooses Advertise, Pepsi earns 80 and Coke earns 80.

- If Pepsi chooses Advertise and Coke chooses Don't Advertise, Pepsi earns 120 and Coke earns 45.

- If Pepsi chooses Don't Advertise and Coke chooses Advertise, Pepsi earns 45 and Coke earns 120.

- If Pepsi chooses Don't Advertise and Coke chooses Don't Advertise, Pepsi earns 100 and Coke earns 100.

In some games, one or more players can have a *dominant strategy*. A dominant strategy is the best strategy for a player regardless of the strategy chosen by the other player.

1. To see if Pepsi has a dominant strategy, answer these questions based on the information in the payoff matrix.

    (A) If Coke decides to advertise, Pepsi's best strategy would be (***Advertise*** / *Don't Advertise*).

    (B) If Coke decides not to advertise, Pepsi's best strategy would be (***Advertise*** / *Don't Advertise*).

    (C) Is Pepsi's best strategy the same regardless of whether Coke advertises or doesn't advertise? Does this mean Pepsi has a dominant strategy?
    Yes, Pepsi's best strategy is to Advertise regardless of what Coke does. Pepsi has a dominant strategy of Advertise.

2. To see if Coke has a dominant strategy, answer these questions based on the information in the payoff matrix.

    (A) If Pepsi decides to advertise, Coke's best strategy would be (***Advertise*** / *Don't Advertise*).

    (B) If Pepsi decides not to advertise, Coke's best strategy would be (***Advertise*** / *Don't Advertise*).

    (C) Is Coke's best strategy the same regardless of whether Pepsi advertises or doesn't advertise? Does this mean Coke has a dominant strategy?
    Yes, Coke's best strategy is to Advertise regardless of what Pepsi does. Coke has a dominant strategy of Advertise.

3. Do the profit values in the payoff matrix make sense? Why would Pepsi's profit be much higher than Coke's profit when Pepsi advertises and Coke does not? Why could both companies' profit be higher if they both don't advertise compared to if they both do advertise?
    If Pepsi advertises and Coke does not, Pepsi will attract some consumers from Coke. This would increase Pepsi's profit and reduce Coke's profit. Since advertising can be very expensive, it is possible that if both companies do not advertise, their profits could be higher than if they both did advertise.

A *dominated strategy* yields a lower payoff than at least one other strategy. In this game, the dominated strategy for Pepsi is Don't Advertise; it is dominated by Advertise. Regardless of the strategy selected by Coke, Pepsi gains more by choosing Advertise. If Pepsi chooses Don't Advertise, the payoff is 45, while a strategy of Advertise has a payoff of 80. Since 45 is less than 80, the dominated strategy is Don't Advertise.

The dominated strategy for Coke is Don't Advertise; it is dominated by Advertise. If Coke chooses Don't Advertise, Coke receives 45 if Pepsi chooses Advertise and 100 if Pepsi chooses Don't Advertise. Since 45 is less than 100, the dominated strategy for Coke is Don't Advertise.

A *Nash Equilibrium* exists when each player is doing his/her best, given what the other player is doing. It is a combination of strategies for each player, such that each chooses his/her best response to the other's strategy choice. In this game, the Nash Equilibrium is both players deciding to Advertise. Although in this example both Coke and Pepsi select the same strategy, in a Nash Equilibrium the players do not have to select the same strategy.

A Nash Equilibrium is similar to a market equilibrium in that there is no incentive for producers and consumers to change from the equilibrium price. Thus a Nash Equilibrium is an "enforceable" equilibrium because the firms do not have an incentive to cheat as they might in a cartel.

Other economic examples of game-theory applications are decisions by firms about what price to charge, whether to enter a market, where to locate, and what kind of product or quality level to produce; decisions by a central bank on monetary policy actions; and decisions by a nation on the optimal tariff policy.

Part B: The Prisoner's Dilemma Game

One classic application of game theory is the *prisoner's dilemma game*. Prisoner's dilemma games are games in which each player has a dominant strategy; and when both players play the dominant strategy, the payoffs are smaller than if each player played the dominated strategy. The dilemma is how to avoid this bad outcome.

The basics of the prisoner's dilemma game are as follows: two prisoners, Charles and Frances, have the option to confess or not confess to a crime they committed. The prosecutor has only enough information to convict both criminals of a minor offense and is, therefore, relying on a confession. The minor offense carries one year in jail. The prisoners are questioned in different cells, without the ability to communicate. They are told that if one prisoner confesses while the other remains silent, the prisoner confessing will go free and the prisoner remaining silent will serve 20 years in jail. If both prisoners confess, both prisoners will serve three years in jail.

If a player goes free, the payoff is 0. If a player serves one year in jail, the payoff is –1. If a player spends 20 years in jail, the payoff is –20. Use these numbers in your payoff matrix. Note that the negative numbers come from losing years of freedom.

4. Determine the three basic elements of the game.

(A) The players: ***Charles and Frances***

(B) The strategies for each player: ***Confess or Not Confess***

(C) The payoffs for each player: ***If one confesses, he or she goes free, and the other prisoner gets 20 years in jail. If both confess, both get three years in jail. If neither confess, both get one year in jail.***

5. Create a payoff matrix for the prisoner's dilemma game.

		Frances	
		Confess	Not Confess
Charles	Confess	–3, –3	0, –20
	Not Confess	–20, 0	–1, –1

6. Are there dominant strategies? Explain.
   Charles and Frances both have Confess as a dominant strategy. This is each prisoner's best strategy no matter what the other prisoner decides to do.

7. Identify any dominated strategies. Explain.
   Not Confess is a dominated strategy for both Charles and Frances. This strategy gives a less desirable outcome than the strategy of Confess for each prisoner.

8. Is there a Nash Equilibrium? Explain.
   Yes, the Nash Equilibrium is for both prisoners to Confess.

Part C: Variation of the Prisoner's Dilemma Game

You are in a class with one other student. It is the end of the semester, and final exams are in a week. Your teacher has said the final exam will be graded so that anyone who scores the class average on the final exam will receive a "B" in the class. Anyone who scores above the average will receive an "A" in the class, and anyone who scores below the average will fail the class. You would certainly score higher on the exam than the other student. You and the other student have made an agreement not to take the final exam so that the class average is zero and you both receive "B" grades.

9. Determine the three basic elements of the game.

   (A) The players: *You and the Other Student*

   (B) The strategies for each player: *Take the Exam or Not Take the Exam*

   (C) The payoffs for each player: *If both of you take the exam, you receive an A and the other student receives an F. If both of you do not take the exam, you both receive a B. If you take the exam and the other student does not take the exam, you receive an A and the other student receives an F. If the other student takes the exam and you do not take the exam, you receive an F and the other student receives an A.*

10. Create a payoff matrix for this game.

		Other Student	
		Take the Exam	Not Take the Exam
You	Take the Exam	A, F	A, F
	Not Take the Exam	F, A	B, B

11. Do you have a dominant strategy? Explain.

Yes, Take the Exam is my dominant strategy because it is my best choice no matter what strategy the other student chooses.

12. Using a four-point scale (A = 4, B = 3, C = 2, and D = 1), which choice results in the highest class GPA?

The highest class GPA will result if neither student takes the exam. If neither student takes the exam, each student will receive a B which results in 6 grade points, or an average GPA of 3.0 per student. Each of the other three strategy combinations will produce one A and one F for a total of 4 grade points, or an average GPA of 2.0 per student.

If you finished Parts B and C correctly, you will realize that when each player chooses his or her dominant strategy, the result is unattractive to the group.

The key to avoiding the prisoner's dilemma outcome of lower payoffs for both players is to find a way for players to credibly commit to playing a dominated strategy. Merely having both prisoners agree to Not Confess or both students to Not Take the Exam will not work. This results because it is always optimal for Prisoner 1 (or Prisoner 2) to still play the Confess strategy, and it is always optimal for the better student to play the Take the Exam strategy. One possible way to have credible commitment in the prisoner's dilemma game would be to have both prisoners reveal another past crime they committed, thus ensuring that if they confess to this crime, the other prisoner will have additional information to punish the prisoner who cheats on an agreement to not confess.

One way to do this is to form a *cartel*. A cartel is a coalition of firms that coordinate their decisions to reach a more optimal solution for all members of the group by finding ways to credibly commit players to play their dominated strategies. Cartels, however, are not always successful in maintaining their agreements because there may be an incentive for a member to cheat on the cartel.

Part D: What Should These Firms Do?

There are two firms that produce fiberglass canoes. Both River Queen and Ace Current must decide whether to market a Premium canoe or a Regular canoe. The profit of a firm depends on the type of canoe produced by the other firm. In this chart, the first value is the profit of River Queen, and the second value is the profit of Ace Current. The firms make their decisions simultaneously in a one-period situation. (The values in the chart are thousands of dollars.)

		Ace Current	
		Premium	Regular
River Queen	Premium	$400, $100	$450, $200
	Regular	$150, $400	$200, $150

13. Does River Queen have a dominant strategy? What decision will River Queen make?
River Queen has a dominant strategy. If Ace Current produces a Premium canoe, River Queen earns a profit of $400,000 by making a Premium canoe compared to only $150,000 by making a Regular canoe. If Ace Current produces a Regular canoe, River Queen earns a profit of $450,000 by making a Premium canoe compared to only $200,000 by making a Regular canoe. No matter what Ace Current decides to do, River Queen has a higher profit if it produces the Premium canoe, so that is River Queen's dominant strategy.

14. Does Ace Current have a dominant strategy? What decision will Ace Current make?
Ace Current does not have a dominant strategy because its optimal strategy depends on the choice made by River Queen. If River Queen produces a Premium canoe, Ace Current's best strategy is to produce a Regular canoe. But if River Queen produces a Regular canoe, the payoff matrix shows Ace Current should produce a Premium canoe. Assuming Ace Current knows that River Queen has a dominant strategy of a Premium canoe, Ace Current will know its best strategy is to produce a Regular canoe.

15. Is there a Nash Equilibrium?
Yes, River Queen will produce a Premium canoe and Ace Current will produce a Regular canoe. Each firm will be doing its best, given what the other firm is doing.

Part E: Questions

16. Is the Coke and Pepsi advertising game a prisoner's dilemma game? Explain why or why not.
Yes, it is optimal for both players to play their dominated strategies and be at the Don't Advertise/Don't Advertise corner, earning 100 each.

17. Interpret "standing at a concert" in terms of the prisoner's dilemma game.
If one person stands, he or she gets a better view of the concert. If the person in front of someone stands, then that person's best response is also to stand, or he or she will not be able to see the concert. However, if all people sat, then everyone would be able to see the concert and would not get tired standing.

18. Explain at least one way the optimal outcome for players, which would be for all players to play the dominated strategy, can be reached in Question 17. What are the possible commitment problems?
The concert hall could require people at the concert to remain seated. However, this implies an external enforcer. If an external enforcer cannot be used, the group may collectively decide ways to punish those who stand. The punishment could range from throwing food at violators to physically assaulting them. The key is to make the commitment credible.

19. A rivalry exists between the U.S. jet producer Boeing and the European jet producer Airbus. Each government has the opportunity to subsidize its jet producer to give it a competitive edge in the global market. Using game theory, explain what you would expect to observe in practice.
Both countries would subsidize their producers. However, this costs money and lowers the price of jets for the rest of the world without either firm ultimately receiving a competitive advantage (the same outcome for both firms if there were no subsidies at all). This is another example of the prisoner's dilemma game.

MICROECONOMICS

Factor Markets

Unit 4

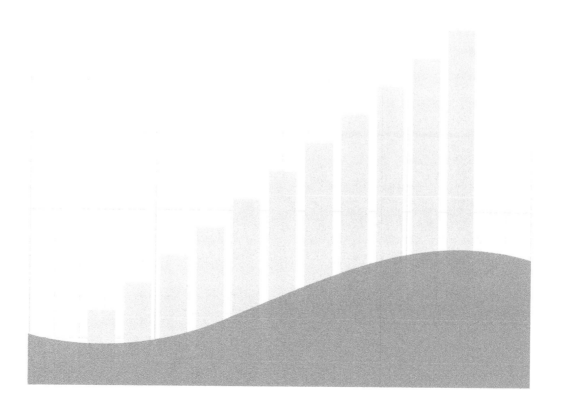

■ Firms are sellers in product markets and buyers in factor (resource) markets.

■ The demand for any resource is derived from the demand for the products that the resource can produce. Thus, resource demand depends on the price of the good or service that the resource produces and on the resource's productivity in producing the good or service.

■ The demand curve for a resource in the short run is downward sloping because the marginal physical product (MPP) of additional inputs of a resource will decrease as a result of the law of diminishing marginal returns. In some textbooks, marginal physical product is called marginal product.

■ A firm will continue to hire factors of production as long as its marginal revenue product (MRP) exceeds its marginal resource cost (MRC). A firm will not hire more resources once MRC exceeds MRP.

■ The marginal revenue product curve for a firm selling its product in an imperfectly competitive market will be steeper than the marginal revenue product curve for a firm selling in a perfectly competitive market. The steeper slope results from both a decrease in the marginal physical product and a decrease in the product price required to permit the firm to sell a larger output.

■ A firm maximizes total profits where a factor's marginal revenue product equals the factor's marginal resource cost. A firm maximizes total profit where MRP = MRC.

■ In a perfectly competitive labor market, a firm can hire all the workers it wants at the current market wage. The firm will hire workers until the last worker's wage (MRC) equals the marginal revenue product of that last worker hired.

■ When a combination of resources is employed in producing a good or service, the profit-maximizing rule is

$$\frac{MRP_a}{MRC_a} = \frac{MRP_b}{MRC_b} = \frac{MRP_n}{MRC_n} = 1.$$

■ When a firm produces the profit-maximizing level of output, it must utilize a least-cost combination of resources. The rule for a least-cost combination of resources is

$$\frac{MPP_a}{MRC_a} = \frac{MPP_b}{MRC_b} = \frac{MPP_n}{MRC_n}.$$

■ For a firm facing a perfectly competitive resource market, resource supply is perfectly elastic and equal to marginal resource cost at a market-determined price (wage) for the resource. Under monopsony or other imperfect conditions of employment, both resource supply and marginal resource cost are positively sloped curves with the marginal resource cost being a value greater than the price (wage) for all units beyond the first unit of the resource employed.

■ Given a downward-sloping marginal revenue product curve and the differences existing between supply and marginal resource cost in perfect competition and monopsony, a monopsonistic employer will pay a lower price (wage) and hire fewer units of a resource than a perfect competitor.

■ Economic rent is any payment to the supplier of a resource that is greater than the minimum amount required to employ the desired quantity of the resource

■ The equilibrium real interest rate influences the level of investment and helps allocate financial and physical capital to specific firms and industries.

- Profits are the return to entrepreneurs for assuming risk and for organizing and directing economic resources.

- Profits allocate resources according to the demands of consumers.

Advanced Placement Economics Microeconomics: Teacher Resource Manual © Council for Economic Education, New York, N.Y.

How Many Workers Should a Firm Hire?

You are the president of Acme Yo-Yo Company, a small manufacturing firm that produces Supersonic Yo-Yos, a popular toy that makes a "supersonic" noise when used.

■ Acme yo-yos are produced by workers operating with two yo-yo-making machines. You have estimated how many yo-yos can be made using different numbers of workers and you must decide how many workers to hire to maximize your firm's total profit.

■ Acme is a perfect competitor in the product market. This means your firm can sell as many yo-yos as you want at the market price of a yo-yo.

■ Acme also is a perfect competitor in the labor resource market. This means you can hire as many workers as you want at the market wage.

■ You will hire each worker who adds more to your firm's total revenue than he/she adds to your total cost. You will not hire a worker who adds less to total revenue than to total cost.

■ Marginal physical product (MPP) is the change in your firm's total output (Q) from adding an extra worker: $MPP = \Delta Q/\Delta L$, where L stands for labor.

■ Marginal revenue product (MRP) is the change in your firm's total revenue (TR) from adding an extra worker: $MRP = \Delta TR/\Delta L$. Because you can sell all the yo-yos you want at the market price (P), $MRP = (MPP)(P \text{ of a yo-yo})$.

■ Marginal resource cost (MRC) is the change in your firm's total cost (TC) from adding an extra worker: $MRC = \Delta TC/\Delta L$. Because you can hire all the workers you want at the market wage, $MRC = Wage$.

■ The profit-maximizing rule for an employer is to hire the number of workers at which $MRP = MRC$. This means the employer hires those workers with $MRP > MRC$ and stops before hiring workers with $MRP < MRC$. (If this rule sounds familiar, it uses the same logic as the $MR = MC$ rule a firm uses to find its profit-maximizing amount of output.)

🛈 *Student Alert:* **Some textbooks use marginal factor cost (MFC) or marginal labor cost (MLC) instead of marginal resource cost (MRC).**

Part A: Creating the Firm's Demand for Labor

 Table 4-1.1
Productivity and Revenue Data for Yo-Yo Workers

L (workers per day)	Q (yo-yos per day)	MPP	P	TR	MRP
0	0	–	*$5*	$0	–
1	20	*+20*	*$5*	*$100*	*+$100*
2	50	+30	*$5*	*$250*	+$150
3	70	*+20*	$5	*$350*	*+$100*
4	85	*+15*	*$5*	$425	*+$75*
5	95	+10	*$5*	*$475*	*+$50*
6	100	*+5*	*$5*	*$500*	*+$25*

1. Complete Table 4-1.1. Assume the market price of a yo-yo is $5.

2. Why does the number of extra yo-yos produced by an additional worker decrease as more workers are added? Is it because the additional workers are less motivated and less talented than previous workers?
   MPP gets smaller due to the principle of diminishing marginal productivity, which says that as a firm adds more workers to a fixed amount of equipment, eventually the MPP diminishes. This is caused by the limited amount of capital and not because some workers are lazy or untrained. Economists assume the firm has homogeneous (identical) labor units.

3. Plot the MRP values in Figure 4-1.1. Connect those values and label the curve as "MRP." Plot each MRP value on the higher of the two L values, not at the midpoint. For example, plot the MRP value of $150 at L = 2 rather than at L = 1.5.

Figure 4-1.1

The Acme Firm's Demand for Labor and Supply of Labor

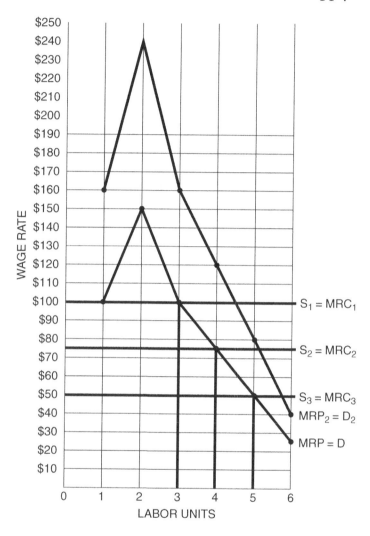

4. If the market wage is $100 per worker per day, your firm can hire all the workers it wants at that wage. This means the supply of labor to your firm can be shown as a horizontal line at the wage of $100. Draw a horizontal line in Figure 4-1.1 at $100 and label the line as "$S_1 = MRC_1$." The MRC to the firm of each extra worker is equal to the wage of $100.

5. At a wage of $100, how many workers should your firm hire? Why?
   The firm will hire 3 workers at a wage of $100. The first worker has MRP = $100, the second has MRP = $150, and the third has MRP = $100. Because the fourth worker has MRP of only $75, that worker will not be hired at a wage of $100.

6. Now assume the market wage drops to $75. Draw a new horizontal line at that wage and label it as "$S_2 = MRC_2$." How many workers will be hired at the wage of $75?
The firm will hire four workers at a wage of $75.

7. Finally, assume the market wage is $50. Draw another horizontal line at that wage and label it as "$S_3 = MRC_3$." How many units of labor will be hired at the wage of $50?
The firm will hire five workers at a wage of $50.

8. The firm's demand for labor shows how many workers it will hire at different wages. Complete Table 4-1.2 based on your work above.

 Table 4-1.2
Acme's Demand for Labor

Wage	Number of workers hired
$100	*3*
$75	*4*
$50	*5*

9. If a firm hires labor in a perfectly competitive factor market, then the downward sloping portion of its MRP curve is its demand (D) curve for labor. If the wage is equal to the MRC, then by going to its MRP curve at a given wage, the firm finds the amount of labor where MRP = MCL. Go back to Figure 4-1.1 and label the MRP curve as "MRP = D."

10. Is the law of demand evident in Table 4-1.2? Why does a firm hire more workers when the wage decreases?
Yes. As the wage decreases, the firm increases the number of workers it wishes to hire. A lower wage makes additional workers profitable.

Part B: The Derived Demand for Labor

We saw in Part A that if a firm operates in perfectly competitive resource markets, its demand for labor is its MRP curve. So what can increase the firm's demand for labor? Remember how we calculate MRP if the product market is perfectly competitive: MRP = (MPP)(price of the good). An increase in the MPP of labor or an increase in the price of the good will increase the MRP of labor, thus increasing the firm's demand for labor. A decrease in the marginal physical product or a decrease in the good's price will reduce the demand for labor.

11. In Table 4-1.3, indicate for each situation whether the product or labor market is being affected, whether the MPP of labor or the price (P) of the good will change, and whether the demand for labor will increase or decrease.

 Table 4-1.3

Factors Changing a Firm's Demand for Labor

Situation	Which market?	Change in MPP?	Change in P?	Change in demand for labor
(A) A new yo-yo machine increases productivity of labor.	Product / **_Labor_**	**_Yes_** / No	Yes / **_No_**	**_Increase_** / Decrease
(B) The price of yo-yos increases.	**_Product_** / Labor	Yes / **_No_**	**_Yes_** / No	**_Increase_** / Decrease
(C) New government safety regulation reduces worker productivity.	Product / **_Labor_**	**_Yes_** / No	Yes / **_No_**	Increase / **_Decrease_**
(D) The demand for yo-yos decreases.	**_Product_** / Labor	Yes / **_No_**	**_Yes_** / No	Increase / **_Decrease_**
(E) New technology increases output of yo-yos.	Product / **_Labor_**	**_Yes_** / No	Yes / **_No_**	**_Increase_** / Decrease
(F) Consumers become tired of yo-yos.	**_Product_** / Labor	Yes / **_No_**	**_Yes_** / No	Increase / **_Decrease_**

The demand for any resource is called a *derived demand* because it is derived from the demand for the good or service that is produced by the resource. It is important that you understand the relationship between demand in the factor market and demand in the product market. (Even if you are a charming individual, unless you produce a good or service that is in demand, you will find it hard to land a good job.)

12. Assume that yo-yos become a hot fad and the increased demand for them drives the market price of a yo-yo up to $8. Complete Table 4-1.4, which has the same productivity data as Table 4-1.1.

Table 4-1.4
Productivity and Revenue Data for Yo-Yo Workers

L (workers per day)	Q (yo-yos per day)	MPP	P	TR	MRP
0	0	–		$0	–
1	20	**+20**	**$8**	**$160**	**+$160**
2	50	+30	**$8**	**$400**	+$240
3	70	+20	$8	**$560**	+$160
4	85	**+15**	**$8**	$680	**+$120**
5	95	+10	**$8**	**$760**	**+$80**
6	100	**+5**	**$8**	**$800**	**+$40**

13. Plot the new MRP data in Figure 4-1.1 and label it as "$D_2 = MRP_2$." Does this represent an increase in Acme's demand for labor? What caused it?
This is an increase in the demand for labor caused by an increase in the price of the good that labor is producing. The productivity of labor is unchanged but the value of the MPP has increased because of the higher price of yo-yos.

14. Based on your new MRP_2 curve in Figure 4-1.1, fill in Table 4-1.5.
Because of the increase in labor's MRP, Acme will increase the number of workers hired at wages of $100 and $75. It still hires 5 workers at a wage of $50 because the MRP of the sixth worker is still less than $50.

Table 4-1.5
Acme's New Demand for Labor

Wage	Number of workers hired
$100	**4**
$75	**5**
$50	**5**

Part C: How Many Workers to Hire?

Figure 4-1.2 shows the MRP curve and the MRC curve for a company that sells its product in a perfectly competitive goods market and hires its labor in a perfectly competitive resource market.

15. You tell your friend that this firm should hire 760 units of labor because that is where MRP = MRC. Your friend is confused and asks how this firm can maximize total profit with 760 labor units since the marginal profit from the 760th labor unit appears to be $0. Can you help your friend understand the logic of the MRP = MRC rule?

Figure 4-1.2
Logic of the MRP = MRC Rule

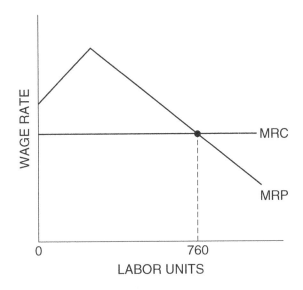

Yes, the marginal profit of the 760th worker is $0 because for that worker we see that MRP = MRC. But by hiring 760 workers, the firm hired the first 759 workers. And each of them had MRP > MRC, which means they each created positive marginal profit for the firm, thus increasing the firm's total profit. By stopping with the 760th unit, the firm did not hire workers with MRP < MRC because they would have negative marginal profit, which would decrease the firm's total profit. The "MRP = MCL" rule is a handy tool that identifies the amount of labor needed to maximize the firm's total profit.

The Optimal Combination of Resources

In Activity 4-1, we assumed the Acme Yo-Yo Company was operating in the short run with a fixed amount of capital (equipment) and with labor as its variable resource. Let's now consider a long-run example where the firm can change its capital as well as its labor. What combination of labor (L) and capital (K) should the firm employ?

Part A: The Least-Cost Combination of Resources

What should a firm do if it wants to produce the most output possible from a given resource budget? What should it do if it wants to produce a given level of output at the lowest total cost? The approach to both of these problems is similar. The firm should allocate its resource budget between units of labor and units of capital in such a way that the following condition is satisfied, where marginal physical product is MPP and marginal resource cost is MRC:

$$\frac{MPP_L}{MRC_L} = \frac{MPP_K}{MRC_K}.$$

If the resource markets are perfectly competitive, the price the firm pays for an extra unit of a resource is equal to its MRC. In that case the condition can be written as

$$\frac{MPP_L}{P_L} = \frac{MPP_K}{P_K}.$$

where P_L is the price of a unit of labor and P_K is the price of a unit of capital.

Another way of stating this condition for *economic efficiency* is that the firm should get the same extra output from the last dollar spent on each type of resource.

Assume a firm has allocated its given resource budget between labor and capital and finds the marginal physical product for the resources to be 200 units from labor and 400 units from capital. That means the last unit of labor increased total output by 200 units while the last unit of capital increased output by 400 units. At first glance, you might think the firm should move some money away from labor and over to capital. But that would totally ignore the prices of the two resources. Assume the prices of labor and capital in competitive resource markets are $10 and $40, respectively.

1. Calculate the "MPP per $1" for each resource.

   Labor: $\frac{200\ units}{\$10} = 20\ units\ per\ \$1.$ **Capital:** $\frac{400\ units}{\$40} = 10\ units\ per\ \$1.$

2. Based on your work in Question 1, is the firm getting the most output possible from its given resource budget? If so, explain why. If not, how should it reallocate its budget between labor and capital?
   No, the firm can do better. It should spend more of its budget on labor and less on capital. Labor is giving more output per $1 on the margin than is capital.

3. Suppose the MPP values are as given in Question 1, but that the prices of labor and capital are $10 and $20, respectively. Is the firm now getting the most output possible from its resource budget? Explain.

$$\text{Labor:} \quad \frac{200 \text{ units}}{\$10} = 20 \text{ units per } \$1. \qquad \text{Capital:} \quad \frac{400 \text{ units}}{\$20} = 20 \text{ units per } \$1.$$

The firm is getting the most output possible from its resource budget. If it moved a dollar from one resource to the other, there would be no net change in output.

4. A different firm has allocated its resource budget between labor and capital and is producing a given output level at the lowest possible total cost. The MPP of labor is 25 units, and the MPP of capital is 20 units. If the price of a unit of labor is $100, what is the price of a unit of capital?
Since we know the firm is using the least-cost combination of resources, we can solve for the price of capital:

$$\frac{25 \text{ units}}{\$100} = \frac{20 \text{ units}}{P_K} \qquad (25 \text{ units})(P_K) = \$2,000 \qquad P_K = \$80.$$

Part B: The Profit-Maximizing Combination of Resources

The economic efficiency condition in Part A is what economists call a "necessary but not sufficient" condition for profit maximization. In other words, if a firm is not using an economically efficient (least-cost) combination of resources, then it cannot possibly be maximizing its total profit. If it is using an economically efficient combination, then it might be profit maximizing, but an additional condition must be satisfied to guarantee that is the case.

Here is the profit-maximizing condition for a combination of two resources:

$$\frac{MRP_L}{MRC_L} = \frac{MRP_K}{MRC_K} = 1.$$

If the resource markets are perfectly competitive, the condition can be written as

$$\frac{MRP_L}{P_L} = \frac{MRP_K}{P_K} = 1.$$

While this condition looks similar to the one in Part A, there are two significant differences.

1. The firm is comparing MRP, not MPP, to MRC.

2. The two ratios must both be equal to 1.

The second difference means the MRP from the last unit of each resource must be equal to its MRC. If the MRP of a unit of labor is greater than its MRC, the firm should hire more labor. If the MRP of a unit of capital is less than its MRC, the firm should get rid of some capital. (This is the rule we used in Activity 4-1 to find the profit-maximizing amount of labor in the short run when capital was fixed: Hire the amount of labor where MRP = MCL.)

5. Suppose the Ebbets Company produces 1,000 units of output with a combination of labor and capital such that the MRP of labor is $30 and the MRP of capital is $40. If this firm is maximizing its total profit at this output, what are the prices of units of labor and capital? (Assume the firm buys resources in perfectly competitive markets.)

$$\frac{\$30}{P_L} = \frac{\$40}{P_K} = 1.$$

The price of labor is $30 and the price of capital is $40.

6. The Shibe Company produces 800 units of output per period. The MRP of labor is $60, and the MRP of capital is $40. The market prices of units of labor and capital are $12 and $8, respectively. Is this firm maximizing its total profit? Explain.

$$Labor: \frac{\$60}{\$12} = \frac{\$5}{\$1}. \qquad Capital: \frac{\$40}{\$8} = \frac{\$5}{\$1}.$$

No, it is not maximizing its total profits. Since the MRP from each resource exceeds the price (MRC) of that resource, the firm should hire more of each resource and expand its output. Don't be fooled by the fact that in this example the two ratios are equal. The point is that both ratios are greater than 1, which means the firm should employ more labor and more capital.

7. The Honus Company currently produces Q_1 units of output each period. It sells its good in a perfectly competitive product market and buys its resources in perfectly competitive factor markets. The MPP of labor is 50 units, and the MPP of capital is 80 units. The prices it pays for units of labor and capital are $100 and $160, respectively.

(A) Is the company operating in an economically efficient manner? Explain.

$$Labor: \frac{50\ units}{\$100} = 0.5\ units\ per\ \$1. \qquad Capital: \frac{80\ units}{\$160} = 0.5\ units\ per\ \$1.$$

Yes, the firm is economically efficient. It is producing its output Q_1 at the lowest possible total cost.

(B) What would the market price of its good have to be for the firm to be maximizing its total profit?
Since it is using an economically efficient combination of resources, the firm might be maximizing its total profit. For profit-maximization to occur, the firm must use a combination of resources such that $MRP_L = P_L$ and $MRP_K = P_K$.

$$MPR_L = P_L \qquad\qquad MPR_K = P_K$$
$$(MPP_L)(P_{good}) = P_L \qquad (MPP_K)(P_{good}) = P_K$$
$$(50\ units)\ (P_{good}) = \$100 \qquad (80\ units)\ (P_{good}) = \$160$$
$$P_{good} = \$2.00 \qquad\qquad P_{good} = \$2.00$$

For profit-maximization, the price of its good would have to be $2.00.

The least-cost and profit-maximization conditions also apply to a firm with more than two resources (W, X, and Y).

Least-cost combination:
$$\frac{MPP_W}{MRC_W} = \frac{MPP_X}{MRC_X} = \frac{MPP_Y}{MRC_Y}.$$

Profit-maximization combination:
$$\frac{MRP_W}{MRC_W} = \frac{MRP_X}{MRC_X} = \frac{MRP_Y}{MRC_Y} = 1.$$

The Only Game in Town

In Activity 4-1, we assumed the Acme Yo-Yo Company sold its product in a perfectly competitive market. Acme could sell all the yo-yos it wanted at the price determined in the market. Now, let's suppose that Acme is a monopolist and controls the yo-yo market. Because it still hires its workers in a perfectly competitive labor market, we will continue to treat its marginal revenue product (MRP) curve as its demand for labor (L). It can hire all the workers it wants at the market wage rate.

What is different in our analysis if Acme is a monopolist in the product market rather than a perfectly competitive seller of yo-yos? The difference is that now the firm must lower its price to sell more yo-yos. That will create a wedge between its price and the marginal revenue it receives from an extra sold unit. And it will make the workers' MRP decrease faster than it did when the firm was perfectly competitive. Now there are two reasons why MRP decreases as more workers are hired: diminishing marginal productivity and diminishing marginal revenue.

Part A: Creating the Monopolist's Demand for Labor

1. Complete Table 4-3.1, which shows the prices at which the Acme monopolist can sell the different quantities of yo-yos it is producing. You can see that the firm must lower the price to sell more of its product. The productivity data are the same as they were in Activity 4-1; the fact that the firm now has no competition in the product market does not affect the productivity of workers.

🛈 *Student Alert:* **You cannot find the MRP of a worker by multiplying the marginal physical product (MPP) by the price (P). That worked in Activity 4-1 because the firm sold its output (Q) at the market price. But now the firm is a monopolist and must lower price to sell more output. MRP is found here as the change in total revenue (TR) when the firm adds an extra worker.**

 Table 4-3.1
Productivity and Revenue Data for Yo-Yo Workers

L (workers per day)	Q (yo-yos per day)	MPP	P	TR	MRP
0	0	–	$8.00	$0	–
1	20	**+20**	$7.25	**$145.00**	**+$145.00**
2	50	+30	$6.00	**$300.00**	+$155.00
3	70	**+20**	$5.25	**$367.50**	**+$67.50**
4	85	**+15**	$4.70	$399.50	**+$32.00**
5	95	+10	$4.30	**$408.50**	+$9.00
6	100	**+5**	$4.00	**$400.00**	**−$8.50**

2. Plot the firm's MRP data in Figure 4-3.1. Connect the MRP values and label the curve as "D = MRP." Plot the MRP values at the new labor amount rather than at the midpoint.

 Figure 4-3.1
The Acme Firm's Demand for Labor and Supply of Labor

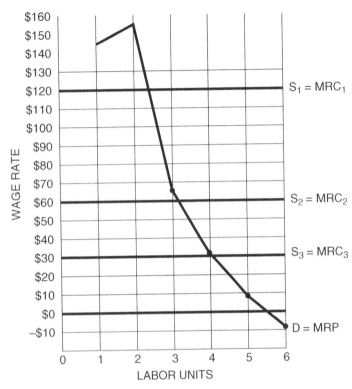

3. Draw three horizontal labor supply curves in Figure 4-3.1 at wages of $120, $60, and $30. Label them as "$S_1$ = MRC_1," "S_2 = MRC_2," and "S_3 = MRC_3."

4. Complete Table 4-3.2, which shows how many workers the firm will hire at each of these wages. *The firm will hire each unit of labor for which MRP is greater than or equal to MRC.*

 Table 4-3.2
Acme's Demand for Labor

Wage	Number of workers hired
$120	*2*
$60	*3*
$30	*4*

5. Does the law of demand apply to this firm, which is a monopolist in the product market?
Yes. This firm, like any other firm, will hire more workers if the wage is reduced.

6. Why can we consider the firm's MRP curve as its labor demand curve? Is it important that the labor market is perfectly competitive? Is it important that the product market is not perfectly competitive?
A demand curve shows how many units of an item are demanded at different prices. Since this firm buys labor in a perfectly competitive factor market, it can get all the workers at the market wage. This means the wage is equal to the firm's marginal resource cost. At any wage, it can go horizontally out to the MRP curve to find the optimal number of workers to hire. The fact that it is a monopolist in the product market does not play a role in stating that the MRP curve is the firm's demand for labor.

7. Other things being equal, would Acme's demand curve for labor be steeper or flatter now than it was when it was in a perfectly competitive goods market? Why?
It will be steeper because there now are two reasons why MRP decreases as more workers are added: (1) diminishing marginal productivity from extra labor units, and (2) diminishing marginal revenue from extra output units. When the product market was perfectly competitive, the only reason MRP decreased as more labor was hired was diminishing marginal productivity.

Factor Market Pricing

A perfectly competitive labor market determines the equilibrium wage and employment in that market. Firms that buy labor in this market will pay the market wage and can hire all the workers they want at this wage. This activity demonstrates how the market wage is set and how a firm interacts with the labor market.

Part A: Labor Demand for the Perfectly Competitive Firm

The Awesome Belt Company (ABC) is a price taker in both the input and output markets. It hires labor in a perfectly competitive resource market and sells its belts in a perfectly competitive product market. The total revenue (TR) the firm receives from each amount of labor is found by multiplying output (Q) by the price (P) at which that level of output can be sold. The marginal revenue product (MRP) of an extra unit of labor is the change in TR resulting from the firm adding the extra labor unit.

1. Complete Table 4-4.1 based on two different possible prices for ABC's belts.

Table 4-4.1
ABC's Productivity and Revenue Data

Labor (L)	Output (Q)	Marginal physical product (MPP) ($\Delta Q/\Delta L$)	Price = $2.00		Price = $3.00	
			TR	MRP	TR	MRP
0	0	–	$0	–	*$0*	–
1	10	+10	*$20*	+$20	*$30*	*+$30*
2	30	+20	$60	*+$40*	*$90*	*+$60*
3	70	*+40*	$140	*+$80*	$210	*+$120*
4	105	*+35*	*$210*	*+$70*	*$315*	+$105
5	135	*+30*	$270	+$60	*$405*	*+$90*
6	160	*+25*	*$320*	*+$50*	$480	*+$75*
7	180	+20	*$360*	+$40	*$540*	+$60
8	195	*+15*	$390	*+$30*	$585	*+$45*
9	205	+10	*$410*	+$20	*$615*	+$30
10	205	+0	*$410*	*+$0*	*$615*	+$0
11	195	*−10*	$390	−$20	*$585*	*−$30*

2. Now complete Table 4-4.2 and Table 4-4.3, which show ABC's demand for labor at two different prices of belts. The demand schedules indicate the highest wage the firm will pay for a given number of workers, based on the MRP of workers in Table 4-4.1.

 Table 4-4.2
ABC's Demand for Labor if the Price of Belts Is $2.00

Wage	Quantity of labor demanded
$20	9
$30	8
$40	7
$50	6
$60	5
$70	4
$80	3

 Table 4-4.3
ABC's Demand for Labor if the Price of Belts Is $3.00

Wage	Quantity of labor demanded
$30	9
$45	8
$60	7
$75	6
$90	5
$105	4
$120	3

Part B: The Perfectly Competitive Labor Market

3. Assuming there are 1,000 firms identical to ABC in the belt industry, complete Table 4-4.4, based on the market price of belts being $2.00. Since the firms are identical, you can simply multiply the quantity of labor demanded by ABC at the different wages by 1,000 to derive the market demand for labor. Table 4-4.4 also has information about the number of workers willing to supply their labor at the different wages. Comparing the quantity of workers demanded and the quantity supplied, indicate whether there is a shortage or a surplus of labor at each wage. One wage is the equilibrium wage in the market.

Table 4-4.4
The Labor Market Based on the Price of Belts Being $2.00

Wage	Quantity of labor demanded	Quantity of labor supplied	State of the labor market
$20	*9,000*	3,000	**Shortage** / Equilibrium / Surplus
$30	*8,000*	4,000	**Shortage** / Equilibrium / Surplus
$40	*7,000*	5,000	**Shortage** / Equilibrium / Surplus
$50	*6,000*	6,000	Shortage / **Equilibrium** / Surplus
$60	*5,000*	7,000	Shortage / Equilibrium / **Surplus**
$70	*4,000*	8,000	Shortage / Equilibrium / **Surplus**
$80	*3,000*	9,000	Shortage / Equilibrium / **Surplus**

4. In Figure 4-4.1, plot the market demand and supply curves for labor from Table 4-4.4. Label the demand curve as "$D_{\$2.00}$" and the supply curve as "S".

Figure 4-4.1
The Labor Market

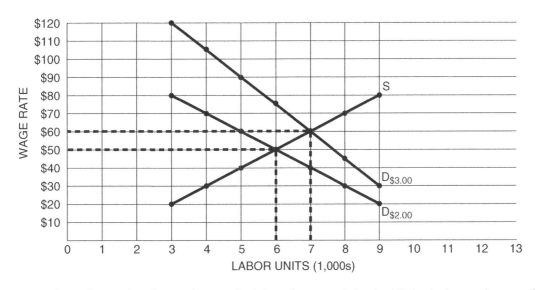

5. Why is the market demand curve for labor downward sloping? Why is the market supply curve of labor upward sloping?
    Firms will hire more workers at a low wage and fewer workers at a high wage. The market demand is the sum of the individual demands of firms, and the MRP (demand) curve of a typical firm is downward sloping. Workers respond positively to a higher wage and will offer more labor as the wage increases. The market supply curve is the horizontal summation of the upward-sloping supply curves of individual workers.

6. Assume the wage is at some level greater than the equilibrium wage. Is there a shortage or surplus of labor? What adjustments take place in the market to move the wage to the equilibrium wage? *At a wage above the equilibrium wage, there will be a surplus of workers. This surplus puts downward pressure on the market wage. As the wage falls, the quantity demanded of workers increases and the quantity supplied decreases, until the surplus is eliminated.*

7. Assume the wage is at some level less than the equilibrium wage. Is there a shortage or surplus of labor? What adjustments take place in the market to move the wage to the equilibrium wage? *At a wage below the equlibrium wage, there will be a shortage of workers. This shortage puts upward pressure on the market wage. As the wage rises, the quantity demanded of workers decreases and the quantity supplied increases, until the shortage is eliminated.*

8. Assuming there are 1,000 firms identical to ABC in the belt industry, complete Table 4-4.5, based on the market price of belts being $3.00.

 Table 4-4.5
The Labor Market Based on the Price of Belts Being $3.00

Wage	Quantity of labor demanded	Quantity of labor supplied*	State of the labor market
$30	**9,000**	4,000	**Shortage** / Equilibrium / Surplus
$45	**8,000**	4,500	**Shortage** / Equilibrium / Surplus
$60	**7,000**	7,000	Shortage / **Equilibrium** / Surplus
$75	**6,000**	8,000	Shortage / Equilibrium / **Surplus**
$90	**5,000**	10,000	Shortage / Equilibrium / **Surplus**
$105	**4,000**	11,500	Shortage / Equilibrium / **Surplus**
$120	**3,000**	13,000	Shortage / Equilibrium / **Surplus**

*Some of the quantity supplied figures are interpolated from the supply data in Table 4-4.4.

9. In Figure 4-4.1, plot the market demand curve for labor from Table 4-4.5. Label the demand curve as "D$_{$3.00}$." (The supply curve is the same as in Table 4-4.4.)

10. Why did the market demand curve for labor shift to the right when the price of belts increased from $2.00 to $3.00? *The increase in price made the output of workers more valuable, thus increasing their MRP, which is the firms' demand for labor.*

11. What happened to the equilibrium wage and the equilibrium quantity of labor when the labor demand curve shifted to the right?
    They both increased.

Part C: The Perfectly Competitive Labor Market and a Firm's Demand for Labor

A perfectly competitive employer takes the market wage and can hire all the labor it wants at that wage. The firm does not have to raise its wage to attract more workers. The labor supply curve for the firm is horizontal at the market wage. This supply curve is perfectly elastic. If the firm drops its wage below the equilibrium wage, it will not be able to hire any workers.

 Figure 4-4.2
The Labor Market and a Typical Firm in That Market

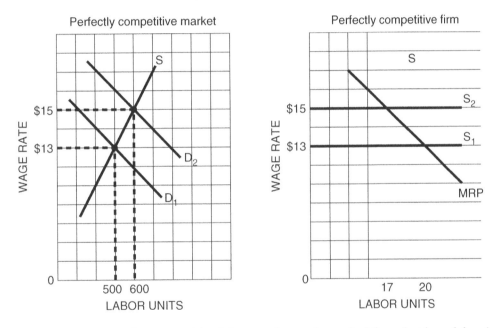

Figure 4-4.2 shows the competitive labor market and a typical firm that buys labor in that market. Answer the following questions based on this graph.

12. If the market demand for labor is D_1, the equilibrium wage will be $ ___*13*___ and the equilibrium quantity of labor will be ___*500*___ workers.

13. How many workers will the firm hire at this market wage? ___*20 workers*___

14. If the market demand for labor increases to D$_2$, the market wage will increase to $ *15*   and the equilibrium number of workers will increase to   *600*   .

15. How many workers will the firm hire at this new market wage?   *17 workers*

16. When the market wage increased, did the firm hire more or fewer workers? Why?
    It hired fewer workers. It dismissed three workers whose MRP made them worth a wage of $13, but not worth a wage of $15.

17. Is the firm's MRP curve also its demand curve for labor? Explain.
    In this situation, the MRP curve is the firm's demand curve for labor. Because the firm hires labor in a perfectly competitive market, the wage is equal to the firm's marginal resource cost (MRC). Since the optimal amount of labor is found where MRP = MCL, the intersection of the horizontal labor supply curve and the firm's MRP curve tells you how many workers the firm should hire at each market wage.

18. Are the workers in this market demanded exclusively by firms that produce the identical good, or are they hired by firms that make a variety of different goods?
    Typically, the workers are demanded by a variety of firms, not just by those in one particular industry.

How Wages Are Determined in Labor Markets

This activity examines how wages and employment are determined in two types of labor markets. A *perfectly competitive labor market* is one in which all buyers and sellers are so small that no one can act alone and affect the market wage. The interaction of market demand (D) and supply (S) determines the wage and the level of employment. A *monopsony* exists if there is only one buyer of labor in the resource market. The monopsonist pays as low a wage as possible to attract the number of workers needed.

🛈 *Student Alert:* **If the monopsonist needs more workers, the wage will have to be raised.**

Part A: A Perfectly Competitive Labor Market

 Figure 4-5.1

A Perfectly Competitive Labor Market

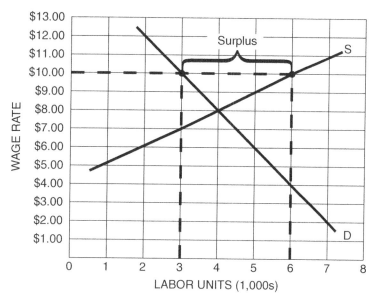

Figure 4-5.1 illustrates a perfectly competitive labor market. Labor is measured in thousands of labor hours. Answer the following questions based on this graph.

1. What are the equilibrium wage and number of labor hours in this labor market?
   $8.00 and 4,000 hours of labor

2. Why is the demand for labor downward sloping?
   Firms will hire more workers if the wage is reduced.

3. Why is the supply of labor upward sloping?
Workers will offer more hours of labor at a high wage than at a low wage.

Part B: A Minimum Wage

4. Why does the government create a minimum wage in a labor market?
It does so to help low-income workers earn a higher income.

5. If the government sets a minimum wage of $10.00 in the labor market shown in Figure 4-5.1, will there be a shortage or surplus of labor? How large is this shortage or surplus? Indicate this on the graph at the wage of $10.00.
There will be a surplus of 3,000 labor hours. At this wage, the quantity supplied is 6,000 labor hours and the quantity demanded is 3,000 labor hours.

6. Are some workers made better off because of the minimum wage? Are some workers made worse off because of it? Explain.
Those workers who keep a job are better off because they receive a higher wage. Those workers who are fired are worse off because a wage of $8.00 is better than no wage at all.

7. Would skilled or unskilled workers be more likely to lose their jobs because of a minimum wage law?
Unskilled workers would be more likely to lose their jobs because their MRP is lower than that of skilled workers.

8. If the demand for labor were more inelastic, would more or fewer workers lose their jobs because of the minimum wage? Explain.
If demand were more inelastic, employers would not have so strong a tendency to reduce their quantity demanded of labor when the wage increases. Thus, fewer workers would lose their jobs as a result of the minimum wage.

Part C: A Monopsonistic Labor Market

Assume the Ross Textile Company is a monopsony in a small town. Because it faces the upward sloping market supply of labor, Ross must raise its wage if it wants to increase the quantity supplied of workers. The company pays the same wage to all its employees, so if it increases the wage to attract another worker, the marginal resource cost of that worker is greater than the wage paid to the worker: MRC > Wage.

 Student Alert: **If the wage is raised to hire another worker, then MRC > Wage.**

9. Table 4-5.1 shows the supply of labor to Ross. Complete the table.

 Table 4-5.1
Labor Supply Schedule

Workers	Wage	Total labor cost	Marginal resource cost
1	$5.00	$5.00	***$5.00***
2	$5.50	$11.00	$6.00
3	$6.00	***$18.00***	***$7.00***
4	$6.50	***$26.00***	***$8.00***
5	$7.00	***$35.00***	$9.00
6	$7.50	$45.00	***$10.00***

10. Plot the Ross Company's labor supply (S) curve and MRC curve in Figure 4-5.2. The firm's marginal revenue product (MRP) curve is already in the graph.

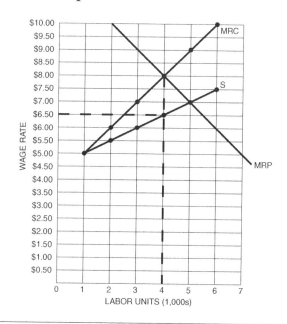 Figure 4-5.2
A Monopsonistic Labor Market

11. Why is the MRC curve above the S curve?
    Because the firm pays all workers the same wage, when it increases its wage to attract another worker then the true cost to the firm of that worker is greater than the wage paid to that worker. The worker's MRC is his or her wage plus the increase in wages for all other workers.

12. What is more important to Ross as it considers hiring another worker—the wage paid to the worker or the worker's MRC? Why?
    The MRC is more important. The firm hires the number of workers where MRP = MRC, not where MRP = Wage, because it is a monopsonist and not a perfectly competitive employer. The extra cost of an additional worker is the worker's MRC, not the worker's wage.

13. How many workers will Ross hire? What wage will it pay to each of these workers?
    The firm will hire 4,000 workers because that is where MRP = MRC. It goes to the labor supply curve to find the wage needed to attract 4,000 workers: $6.50.

14. Is the MRP curve the firm's D curve for labor?
    No. Because the firm is a monopsonist, the wage is not equal to the MRC. The firm finds its profit-maximizing amount of labor where MRP = MRC, but it does not get the wage from the intersection of the MRP and MRC curves; it must go to the labor supply curve for the wage. A monopsonist in the resource market does not have a labor demand curve, similar to the way a monopsonist in the product market does not have a supply curve.

15. What would be the equilibrium wage and employment if this were a perfectly competitive market? How do these values compare with those of the monopsonist?
    In a perfectly competitive market, equilibrium would be where the MRP curve intersects the S curve. The wage would be $7.00 and the employment would be 5,000 workers. The wage and employment would be higher than in the case of monopsony.

16. If any firm hires the amount of labor at which MRP = MRC, is it also true that the firm is producing the output level at which MR = MC? Does the answer depend on whether the firm is perfectly competitive or monopolistic in the goods market, or whether it is perfectly competitive or monopsonistic in the labor market?
    Hiring the amount of labor at which MRP = MCL is the rule a firm follows to maximize its total profit. Thus, it must mean the firm is producing the profit-maximizing quantity of its product, which is found by producing where MR = MC. The degree of competition in the product and resource market does not change these two profit-maximizing rules.

Wages and Employment in Competitive and Monopsonistic Labor Markets

This activity asks you to show how changes in economic conditions, government policy, and union activity affect different types of labor markets. The impact of such changes depends on the degree of competition on the demand and supply sides of the labor market. The symbols W_C, L_C, W_M, and L_M refer to the wages and labor in the competitive and monopsonistic labor markets. You are to consider the short-run effects in the specified labor market.

Part A: Perfect Competition and Monopsony

 Figure 4-6.1
Perfectly Competitive and Monopsonistic Labor Markets

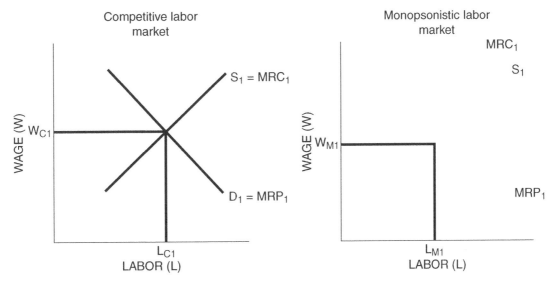

Figure 4-6.1 presents the basic setup of a perfectly competitive labor market and a monopsonistic labor market. Answer the following questions based on this figure.

1. Why is the marginal revenue product (MRP) curve equal to the market demand (D) curve for labor in the perfectly competitive labor market?
   Because the firm hires labor in a perfectly competitive labor market, the wage it pays each worker is equal to the marginal resource cost of a worker. This means that by going to the marginal revenue product curve at each wage, the firm determines the number of workers to hire. This means the MRP curve is the firm's demand curve for labor.

2. Why is the MRP curve not equal to the market D curve for labor in the monopsonistic labor market?
   A monopsonist does not have a labor demand curve because there is no one curve the firm can go to at a given wage to find its optimal number of workers. It uses the MRP and MRC curves to determine the number of workers, then uses the labor supply curve to find the wage.

3. Why is the marginal resource cost (MRC) curve equal to the market labor supply (S) curve in the perfectly competitive labor market?

In a perfectly competitive labor market, the market wage is the firm's MRC of an extra worker. The firm can hire all the workers it wants at the market wage and does not have to increase the wage to attract another worker.

4. Why is the MRC curve not equal to the market labor S curve in the monopsonistic labor market?

The monopsonist must increase its wage to attract another worker. Since it pays this higher wage to all workers, the MRC of an extra worker exceeds the wage paid to that worker.

5. In the appropriate graph, indicate by W_{C1} and L_{C1}, or W_{M1} and L_{M1}, the market wage and quantity of labor.

Part B: Analyzing Changes in the Labor Market

For each of the following scenarios, analyze the short-run effect of the specified event on each labor market. In the perfectly competitive labor market graph, indicate by W_{C1} and W_{C2} the market wage before and after the event. Indicate by L_{C1} and L_{C2} the equilibrium quantity of labor before and after the event. In the monopsonistic labor market graph, indicate by W_{M1} and W_{M2} the market wage before and after the event. Indicate by L_{M1} and L_{M2} the equilibrium quantity of labor before and after the event. State whether the event increases, decreases, or does not change the market wage and labor. Be sure to shift the curves that are affected by the events, leading to the changes in wage and labor.

6. Event: The state passes legislation requiring new teachers to pass a competency test in order to be employed by any school in the state. (The graphs refer to the labor market for teachers.)

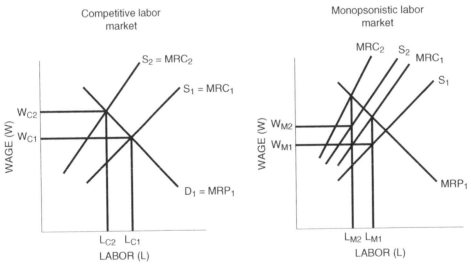

Competitive labor market

Monopsonistic labor market

Competitive labor market: wage increases, labor decreases
Monopsonistic labor market: wage increases, labor decreases

7. Event: New training methods increase the productivity of workers in the automobile industry. (The graphs refer to the labor market for automobile workers.)

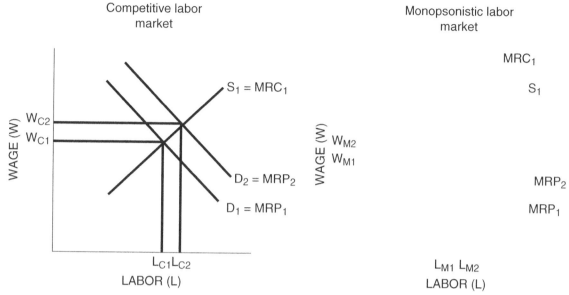

Competitive labor market: wage increases, labor increases
Monopsonistic labor market: wage increases, labor increases

8. Event: The U.S. government relaxes a tough immigration law, making it easier for construction workers from other countries to enter the United States. (The graphs refer to the American labor market for construction workers.)

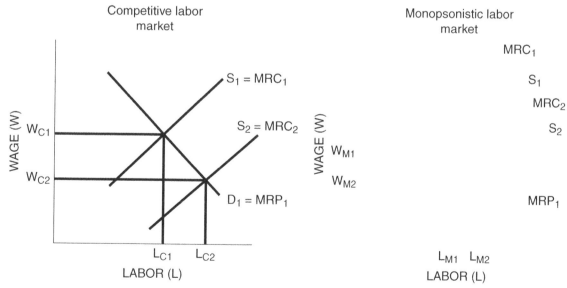

Competitive labor market: wage decreases, labor increases
Monopsonistic labor market: wage decreases, labor increases

9. Event: The German government lowers tariffs on shoes imported into Germany. (The graphs refer to the labor market for shoe workers in Germany.)

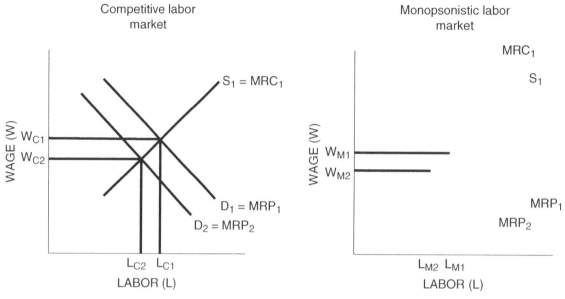

Competitive labor market: wage decreases, labor decreases
Monopsonistic labor market: wage decreases, labor decreases

10. Event: Labor unions conduct a successful advertising campaign urging people to buy goods and services produced by American workers. (The graphs refer to the labor market for all American workers.)

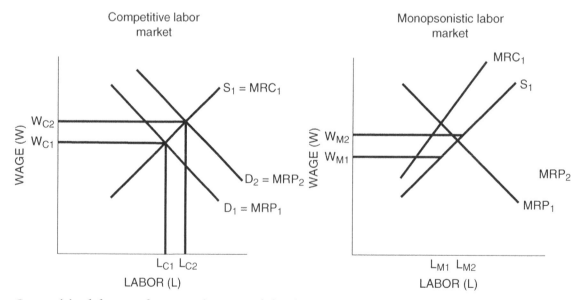

Competitive labor market: wage increases, labor increases
Monopsonistic labor market: wage increases, labor increases

Advanced Placement Economics Microeconomics: Teacher Resource Manual © Council for Economic Education, New York, N.Y.

Part B: Monopsony and a Minimum Wage

Figure 4-6.2 illustrates the labor market in which there is only one employer. This monopsonist sells its good in a perfectly competitive product market.

Figure 4-6.2

A Monopsonistic Labor Market

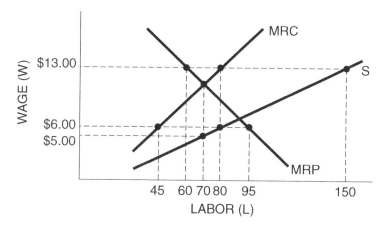

1. What is the profit-maximizing amount of labor for this monopsonistic firm? Why?
   The firm will hire 70 units of labor because that is where MRP = MRC.

2. What wage will it pay each unit of labor? Why?
   It will pay a wage of $5.00, as shown on the S curve at 75 units of labor.

3. If the government sets a minimum wage of $13.00, how many units of labor would be hired? How many units of labor will be unemployed with this minimum wage? Explain.
   At a minimum wage of $13.00, 60 units of labor will be hired where the MRP curve intersects the revised MRC curve. The MRC of labor will be shown as a horizontal line at $13.00 out to the labor supply curve at 150 units because the firm can attract up to 150 labor units at a wage of $13.00. To attract more than 150 labor units, the firm will have to offer a wage higher than $13.00. The cost of an extra unit of labor jumps up to the original MRC curve beyond 150 labor units. At the high minimum wage of $13.00, 150 labor units are supplied but only 60 units are hired. The result is unemployment of 90 labor units.

4. If the government sets a minimum wage of $6.00, how many units of labor would be hired? How many units of labor will be unemployed with this minimum wage? Explain.
   At a minimum wage of $6.00, 80 units of labor will be hired where the MRP curve intersects the revised MRC curve. The MRC of labor will be shown as a horizontal line at $6.00 out to the labor supply curve at 80 units because the firm can attract up to 80 labor units at a wage of $6.00. To attract more than 80 labor units, the firm will have to offer a wage higher than $6.00. The cost of an extra unit of labor jumps up to the original MRC curve beyond 80 labor units. At the minimum wage of $6.00, 80 labor units are supplied and all 80 units are hired. The result is zero unemployment at a minimum wage of $6.00.

Problems Dealing with Factor Markets

Part A: Factor Market Questions

Answer the questions and briefly explain your answers. Feel free to use diagrams to illustrate your points.

1. Why are some basketball players paid more than brain surgeons? Explain using the concept of marginal revenue product.
Because there is such a high demand of fans to watch star basketball players, their MRPs are very high. There are few close substitutes for a great basketball player. As teams compete for the best players, the star players receive salaries approximately equal to their high MRPs. Brain surgeons perform a valuable service and receive high salaries, but the number of brain surgeons compared to the demand for them means some star basketball players receive relatively higher salaries.

2. True, false, or uncertain, and explain why? "If it were not for unions pushing up wages, we'd all be working 60 hours a week for $100 a month just like people did a century ago."
False. Although unions may raise the wages of their members, the biggest factor in increasing real wages is higher productivity. Increases in real wages depend on increases in real output. Unions may have been responsible for social legislation, but increasing MRP is more important.

3. Use a graph to explain why a firm that wants to maximize its total profits uses a resource until the marginal revenue product of this resource equals the marginal resource cost.

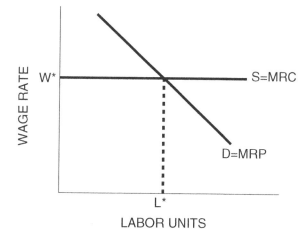

This graph shows a firm that hires labor in a perfectly competitive resource market. By hiring L* labor units, the firm hires all the labor units with MRP > MRC. These are the units that generate positive marginal profit for the firm. By stopping at L* units, the firm does not hire labor units with MRP < MRC, units that would decrease the firm's total profit.

4. True, false, or uncertain, and why? "American workers who are paid $10 an hour cannot possibly compete with workers who are paid $1 an hour in developing countries."
False. American workers tend to be paid more because their productivity is high. Increases in real wages depend on increases in real output.

5. Why might a university pay a Nobel Prize-winning faculty member more than its president? Does this make sense economically for the university? Support your answer.
   The Nobel Prize winner increases the reputation of the university and attracts more students, thus increasing the university's total revenue. Because the MRP of the professor is greater than the MRP of the president, the salary of the professor could be greater than the salary of the president.

6. What are the effects of a minimum wage that is above the equilibrium wage in a perfectly competitive market? What about in a market in which the employer is a monopsonist? Give an example of a relatively competitive labor market and a less competitive labor market.
   In a competitive labor market, a minimum wage above the equilibrium wage increases the number of workers who want to work (quantity supplied) and decreases the number of workers firms want to hire (quantity demanded). The result is a surplus of workers at the minimum wage: unemployment. For a monopsonist, the MRC curve is located above the labor supply curve. This results in a lower wage and lower employment than in a perfectly competitive labor market. Raising the minimum wage in a monopsonistic labor market will increase employment and wages as long as the minimum wage is less than the wage where MRP = MRC. Most economists believe that labor markets are closer to perfect competition than to monopsony. There are numerous examples of competitive labor markets, such as the market for accountants in a large metropolitan area. Examples of monopsonistic labor markets would be a specialized company in a small town or a supplier to a rural military base.

7. The National Collegiate Athletic Association (NCAA) regulates all college athletics in the United States. It sets the amount of scholarships, the number of scholarships granted, and the regulations for recruiting athletes. The NCAA has hundreds of rules regulating intercollegiate athletics.

   (A) What effect do these regulations have on who receives the economic rent from college athletics?
   They set the level of the athletes' benefits and salaries so the universities receive the economic rent.

   (B) Which colleges have greater incentives to cheat? Why?
   Colleges with increased incentives to violate NCAA rules could include those that do not have national academic prestige and cannot recruit against the colleges that do. Colleges with big arenas and stadiums that they need to fill also can be tempted to break rules to sign a star athlete who can boost the school's reputation and revenue.

   (C) Who would gain if the NCAA could no longer set rules for college athletics? Why?
   Top athletes at major universities would receive substantial salaries rather than standard scholarships. Players in major revenue sports would benefit, while players in low-revenue sports will be hurt.

   (D) Who would lose if the NCAA could no longer control college athletics? Why?
   Universities would see their expenses increase as they would have to compete with other institutions for the best athletes.

   (E) True, false, or uncertain, and why? "The NCAA is a champion for amateur athletics, and its rules protect the rights of college athletes."
   False or uncertain. The NCAA does champion the cause of amateur athletics, but this may benefit the universities more than the athletes. A case can be made that the NCAA is a champion for the majority of amateur athletes who are not in the major revenue sports. In the absence of the NCAA, athletes who are less successful would not be able to participate.

Part B: How Many Workers to Hire?

Table 4-7.1 gives you information about a firm operating in a perfectly competitive product market. Consider all factors of production fixed, with the exception of labor. The other factors of production cost the firm $50 a day, which may be thought of as the firm's total fixed cost. Assume the firm is a profit maximizer.

 Table 4-7.1

Firm Operating in a Competitive Product Market

Labor (L) (workers per day)	Output (Q) (units per day)	Marginal physical product (MPP)	Total revenue (TR)	Marginal revenue product (MRP)
0	0	–	$0	–
1	22	*+22*	*$66*	*+$66*
2	40	+18	$120	+$54
3	56	*+16*	*$168*	*+$48*
4	70	*+14*	*$210*	*+$42*
5	82	+12	*$246*	+$36
6	92	*+10*	$276	*+$30*
7	100	+8	$300	*+$24*
8	106	+6	$318	+$18

Fill in the answer blanks or underline the correct words in parentheses.

8. Assume the firm sells its output at $3 per unit. Complete Table 4-7.1.

(A) If the equilibrium market wage is $36 per day, the firm will hire ___5___ workers per day and produce ___82___ units of output.

(B) Given your answer to the preceding question, the firm will have total revenue of ___$246___ per day and total cost of ___$230___ per day.
Total cost = (5 workers)($36) + $50 = $230.

(C) The above will result in a (**profit** / loss) of ___$16___ per day.

9. Suppose you work for a firm that sells its output in a monopolistic market. Answer the following questions.

(A) If you hire an additional worker, output goes up from 75 to 125 units per day. If you want to sell the additional 50 units, you must lower your price from $3 per unit to $2 per unit. What is the highest wage you would be willing to pay the additional worker?
The highest wage you would be willing to pay is equal to the worker's MRP. The total revenue from 75 units is (75)($3) = $225. The total revenue from 125 units is (125)($2) = $250. The MRP of the extra worker is +$25, so this is the highest wage you would pay.

(B) Assume that you hired the additional worker and output now stands at 125 units per day. If you hire another worker, output rises to 165 units per day. Given the demand curve for your product, you know that to sell the additional output, price will have to be dropped from $2 per unit to $1 per unit. What is the maximum wage you would be willing to pay *this* additional worker? Would you hire this additional worker? Why or why not?
The total revenue from 125 units is $250. The total revenue from 165 units is (165)($1) = $165. The MRP of this extra worker is –$85. There is no wage at which you would find this worker profitable because MRP is negative.

10. Use a graph to explain why monopsonists will always hire fewer workers and pay lower wages than firms operating in competitive labor markets. (Assume that the monopsonistic and competitive firms have the same costs.)

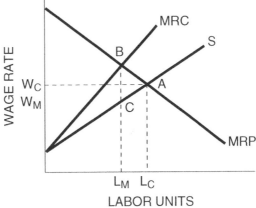

If this were a monopsonistic labor market, the optimal quantity of labor would be L_M because that is where the MRP curve intersects the MRC curve at point B. The monopsony wage would be W_M, found on the labor supply curve at point C for quantity L_M. L_M is the optimal number of labor units for a monopsony because to the left of point B, MRP > MRC, and to the right of point B, MRP < MRC. In a perfectly competitive labor market, the MRP curve would represent the demand for labor curve and the S curve would represent the MRC curve. Equilibrium would be at point A where the S curve intersects the MRP curve, with labor quantity L_C and wage W_C. For labor units to the left of point A, MRP > MRC, and for units to the right of point A, MRP < MRC. The labor quantity is smaller in the monopsonistic labor market than in the perfectly competitive labor market because the MRC of labor is greater in the monopsonistic market. The wage is lower in the monopsonistic labor market because the wage the monopsony must pay for only L_M units is less than the wage needed to attract L_C units.

MICROECONOMICS

The Role of Government

Unit 5

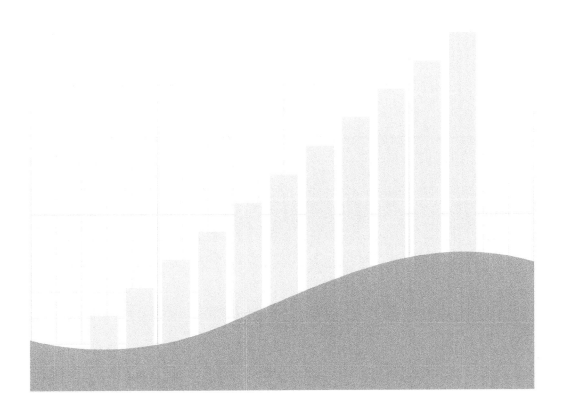

■ The economic functions of government include enforcing laws and contracts, maintaining competition, redistributing income, providing public goods, correcting allocations for externalities, and stabilizing the economy.

■ Government must provide public goods because a private market will not provide them. Pure public goods must meet the criteria of nonrivalrous (shared consumption) and nonexclusion.

■ Even a perfectly competitive market sometimes produces too little of some goods and too much of others; economists call this situation a market failure.

■ The market overproduces goods that create negative externalities. A negative externality is created when part of the cost of a transaction is borne by third parties who are not directly involved in the transaction. Negative externalities include pollution and harmful effects of pesticides and smoking. Negative externalities are sometimes called spillover costs.

■ The market underproduces goods that create positive externalities. A positive externality is created when benefits of a transaction or activity are received by third parties who are not directly involved in the transaction. Positive externalities include education, vaccinations against diseases, and flood control. Positive externalities are sometimes called spillover benefits.

■ Government tries to discourage the production of goods that involve negative externalities and encourage the production of goods that involve positive externalities.

■ Cleaning up the environment would be efficient if it were cleaned up to the point where the marginal social benefits of the cleanup were equal to the marginal social costs, and the cleanup were done at the least possible cost.

■ Most economists believe the environment can be cleaned up at a lower cost by substituting market incentives for command and control policies.

■ Sometimes buyers and sellers do not have perfect information, so the market outcome is not efficient. In these cases, it may be necessary for government to intervene in the market.

■ The theory of public choice uses economic analysis to evaluate government operation and policies.

■ Public-choice theorists believe politicians and government officials are as self-interested as business people. However, instead of trying to maximize profits, "political entrepreneurs" seek to maximize power, salaries, prestige, and votes. This behavior results in government waste and inefficiency.

■ Governments tax to raise revenue. Some taxes are based on the ability-to-pay theory, while others are based on the benefits-received theory.

■ Tax rates can be progressive, proportional, or regressive.

■ Government taxing and spending policies can change a society's distribution of income.

■ The incidence of a tax can be shifted from the person paying the government to someone else. This is accomplished through changes in prices, income, and outputs.

Private or Public? Public Goods and Services

Our Economic System

An economic system is the way in which people and societies organize economic life to answer three basic questions: *What* goods and services will be produced? *How* will they be produced? *For whom* will they be produced?

In many countries, most production decisions—what, how, and for whom to produce—are made in the marketplace through interactions of buyers and sellers. This is called the *private sector* of the economy. Other decisions are made by different levels of government. This is called the *public sector* of the economy. Many economic systems are called *mixed* systems since they produce a combination of private and public goods and services.

What Goods and Services Should Governments Provide?

While many goods and services can be provided by the private or the public sector, a few can be provided effectively only by governments. Generally, governments try to provide the goods and services that are necessary but that individual consumers might not purchase directly on their own. There are two criteria that can be used in judging whether something should be provided by governments: *nonexclusion* and *nonrivalrous* (*shared consumption*).

Nonexclusion

In some situations people cannot be excluded from the benefits of a good or service even if they do not pay for it. If only some of the people paid for national defense, for example, others could not be excluded from the benefits of national defense if it is provided. The nonpurchasers of national defense would be protected just as much as the purchasers. People who receive the benefit of a good but don't pay for it are called *free riders*.

Nonrivalrous (Shared Consumption or Joint Use)

In some situations one person's use or consumption of a good or service does not reduce its usefulness to others. The security one person receives from a street light is not diminished by a neighbor receiving the same security. The protection the street light provides is not reduced by additional people using it.

Private businesses will not produce things that people are not willing to buy, and individual consumers are reluctant to pay for goods and services from which others who do not pay will reap the benefits: "Why should I be the one to buy the street light if everyone else also is getting the benefits?" Governments therefore must provide some goods and services such as national defense, flood control, and judicial and legal systems that are characterized by shared consumption and are necessarily or should be nonexclusive. Public goods are goods that are provided by government and will not be provided by the private sector.

Private and Public Goods

Pure private goods are subject to exclusion and rivalry. Nonbuyers cannot consume the good, and if one person consumes a unit of the good, someone else cannot consume that unit. They are purchased directly in the marketplace. *Pure public goods* are subject to nonexclusion and shared consumption. They are purchased indirectly through tax dollars.

Some goods have elements of both private goods and public goods. Fishing in the ocean, for example, is generally not subject to exclusion; but once one person catches a fish, it is not available to others. Likewise, it is sometimes possible to exclude people from theaters, national parks, or even roads by charging admission fees or tolls. But one person camping in a park or driving on a highway usually does not reduce the usefulness of these places to others. Controversy often arises over how these *mixed goods*—sometimes called *common-pool resources* and *toll goods*—should be provided and who should pay for them. Some goods do not fall into neat boxes, but show degrees of nonexclusion and shared consumption.

 Table 5-1.1
Combinations of Exclusion and Shared Consumption

		Shared consumption	
		No	Yes
Exclusion	Yes	Pure private goods: haircuts, bread, ice cream	Toll goods: theaters, cable TV, parks, toll roads
	No	Common-pool resources: fish taken from the ocean, irrigation water taken from a river, congested roads	Pure public goods: national defense, flood control, street lights, mosquito abatement, judicial and legal system

1. What is the difference between the private and public sectors of our economy?
   The public sector is government: federal, state, and local. The private sector consists of decisions in the marketplace made between buyers and sellers.

2. What are the characteristics of a pure private good?
   It is traded through voluntary exchange. People who are not part of the transaction can be excluded from the transaction. Pure private goods, such as haircuts, cannot be characterized by shared consumption.

3. What are the characteristics of a pure public good?
   Nonexclusion, shared consumption

4. Place each of the goods and services in the list below into one of the four boxes in Table 5-1.2.

   Circle the box that contains pure private goods. Then draw two circles around the box that contains pure public goods.

   (A) A college education

   (B) Electric power

   (C) A haircut

   (D) National defense

   (E) A private amusement park

   (F) Spraying for mosquitoes

   (G) Cable television

   (H) Canine rabies shots

   (I) Street lights

   (J) The Panama Canal

   (K) Public toll roads and bridges

   (L) Police and fire protection

   (M) Health care

   (N) National forest campgrounds

   (O) Potato chips

   (P) Auto airbags

Table 5-1.2

Determining Combinations of Exclusion and Shared Consumption

		Shared consumption	
		No	Yes
Exclusion	Yes	*(B) Electric power* *(C) A haircut* *(H) Canine rabies shots* *(O) Potato chips* *(P) Auto airbags*	*(A) A college education* *(E) A private amusement park* *(G) Cable television* *(J) The Panama Canal* *(K) Public toll roads and bridges* *(M) Health care* *(N) National forest campgrounds*
	No		*(D) National defense* *(F) Spraying for mosquitoes* *(I) Street lights* *(L) Police and fire protection*

5. What is a free rider? Select three goods from the list in Question 4 that could have free riders. *Someone who uses the good or service but doesn't pay for it. Free riders occur when there are nonexclusion and shared consumption. This occurs for all public goods. Examples from the list are spraying for mosquitoes, police and fire protection, national defense, and street lights.*

Externalities

A *market externality* refers to a situation where some of the costs or benefits from an activity fall on someone other than the people directly involved in the activity. Externalities may be either positive (the activity provides a benefit to someone else) or negative (the activity places a cost on someone else). Costs that fall on someone else are called *external costs*, and benefits that fall on someone else are called *external benefits*. These external effects of an activity are also called *social spillover costs* and *social spillover benefits*, or *third-party costs* and *third-party benefits*.

The demand curve for a good or service shows the *marginal private benefit (MPB)* to those individuals who are consuming the product. It shows how many units will be demanded by consumers at different prices. The demand curve also shows the highest prices consumers will pay for different quantities of the product. The supply curve of a good or service shows the *marginal private cost (MPC)* to those individuals who are producing the product. It shows how many units will be supplied by producers at different prices. The supply curve also shows the lowest prices producers will accept for different quantities of the product.

If there are no positive externalities associated with the activity, then the marginal private benefit from an additional unit will be equal to the *marginal social benefit (MSB)*. The marginal social benefit shows the benefit to society from an extra unit of the activity. If no one other than the person associated with the activity receives any benefit from the extra unit, then MPB = MSB.

If there are no negative externalities associated with the activity, then the marginal private cost from an additional unit will be equal to the *marginal social cost (MSC)*. The marginal social cost shows the cost to society from an extra unit of the activity. If no one other than the person associated with the activity incurs any cost from the extra unit, then MPC = MSC.

Consumers of a product buy according to their marginal private benefits as shown by the demand curve, and producers of the item produce according to their marginal private costs as shown by the supply curve. The equilibrium quantity of the product in a perfectly competitive market will be the quantity where MPB = MPC. This is where the market demand curve intersects the market supply curve. *If there are no externalities, the competitive market output is the socially optimal (efficient) quantity because it is where MSB = MSC.* Society feels the market is producing exactly the right amount of the product. Given the marginal benefit society is receiving from the last unit, it feels the correct amount of its scarce resources is being allocated to the provision of that unit.

The competitive market results in *market failures*, however, if there are positive or negative externalities associated with the consumption or production of the good or service. These spillover benefits or costs, if not corrected, will result in the market producing either too much or too little of the activity from society's perspective. The externalities drive a wedge between the MSB and the MPB, or between the MSC and the MPC. Because the market will produce the output where MPB = MPC, these differences yield a quantity of the product at which MSB is not equal to MSC. We often turn to the government to attempt to correct these market failures.

To understand how externalities can result in market failures, it is important that you know these relationships:

■ Marginal Social Benefit = Marginal Private Benefit + Marginal External Benefit

$$MSB = MPB + MEB$$

■ Marginal Social Cost = Marginal Private Cost + Marginal External Cost

$$MSC = MPC + MEC$$

Summary of key points:

■ Society wants a market to produce the quantity where $MSB = MSC$.

■ Private decision makers want to have the quantity where $MPB = MPC$.

■ As long as MEB and MEC are zero (no externalities), the market quantity will be the socially optimal (efficient) quantity.

■ If MEB or MEC is not zero, we will have a market failure.

 Student Alert: Some textbooks use slightly different approaches to the topic of externalities. While the end results with regard to the effects of externalities are the same, be sure you understand the approach and terminology that are being used.

Part A: How Much Music?

Figure 5-2.1
External Benefits

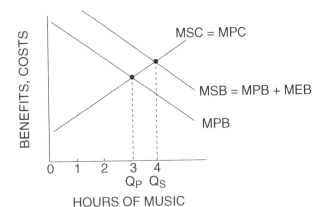

1. Margaret has Wendy as her roommate in a college residence hall. Wendy has brought an expensive stereo system to play in the room. Figure 5-2.1 shows Wendy's MPB and MPC curves for music played on the stereo system. Based on Figure 5-2.1, answer the following questions.

(A) If Wendy considers only the MPB and MPC from playing music, how many hours of music will be played? Label the number of hours in Figure 5-2.1 as Q_p to indicate the private market quantity.
Three hours, where MPB = MPC.

(B) Assume that Wendy plays music only at times that do not disturb Margaret and plays only music that Margaret also enjoys. The "MSB = MPB + MEB" curve in Figure 5-2.1 shows the MSB from the music, including the MEB to Margaret. If Wendy considers the MSB from playing music rather than only the MPB, what happens to the quantity of music played? Label the number of hours as Q_s in Figure 5-2.1 to indicate the socially optimal quantity.
It increases to 4 hours, where MSB = MSC. This is the socially optimal amount.

(C) In Figure 5-2.1, what does the vertical gap between the MSB and MPB curves represent?
The vertical gap represents the marginal external benefit (MEB) of the music. This is the social spillover benefit of the music to Margaret.

(D) Assuming there are no external costs from the music, when Wendy does not consider the MEB from playing music, the number of hours played is (*greater than / equal to / **less than***) the socially efficient number of hours.

 Figure 5-2.2
External Costs

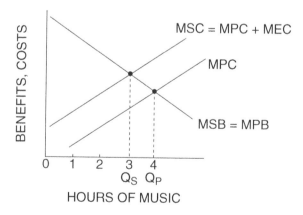

2. Again, Wendy has a new stereo system and Margaret is her roommate.

(A) In Figure 5-2.2, assume Wendy only considers her MPB and MPC from music. How many hours of music will be played? Label the number of hours in Figure 5-2.2 as Q_p to indicate the private market quantity.
Four hours, where MPB = MPC.

(B) Now assume that Wendy plays music only at times that Margaret is trying to study and plays only music that Margaret hates. In Figure 5-2.2, the "MSC = MPC + MEC" curve shows the

MSC from the music, including the MEC to Margaret. If Wendy considers the MSC from playing music rather than only the MPC, what happens to the quantity of music played? Label the number of hours as Q_S in Figure 5-2.2 to indicate the socially optimal quantity.
It decreases to 3 hours, where MSB = MSC. This is the socially optimal amount.

(C) In Figure 5-2.2, what does the vertical gap between the MSC and MPC curves represent?
The vertical gap represents the marginal external cost (MEC) of the music. This is the social spillover cost of the music to Margaret.

(D) Assuming there are no external benefits from the music, when Wendy does not consider the MEC from playing music, the number of hours played is (**greater than** / *equal to* / *less than*) the socially efficient number of hours.

3. How can government regulation (in this case, residence hall rules) assure the efficient quantity of music? Consider the circumstances under which prohibiting stereos or imposing daily "quiet hours" are efficient ways to regulate stereo use in the hall. Does economics suggest a more efficient approach to stereo regulation?
Prohibiting stereos or imposing quiet hours will not result in an efficient level since marginal external benefits and marginal external costs are not considered. A more efficient approach would be to issue "rights" to play stereos. You could issue property rights and negotiate how many hours the stereo could be played. For example, Wendy could pay Margaret if there is a negative externality, and Wendy could charge Margaret if there is a positive externality.

Part B: More Externalities Examples

4. For each of these activities, explain whether there is a positive or negative externality.

(A) Private high school education
Positive. The students become better citizens.

(B) Smog from an electric power plant
Negative. The pollution causes health problems for people living near the power plant.

(C) Your neighbor's yappy dog
Negative. The dog's barking keeps the neighbors awake at night.

(D) Pre-kindergarten measles vaccinations
Positive. There is less spread of disease.

Part C: Applying Your Knowledge of Externalities

The Women's National Basketball Association (WNBA) is considering awarding a new franchise to the city of Metropolis, but only if the team has a new arena in which to play. Proponents of the franchise argue that the team will generate new businesses, provide jobs, increase tax revenue, and promote tourism in Metropolis. Opponents argue that most of the money spent on basketball games will come from Metropolis-area residents who will simply reduce their spending on other activities. The opponents claim there will be few new jobs, little increase in tax revenue, and few new tourists coming to Metropolis. They also say the new arena will cause property values to fall in the area and create traffic congestion and noise pollution.

Voters have the following three proposals before them:

Proposal #1: No city money should be used to construct the arena. Team owners should pay the full cost of building the facility and include that cost in the price of game tickets.

Proposal #2: The city should place a tax on each ticket sold to pay the full cost of the arena.

Proposal #3: The city should build the arena and lease the right to play there to the basketball club at a subsidized rate.

For the analysis that follows, assume the output of the team is the number of tickets sold.

5. What assumption does Proposal #1 make about external costs and external benefits associated with the new franchise?
It assumes there are no positive or negative externalities. The benefits of the franchise go to the people who buy the tickets and there are no spillover benefits to others. It assumes the team incurs the cost of the franchise and arena and there are no spillover costs to others. Under these assumptions, MPB = MSB and MPC = MSC. When the market produces the output where MPB = MPC, it also will be producing the socially optimal output where MSB = MSC.

Figure 5-2.3 can be used to illustrate the position of opponents to the franchise. Answer the following questions based on this graph.

 Figure 5-2.3
Social Spillover Costs

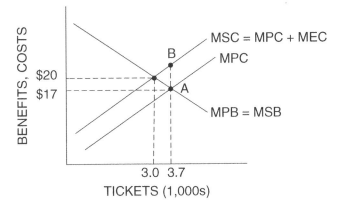

6. What assumption is made about social spillover benefits from the franchise? Explain.
It assumes there are no spillover benefits because MSB = MPB.

7. What assumption is made about social spillover costs from the franchise? Explain.
It assumes there are spillover costs (such as traffic congestion). The MSC curve is above the MPC curve, with the difference between them being the marginal external cost (MEC).

8. How many tickets will be sold based on the MPB and MPC?
   The market will result in 3,700 tickets per game because that is where MPB = MPC. The price of tickets will be $17.

9. What is the socially optimal number of tickets?
   The socially optimal number of tickets is 3,000 because that is where MSB = MSC. The price would be $20.

10. What does the vertical gap "AB" represent?
    This gap represents the marginal external cost of the franchise.

11. What can the Metropolis city government do to make the market output be equal to the socially efficient output? Explain, using the graph to illustrate your answer.
    The government can place a tax on each ticket equal to the MEC (shown as "AB"). This will put the external cost on the team owners, thus making the MPC shift up to where the MSC curve is positioned. The team will sell 3,000 tickets at a price of $20.

Figure 5-2.4 can be used to illustrate the position of supporters of the franchise. Answer the following questions based on this graph.

 Figure 5-2.4
Social Spillover Benefits

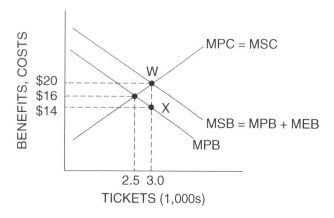

12. What assumption is made about social spillover benefits from the franchise? Explain.
    It assumes there are spillover benefits (such as more tax revenue to the city). The MSB curve is above the MPB curve, with the difference between them being the marginal external benefit (MEB).

13. What assumption is made about social spillover costs from the franchise? Explain.
    It assumes there are no spillover costs because MSC = MPC.

14. How many tickets will be sold based on the MPB and MPC?
    The market will result in 2,500 tickets per game because that is where MPB = MPC. The price of tickets will be $16.

15. What is the socially optimal number of tickets?
The socially optimal number of tickets is 3,000 because that is where MSB = MSC. The price would be $20.

16. What does the vertical gap "WX" represent?
This gap represents the marginal external benefit of the franchise.

17. What can the Metropolis city government do to make the market output be equal to the socially efficient output? Explain, using the graph to illustrate your answer.
The government can provide team owners with a $6 subsidy for each ticket equal to the MEB (shown as "WX"). The purpose of this incentive is to encourage owners to provide more of the product. There are two ways this subsidy of $6 can be demonstrated graphically.

(1) The subsidy can be viewed as a reduction of the MPC of the team owners, thus making the MPC shift down to an "MPC – subsidy" curve that intersects the MPB curve at 3,000 tickets. The team will sell these tickets at a price of $14 and receive a subsidy of $6 for each ticket.

(2) Or, the subsidy can be seen as an upward shift of the owner's extra revenue per ticket by the amount of the subsidy so it is in the same position as the MSB curve. The result is that 3,000 tickets will be sold. Since fans will only pay a price of $14 for 3,000 tickets (based on their MPB curve), that is the price received by owners. The owners will also receive a subsidy of $6 for each ticket. This makes the revenue received from the last ticket equal to $20, which is the same as the MPC of providing that unit.

Part D: Per Unit or Lump Sum? Which Type of Tax or Subsidy to Use?

 Student Alert: Which form of a tax or subsidy should the government use to correct the effects of an externality? Should it apply a per-unit or a lump-sum adjustment?

Figure 5-2.5 shows the average total cost (ATC), average variable cost (AVC), marginal cost (MC), demand (D), marginal revenue (MR), and average revenue (AR) functions of a perfectly competitive firm. The firm is producing Q_1 units because that is where $MR = MC$. Assume there is a negative externality associated with the firm's product and the government would like to have the firm reduce its output.

Figure 5-2.5
A Profit-Maximizing Perfectly Competitive Firm

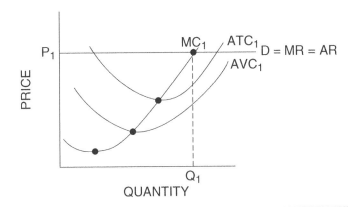

18. Suppose the government places a per-unit tax of "t" on the firm's product. Which cost measures will be affected by this per-unit tax: ATC, AVC, average fixed cost (AFC), or MC? Show in Figure 5-2.6 how the cost curves will look after the tax is imposed. What happens to the output level the firm wants to produce? Was the per-unit tax successful in having the firm reduce its quantity?

 Figure 5-2.6

The Government Levies a Per-Unit Tax of "t"

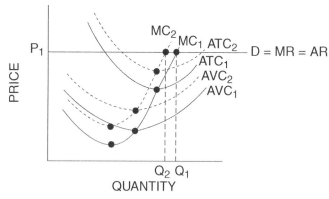

Because this is a per-unit tax, it will affect the firm's MC and AVC curves, which means it also will affect the ATC curve. The AFC will not be affected because a per-unit tax does not change TFC. Each of the MC, AVC, and ATC curves shifts up vertically by the distance "t" at all output levels. The output levels where these three cost curves have their minimum points are the same as before. Because the firm's MC curve has shifted up, the firm's optimal output level where MR = MC (shown as Q_2) will be less than the original level of Q_1. The per-unit tax did result in a smaller quantity being produced by the firm. The demand facing the firm is not changed by the tax.

19. Suppose the government places a one-time, lump-sum tax of "T" on the firm's product. Which of these cost measures will be affected by this lump-sum tax: ATC, AVC, AFC, or MC? Show in Figure 5-2.7 how the graph will look after the tax is imposed. What happens to the output level the firm wants to produce? Was the lump-sum tax successful in having the firm reduce its quantity?

 Figure 5-2.7

The Government Levies a Lump-Sum Tax of "T"

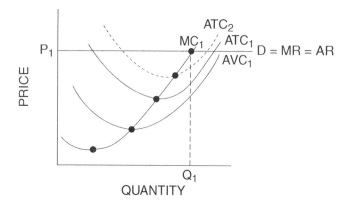

Because this is a lump-sum tax and not dependent on how many units the firm produces, it amounts to an increase in the firm's TFC. This means the firm's AFC will increase as well. Because it is not a per-unit tax, the firm's MC and AVC curves are not affected. The ATC curve will increase because of the increase in AFC. The upward shift of the ATC curve gets smaller as quantity rises because as the lump-sum tax is spread over more output units, the increase in AFC is reduced. Because the firm's MC curve is unchanged, the firm's optimal output level where MR = MC remains at Q_1. The lump-sum tax reduced the firm's total profit but it did not result in a smaller quantity being produced by the firm. The demand facing the firm is not changed by the tax.

20. Assume a firm produces a product for which there is a positive externality. As an incentive to the firm to produce more of its product, should the government give the firm a per-unit subsidy or a lump-sum subsidy? Explain.

    Using the same logic as for the per-unit tax and lump-sum tax, if the government wants the firm to increase its quantity, it should use a per-unit subsidy. A per-unit subsidy can be viewed as a decrease in the firm's MC of production, or as an increase in the firm's per-unit revenue. In either case, the output level where MR = MC will be larger than before.

Part E: Summary

21. When positive externalities are involved, private markets produce (*more than* / *exactly* / **less than**) the socially optimal amount of the product.

22. When negative externalities are involved, private markets produce (**more than** / *exactly* / *less than*) the socially optimal amount of the product.

23. Why do economists say the presence of an externality results in a market failure?

    Externalities make MPB different from MSB, or MPC different from MSC. Since the market output will be where MPB = MPC, the externality results in the market producing a quantity that is not the socially efficient level at which MSB = MSC. The result is either too many or too few of society's scarce resources being devoted by the market to the activity.

24. How can a tax be used to remedy a negative externality?

    The tax raises the MPC of production and thus reduces the quantity.

25. How can a subsidy mitigate an inefficient output level in the presence of a positive externality?

    The subsidy increases the quantity by providing an incentive to producers to provide a larger quantity. The subsidy can be viewed either as a reduction of the producers' MPC, or as an increase in the producers' marginal revenue from the last unit.

Private or Public? The Coase Theorem

When an activity results in a negative externality (external cost), the market outcome will not be efficient. In these cases, the government may choose to intervene in the market and impose some form of regulation, for example, a legal restriction or a tax. If the external cost the activity creates is borne by those who conduct the activity, the market outcome will be efficient.

For example, if a firm dumps its waste into a river, it pollutes the river and creates a negative externality (external cost) for those downstream. The government may intervene to restrict dumping in the river, or it may impose an effluent tax (a tax on each unit of pollution released into the river). If the firm is forced to pay for the pollution it releases into the river, it will dump less. A sufficiently high tax will lead to the optimal reduction in river pollution from the firm. Thus, the firm has internalized the externality.

However, in some situations, it may not be necessary to regulate a market to achieve an efficient outcome. It may be possible for the parties affected by an externality to negotiate an efficient outcome on their own. For example, if people who use the river downstream can negotiate with the polluting firm, they may be willing to pay the firm to stop polluting. This idea is embodied in the *Coase Theorem*, which states that if those who are affected by an externality can negotiate, they may arrive at an efficient solution to the externality problem.

Two firms are involved in a dispute. Grunge, Inc., a manufacturing firm, pollutes a nearby river. The pollution travels downstream past White Water Expeditions, a company that provides river rafting trips. Dumping its waste into the river cuts Grunge's waste-disposal costs, while decreasing the number of people who want to raft on the river. The total profits of the two firms (both with and without waste dumping) are shown in Table 5-3.1.

 Table 5-3.1
Total Profits per Month

	With dumping	Without dumping
Grunge, Inc.	$2,300	$2,000
White Water Expeditions	$1,500	$2,000

1. What are the total returns to both companies with and without dumping? Which situation (dumping or no dumping) is socially optimal—in other words, provides the highest combined returns?
   The combined total profits with dumping: $3,800
   The combined total profits without dumping: $4,000
   The highest combined profits result when Grunge does not dump its waste into the river.

2. If there is no government intervention in the market, and the two companies do not communicate, will Grunge dump waste into the river? Why or why not?
   Yes. Grunge has greater total profits if it dumps its waste and reduces its total costs.

3. What is the cost to Grunge not to dump waste into the river?
   Since its total profits are $300 lower if it does not dump its waste, the cost to Grunge of not polluting the river is $300.

4. What is the cost of the pollution to White Water each month? How much would White Water be willing to pay Grunge to stop dumping waste into the river?
   White Water's total profit is $500 higher each month if the river is clean. That means White Water should be willing to pay Grunge up to $500 each month not to dump its waste into the river.

5. If Grunge and White Water could negotiate, at no cost, could they come to an agreement that would eliminate the externality problem and result in the efficient outcome? If not, why not? If so, what would be the payment from White Water to Grunge?
   If the two sides consider their potential increase in total profits, they have room to reach an agreement that will benefit both sides. If White Water will pay Grunge some amount between $301 and $499, each side will gain.

6. Does it matter who has the property right: Grunge to dump or White Water to have clean water? Explain.
   No, it does not matter. If Grunge has the property right, White Water will pay Grunge not to dump. If White Water has the right, Grunge will clean up its waste at a cost of $300.

Economic Efficiency and the Optimum Amount of Pollution Cleanup

! *Student Alert:* **Does it make sound economic sense to clean up all pollution?**

The human and environmental damage caused by industrial pollution often arouses public attention. Although it might be nice to restore our environment to its pristine state, pollution cleanup is costly and dollars used for cleanup might be spent elsewhere. It seems, then, that some sort of balance must be struck between undesirable pollution and its costly cleanup. Let's apply marginal analysis to determine an optimal amount of pollution and environmental cleanup.

The marginal social benefit (MSB) of cleaning up pollution tends to decline as additional units of pollution are cleaned up. The marginal social cost (MSC) of cleaning up pollution tends to increase as additional units of pollution are cleaned up. If society has accurate information about the total social (public and private) benefits and costs of various amounts of cleanup, society should be able to get close to the most efficient, or optimum, level of cleanup (and/or pollution) where the marginal social benefits equal the marginal social costs (MSB = MSC).

Imagine a community in which two firms emit foul sludge into two local lakes (one for each firm). Natural processes gradually break down the sludge, rendering it harmless. But as long as emissions continue, a certain equilibrium level of harmful sludge remains in the lake. If emissions are lowered, this equilibrium level will be reduced. The opposite occurs if emissions are increased. Currently each firm emits five units of sludge each week.

Given the information in Tables 5-4.1 and 5-4.2, you should be able to determine the optimal level of emissions for this community. Fill in the blanks in the tables, and use this information to answer Questions 1 through 4. Assume that benefits obtained and costs incurred for cleanup at one lake have no impact on costs and benefits at the other lake.

 Table 5-4.1
Firm 1

Reduction of foul sludge emissions	Total social benefit of cleanup	Marginal social benefit of cleanup	Total social cost of cleanup	Marginal social cost of cleanup
0	$0	—	$0	—
1	$350	$350	$160	$160
2	$650	*$300*	$370	*$210*
3	$900	*$250*	$630	*$260*
4	$1,100	*$200*	$940	*$310*
5	$1,250	*$150*	$1,300	*$360*

1. Using the data from Table 5-4.1, fill in the blanks or underline the correct words in parentheses.

(A) The marginal social benefit (MSB) of reducing emissions by the first unit of foul sludge is **$350**, and the marginal social cost (MSC) of reducing pollution emissions by the first unit is **$160**. The MSB is (**greater than** / equal to / less than) the MSC, so it (**would** / would not) be economically efficient from society's perspective to require Firm 1 to reduce pollution emission by the first unit.

(B) The MSB of eliminating the last (fifth) unit of foul sludge is **$150**, and the MSC of reducing pollution emissions by the last (fifth) unit is **$360**. The MSB is (greater than / equal to / **less than**) the MSC, so it (would / **would not**) be economically efficient from society's perspective to require Firm 1 to reduce pollution emission by the fifth unit.

 Table 5-4.2
Firm 2

Reduction of foul sludge emissions	Total social benefit of cleanup	Marginal social benefit of cleanup	Total social cost of cleanup	Marginal social cost of cleanup
0	$0	—	$0	—
1	$350	$350	$130	$130
2	$650	*$300*	$280	*$150*
3	$900	*$250*	$450	*$170*
4	$1,100	*$200*	$640	*$190*
5	$1,250	*$150*	$850	*$210*

2. Using the data from Table 5-4.2, fill in the blanks or underline the correct words in parentheses.

(A) The MSB of eliminating the fourth unit of foul sludge is ____**$200**____, and the MSC of reducing pollution emissions by this fourth unit is ____**$190**____. The MSB is (**greater than** / equal to / less than) the MSC, so it (**would** / would not) be economically efficient from society's perspective to require Firm 2 to reduce pollution emissions by four units.

(B) The MSB of eliminating the fifth (last) unit of foul sludge is ____**$150**____, and the MSC of reducing pollution emissions by this fifth (last) unit is ____**$210**____. The MSB is (greater than / equal to / **less than**) the MSC, so it (would / **would not**) be economically efficient from society's perspective to require Firm 2 to reduce pollution emissions by five units.

3. If this community decides to adopt a pollution control ordinance aimed at maximizing economic efficiency, how should it evaluate each of the following three proposals, all of which are based on the data presented above? Write a brief economic evaluation in the space provided after each of the proposals. Be sure to use the concepts of marginal social benefit and marginal social cost in your analysis.

Proposal A. "Foul sludge emissions should be reduced (by five units) to zero for each firm because we should eliminate all pollution from our lakes regardless of the cost."

This proposal (*would* / ***would not***) maximize economic efficiency.
Economic efficiency considers marginal social costs and marginal social benefits:
   MSB < MSC after Firm 1 reduces two units.
   MSB < MSC after Firm 2 reduces four units.
   For five units, MSC > MSB for both firms.
Therefore, it would not be economically efficient to make either firm reduce five units because the MSB would be less than the MSC.

Proposal B. "Firm 2 should be forced to reduce emissions from five units to zero because the total social benefit of cleanup ($1,250) exceeds the total social cost of cleaning up ($850). But Firm 1 should not be forced to clean up at all, because the total social benefit of cleanup ($1,250) is less than the total social cost of reducing emissions to zero ($1,300)."

This proposal (*would* / ***would not***) maximize economic efficiency.
It is marginal (not total) benefits and marginal (not total) costs that count in finding the optimum point of economic efficiency. If Firm 2 reduces five units and Firm 1 reduces zero units, the total net gain is $400 ($1,250 – $850) from Firm 2. However, if Firm 2 reduces only four units and Firm 1 reduces two units, the total net gain is $740:
   Firm 1: $650 – $370 = $280
   Firm 2: $1,100 – $640 = $460
          $740

Proposal C. "In the interest of equal treatment for all, each firm should be forced to clean up (reduce emissions) by three units."

This proposal (*would* / ***would not***) maximize economic efficiency.
Making Firm 1 reduce a third unit would result in MSB < MSC. Stopping Firm 2 at three units would leave MSB > MSC. Efficiency would increase if Firm 1 cut back to reducing two units, and Firm 2 continued reducing to a fourth unit. With each firm reducing three units, the total net gain is $720:
   Firm 1: $900 – $630 = $270
   Firm 2: $900 – $450 = $450
          $720

With Firm 1 reducing two units and Firm 2 reducing four units, the total net gain is $740:
   Firm 1: $650 – $370 = $280
   Firm 2: $1,100 – $640 = $460
          $740

4. Using the data presented above, what do you think is the socially optimal level of emissions reduction for each firm? Explain why you chose these numbers.

   Firm 1:   **2**   units

   Firm 2:   **4**   units

   The optimal level of emissions is the output where MSB = MSC. For Firm 1, MSB > MSC up to a reduction of two units; beyond this point MSB < MSC. For Firm 2, MSB > MSC up to a reduction of four units; beyond this point MSB < MSC. No other combination yields a net gain greater than $740.

5. What would you say to someone who makes the following statement? "Society should do all it can to eliminate all pollution."
   I would say that the person is wrong. The optimal amount of pollution elimination is the amount at which the MSB = MSC of pollution reduction. Any units of pollution elimination that have MSB < MSC should not be provided.

      Advanced Placement Economics Microeconomics: Teacher Resource Manual © Council for Economic Education, New York, N.Y.

What Is a Fair Tax?

Almost everyone is concerned about how much we pay in taxes. The best way to determine how much tax you pay is to state your tax as an *effective tax rate*. An effective tax rate is the percentage of your income you pay in taxes. This differs from a *nominal tax rate* or *legal tax rate*. For example, a sales tax rate may be 5 percent (the nominal rate), but this does not mean that all people pay 5 percent of their income in sales taxes. Outlays for rent, insurance, and medical bills, among other things, may not be subject to sales taxes. Neither, of course, are savings.

Let's look at the effective tax rate of Joanne Walters. If she made $30,000 a year and paid $6,000 in taxes, her effective tax rate would be 20 percent. You can figure this by dividing $6,000 by $30,000:

$$\frac{\$6,000}{\$30,000} = 20\%.$$

There are three kinds of effective tax rates. If a tax is *progressive*, the effective tax rate increases as a person's income goes up. For example, a person who makes $30,000 a year may have an effective tax rate of 10 percent, while a person who makes $45,000 a year may have an effective rate of 18 percent.

If a tax is *proportional*, the effective tax rate stays the same regardless of income. In this case, a person making $30,000 a year and a person making $45,000 a year would both be taxed at an effective rate of, say, 10 percent. Of course, the person making $45,000 a year would pay more total dollars in taxes. A proportional tax is sometimes called a *flat tax*.

If a tax is *regressive*, the effective tax rate decreases as income goes up. For example, a person making $30,000 a year might pay an effective tax rate of 10 percent, while a person who makes $45,000 a year might pay an effective tax rate of 8 percent.

Now answer these questions to see if you understand progressive, proportional, and regressive tax rates.

1. A tax that requires each person to pay 3 percent of income regardless of the level of income is a **proportional** tax.

2. A tax levied at 1 percent on the first $1,000 of income, 2 percent on the next $1,000, and so on is a **progressive** tax.

3. A tax levied at 15 percent on the first $1,000 of income, 12 percent on the next $1,000, and so on is a **regressive** tax.

4. If it is true that a person with an income of $20,000 a year typically buys 10 gallons of gasoline per week and a person with an income of $40,000 typically buys 15 gallons of gasoline per week, this sugests that an excise tax of 40 cents per gallon would be a *regressive* tax. Explain.
The richer person has double the income but buys only 50 percent more gasoline. Therefore, the poorer person pays a greater percentage of his or her income on the gasoline tax.

5. Rick Morales has an income of $50,000 but spends only $40,000 on taxable goods. Chet Burton has an income of $25,000 and spends it all on taxable goods. Assuming an 8 percent sales tax, Mr. Morales will pay *$3,200* in sales taxes, which is *6.4* percent of his total income. On the other hand, Mr. Burton will pay ___*$2,000*___ in sales taxes, which is ___*8.0*___ percent of his total income. Therefore, we can conclude that the sales tax is *(progressive / proportional / **regressive**)*.

6. Since the sales tax has the same nominal or legal rate based on sales, why is it regressive? What steps could be taken to make it less regressive?
The sales tax base is consumption, not income. Most states do not include services in their sales tax base. Since the rich purchase more services, taxing services would make the tax less regressive. It would also raise more revenue. Since the poor pay a greater percentage of their income on food, exempting food also makes the tax less regressive. Several states exempt food from sales taxes. The government could tax income, or exempt the first portion of expenditures, or eliminate the sales tax on necessities such as food.

7. Suppose that the government runs a pension fund to which all workers must contribute. The employee contribution rate is 6.2 percent on the first $84,900 of income. All income in excess of $84,900 is not taxed for pension purposes.

   (A) What is the effective pension tax rate for a person earning $20,000 a year? *6.2%*

   (B) What is the effective pension tax rate for a person earning $84,900? *6.2%*

   (C) What is the effective pension tax rate for a person earning $169,800? *3.1%*
   The first $84,900 is taxed at 6.2 percent = ($84,900)(0.062) = $5,263.80. The remaining income of $84,900 is not taxed for this person. The effective tax rate is $5,263.80/$169,800 = 0.031 = 3.1 percent.

   (D) Therefore, the pension tax is a *(progressive / **proportional** / regressive)* tax up to $84,900 of income. For incomes above ___*$84,900*___, the tax is *(progressive / proportional / **regressive**)*.

   (E) In addition to the pension tax, assume people must pay 1.45 percent of their income for medical benefits. There is no income limit on the medical care tax. Does this make the total tax for pension and medical care more or less regressive? Why?
   Less regressive because high-income people must pay the medical care tax on their entire income, but they must pay the pension tax on their income up to only $84,900.

Who Pays the Income Tax?

Who actually pays the income tax? Do "the rich" escape paying their "fair" share of taxes? Is most of the income tax paid by middle-income people? Who are the rich? These questions are important for several reasons:

■ Taxes can redistribute income. Like Robin Hood, government can tax the rich and redistribute this money to the poor. Instead of money, most tax revenue is redistributed in the form of college scholarships, food stamps, medical care, housing assistance, and other services for lower-income families. While the merits of these programs can be debated, almost no one would agree that a "Robin Hood in reverse" policy would be beneficial: taxing the poor and redistributing tax revenue to the wealthy.

■ Some people think taxes should have *vertical equity*, that is, the tax burden should be distributed fairly across people according to their ability to pay. This argument for progressive taxation maintains that the rich have more ability to pay taxes, and therefore should bear a larger tax burden than low-income families.

■ Some people think that income should be distributed more equally than it is today.

Part A: Examining the Tax Data

Tables 5-6.1 and 5-6.2 contain information regarding shares of income, taxes, and tax rates for federal income tax returns for 1997 and 2009. Use the tables to answer the questions that follow.

 Table 5-6.1
Federal Income Tax Return Data: 2009

Percent of all taxpayers	Income range	Group's share of total income (adjusted gross income)	Group's share of total income taxes	Group's average tax rate
Top 1%	Above $343,927	16.9%	36.7%	24.0%
Top 5%	Above $154,643	31.7%	58.7%	20.5%
Top 10%	Above $112,124	43.2%	70.5%	18.1%
Top 25%	Above $66,193	65.8%	87.3%	14.7%
Top 50%	Above $32,396	86.5%	97.7%	12.5%
Bottom 50%	Below $32,396	13.5%	2.3%	1.8%
All taxpayers		100.0%	100.0%	11.1%

Source: Tax Foundation

Table 5-6.2
Federal Income Tax Return Data: 1997

Percent of all taxpayers	Income range	Group's share of total income (adjusted gross income)	Group's share of total income taxes	Group's average tax rate
Top 1%	Above $250,736	17.4%	33.2%	27.6%
Top 5%	Above $108,048	31.8%	51.9%	23.6%
Top 10%	Above $79,212	42.8%	63.2%	21.4%
Top 25%	Above $48,173	65.0%	81.7%	18.2%
Top 50%	Above $24,393	86.2%	95.7%	16.1%
Bottom 50%	Below $24,393	13.8%	4.3%	4.5%
All taxpayers		100.0%	100.0%	14.5%

Source: Tax Foundation

1. Suppose you define "the rich" as the top 10 percent of all income earners. In 2009, what was the minimum income you had to earn to be "rich"?
   $112,124

2. What percentage of total income taxes did the top 1 percent of income earners pay in 2009?
   36.7 percent

3. In 2009, what percentage of total income taxes was paid by the bottom half of all income earners?
   2.3 percent

4. In 2009, the average U.S. taxpayer paid 11.1 percent of his/her income in taxes. Based on the information in the table, would you classify the U.S. income tax system as progressive, proportional, or regressive? Why?
   The U.S. income tax system is progressive because the tax rate increases as a person's income level increases.

5. Compare 1997 with 2009. What is the best description of what happened to the income tax burden in the United States over this 12-year period?

The income tax remained progressive. The share of total income taxes paid by the top 50 percent increased while the share paid by the bottom 50 percent decreased.

Part B: Equity Questions

Many people are concerned that "the rich are getting richer and the poor are getting poorer." Using the income tax data from Tables 5-6.1 and 5-6.2, answer the following questions.

6. Is there evidence that the rich got richer and the poor got poorer between 1997 and 2009? Explain.

The evidence is subject to interpretation. To be in the top 1 percent of income earners required an income of $250,736 in 1997 and an income of $343,927 in 2009. This is an increase of 37.2 percent. In an absolute sense, the rich got richer over this period. However, the share of total income earned by the top 1 percent decreased from 17.4 percent in 1997 to 16.9 percent in 2009. In a relative sense, the rich did not get richer. To be in the bottom 50 percent of income earners required an income of $24,393 in 1997 and an income of $32,396 in 2009. This is an increase of 32.8 percent. The bottom 50 percent of income earners accounted for 13.8 percent of income in 1997 and 13.5 percent in 2009.

7. Some politicians argue that the wealthy are not paying their "fair" share of taxes. Based on the data in the two tables, do you agree or disagree? Explain.

In 1997, the top 1 percent of income earners received 17.4 percent of all income and paid 33.2 percent of all income taxes. In 2009, the top 1 percent earned 16.9 percent of all income and paid 36.7 percent of all income taxes. For this top income-bracket group, the share of income decreased, but their share of the tax burden increased. One could argue that the rich have a much higher ability to pay taxes, and that even 36.7 percent is not their fair share of taxes.

8. Would you argue that the U.S. income tax system promotes or hinders greater income equality? Why?

The U.S. income tax system appears to promote equality because it increases the tax burden as one's income level grows. The higher the income, the higher the effective tax rate. However, this also makes it hard to move up the income ladder: as you work hard and start to earn more income, the government takes more of your earnings. Also, redistribution results from both taxing and spending; the data in Tables 5-6.1 and 5-6.2 deal only with the tax side. If tax revenue is not redistributed to people with lower incomes, then the system will not be as effective at promoting equality. Overall, other things being equal, the U.S. progressive income tax system promotes equality.

Microeconomics

The Lorenz Curve and Gini Coefficient

The labor markets often fail to allocate income equally. Some households earn much income while many more earn little income. Differences in worker productivity, varying trade patterns, patterns of past discrimination, and tax policies are some of the reasons for what economists call *income inequality*. For example, increased demand for workers with at least bachelor's degrees and decreased demand for workers with only high school diplomas have resulted in income inequality as college-educated laborers' income has risen and high school-educated laborers' income has fallen.

Two important measures of income inequality are the Lorenz curve and the Gini coefficient. The *Lorenz curve* is a graph of income inequality that shows what percentage of a country's income is being earned by a percentage of the country's households.

 Figure 5-7.1
Lorenz Curve #1

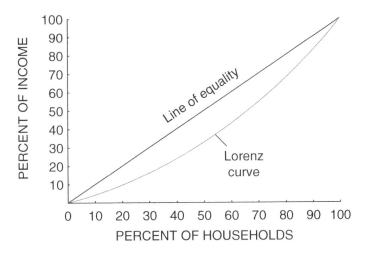

In Figure 5-7.1, the line of equality represents a perfectly even distribution of income. A perfectly even distribution means that 10 percent of the households earn 10 percent of the income, 20 percent of the households earn 20 percent of the income, and so on. The Lorenz curve shows the actual distribution of income. The closer the Lorenz curve is to the line of equality, the more evenly distributed is the income. The more the Lorenz curve sags away from the line of equality, then the more unevenly income is distributed. Figure 5-7.2 shows more income inequality than Figure 5-7.1.

Figure 5-7.2
Lorenz Curve #2

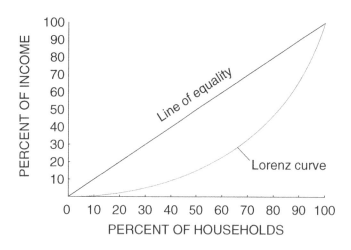

1. In Figure 5-7.3, determine the amount of income that is being earned by 50 percent of the households in the country of Maxopia.
   33 percent

Figure 5-7.3
Lorenz Curve for the Country of Maxopia

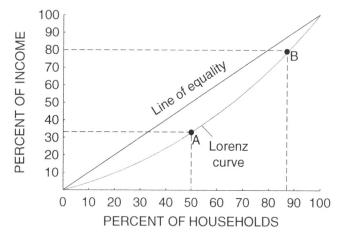

2. Now, determine the percentage of income being earned by 88 percent of the households.
   80 percent

3. Using Figure 5-7.4, determine the percentage of income being earned by 50 percent of the households and then by 88 percent of the households in the country of Minopia. You may want to use a ruler to help you.

(A) 50 percent of households earn *about 12 percent* of the income.

(B) 88 percent of households earn *about 62 percent* of the income.

Figure 5-7.4
Lorenz Curve for the Country of Minopia

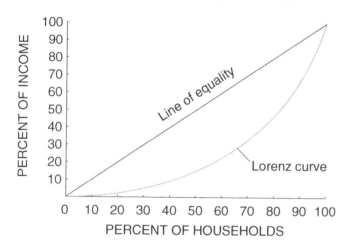

4. Compare your results from Questions 1 and 2 with your results from Questions 3A and 3B. Which country has more income equality—Maxopia or Minopia?
Maxopia has more income equality; its Lorenz curve is closer to the line of equality.

Another measure of income inequality is the *Gini coefficient*. The Gini coefficient compares the area between the line of equality and the Lorenz curve (as seen in area A in Figure 5-7.5) with the total area under the line of equality (the sum of areas A and B in Figure 5-7.5).

Figure 5-7.5
Lorenz Curve #5

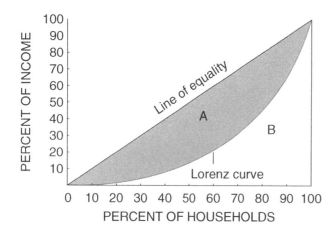

In Figure 5-7.5, the Gini coefficient = A/(A + B). The coefficient ranges from 0 to 1. A Gini coefficient of 0 indicates perfect income equality, while a Gini coefficient of 1 indicates perfect income inequality because just one household is earning 100 percent of the income.

5. As the area of A increases relative to the area of B, what is happening to income inequality?
   Income inequality is increasing.

6. If the country Economica has a Gini coefficient of 0.5, while the country Graphland has a Gini coefficient of 0.75, then in which country is income more evenly distributed?
   Economica's income is more evenly distributed.

7. Assume that Economica has a Gini coefficient of 0.5. If Economica's government imposes a redistributive income tax on the top 50 percent of households, then how will the following change:

   (A) The Lorenz curve *will move closer to the line of equality.*

   (B) The Gini coefficient *will get closer to zero.*

   (C) The line of equality *will not change.*

   (D) The income distribution of Economica *will be more equal.*

MICROECONOMICS

Sample AP Exam
Multiple-Choice Question
Answer Keys

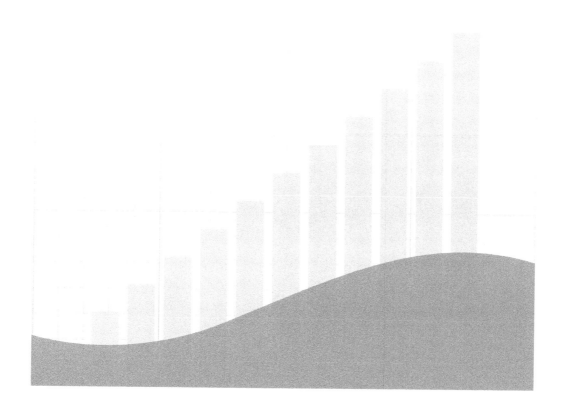

Answer Key to Multiple-Choice Questions

1. *D*	12. *C*	23. *A*
2. *B*	13. *C*	24. *C*
3. *E*	14. *C*	25. *A*
4. *C*	15. *D*	26. *B*
5. *C*	16. *C*	27. *B*
6. *B*	17. *B*	28. *C*
7. *E*	18. *C*	29. *C*
8. *B*	19. *D*	30. *E*
9. *B*	20. *E*	31. *B*
10. *B*	21. *C*	32. *C*
11. *A*	22. *C*	33. *D*

Circle the letter of each correct answer.

1. The crucial problem of economics is
   (A) establishing a fair tax system.
   (B) providing social goods and services.
   (C) developing a price mechanism that reflects the relative scarcities of products and resources.
   (D) allocating scarce productive resources to satisfy unlimited wants.
   (E) enacting a set of laws that protects resources from overuse.

2. When one decision is made, the next best alternative not selected is called
   (A) economic resource.
   (B) opportunity cost.
   (C) scarcity.
   (D) comparative disadvantage.
   (E) production.

3. Which of the following is true if the production possibilities curve is a curved line concave to the origin?
   (A) Resources are perfectly substitutable between the production of the two goods.
   (B) It is possible to produce more of both products.
   (C) Both products are equally capable of satisfying consumer wants.
   (D) The prices of the two products are the same.
   (E) As more of one good is produced, increasing amounts of the other good must be given up.

4. Which of the following will *not* change the demand for oranges?
   (A) A change in consumers' incomes
   (B) A change in the price of grapefruits, a substitute for oranges
   (C) A change in the price of oranges
   (D) A change in consumers' taste for oranges
   (E) An expectation that the price of oranges will change in the future

5. To be considered scarce, an economic resource must be
   (A) limited but not free or desirable.
   (B) limited and free, but not desirable.
   (C) limited and desirable, but not free.
   (D) limited, free, and desirable.
   (E) free and desirable, but not limited.

6. If there is an increase in demand for a good, what will most likely happen to the price and quantity of the good exchanged?

	Price	Quantity
(A)	No change	No change
(B)	**Increase**	**Increase**
(C)	Increase	Decrease
(D)	Decrease	Increase
(E)	Decrease	Decrease

7. Which of the following items would be considered scarce?
   (A) Education
   (B) Gold
   (C) Time
   (D) Education and gold
   (E) Education, gold, and time

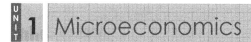

8. An increase in the price of gasoline will cause the demand curve for tires to shift in which direction?

   (A) To the left, because gasoline and tires are substitutes

   (B) To the left, because gasoline and tires are complements

   (C) To the right, because gasoline and tires are substitutes

   (D) To the right, because gasoline and tires are complements

   (E) To the right, because an increase in the price of gasoline makes consumers poorer and thus not willing to pay as much for tires

9. Which of the following problems do all economic systems face?

   I. How to allocate scarce resources among unlimited wants
   II. How to distribute income equally among all the citizens
   III. How to decentralize markets
   IV. How to decide what to produce, how to produce, and for whom to produce

   (A) I only

   (B) I and IV only

   (C) II and III only

   (D) I, II, and III only

   (E) I, II, III, and IV

10. In which way does a straight-line production possibilities curve differ from a concave production possibilities curve?

    (A) A straight-line production possibilities curve has a decreasing opportunity cost.

    (B) A straight-line production possibilities curve has a constant opportunity cost.

    (C) A straight-line production possibilities curve has an increasing opportunity cost.

    (D) A straight-line production possibilities curve does not show opportunity cost.

    (E) There is no difference between the two production possibilities curves.

11. The law of increasing opportunity cost is reflected in the shape of the

    (A) production possibilities curve concave to the origin.

    (B) production possibilities curve convex to the origin.

    (C) horizontal production possibilities curve.

    (D) straight-line production possibilities curve.

    (E) upward-sloping production possibilities curve.

The figure below is used for questions 12 through 15. It shows the production possibilities curve for a country with full employment of a given-size labor force.

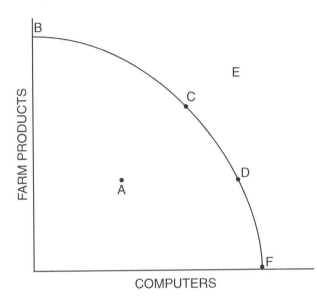

12. If the country is currently producing at Point C, it can produce more computers by doing which of the following?

   (A) Moving to Point A

   (B) Moving to Point B

   (C) Moving to Point D

   (D) Moving to Point E

   (E) Remaining at Point C

13. Which of the following statements about the production possibilities curve is true?

   (A) Point A is not attainable in a developed society.

   (B) Point D is not attainable given the society's resources.

   (C) The relative position of Points C and D reflect production alternatives rather than relative prices.

   (D) Elimination of unemployment will move the production possibilities curve to the right, closer to Point E.

   (E) Point E lies outside the production possibilities curve because it represents a combination of resources not desired by the citizens of the country.

14. How might Point E be attained?

   (A) If the country's resources were more fully employed

   (B) If the country's resources were shifted to encourage more efficient use of scarce resources

   (C) If improvements in technology occurred in either the computer sector or the farm products sector

   (D) If firms decreased their output of computers

   (E) If the nation used more of its scarce resources to produce farm products

15. The production possibilities curve of the country would be most likely to shift to the right if the country were currently producing at which of the following points?

   (A) Point A

   (B) Point B

   (C) Point C

   (D) Point D

   (E) Point E

The figure below is used for questions 16, 17, and 18. It shows the production possibilities curve for two types of goods for a country with full employment of a given-size labor force.

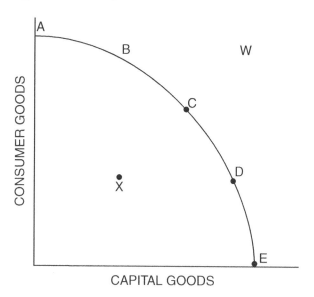

16. If the country is currently producing at Point C, it can produce more capital goods by moving in the direction of

    (A) Point A.

    (B) Point B.

    (C) Point D.

    (D) Point W.

    (E) Point X.

17. If the country moves from Point C to Point D, future economic growth will

    (A) decrease.

    (B) increase.

    (C) not change, but consumer satisfaction will increase.

    (D) not change, but unemployment will increase.

    (E) not change, but inflation will increase.

18. Which of the following is most likely to cause the production possibilities curve to shift outward toward Point W?

    (A) Employing the country's resources more fully

    (B) Shifting the country's resources to encourage more efficient use of scarce resources

    (C) Improving the technology for the production of either consumer or capital goods

    (D) Decreasing production of capital goods

    (E) Shifting some scarce resources to produce consumer goods in the current period

19. The opportunity cost of producing an additional unit of product J is

    (A) the dollar value of resources used to make the extra unit of product J.

    (B) the retail price paid for product J.

    (C) the wholesale price of product J.

    (D) the amount of product K that could have been produced with the resources used to make the unit of J.

    (E) the profit that was earned from producing product J.

20. Which of the following would cause a leftward shift of the production possibilities curve?

    (A) An increase in unemployment

    (B) An increase in inflation

    (C) An increase in capital equipment

    (D) A decrease in consumer demand

    (E) A decrease in working-age population

21. Which of the following would cause an outward or rightward shift in the production possibilities curve?

    (A) An increase in unemployment

    (B) An increase in inflation

    (C) An increase in capital equipment

    (D) A decrease in natural resources

    (E) A decrease in the number of workers

Use the following table for questions 22, 23, and 24.

Mars		Venus	
Food	Clothing	Food	Clothing
0	30	0	40
2	24	4	32
4	18	8*	24*
6*	12*	12	16
8	6	16	8
10	0	20	0

Two nations, Mars and Venus, each produce food and clothing. The table above gives points on each nation's production possibilities curve. The asterisks indicate their current point of production.

22. In Mars, the opportunity cost of obtaining the first two units of food is how many units of clothing?

(A) 2   (D) 8

(B) 3   (E) 12

(C) 6

23. In Venus, the opportunity cost of the first unit of

(A) food is two units of clothing.

(B) food is eight units of clothing.

(C) clothing is two units of food.

(D) clothing is four units of food.

(E) clothing is eight units of food.

24. Which of the following statements is correct based on the concept of comparative advantage?

(A) Mars and Venus should continue producing the quantities indicated by the asterisks.

(B) Mars should specialize in the production of food.

(C) Mars should specialize in the production of clothing.

(D) Venus has the comparative advantage in clothing.

(E) Mars has an absolute advantage in the production of food.

25. The table below shows the number of hours needed to produce one bushel of soybeans and one bushel of rice in each of two countries.

Country	One bushel of soybeans	One bushel of rice
U.S.	5 hours	7 hours
Japan	15 hours	10 hours

Which of the following statements must be true?

(A) The U.S. has both the absolute and comparative advantage in producing soybeans.

(B) Japan has both the absolute and comparative advantage in producing soybeans.

(C) The U.S. has both the absolute and comparative advantage in producing rice.

(D) Japan has both the absolute and comparative advantage in producing rice.

(E) Japan has the absolute advantage in producing soybeans and the comparative advantage in producing rice.

26. A rational decision maker will choose to act only if

(A) the marginal benefit of the action is greater than the average cost of that action.

(B) the marginal benefit of the action is greater than the marginal cost of that action.

(C) the marginal benefit of the action is less than the average cost of that action.

(D) the average benefit of the action is less than the average cost of that action.

(E) the average benefit of the action is greater than the marginal cost of that action.

27. According to the theory of comparative advantage, a good should be produced where

    (A) its explicit costs are least.

    (B) its opportunity costs are least.

    (C) the cost of real resources used is least.

    (D) production can occur with the greatest increase in employment.

    (E) production can occur with the lowest increase in employment.

28. Which of the following statements violates the economic concept of matching marginal benefits with marginal costs in test taking?

    (A) "My grade in this course is already an A and the final examination is optional, so I'm not taking the final examination in this class."

    (B) "My grade going into the final examination for math is B-plus. The final exam constitutes half of the course grade, so I'm going to study more for the final in this class than in solid-state genetics, where I have a solid A."

    (C) "Most of my grades are B-minus, but in fluid dynamics I have an A. I'm going to study only for the final exam in fluid dynamics."

    (D) "If I spend two extra hours a week reading English literature, my scores on standardized tests of verbal skills will improve by 20 percent. Since my verbal skills are average, I'm going to reallocate my time into reading more literature."

    (E) All the statements violate the concept of matching marginal benefits with marginal costs in test taking.

29. "If you want to have anything done correctly, you have to do it yourself." This quote violates the principle of which of the following economic concepts?

    (A) Scarcity

    (B) Supply

    (C) Comparative advantage

    (D) Diminishing marginal returns

    (E) Demand

30. Which of the following will *not* cause the demand curve for athletic shoes to shift?

    (A) A change in tastes for athletic shoes

    (B) Widespread advertising campaign for athletic shoes

    (C) Increase in money incomes of athletic-shoe consumers

    (D) Expectations that the price of athletic shoes will decrease in the future

    (E) A decrease in the price of athletic shoes

31. Assume that the demand for apples is downward sloping. If the price of apples falls from $0.80 per pound to $0.65 per pound, which of the following will occur?

    (A) A smaller quantity of apples will be demanded.

    (B) A larger quantity of apples will be demanded.

    (C) Demand for apples will decrease.

    (D) Demand for apples will increase.

    (E) Supply of apples will decrease.

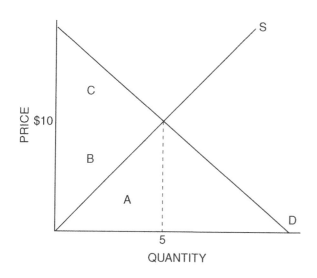

33. Producer surplus is the

    (A) area under the supply curve to the left of the amount sold.

    (B) area under the supply curve to the right of the amount sold.

    (C) amount the seller is paid plus the cost of production.

    (D) amount the seller is paid less the cost of production.

    (E) cost to sellers of participating in a market.

32. On the graph above, what area represents consumer surplus when the price is $10?

    (A) A   (D) A and B

    (B) B   (E) B and C

    (C) C

Answer Key to Multiple-Choice Questions

1. *E*	9. *D*	17. *E*
2. *D*	10. *A*	18. *B*
3. *A*	11. *A*	19. *A*
4. *D*	12. *E*	20. *A*
5. *D*	13. *C*	21. *D*
6. *C*	14. *A*	22. *D*
7. *C*	15. *E*	23. *A*
8. *E*	16. *B*	

Circle the letter of each correct answer.

1. A downward sloping demand curve can be explained by
   I. diminishing marginal utility.
   II. diminishing marginal returns.
   III. the substitution effect.
   IV. the income effect.
   (A) I only
   (B) II only
   (C) I and III only
   (D) I and IV only
   (E) I, III, and IV only

2. If hot dogs are an inferior good, an increase in income will result in
   (A) an increase in the quantity demanded for hot dogs.
   (B) an increase in the demand for hot dogs.
   (C) a decrease in the quantity demanded for hot dogs.
   (D) a decrease in the demand for hot dogs.
   (E) no change in the demand for hot dogs.

3. Assume that coal is a normal good. If the price of coal increases and the quantity sold increases, which of the following is consistent with these observations?
   (A) The price of oil, a substitute for coal, increased.
   (B) A wage increase was given to coal miners.
   (C) New machinery made coal mining more efficient.
   (D) Consumers' incomes fell.
   (E) The demand curve is inelastic.

4. During a football game, it starts to rain and the temperature drops. The senior class, which runs the concession stand and is studying economics, raises the price of coffee from 50 cents to 75 cents a cup. They sell more than ever before. Which answer explains this?
   (A) The supply of coffee increased.
   (B) The demand curve for coffee was elastic.
   (C) The supply of coffee decreased.
   (D) The demand for coffee increased.
   (E) The demand curve for coffee was inelastic.

5. Which of the following statements best reflects the law of *diminishing marginal utility*?
   (A) "I have to have a scoop of ice cream on my pie."
   (B) "I'll never get tired of your cooking."
   (C) "The last bite tastes just as good as the first."
   (D) "I couldn't eat another doughnut if you paid me."
   (E) "I prefer to eat several small meals a day, rather than three large ones."

6. If the cost of producing automobiles increases, the price, equilibrium quantity, and consumer surplus will most likely change in which of the following ways?

	Price	Quantity	Consumer surplus
(A)	Increase	Increase	Increase
(B)	Increase	Decrease	Increase
(C)	**Increase**	**Decrease**	**Decrease**
(D)	Decrease	Increase	Decrease
(E)	Decrease	Decrease	Decrease

7. Compare 2011 with 2012. Which of the following statements is (are) true?

Year	Quantity sold	Price
2011	30,000	$10
2012	50,000	$20

   I.   Demand has increased.

   II. Quantity demanded has increased.

   III. Supply has increased.

   IV. Quantity supplied has increased.

   V. Supply has decreased.

(A) I only

(B) V only

(C) I and IV only

(D) I and V only

(E) I, II, and III only

8. During the 1990s, the price of VCRs fell by about 30 percent, and quantity sold decreased by the same amount. The demand for VCRs must

(A) be inelastic.

(B) be elastic.

(C) be unit elastic.

(D) have shifted to the right.

(E) have shifted to the left.

9. Which of the following will occur if a legal price floor is placed on a good below its free-market equilibrium?

(A) Surpluses will develop.

(B) Shortages will develop.

(C) Underground markets will develop.

(D) The equilibrium price will ration the good.

(E) The quantity sold will increase.

10. A marketing survey shows that gate receipts would increase if the price of tickets to a summer rock concert increased, even though the number of tickets sold would fall. What does this imply about the price elasticity of demand for concert tickets?

(A) Demand is inelastic.

(B) Demand is elastic.

(C) Demand is unit elastic.

(D) Demand is perfectly inelastic.

(E) Demand is perfectly elastic.

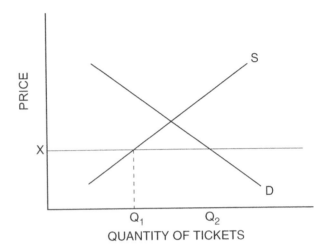

11. According to the graph above, which of the following will occur if a legal price ceiling is imposed at price X?

(A) Shortages will occur.

(B) Surpluses will occur.

(C) Demand will increase.

(D) Q_2 will be purchased.

(E) Supply will decrease.

12. Which of the following statements about price controls is true?

(A) A price ceiling causes a shortage if the ceiling price is above the equilibrium price.

(B) A price floor causes a surplus if the price floor is below the equilibrium price.

(C) A price ceiling causes an increase in demand if the ceiling price is set below the equilibrium price.

(D) A price ceiling causes a decrease in demand if the price floor is set above the equilibrium price.

(E) Price ceilings and price floors result in a misallocation of resources.

13. If the price of lunch at the school cafeteria increases and cafeteria revenue remains constant, the price elasticity of demand for a school lunch must be

(A) elastic.

(B) perfectly elastic.

(C) unit elastic.

(D) inelastic.

(E) perfectly inelastic.

14. If an excise tax is imposed on a product, consumer surplus and producer surplus for this good will most likely change in which of the following ways?

	Consumer surplus	Producer surplus
(A)	*Decrease*	*Decrease*
(B)	Decrease	Increase
(C)	Decrease	Not change
(D)	Not change	Increase
(E)	Not change	Not change

15. If the price of paperback books increases and consumer expenditures on paperback books also increase, which of the following is necessarily true?

(A) Paperback books are normal goods.

(B) Paperback books are inferior goods.

(C) The demand for paperback books is unit elastic.

(D) The demand for paperback books is elastic.

(E) The demand for paperback books is inelastic.

16. The substitution effect causes a consumer to buy less of a product when the price increases because the

(A) product is now less expensive compared to similar products.

(B) product is now more expensive compared to similar products.

(C) consumer's real income has decreased.

(D) consumer's real income has increased.

(E) consumer will buy more inferior goods and fewer normal goods.

Product	% Change in income	% Change in quantity
A	+5	+5
B	+5	−5
C	−10	−5
D	−10	+10

17. Based on the information in the table above, which product(s) is/are inferior?

(A) Product A only

(B) Product B only

(C) Product D only

(D) Product A and C only

(E) Product B and D only

18. Brooke is spending all of her income consuming products X and Y. If $MU_x/P_x = 10$ and $MU_y/P_y = 6$, what should Brooke do to maximize her satisfaction?

(A) Buy more X and more Y.

(B) Buy more X and less Y.

(C) Buy less X and less Y.

(D) Buy less X and more Y.

(E) Make no changes.

19. If the price of a good decreases by 3 percent and total revenue increases, the absolute value of the price elasticity of demand for the good could possibly be

(A) 1.3   (D) 0.2

(B) 1   (E) 0

(C) 0.8

20. Advocates of higher minimum wages for unskilled labor defend their position by arguing that

(A) low-income workers deserve to earn incomes above the poverty level.

(B) higher wages boost worker productivity and efficiency.

(C) higher wages will cause employers to reduce the payroll, but the total wages of remaining workers will be higher.

(D) higher wages induce more workers into the labor market and thus reduce unemployment.

(E) it is more efficient for the private sector to provide a higher wage than for the government to provide transfer payments to low-income workers.

21. A paper mill located on a scenic river decides to dump its untreated waste products into the river. Which of the following is the likely result of this action?

(A) The marginal private cost and marginal social cost of paper production will be equal.

(B) The marginal private cost will be greater than the marginal social cost of paper production.

(C) The price of paper produced by the mill will increase.

(D) The mill will produce more paper than society would like it to produce.

(E) The mill will produce the socially optimal amount of paper.

Answer Questions 22 and 23 based on this graph of the market for Good X.

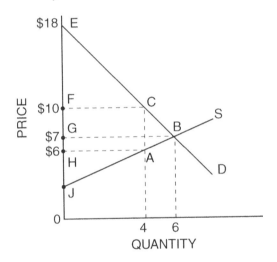

22. In a competitive market the value of consumer surplus is

(A) $0.   **(D) $33.**

(B) $11.   (E) $42.

(C) $18.

23. If the government decided that only 4 units of Good X could be sold, the deadweight loss of this policy would be shown by area

(A) ABC.   (D) CFE.

(B) ACEJ.   (E) BGJ.

(C) AHJ.

Answer Key to Multiple-Choice Questions

1. *E*	16. *C*	31. *C*
2. *C*	17. *E*	32. *A*
3. *D*	18. *C*	33. *C*
4. *C*	19. *C*	34. *D*
5. *C*	20. *B*	35. *E*
6. *D*	21. *D*	36. *B*
7. *E*	22. *C*	37. *E*
8. *A*	23. *B*	38. *E*
9. *E*	24. *D*	39. *A*
10. *E*	25. *D*	40. *C*
11. *D*	26. *B*	41. *A*
12. *C*	27. *D*	42. *E*
13. *D*	28. *D*	43. *A*
14. *B*	29. *D*	44. *B*
15. *B*	30. *C*	45. *A*

Circle the letter of each correct answer.

1. True statements about the theory of the firm in the short run and long run include which of the following?

    I. All input quantities are fixed in the short run.

    II. All input quantities are variable in the long run.

    III. At least one input quantity is fixed in the short run.

    (A) I only

    (B) II only

    (C) III only

    (D) I and II only

    (E) II and III only

3. Which of the following statements about a firm's production function are true?

    I. When total product is at its maximum, marginal product is zero.

    II. When total product rises, marginal product is rising.

    III. When marginal product is greater than average product, average product is rising.

    IV. When marginal product is less than average product, average product is falling.

    (A) I and II only

    (B) II and III only

    (C) II and IV only

    (D) I, III, and IV only

    (E) I, II, III, and IV

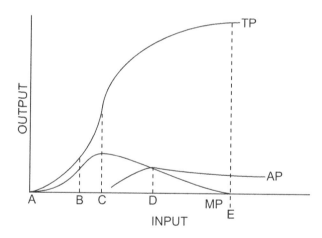

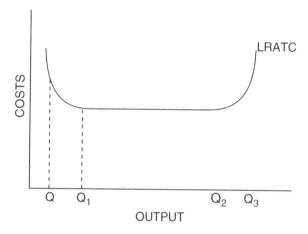

2. On the graph above, the onset of diminishing marginal returns occurs beyond

    (A) Point A.

    (B) Point B.

    (C) Point C.

    (D) Point D.

    (E) Point E.

4. According to the graph above, if the firm is producing any quantity greater than Q_2, the firm is experiencing

    (A) economies of scale.

    (B) minimum efficient scale.

    (C) diseconomies of scale.

    (D) constant returns.

    (E) increasing returns.

5. For a perfectly competitive firm, if the market price is $8, then

   (A) marginal revenue is greater than $8.

   (B) marginal revenue is less than $8.

   (C) marginal revenue is equal to $8.

   (D) average revenue is greater than $8.

   (E) average revenue is less than $8.

6. A firm's short-run marginal cost curve will eventually increase because of

   (A) more efficient production.

   (B) economies of scale.

   (C) diseconomies of scale.

   (D) diminishing marginal returns.

   (E) increasing marginal returns.

7. Assume that in the short run at the profit-maximizing output, the price is lower than average variable cost. The perfectly competitive firm should

   (A) increase its price.

   (B) decrease its price.

   (C) increase its output.

   (D) decrease its output.

   (E) shut down.

8. Assume that a perfectly competitive firm is operating where marginal revenue is greater than marginal costs. To increase total profits, the firm should

   (A) increase production.

   (B) decrease production.

   (C) increase price.

   (D) decrease price.

   (E) do nothing.

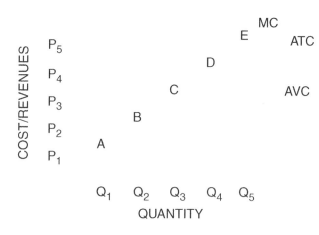

Use the graph above to answer Questions 9, 10, and 11.

9. If the firm is in short-run equilibrium at a price of P_5, a perfectly competitive firm will maximize total profits by producing at which of the following levels of output?

   (A) Q_1 (D) Q_4

   (B) Q_2 *(E) Q_5*

   (C) Q_3

10. At which price will this perfectly competitive firm make an economic profit?

   (A) P_1 (D) P_4

   (B) P_2 *(E) P_5*

   (C) P_3

11. Which price-quantity combination represents long-run equilibrium for this perfectly competitive firm?

   (A) Point A   *(D) Point D*

   (B) Point B   (E) Point E

   (C) Point C

12. If the average variable cost of producing five units of a product is $100 and the average variable cost of producing six units is $125, then the marginal cost of producing the sixth unit is

   (A) $25.   (D) $500.

   (B) $125.   (E) $750.

   (C) $250.

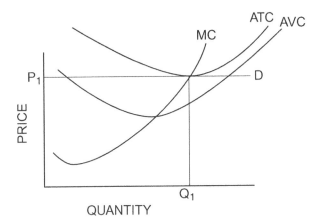

13. According to the graph above, if the firm is producing at Q_1, the firm is

   (A) losing money because the firm is operating at the shutdown point.

   (B) losing money because the price does not cover average fixed cost.

   (C) making profits because the price is above average variable cost.

   (D) making normal profits because the price just covers average total cost.

   (E) making normal profits because the price is above average variable cost.

14. Which of the following represents the correct relationship between the demand curve for a perfectly competitive industry and the demand curve for a perfectly competitive firm?

	PC industry demand	PC firm demand
(A)	Downward slope to the right	Downward slope to the right
(B)	*Downward slope to the right*	*Perfectly elastic*
(C)	Perfectly elastic	Downward slope to the right
(D)	Perfectly elastic	Perfectly elastic
(E)	Perfectly inelastic	Perfectly elastic

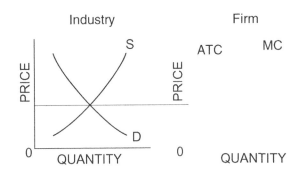

15. According to the graphs above, in which of the following ways are the industry supply curve and the equilibrium price most likely to change in the long run?

	Industry supply	Equilibrium price
(A)	Decrease	Decrease
(B)	*Decrease*	*Increase*
(C)	Increase	Decrease
(D)	Increase	Increase
(E)	Not change	Decrease

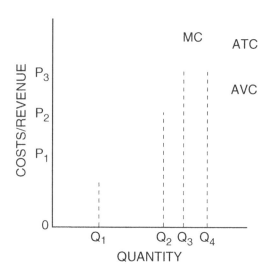

Use the graph above to answer Question 16.

16. If price is P_3, the firm will

   (A) produce Q_2 units and earn only a normal profit.

   (B) produce Q_1 units and earn an economic profit.

   (C) produce Q_3 units and earn an economic profit.

   (D) produce Q_4 units and earn an economic profit.

   (E) shut down.

17. Which of the following is true of a pure monopolist's demand curve?

   (A) It is perfectly inelastic.

   (B) It is perfectly elastic.

   (C) It coincides with its marginal revenue curve.

   (D) It lies below its marginal revenue curve.

   (E) It lies above its marginal revenue curve.

18. Average fixed cost is shown as the vertical distance between

   (A) marginal cost and average variable cost.

   (B) marginal cost and average total cost.

   (C) average variable cost and average total cost.

   (D) average total cost and the horizontal axis.

   (E) marginal cost and the horizontal axis.

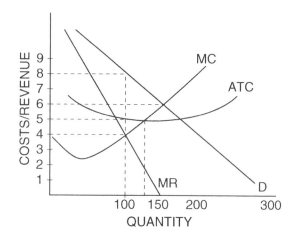

Use the graph above to answer Questions 19, 20, and 21.

19. Assume that the firm in the graph above is an unregulated monopolist. It will produce

   (A) 175 units at a price of $7.00.

   (B) 100 units at a price of $6.00.

   (C) 100 units at a price of $8.00.

   (D) 150 units at a price of about $5.00.

   (E) about 210 units at a price of about $4.00.

20. Assume that the firm in the graph is an unregulated monopolist. It will earn long-run profits of

   (A) $0.   (D) $500.

   (B) $300.   (E) $900.

   (C) $400.

21. At 100 units of output, the firm's average revenue is

   (A) $0.   **(D) $8.**
   (B) $4.   (E) $800.
   (C) $6.

25. Total revenue will be maximized when price is equal to

   (A) P_1.   **(D) P_4.**
   (B) P_2.   (E) P_5.
   (C) P_3.

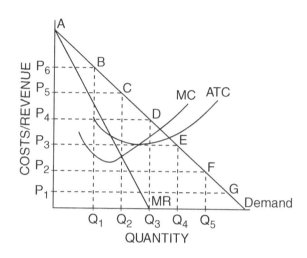

Use the graph above to answer Questions 22 through 25.

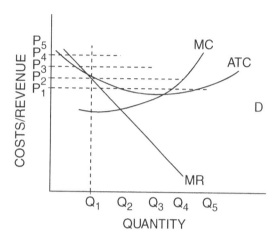

Questions 26, 27, and 28 are based on the graph above of cost and revenue curves for a monopoly firm.

22. For the firm in the graph—an unregulated monopolist—the price elasticity of demand is unit elastic at a price and an output of

   (A) P_6 and Q_1.   (D) P_3 and Q_4.
   (B) P_5 and Q_2.   (E) P_3 and Q_4.
   (C) P_4 and Q_3.

26. To maximize total profit, this monopolist should produce at which of the following levels of output?

   (A) Q_1 (D) Q_4
   (B) Q_2   (E) Q_5
   (C) Q_3

23. Consumer surplus for this profit-maximizing monopolist will be represented by area

   (A) ABP_6.   (D) AEP_3.
   (B) ACP_5.   (E) AGP_1.
   (C) ADP_4.

27. The price the monopolist charges at the profit-maximizing level of output will be

   (A) P_1.   **(D) P_4.**
   (B) P_2.   (E) P_5.
   (C) P_3.

24. The profit-maximizing price for this firm is

   (A) P_2.   **(D) P_5.**
   (B) P_3.   (E) P_6.
   (C) P_4.

28. When the firm maximizes total profit, the profit per unit will be

   (A) $P_2 - P_1$.   **(D) $P_4 - P_1$.**
   (B) $P_3 - P_2$.   (E) $P_1 - 0$.
   (C) $P_4 - 0$.

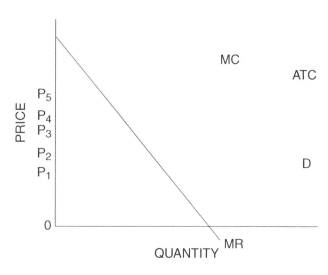

Use the graph above to answer Questions 29 and 30.

29. If this monopoly is regulated so as to have it produce the socially optimal output level, what price should the firm charge?

(A) P$_1$

(B) P$_2$

(C) P$_3$

(D) P$_4$

(E) P$_5$

30. If a regulating agency requires this monopoly to charge a price that allows the firm to have a fair return (where all costs are covered, including a normal profit), the price would be

(A) P$_1$.

(B) P$_2$.

(C) P$_3$.

(D) P$_4$.

(E) P$_5$.

31. What happens to a monopolist's price, profits, and output if its total fixed costs decrease?

	Price	Profits	Output
(A)	Decrease	Increase	Decrease
(B)	Decrease	Decrease	Decrease
(C)	*No change*	*Increase*	*No change*
(D)	Increase	Increase	Increase
(E)	Decrease	No change	Increase

32. The presence of both allocative and productive efficiency is possible in which of the following market structures?

I. Perfectly competitive

II. Monopolistic

III. Oligopolistic

IV. Monopolistically competitive

(A) I only

(B) II only

(C) III only

(D) I and IV only

(E) II and IV only

33. Which of the following is true of monopolists that practice price discrimination?

(A) They charge all customers the same price.

(B) They earn a smaller profit than those that do not practice price discrimination.

(C) They charge customers different prices according to different elasticities of demand.

(D) They produce lower quantities than pure monopolists.

(E) They produce the same quantity of output as pure monopolists.

34. Characteristics of an oligopolistic market include which of the following?

I. Easy entry and exit of firms

II. Few firms

III. Interdependence among firms

(A) I only

(B) II only

(C) III only

(D) II and III only

(E) I, II, and III

35. In the long run, a monopolistically competitive firm will make

    (A) more economic profit than a perfectly competitive firm.

    (B) less economic profit than a perfectly competitive firm.

    (C) more economic profit than a monopoly.

    (D) more economic profit than an oligopolist.

    (E) zero economic profit.

36. If all of the firms in an oligopoly could, without any additional cost, form an industry-wide cartel to jointly maximize profits, the demand curve facing the cartel would be

    (A) less elastic than the industry demand curve.

    (B) the same as the industry demand curve.

    (C) more elastic than the industry demand curve.

    (D) perfectly inelastic.

    (E) horizontal at the market-clearing price.

37. Characteristics of an oligopoly include which of the following?

    I.   Collusion can increase oligopolists' profits.

    II. Oligopolistic firms are interdependent.

    III. Independent price decision making leads to lower returns.

    (A) I only

    (B) II only

    (C) III only

    (D) I and II only

    (E) I, II, and III

38. The shapes of the marginal product curve and the total product curve are best explained by the

    (A) law of demand.

    (B) law of supply.

    (C) principle of diminishing marginal utility.

    (D) least-cost rule.

    (E) law of diminishing marginal returns.

Royal's Burgers and Fries

		Concentrate on fries	Concentrate on burgers
Brewer's Fries and Burgers	Concentrate on fries	120, 85	150, 120
	Concentrate on burgers	65, 100	50, 80

Use the payoff matrix above and the information below to answer Questions 39 and 40.

Two competing fast-food restaurants in a small town, Royal's Burgers and Fries and Brewer's Fries and Burgers, realize that each must consider the method of attracting customers that the other is using. The payoff matrix above illustrates the firms' possible strategies and the profits to each restaurant under each possible outcome. (The first number in each box represents the payoff to Brewer's; the second the payoff to Royal's.)

39. Based on the payoffs above, which of the following statements is true?

   (A) Brewer's has a dominant strategy to concentrate on fries.

   (B) Brewer's has a dominant strategy to concentrate on burgers.

   (C) Royal's has a dominant strategy to concentrate on fries.

   (D) Royal's has a dominant strategy to concentrate on burgers.

   (E) Neither restaurant has a dominant strategy.

40. What is the Nash Equilibrium in this game?

   (A) Both fast-food restaurants should choose to concentrate on fries.

   (B) Both fast-food restaurants should choose to concentrate on burgers.

   (C) Brewer's should choose to concentrate on fries, and Royal's should choose to concentrate on burgers.

   (D) Brewer's should choose to concentrate on burgers, and Royal's should choose to concentrate on fries.

   (E) There is no Nash Equilibrium in this game.

41. Which of the following is true of a cartel?

   (A) A cartel is a coalition of firms that seek to coordinate their decisions so all firms can earn a higher economic profit.

   (B) A cartel is a way for firms to earn more by playing their dominant strategies.

   (C) A cartel is considered stable.

   (D) A cartel seeks to maximize total revenue of its members.

   (E) A cartel sets price and output of its members in the same way that a price discriminating monopolist would.

42. Which of the following best characterizes the firms in an oligopoly industry?

   (A) Firms can easily enter the industry when profits are high.

   (B) There are more firms than in a monopolistically competitive industry.

   (C) They are independent.

   (D) They always collude to increase profits.

   (E) They use strategic decision making.

Acme

		Advertise	Don't advertise
AAA	Advertise	Acme: 150 AAA: 150	Acme: –100 AAA: 400
	Don't advertise	Acme: 400 AAA: –100	Acme: 0 AAA: 0

Use the payoff matrix above and the information below to answer Questions 43, 44, and 45.

Acme and AAA are the two major firms in the industry. Each must decide whether to conduct a television advertising campaign. The returns from each firm's decision depend on the decision of the other. The profits resulting from each possible combination of the firms' decisions are given in the payoff matrix above.

43. If AAA advertises and Acme does not, Acme's profits will be

(A) *–$100.*   (D) $300.

(B) $0.   (E) $400.

(C) $150.

44. If AAA advertises, Acme will

(A) decide not to advertise because this is its dominant strategy.

(B) *advertise because this is its dominant strategy.*

(C) not have a dominant strategy.

(D) lose money.

(E) increase its profit by $400 if it advertises.

45. Which of the following statements is true?

(A) *If AAA advertises, Acme's dominant strategy is to advertise.*

(B) If Acme advertises, AAA's dominant strategy is NOT to advertise.

(C) The two firms are in a prisoner's dilemma game.

(D) The two firms would be better off to agree to save their money and NOT advertise.

(E) A collusive agreement to advertise would benefit both firms.

Answer Key to Multiple-Choice Questions

1. *A*
2. *B*
3. *E*
4. *D*
5. *D*
6. *A*
7. *E*
8. *E*
9. *E*

10. *D*
11. *C*
12. *B*
13. *B*
14. *D*
15. *E*
16. *B*
17. *D*
18. *A*

19. *C*
20. *E*
21. *B*
22. *C*
23. *C*
24. *C*
25. *B*

Circle the letter of each correct answer.

1. Derived demand is

   (A) demand for an input used to produce a product.

   (B) demand derived from the satisfaction of a buyer for the product.

   (C) caused by monopoly control of the inputs.

   (D) derived from government policy.

   (E) dependent on the demand for a substitute or a complementary input.

Use the following information to answer Questions 2, 3, and 4.

Number of chefs	Number of pizzas that can be made in an hour
0	0
1	10
2	18
3	24
4	28
5	30
6	29

2. The law of diminishing marginal returns occurs with the hiring of which chef?

   (A) First   (D) Fourth

   (B) Second   (E) Fifth

   (C) Third

3. The marginal productivity of the third chef is

   (A) 24 pizzas   (D) 8 pizzas

   (B) 18 pizzas   **(E) 6 pizzas**

   (C) 10 pizzas

4. If the price per pizza is $10 and if each chef receives $20 an hour, how many chefs will the owner hire to maximize total profits?

   (A) 2   **(D) 5**

   (B) 3   (E) 6

   (C) 4

5. Which of the following would determine the marginal revenue product of an input used in a perfectly competitive output market?

   I. Dividing the change in total revenue by the change in the input
   II. Dividing the change in marginal revenue by the change in the output
   III. Multiplying the marginal product by the price of the output
   IV. Multiplying marginal revenue by the price of the output

   (A) I only   **(D) I and III only**

   (B) II only   (E) II and IV only

   (C) III only

6. Which of the following explains why the marginal revenue product of an input in a perfectly competitive product market decreases as a firm increases the quantity of an input used?

   (A) Diminishing marginal productivity from labor

   (B) Diminishing marginal utility

   (C) The homogeneity of the product

   (D) The free mobility of resources

   (E) Diminishing marginal revenue from output

7. A profit-maximizing firm should hire an input as long as the

   (A) firm can increase its total revenue.

   (B) price of the input doesn't exceed the price of the other inputs used in the firm's production.

   (C) marginal revenue product of the input is less than the cost of hiring the input.

   (D) marginal revenue product of the input is greater than the marginal revenue products of other inputs the firm is using.

   (E) marginal revenue product of the input is at least as much as the marginal cost of hiring the input.

8. The demand for labor will decrease in response to which of the following?

   (A) Increased productivity of labor

   (B) Better training of all laborers

   (C) A decrease in the supply of labor

   (D) An increase in the supply of labor

   (E) Decreased demand for goods and services produced by labor

9. A firm hiring inputs in a perfectly competitive market will hire up to the point where

   (A) marginal physical product of the input is at a minimum.

   (B) marginal physical product of the input is at a maximum.

   (C) the price of the input equals the price of the output.

   (D) the price of the input equals the marginal physical product of the input.

   (E) the price of the input equals the marginal revenue product of the input.

10. A firm is a competitive seller of output at a market price of $3. The only resource it requires to create its product is labor, which it purchases competitively at a wage rate of $8 per hour. The last worker it employs increases total output from 36 to 40 units per hour. What is the marginal revenue product for this worker?

    (A) $3   **(D) $12**

    (B) $4   (E) $24

    (C) $8

Use the following information to answer Questions 11, 12, and 13.

Units of workers	Total product	Product price
0	0	$5.00
1	10	$4.50
2	19	$4.00
3	27	$3.50
4	34	$3.00
5	40	$2.50

11. The marginal revenue product of the third worker is equal to

    (A) $3.50   (D) $28.00

    (B) $10.50   (E) $94.50

    (C) $18.50

12. Which of the following is true according to the information in the table?

    (A) The firm is selling its product in a purely competitive market.

    (B) The firm is selling its product in an imperfectly competitive market.

    (C) There is no level of output at which this firm can earn a profit.

    (D) The law of diminishing returns is not applicable to this firm.

    (E) The firm is hiring its workers in an imperfectly competitive labor market.

13. If the wage rate is constant and equal to $21, how many workers will the profit-maximizing firm hire?

(A) 1

(B) 2

(C) 3

(D) 4

(E) 5

14. Which of the following will cause an increase in the demand for labor?

I.   Increase in the price of the output
II. Increase in worker productivity
III. Increase in wages
IV. Increase in the supply of workers

(A) I only

(B) II only

(C) III only

(D) I and II only

(E) III and IV only

15. A firm requires labor and capital to produce a given output. Labor costs $8 per hour, and capital costs $12 per hour. At the current output level, the marginal physical product of labor is 40 units, and the marginal physical product of capital is 60 units. To minimize its production costs at the current level of output, in which of the following ways should the firm change the amount of labor and capital?

	Labor	Capital
(A)	Increase	Increase
(B)	Increase	Decrease
(C)	Decrease	Increase
(D)	Decrease	No change
(E)	**No change**	**No change**

16. In a competitive industry, suppose the marginal revenue product of the last donut baker hired is $35 and the marginal revenue product of the last bagel maker hired is $15. A bakery must pay donut bakers $40 a day and bagel makers $10 a day. Which of the following should the bakery hire to maximize profits?

(A) More donut bakers and fewer bagel makers

(B) Fewer donut bakers and more bagel makers

(C) Fewer of both donut bakers and bagel makers

(D) More of both donut bakers and bagel makers

(E) Neither more nor fewer donut bakers or bagel makers

Use the graph below to answer Questions 17, 18, and 19.

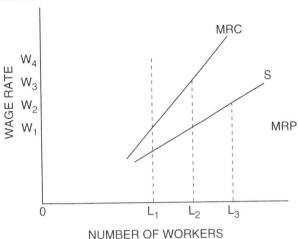

17. Under perfectly competitive conditions in the product and labor markets, the wage rate will be

(A) W_1, and L_2 workers will be hired.

(B) W_2, and L_2 workers will be hired.

(C) W_3, and L_2 workers will be hired.

(D) W_2, and L_3 workers will be hired.

(E) W_4, and L_2 workers will be hired.

18. Now suppose that through an employers' association, firms in this industry establish a monopsony in the hiring of labor. In this case, the wage rate will be

(A) W_1, and L_2 workers will be hired.

(B) W_2, and L_2 workers will be hired.

(C) W_3, and L_2 workers will be hired.

(D) W_3, and L_3 workers will be hired.

(E) W_4, and L_1 workers will be hired.

19. Now assume that workers react to the formation of this monopsony by establishing a union. To what level can this union increase the wage rate without causing the number of jobs to decline below that which the monopsony would otherwise provide?

(A) W_1 (B) W_2 *(C) W_3*   (D) W_4

(E) Unions can never increase real wage rates.

20. If the wage paid to labor, the only variable input, is $20, and the marginal physical product of labor is four units per hour, the marginal cost of a unit of output is

(A) $20.   (D) $10.

(B) $16.   *(E) $5.*

(C) $12.

21. Pure economic rent refers to the

(A) capital gains received from the sale of property.

(B) payment to any resource over and above what is required to keep the resource in supply at its current level in the long run.

(C) difference between the return to owners of land and the market rate of interest.

(D) implicit value of owner-occupied housing in the long run.

(E) price paid for a resource that has a perfectly elastic supply.

22. Under what conditions is a firm's marginal revenue product of labor curve the same thing as its demand curve for labor?

    (A) If the firm sells its output in a perfectly competitive product market

    (B) If the firm sells its output in an imperfectly competitive product market

    (C) If the firm hires labor in a perfectly competitive resource market

    (D) If the firm hires labor in an imperfectly competitive resource market

    (E) The marginal revenue product curve is never the same thing as a firm's demand curve for labor.

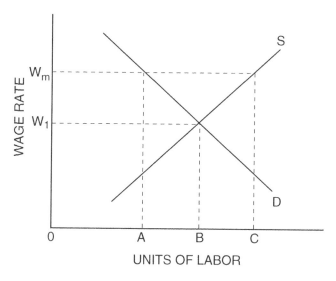

23. The competitive labor market shown above is initially in equilibrium. If a minimum wage level is set at W_m, employment will

    (A) increase from A to B.

    (B) increase from B to C.

    (C) decrease from B to A.

    (D) decrease from C to A.

    (E) decrease from C to B.

24. One reason why the supply of carpenters is greater than the supply of physicians is that

    (A) carpenters demand less income.

    (B) physicians do not belong to a union.

    (C) physicians must make a greater investment in human capital.

    (D) carpenters belong to unions.

    (E) carpenters are in greater demand than are doctors.

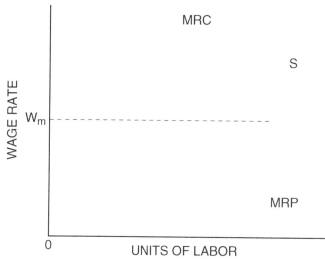

25. The monopsonistic labor market shown above is initially in equilibrium. If a minimum wage is set at W_M, the level of employment will

    (A) decrease.

    (B) increase.

    (C) stay the same.

    (D) increase or decrease depending on how the supply curve shifts as a result of the change in the wage rate.

    (E) be indeterminant under monopsonistic labor markets.

Answer Key to Multiple-Choice Questions

1. *B*	9. *D*	17. *D*
2. *D*	10. *C*	18. *C*
3. *C*	11. *D*	19. *A*
4. *B*	12. *C*	20. *C*
5. *E*	13. *B*	21. *D*
6. *B*	14. *C*	22. *C*
7. *A*	15. *C*	23. *C*
8. *C*	16. *E*	24. *B*

Circle the letter of each correct answer.

1. Which of the following characterizes a public good?

    (A) People who do not pay for the good can be excluded from using it.

    (B) If one person uses the good, it does not prevent others from using it.

    (C) It is easy to determine who must pay for the good.

    (D) The good exhibits negative externalities.

    (E) The good exhibits positive externalities.

2. The free rider problem is associated with

    (A) all market goods.

    (B) goods that are exclusionary.

    (C) bus transportation.

    (D) the production of public goods.

    (E) the production of public transportation.

3. Which of the following best meets the criteria of a public good?

    (A) A phone card

    (B) An airline ticket

    (C) National defense

    (D) A college education

    (E) A restaurant

4. The market system fails to produce public goods because

    (A) there is no need or demand for such goods.

    (B) private firms cannot restrict the benefits of such goods only to consumers who are willing to pay for them.

    (C) public enterprises can produce such goods at lower cost than can private enterprises.

    (D) their production seriously distorts the distribution of income.

    (E) a person unwilling to pay can be excluded from the benefits that the product provides.

5. Which of the following are economic functions of government?

    I. Enforcing laws and contracts

    II. Providing public goods

    III. Correcting market failures

    (A) I only

    (B) II only

    (C) III only

    (D) II and III only

    (E) I, II, and III

6. In a market economy, the distribution of income is

    (A) equitable because people who are willing to work earn income.

    (B) primarily determined by the prices of scarce resources people own.

    (C) primarily determined by the government through its power to tax.

    (D) based on need.

    (E) always more equal than in a command economy.

7. If the production of a good creates negative externalities, the private market will produce

    (A) too much of the good at too low a price.

    (B) too much of the good at too high a price.

    (C) too little of the good at too high a price.

    (D) too little of the good at too low a price.

    (E) the right amount of the good at the correct price.

8. If the production of a good creates positive externalities, the private market will produce

    (A) too much of the good at too high a price.

    (B) too much of the good at too low a price.

    (C) too little of the good at too low a price.

    (D) too little of the good at too high a price.

    (E) the right amount of the good at the correct price.

Use the supply and demand graph below to answer Questions 9, 10, and 11. In the graph, S$_1$ shows the marginal private cost to producers of the product, S$_2$ shows the marginal social cost, and D shows both the marginal private benefit and the marginal social benefit.

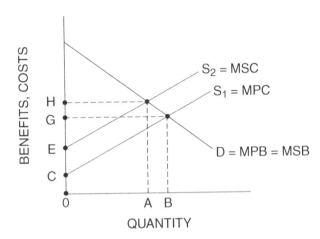

9. Based on the graph,

   (A) the market will produce A units, which is the socially efficient quantity.

   (B) the market will produce B units, which is the socially efficient quantity.

   (C) the market will produce A units while the socially efficient quantity is B.

   (D) the market will produce B units while the socially efficient quantity is A.

   (E) we cannot determine the socially efficient quantity.

10. One solution to the externality problem in this market is to

    (A) give consumers a subsidy equal to H – G.

    (B) give producers a subsidy of the amount C – 0.

    (C) tax producers by the amount E – C.

    (D) tax producers by the amount H – G.

    (E) tax consumers by the amount H – C.

11. If the government corrects this externality problem with a tax so that all costs are included in the cost of producing the item, then the product price will be

    (A) C.

    (B) E.

    (C) G.

    (D) H.

    (E) H – G.

Use the supply and demand graph below to answer Questions 12 and 13. In the graph, D$_1$ shows the marginal private benefit to consumers of the product, D$_2$ shows the marginal social benefit, and S shows both the marginal private cost and the marginal social cost.

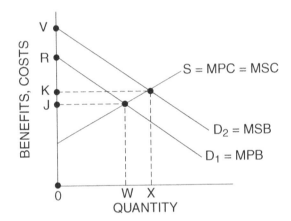

12. Based on the graph,

    (A) the market will produce W units, which is the socially efficient quantity.

    (B) the market will produce X units, which is the socially efficient quantity.

    (C) the market will produce W units while the socially efficient quantity is X.

    (D) the market will produce X units while the socially efficient quantity is W.

    (E) we cannot determine the socially efficient quantity.

13. One solution to the externality problem in this market is to

    (A) give consumers a subsidy equal to K – J.

    (B) give producers a subsidy of the amount V – R.

    (C) give producers a subsidy of the amount R – K.

    (D) tax producers by the amount R – J.

    (E) tax consumers by the amount J – 0.

14. Which of the following best summarizes most economists' position on allocating resources to control pollution?

    (A) All forms of air and water pollution should be eliminated.

    (B) Government policies to reduce pollution have zero opportunity costs.

    (C) Pollution should be reduced to the point where the marginal social cost of pollution control equals the marginal social benefit of pollution control.

    (D) Pollution should be reduced to the point where the total social cost of pollution control equals the total social benefit of pollution control.

    (E) Pollution should be reduced to the point where the average social cost of pollution control equals the average social benefit of pollution control.

15. Public-choice theory is based on the idea that

    (A) self-interest motivates participants only in the private sector of the economy.

    (B) self-interest motivates participants only in the public sector of the economy.

    (C) self-interest motivates participants in both the public and private sectors of the economy.

    (D) the interests of society are the main interest of participants in the public sector of the economy.

    (E) the interests of society are the main interest of participants in the private sector of the economy.

16. Government may attempt to reduce income inequality by doing which of the following?

    I.   Provide transfer payments to the poor

    II. Directly influence market prices, such as establishing a minimum wage

    III. Tax high-income earners at a higher rate than low-income earners

    (A) I only   (D) I and II only

    (B) II only   **(E) I, II, and III**

    (C) III only

17. Which of the following is the best example of a tax based on the ability-to-pay theory of taxation?

    (A) Sales tax

    (B) Property tax

    (C) Excise tax on gasoline

    (D) Federal income tax

    (E) Highway tolls

18. In which of the following taxes is the benefits-received principle of taxation most evident?

    (A) Corporation income tax

    (B) Personal income tax

    (C) Excise tax on gasoline

    (D) Inheritance taxes

    (E) Progressive tax rates

19. Which of the following taxes is considered regressive?

    (A) Sales tax

    (B) Personal income tax

    (C) Corporation income tax

    (D) Federal estate tax

    (E) Inheritance taxes

20. An excise tax will generate more revenue for government if

    (A) demand is unit elastic.

    (B) demand is elastic.

    (C) demand is inelastic.

    (D) supply is inelastic.

    (E) supply is perfectly elastic.

21. "The President's proposal to increase the federal tax on gasoline is intended to reduce the amount of gasoline purchased and raise more revenue." The second goal would be best served (and the first goal least served) if the demand for gasoline were which of the following?

    (A) Unit elastic

    (B) Relatively elastic

    (C) Relatively inelastic

    (D) Perfectly inelastic

    (E) Decreased by the tax

22. A motel owner is upset that the scenic view provided by the neighboring wooded property will be destroyed because the property's owner plans to cut and sell the trees to a commercial lumber company. The Coase Theorem suggests that this dispute could be resolved by

    (A) a law passed by the government.

    (B) a zoning ordinance against commercial lumbering.

    (C) the owners themselves.

    (D) a government fine for cutting trees.

    (E) an environmental campaign against altering wildlife habitat.

23. If the government increases the amount of government insurance on bank deposits, this action would

    (A) increase the probability of adverse selection.

    (B) lessen the probability of adverse selection.

    (C) increase the probability of a moral hazard problem.

    (D) lessen the probability of a moral hazard problem.

    (E) eliminate the probability of adverse selection or moral hazard.

24. Which of these statements indicates that a country has a more equal distribution of income today than it did ten years ago?

    (A) Its Lorenz curve is closer to the 45-degree line and its Gini coefficient is larger.

    (B) Its Lorenz curve is closer to the 45-degree line and its Gini coefficient is smaller.

    (C) Its Lorenz curve is farther from the 45-degree line and its Gini coefficient is larger.

    (D) Its Lorenz curve is farther from the 45-degree line and its Gini coefficient is smaller.

    (E) Its Lorenz curve and Gini coefficient are unchanged.

Made in the USA
Monee, IL
24 August 2023